Reading Cultural Anthropology

Reading Cultural Anthropology

An Ethnographic Introduction

Pamela Stern

With a Foreword by Roberta Robin Dods

OXFORD

UNIVERSITY PRESS

OXFORD
UNIVERSITY PRESS

Oxford University Press is a department of the University of Oxford.
It furthers the University's objective of excellence in research, scholarship,
and education by publishing worldwide. Oxford is a registered trade mark of
Oxford University Press in the UK and in certain other countries.

Published in Canada by
Oxford University Press
8 Sampson Mews, Suite 204,
Don Mills, Ontario M3C 0H5 Canada

www.oupcanada.com

Library and Archives Canada Cataloguing in Publication

Reading cultural anthropology : an ethnographic
introduction / edited by Pamela Stern.

Includes bibliographical references and index.

ISBN 978-0-19-901312-8 (paperback)

1. Ethnology. 2. Ethnology -- Methodology.
I. Stern, Pamela R., 1958-, editor

GN316.R42 2015   306   C2015-903462-0

Cover image: © Ingetje Tadros/Getty Images

Oxford University Press is committed to our environment.
This book is printed on Forest Stewardship Council® certified paper
and comes from responsible sources.

Printed and bound in Canada
1 2 3 4 — 19 18 17 16

Contents

List of Maps

List of Photographs

Acknowledgements

In the last several years, I have been examining anthropology textbooks as sites where anthropologists convey specialist knowledge to non-specialists. In the course of this research, which was supported by the Social Sciences and Humanities Research Council of Canada, I have had the pleasure of interviewing the authors of many of the most widely used anthropology textbooks in the United States and Canada. The idea for this reader came about during my interview with Roberta Robin Dods, and she encouraged me to pursue the project. Simon Fraser University students from SA201: Anthropology and Contemporary Life read several of the articles I have included in this reader in their full, unabridged forms. Their excitement and cogent discussion of the ethnography and theory gave me confidence that this was a worthwhile effort.

At Oxford University Press Canada, acquisitions editor Caroline Starr, developmental editor Tanuja Weerasooriya, editorial assistant Danielle Pacey, and senior editor Janice Evans have been amazing to work with.

At various points along the way, several people answered my questions or pointed me to sources. These individuals include Kimberly Condon, Morgan Paige Condon, Noel Dyck, and Sandy Ervin. Peter V. Hall, as always, makes life better.

Pamela Stern
Simon Fraser University
2015

Foreword

by Roberta Robin Dods

R *eading Cultural Anthropology: An Ethnographic Introduction*, so skillfully and sympathetically edited by Pamela Stern, brings recognition of the maturity that anthropology has reached as a discipline in the Canadian context. This statement does not diminish the quality of work done by the early anthropologists in various Canadian institutions and research contexts—from museums, to universities, to governmental departments at both the federal and the provincial levels (see, for example, Rogers 1962, 1972; Speck 1915; and Black 1970). However, the researchers of those days were relatively few in number in a land of immense size, and many conducted their research through organizations whose primary aims were not anthropological study (e.g., the Geological Survey of Canada, federal and provincial ministries of natural resources).

Although anthropology in Canada can be traced back to the work of Sir Daniel Wilson (1816–1892), it was not until the 1930s that the first Canadian department of anthropology was formalized at the University of Toronto. In the next decade, the University of British Columbia instituted the second such department, and we have grown from there. Initially, academics of diverse backgrounds and training were brought to Canada to teach anthropology. These academics came from many of the older schools of anthropology, most of which were based in the United States and Great Britain. In time, the universities began to promote more and more graduate students, and significant numbers of these Canadian-educated PhDs were hired into diverse positions throughout Canadian institutions engaged in cultural research and the dissemination of anthropological knowledge. Undoubtedly, the quality of the works presented in this book reflects the strong foundation laid by the many dedicated academics and researchers who shaped the study of anthropology in Canada in the early decades of its development.

One of the central features of the early developmental period in Canadian anthropology was the influence of the Boasian perspective. Although Franz Boas (1858–1942) was from Europe, he came to be known, in his day, as the quintessential North American anthropologist. He worked with First Nations Peoples in the Northwest Coast region of North America during the late nineteenth century and the first decades of the twentieth century collecting cultural, linguistic, archaeological, and physical data. Indeed, some of his ethnographic notes, as well as his recordings of vocabulary and songs and the material items that he uncovered, continue to inform our understandings of late nineteenth- and early twentieth-century realities for the peoples of the Northwest Coast. Further, his cultural relativism and empiricism continue to inform anthropological study today, even though some of his work—such as his collection of human skeletal remains—now stands as an example of our need for sensitivity and a reminder of our professional and ethical obligations. His influence, direct and indirect, led many North American anthropology departments to divide the study of anthropology into four subdisciplines: cultural anthropology, linguistic anthropology, physical (or biological) anthropology, and anthropological archaeology. If we subscribe to the concept of holism in the study of humanity—that is, if we accept the idea that different areas within this study are closely related and cannot exist independently of one another—then we recognize that each subdiscipline informs the others. The importance of a holistic perspective has been augmented in recent years by the inclusion of applied anthropology as the fifth spoke in our wheel of knowing. Regardless, the core was and remains cultural anthropology and a dedication to ethnography and ethnology. This book offers students a strong orientation to this core.

The historical perspective outlined above is alluded to by Stern in several places. In her introduction to the work of Aaron Glass in Chapter 2, for example, she notes:

> Anthropology in Canada once concentrated on documenting the cultures of Aboriginal peoples, and on collecting tools, items of clothing, and religious objects connected to these peoples' cultures as they existed prior to European colonization. Initially, anthropologists focused on these tasks because they assumed that Aboriginal cultures would disappear. . . . In fact, many early ethnographic reports include descriptions of practices that no longer exist, and Canadian museums contain objects that might have been destroyed if not collected.

In a sense, the early anthropologists were right—people and things can disappear, indeed do disappear, and anthropology gives us the chance to preserve a record of our human past while also bearing witness to our human present.

The readings in this book are on serious, complex issues, but they have been made accessible to all through the compassionate and informed editing of Pamela Stern. There is a sense of immediacy in the range of subjects and areas represented here—some of which I touch on below. This immediacy is similar to that expressed by Boas and many other nineteenth-century anthropologists. Just as those researchers felt a sense of loss when faced with the overwhelming changes of their times, so too do we experience a sense of loss when confronted with the radical changes that are transforming our natural and cultural environments—there goes another honeybee, there goes another language.

By looking closely at how humans in a variety of settings respond to some of our age's most pressing issues, these readings call us to recognize the depth and breadth of the work being done in a world where we all confront great challenges and changing circumstances. The authors are careful to avoid subsuming these challenges under the latest buzzword of *globalization* alone. Indeed, what does *globalization* actually mean in a cross-cultural perspective if we see it as a "plastic" word, as German linguist Uwe Poerksen (1995) would describe it—one of those words that seem to convey so much but that are, at the same time, used so broadly that they mean very little? Anthropological study requires a greater specificity and attention to detail than such plastic words can convey on their own. After all, general, imprecise descriptions cannot adequately represent what it is like for real people facing real-world situations—Palestinian olive-oil producers endeavouring to make a living in the West Bank amid changing Israeli policies (Meneley, Chapter 4), transgender individuals seeking to formulate a culturally acceptable gender identity in Indonesia (Blackwood, Chapter 6), people in relatively affluent nations struggling with the often misunderstood disorder anorexia (O'Connor and Van Esterik, Chapter 8), immigrant South Asian women striving to establish places for themselves in a major Canadian city (Ameeriar, Chapter 9), or Canadian youth trying to exercise control over their lives as they travel to foreign countries before "settling down" (Amit, Chapter 18).

Many of the themes explored in the readings are universal or nearly universal, echoing our shared human experience. Consider the following observation, which Pamela Stern makes in the introduction to her article on Inuit communities in Chapter 13:

> Few non-Aboriginal Canadians could or would want to live as their grandparents did; similarly, it is not realistic to think that Inuit or other Aboriginal peoples could take up the lifestyles of their ancestors as a way to improve their circumstances.

In such passages, this book goes a distance to directly challenge ethnocentricity and place all of us in the context of present circumstances rather than in exotic examples of past realities. The shared experiences touched on in the readings range from age-old interests in establishing and defining kinship (Phinney, Chapter 10; Collard and Kashmeri, Chapter 12) to relatively new concerns about how emerging technologies are redefining how we communicate with and relate to others (Luehrmann, Chapter 11). In addition, change in market economy (Cahn, Chapter 14); Aboriginal management of the boreal forest (Willow, Chapter 15), a topic close to my interest (see Dods 1998, 2000, 2002, 2003, 2004, 2007); and the instability of boom–bust mining economies (Walsh, Chapter 17) all speak to worldwide concerns. So too does the article on domestic tourism in Japan (Graburn, Chapter 20), where a theme that sticks out for me is the issue of urban vs rural—or more closely, the loss of the countryside. In this I tend to see humans as shapers of their worlds—both cultural and natural—with each world being a fully cultural construct that is, in every case, defined in a culturally specific way. At the same time, because no human culture exists in isolation, this definition is always open to change through cultural borrowing, cross-cultural diffusion, or reclamation of past cultural constructs.

I have not touched on all articles specifically, but note that they all support the content in many of the introductory anthropology textbooks used in Canadian universities today. Such a reader with Canadian focus has the potential to enrich all of our programs. Further, it sets a tone for students—the "stories" we tell from our fieldwork are the gifts of insight into being human from *others* to us. They are blessings given to us, and in this book these blessings are wrapped in the words of Stern's illuminating introductions. These stories are also invitations to reflexivity, daring us to be applied anthropologists and, as such, to act as agents of positive change.

Roberta Robin Dods
University of British Columbia, Okanagan Campus
2015

Introduction

What images came to mind when you decided to register for an anthropology class? The chances are that you envisioned a course that would teach you about the traditions, folk beliefs, rituals, **foodways**, and technologies of people who live far away or whose day-to-day experiences seem strange, or at least different from your own. To an extent, that might have been true of anthropology several decades ago. Though anthropology is a relatively young discipline—Edward Tylor (1832–1917), often called the first anthropologist, published his definition of culture as "a complex whole" in 1871—it has changed considerably in its short history. Some of the most substantial changes have occurred since the 1980s. Contemporary anthropologists continue to study the lives and **lifeways** of people in distant places, but we also do research at home. Most importantly, contemporary sociocultural anthropologists are concerned with the practices and experiences of all peoples as they live in the world today. The articles collected in this reader reflect the current state of the discipline in Canada.

Colonialism and Salvage Ethnography

As anthropology developed in Canada, it drew on both American cultural anthropology and British social anthropology, and it continues to bear similarities to both without being identical to either. Anthropology originated with European colonialism. Colonial governments often needed ethnographic information about diverse peoples in order to administer the colonized peoples and their lands, and these governments often facilitated the work of anthropologists in order to advance colonial goals. In Canada (as in the United States), the colonized were **Aboriginal peoples** living within the country's borders, and thus most anthropologists working in Canada up until the last quarter of the twentieth century studied **Inuit** and **First Nations** communities.

Throughout the world, colonization caused massive changes in the lives, life expectancies, and practices of colonized peoples. In many parts of the world, colonized peoples were enslaved by their colonizers. In other places, colonized peoples reorganized their activities in order to benefit from trade with the colonizers. Yet, even where Aboriginal peoples welcomed newcomers as trading partners, colonization was a devastating experience involving forcible religious conversion, the introduction and spread of new diseases, and the loss of land and autonomy. Given the immense changes brought about by colonialism, the earliest anthropologists in Canada believed it was essential to record what remained of Aboriginal cultures. This documentation, called **salvage ethnography**, recorded many traditions and preserved in museums many artifacts that might otherwise have been lost. These records and artifacts are greatly valued today. But salvage ethnographers collected only what they mistakenly believed to be *genuine* cultural materials, often ignoring or disregarding imported technologies and new and hybrid practices. This approach helped to create a persistent public misperception that culture change—at least among the less powerful—equals culture loss.

The notion that any culture is inauthentic is absurd. At the same time, there are no peoples (and never have been any) whose culture is uninfluenced by other people. All peoples everywhere, modern and traditional, learn from and sometimes adopt the practices, technologies, and beliefs of others. Much of contemporary anthropology concerns those connections.

An Anthropology of Global Connections

In a classic satirical essay, American anthropologist Ralph Linton (1893–1953) imagined a typical day of a man he identified as "100 per cent American." Notably, without changing his meaning or his intent, Linton could have called this American a Canadian, an Australian, a Scottish or British person, or a white South African, among others. Linton's protagonist slept in pajamas, a garment that originated in India. For breakfast, he ate bacon from pigs, which were originally domesticated in East Asia, prepared according to a recipe originating in Northern Europe; eggs from chickens, which were originally domesticated in Southeast Asia; and coffee from the Horn of Africa. The glass of his windows was invented in ancient Egypt, as was the process for tanning the leather of his shoes. His necktie derived from shawls worn by seventeenth-century Croatians, while his rain boots were made of rubber first discovered by Indigenous people in Central America. The brief essay concludes that as this consumer of global commodities reads the daily newspaper and "absorbs the account of foreign troubles he will, if he is a good conservative citizen, thank a Hebrew deity in an Indo-European language that he is 100 per cent American" (Linton 1936: 327). Linton meant the essay to challenge **ethnocentrism**, but like the cartoon above, it is also a useful reminder that there are not—and have never been—any cultures so remote and so isolated that they have not traded with and exchanged ideas with other peoples. Just as few, if any, Canadians use the same technologies or live in the same ways as their grandparents did, so it is with all peoples. We may adopt new technologies or borrow ideas and practices from other places, but we continue to be able to recognize our ancestors' cultures in our contemporary practices and beliefs. What is distinctive about different cultures cannot be found in lists of practices, beliefs, or **material culture**, but rather in the unique ways that these traits are joined together and change over time.

The methodology of anthropology—that is, close examination of the lives of people in context—is especially well suited to documenting cultural similarities as well as the distinctive ways that cultures are configured. Where anthropologists of the past concentrated on documenting the lives and cultures of non-Western peoples and people living in what have been called small-scale societies (in other words, Indigenous communities and other minority groups), this is no longer the case. Anthropology is a way of learning about the human world that is not limited to certain kinds of places, types of peoples, or topics. Indeed, there is probably no question about human life that is not or cannot be studied anthropologically. Today, anthropologists examine such diverse situations and practices as risk-taking by commodities traders (Ho 2009; Zaloom 2006), electronics factories that are sometimes invaded by evil spirits (Ong 1987), the spiritual practices of evangelical Christians in North America (Luhrmann 2012), trash picking in Brazil (Millar 2012) and trash collecting in New York City (Nagle 2013), small-scale urban drug dealing (Bourgois 2003), romantic love (Jankowiak 1995), labour migration (Constable 2007), and anything and everything else that people do.

Within our varied interests, anthropology has three organizing principles: it is *holistic*, it is *comparative*, and it is *field based*.

To say that anthropology is *holistic* means that we look at the human condition in its entirety as a system in which each part is integrated with and integral to all of the other parts. We regard all aspects of being human as tied together, and we recognize that we cannot understand any one attribute or practice out of the context of the whole; economic systems are connected to religious practices, which are connected to family forms, which are connected to the physical environment and historical events, and so on.

Anthropology developed in the context of a desire to document and explain human cultural differences. *Comparison* offers us an opportunity to consider similarities and differences across time and space. Just as people in similar situations may engage in different cultural practices, people in very different situations may find similar cultural solutions to their problems. One way that we, as anthropologists, engage in comparison is by using the insights gained from studying other peoples to understand and sometimes critique our own cultures.

Finally, anthropology is *field based*. That is, we generally collect our data not in laboratories or libraries, but by going out and spending time closely interacting with the people we study. This mode of data collection, called **ethnography**, ordinarily involves long-term, close, in-depth efforts to learn about the mundane, taken-for-granted thoughts and practices of a group of people. The goal of ethnography is to become immersed in the lives of people in a way that allows us to see and understand the world from their perspectives and in context.

Ethnographic **fieldwork** involves many data-collection activities, including making maps, administering censuses, carrying out surveys, taking photographs, and conducting interviews— all techniques employed by social scientists from other disciplines as well as by anthropologists. Anthropologists are known for using another ethnographic data-collection method as well: **participant observation**. In participant observation, the ethnographer lives with and/or works alongside the people he or she is studying, learning to be a cultural insider in order to gain some of the perspective of a member of a particular culture. Of course, it is not usually possible to become a complete cultural insider. As well, participant observation is not always possible or necessary in some ethnographic research situations. Hugh Gusterson (1996), for example, conducted ethnographic research with nuclear weapons scientists without becoming a nuclear physicist or even setting foot in their secured laboratories. Ethnography involves close examination of social and cultural phenomena to interpret the worlds of our subjects.

Using the tools afforded by holism, comparison, and fieldwork, anthropologists ask: Why do people collectively think the ways they do, act the ways they do, form the social groups they do, and engage in the cultural practices they do? The articles in this reader are meant to illustrate how anthropologists employ a variety of anthropological theories and data-collection methods to address contemporary questions. At the same time, the articles offer a look at the lives, practices, and concerns of a wide variety of peoples around the world.

Organization of This Book

I have grouped the articles in this reader into five sections that correspond to themes that are frequently included in introductory sociocultural anthropology courses. Your professor, of course, may decide to assign the readings in a different order that better suits the organization of your class.

Part I, "Anthropological Traditions/Contemporary Practice," contains five articles that reflect the dynamic nature of anthropological thinking and theorizing. Each of the articles draws on and advances some of the ideas and theories that are part of the discipline's history. Chapters 1 and 2 present cultural groups whose ethnographies have long been part of the anthropological canon, the Ju/'hoansi or San people of southern Africa and the Kwakwaka'wakw people of Canada's west coast. Chapters 3 and 4 concern language and time, two topics that have long interested anthropologists. Chapter 5 shows how ethnographic forms of analysis can be applied to understand political activism.

Several of the articles in this section also concern the fieldwork process. In the past, "the field" was likely to be far from home, and for many anthropologists—including Renée Sylvain (Chapter 1), Aaron Glass (Chapter 2), and Anne Meneley (Chapter 4)—this remains true. There are some intellectual benefits to separation from the familiar. For one thing, it encourages the anthropologist to become immersed in the community he or she is studying. Separation also makes it easier to overcome some of the taken-for-granted notions we all have about how things are done. But not all ethnographic field sites are far from home. For example, beginning in the 1910s, pioneering Canadian ethnographer Marius Barbeau (1883–1969) conducted fieldwork (salvage ethnography, in fact) near his childhood home in rural Quebec, collecting oral traditions as well as examples of music, songs, and dance. Following this tradition, the articles written by Monica Heller (Chapter 3) and Alexander Ervin (Chapter 5) describe fieldwork done at home. Ervin's article is different from the other articles in this reader, in part because Ervin is an **applied** or **practising anthropologist**. That is, he uses anthropological insights and forms of analysis to promote social change. While the article in Chapter 5 does not represent applied anthropology per se, Ervin wrote it to show others how a protest movement can achieve its goals.

Part II, "Gender/Embodiment," focuses on the human body and the ways in which social and cultural forces are expressed in and on individual human bodies. We tend to think of **embodiment** as natural and individual, and it is often extremely difficult to recognize how particular forms of embodiment are both culturally shared and socially reinforced. British anthropologist Stephen Hugh-Jones (2005) tells a humorous story that illustrates this point. As young children at an English boarding school in the 1950s, Hugh-Jones and his classmates were told that it was important to defecate every morning, and that they should report whether or not they had to the boarding-house matron. Regular morning bowel movements were regarded as a sign of good health and good character; thus, boys who did not defecate were given a foul-tasting laxative. Hugh-Jones marvels at the fact that they each dutifully reported their bowel movements to the matron. Still, he did not question the naturalness of daily morning defecation, which became part of his embodied practice. In the 1970s, Hugh-Jones conducted ethnographic fieldwork in an Indigenous village in the Amazonia region of Colombia. The village houses did not have indoor plumbing, and residents defecated in the bushes. As was his routine, Hugh-Jones awoke in the morning and went into the bushes to relieve himself, only to be told by his hosts that morning defecation was disgusting; going to sleep with filth still in one's body was, in their view, unhealthy and a sign of poor habits.

The four articles in Part II concern the malleability of the human body, as well as the ways in which we perceive our bodies. In Chapter 6, Evelyn Blackwood contrasts her sense of herself as a "women-loving woman" with that of her Sumatran lover, who perceived herself not as a lesbian woman but as male. Anne Irwin (Chapter 7) also considers how bodies present as masculine, concluding that military service in a war zone has the power to alter men's bodies in ways that make them seem less manly. In Chapter 8, Richard O'Connor and Penny Van Esterik challenge the widely held assumption that anorexia is a disorder of bodily image. Finally, Lalaie Ameeriar (Chapter 9) exposes the contradictory messages South Asian immigrant women in Toronto receive about their bodily presentations.

The articles that constitute Part III, "Kinship/Marriage/Family," move from individual bodies to kinship and the family, and they reflect contemporary anthropological investigations of these institutions. Beginning with early American anthropologist Louis Henry Morgan (1818–1881) in the nineteenth century, anthropologists have laid special claim to the study of kinship. Indeed, nearly every anthropology textbook has a chapter on the subject. Not surprisingly, the questions that anthropologists ask about kinship have changed over time, from focusing on how a group's kinship system serves as a model of the culture as a whole to investigating how people create and mobilize kin relationships to serve a variety of purposes. The four articles in Part III concern kinship, marriage, child rearing, and household formation. Each author, in her own way, interrogates what happens when individuals bump up against political, economic, and religious structures in their societies. Pamela Stern (Chapter 13) and Harriet Phinney (Chapter 10) each explore how government programs meant to strengthen families produce unintended consequences in those families. In contrast, Sonja Luehrmann (Chapter 11) describes how some Russian women employ new communications technologies to solve a marriage problem made worse by the withdrawal of state support for the rural economy. Technological innovation also figures in the article by Chantal Collard and Shireen Kashmeri (Chapter 12). These ethnographers investigate how couples making use of new reproductive technologies employ their religious beliefs and cultural models to create new forms of relatedness.

Cultural holism is apparent in the four articles in Part IV, "Rituals/Environment/Economy." Each of the articles presents the deep connections that exist between peoples' religious practices and beliefs, their relationships with the local environment, and their economic strategies. In each case, the authors describe people struggling to make a living in uncertain and changing conditions. The urban Mexicans described by Peter Cahn (Chapter 14) have come to believe that individuals can, with the right attitudes, prosper economically. In contrast, the Anishinaabe of Northern Ontario discussed in Chapter 15, the rural Peruvians described in Chapter 16, and the Malagasy villagers discussed in Chapter 17 are less certain of their ability to manage the future. Still, the ethnographies of each group show how they cope with and try to mitigate the uncertainties they face.

The final section, Part V, "Global Lives/Local Identities," contains four articles that examine the intersection of global and local phenomena. Each article concerns **globalization**—those processes that link widely dispersed peoples in ways such that "local happenings are shaped by events occurring many miles away and vice versa" (Giddens 1990: 64). Many scholars assert that the phenomena that we have come to associate with globalization—increased and increasingly rapid flows of ideas, finance, and media, as well as the fragmentation of manufacturing—are recent developments, permitted by newly developed information technologies. Others claim that the contemporary changes we label as globalization are actually changes in the speed and scale of connections rather than changes in the types of connections being made. What is clear, however, is that however the connections occur, globalization is a process of differentiation rather than one of homogenization. The four articles in Part V show how globalization plays out in particular places and among particular segments of the population. John Osburg (Chapter 19) describes the networking practices of men in Chengdu, China, made necessary by globalization. Alexandrine Boudreault-Fournier's (Chapter 21) ethnography of Afro-Cuban musicians shows how globalization holds out the possibility of individual fame and fortune within a relatively unstable society. Finally, both Vered Amit (Chapter 18) and Nelson Graburn (Chapter 20) consider if and how travel is transformative.

Professional anthropologists were the original audience for all of the articles included in this reader. Accordingly, the present volume gives students the opportunity to read, to analyze, and to interrogate actual anthropological writings. In order to make these materials accessible to beginning undergraduates, I have abridged, and in a few cases also annotated, the articles. In addition, I have written introductions to the articles; these introductions provide contextual information and explain many of the theoretical concepts used by the authors. Finally, I have provided definitions—in a glossary at the end of this book—for many of the more advanced or discipline-specific terms used in the articles. If your instructor has assigned a textbook in addition to this reader, that book will also cover many of the theories and specialized terms employed in the readings.

As you work your way through this reader, I encourage you to engage in further explorations of topics that excite you by consulting some of the suggested readings provided at the end of each chapter. For students and instructors interested in particular topics, the table below identifies some of the themes addressed in various chapters.

Themes Covered by Chapter

Theme/Subject	Chapter and Reading	Location
Advocacy by Anthropologists	Chapter 4, "Time in a Bottle"	Palestine
	Chapter 5, "A Green Coalition versus Big Uranium"	Canadian Prairies
Applied and Practising Anthropology	Chapter 5, "A Green Coalition versus Big Uranium"	Canadian Prairies
	Chapter 8, "De-medicalizing Anorexia"	North America
Canadian Peoples and Cultures	Chapter 2, "The Thin Edge of the Wedge"	British Columbia
	Chapter 3, "Brewing Trouble"	Quebec
	Chapter 5, "A Green Coalition versus Big Uranium"	Canadian Prairies
	Chapter 7, "'There Will Be a Lot of Old Young Men Going Home'"	Canada and Afghanistan
	Chapter 9, "The Sanitized Sensorium"	Ontario
	Chapter 13, "The Nucleation of Inuit Households"	Canadian Territories
	Chapter 15, "Re(con)figuring Alliances"	Ontario
	Chapter 18, "'Before I Settle Down'"	Canada and the World

Theme/Subject	Chapter and Reading	Location
Citizenship	Chapter 4, "Time in a Bottle"	Palestine
	Chapter 5, "A Green Coalition versus Big Uranium"	Canadian Prairies
	Chapter 9, "The Sanitized Sensorium"	Ontario
	Chapter 10, "Asking for a Child"	Vietnam
	Chapter 15, "Re(con)figuring Alliances"	Ontario
Economic Development and Modernization	Chapter 4, "Time in a Bottle"	Palestine
	Chapter 13, "The Nucleation of Inuit Households"	Canadian Territories
	Chapter 14, "Building Down and Dreaming Up"	Mexico
	Chapter 16, "Negotiating Livelihoods"	Peru
	Chapter 17, "After the Rush"	Madagascar
	Chapter 19, "Meeting the 'Godfather'"	China
Embodiment	Chapter 6, "*Tombois* in West Sumatra"	Indonesia
	Chapter 7, "'There Will Be a Lot of Old Young Men Going Home'"	Canada and Afghanistan
	Chapter 8, "De-medicalizing Anorexia"	North America
	Chapter 9, "The Sanitized Sensorium"	Ontario
Environment and Ecology	Chapter 5, "A Green Coalition versus Big Uranium"	Canadian Prairies
	Chapter 15, "Re(con)figuring Alliances"	Ontario
	Chapter 16, "Negotiating Livelihoods"	Peru
Ethnographic Fieldwork	Chapter 1, "Loyalty and Treachery in the Kalahari"	Namibia
	Chapter 3, "Brewing Trouble"	Quebec
	Chapter 6, "*Tombois* in West Sumatra"	Indonesia
	Chapter 19, "Meeting the 'Godfather'"	China
Expressive Culture	Chapter 2, "The Thin Edge of the Wedge"	British Columbia
	Chapter 20, "Work and Play in the Japanese Countryside"	Japan
	Chapter 21, "Positioning the New Reggaetón Stars in Cuba"	Cuba
Gender	Chapter 6, "*Tombois* in West Sumatra"	Indonesia
	Chapter 7, "'There Will Be a Lot of Old Young Men Going Home'"	Canada and Afghanistan
	Chapter 9, "The Sanitized Sensorium"	Ontario
	Chapter 10, "Asking for a Child"	Vietnam
	Chapter 11, "Mediated Marriage"	Russia
	Chapter 16, "Negotiating Livelihoods"	Peru
Globalization	Chapter 4, "Time in a Bottle"	Palestine
	Chapter 6, "*Tombois* in West Sumatra"	Indonesia
	Chapter 9, "The Sanitized Sensorium"	Ontario
	Chapter 11, "Mediated Marriage"	Russia
	Chapter 17, "After the Rush"	Madagascar
	Chapter 18, "'Before I Settle Down'"	Canada and the World
	Chapter 19, "Meeting the 'Godfather'"	China
	Chapter 20, "Work and Play in the Japanese Countryside"	Japan

Continued

Theme/Subject	Chapter and Reading	Location
Governance	Chapter 2, "The Thin Edge of the Wedge"	British Columbia
	Chapter 4, "Time in a Bottle"	Palestine
	Chapter 10, "Asking for a Child"	Vietnam
	Chapter 13, "The Nucleation of Inuit Households"	Canadian Territories
	Chapter 21, "Positioning the New Reggaetón Stars in Cuba"	Cuba
Indigenous Peoples	Chapter 1, "Loyalty and Treachery in the Kalahari"	Namibia
	Chapter 2, "The Thin Edge of the Wedge"	British Columbia
	Chapter 13, "The Nucleation of Inuit Households"	Canadian Territories
	Chapter 15, "Re(con)figuring Alliances"	Ontario
Kinship and Family	Chapter 10, "Asking for a Child"	Vietnam
	Chapter 11, "Mediated Marriage"	Russia
	Chapter 12, "Embryo Adoption"	United States
	Chapter 13, "The Nucleation of Inuit Households"	Canadian Territories
	Chapter 16, "Negotiating Livelihoods"	Peru
Life Course	Chapter 7, "'There Will Be a Lot of Old Young Men Going Home'"	Canada and Afghanistan
	Chapter 12, "Embryo Adoption"	United States
	Chapter 18, "'Before I Settle Down'"	Canada and the World
Medical Anthropology	Chapter 8, "De-medicalizing Anorexia"	North America
	Chapter 12, "Embryo Adoption"	United States
Multiculturalism/Cultural Pluralism	Chapter 3, "Brewing Trouble"	Quebec
	Chapter 9, "The Sanitized Sensorium"	Ontario
	Chapter 13, "The Nucleation of Inuit Households"	Canadian Territories
Race and Racism	Chapter 1, "Loyalty and Treachery in the Kalahari"	Namibia
	Chapter 2, "The Thin Edge of the Wedge"	British Columbia
	Chapter 4, "Time in a Bottle"	Palestine
	Chapter 9, "The Sanitized Sensorium"	Ontario
	Chapter 15, "Re(con)figuring Alliances"	Ontario
	Chapter 21, "Positioning the New Reggaetón Stars in Cuba"	Cuba
Rites of Passage	Chapter 1, "Loyalty and Treachery in the Kalahari"	Namibia
	Chapter 7, "'There Will Be a Lot of Old Young Men Going Home'"	Canada and Afghanistan
	Chapter 10, "Asking for a Child"	Vietnam
	Chapter 11, "Mediated Marriage"	Russia
	Chapter 12, "Embryo Adoption"	United States
	Chapter 18, "'Before I Settle Down'"	Canada and the World
Religion and World View	Chapter 2, "The Thin Edge of the Wedge"	British Columbia
	Chapter 14, "Building Down and Dreaming Up"	Mexico
	Chapter 15, "Re(con)figuring Alliances"	Ontario

Theme/Subject	Chapter and Reading	Location
Sexuality	Chapter 6, "*Tombois* in West Sumatra"	Indonesia
	Chapter 10, "Asking for a Child"	Vietnam
Social and Economic Stratification	Chapter 1, "Loyalty and Treachery in the Kalahari"	Namibia
	Chapter 4, "Time in a Bottle"	Palestine
	Chapter 9, "The Sanitized Sensorium"	Ontario
Warfare	Chapter 7, "'There Will Be a Lot of Old Young Men Going Home'"	Canada and Afghanistan
	Chapter 10, "Asking for a Child"	Vietnam

PART I

Anthropological Traditions/
Contemporary Practice

Chapter 1

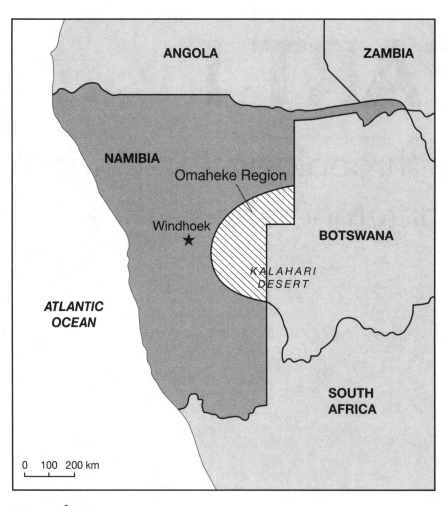

Namibia

Introduction

All cultures change. One of the ways anthropologists document cultural change is by conducting new research among groups that have been studied previously. The article below, by Renée Sylvain, concerns a group of people known as San (or Ju/'hoansi) who live in the southern African country of Namibia. Some aspects of Ju/'hoansi culture are well known through **ethnographic** studies conducted in the 1950s and 1960s. Those important studies, particularly among Ju/'hoansi living in neighbouring Botswana, helped transform the way that anthropologists and others understand **hunting and gathering** as a way of life (Lee 1968). Previously, **foragers** were thought to live difficult, almost destitute lives. But as a result of this research, anthropologists began to think about the San and other hunting and gathering peoples as the "original affluent societies." While we usually think of affluent people as having many material possessions, many hunting and gathering peoples had few possessions; yet they lived well. The Ju/'hoansi in Botswana studied by Canadian anthropologist Richard Lee in the 1960s had nutritious, calorie-rich diets, and the men, especially, worked very few hours each day. Lee's research helped anthropologists understand that all peoples' material needs are learned rather than absolute or universal. Although they had few material possessions, the Ju/'hoansi were described as "affluent" because they had few unmet needs.

The Ju/'hoansi discussed in the article below, who live in the Omaheke Region of Namibia, are part of the same cultural group as the Botswana Ju/'hoansi, but their lives are very different from those of the affluent foragers described by Lee. (Indeed, today the San in Botswana do not live the hunting and gathering life they did in the 1960s.) San in the Omaheke Region of Namibia have not lived by hunting and gathering for more than a century. This is because their traditional lands were confiscated to be used as farmland by German, and later Afrikaner, colonists.[1] In order to survive, most of the Omaheke San became farm labourers and domestic servants. Today about half the Omaheke San live and work on Afrikaner-owned farms. Many officials in Namibia mistakenly regard wage-labouring San as having "lost" their culture because they do not live the ways their ancestors did. Some told Sylvain that there are no San in the Omaheke area.

The article below presents some of the dilemmas that Sylvain faced in planning and conducting her research. For many people, carrying out ethnographic **fieldwork** is the very essence of what it means to be an anthropologist. Anthropological fieldwork often involves spending long periods—often a year or more—living away from home, speaking a different language, and learning about the lives of those being studied from their perspective. Fieldwork is transformative for the anthropologist, but it can also have important consequences for the people studied. Sometimes anthropologists help the people they study, but sometimes they cause problems by meddling in or disturbing existing relationships. Over time, the social science research community in Canada has developed a set of ethical guidelines and procedures meant to help anthropologists and other social scientists conduct research in ways that avoid causing harm to **informants**. But as the article reveals, an abstract set of ethical guidelines does not always provide the tools to resolve real ethical dilemmas encountered in the field.

As Sylvain describes, she designed a research project to study some of the causes and consequences of **racial**, **gender**, and **class** inequality in southern Africa. Anthropologists often have both grand and specific aims in their research. One of Sylvain's general, yet primary, aims was to conduct research that would advance social and economic justice. Her specific project was to study a group of San (formerly known as Bushmen) in Namibia. Namibia is one of four countries in southern Africa where San people live, the others being Angola, Botswana, and South Africa.

Namibia was a good choice for studying the complexities of inequality. From 1915 to 1990, Namibia was a colony of South Africa, which imposed its strict racial segregation laws known as **apartheid**. The system of racial classifications was primarily cultural, but skin colour was also invoked to create artificial boundaries between different groups of people. Under this system, the brown-skinned San were lumped together with mixed-race people, as well as descendants of Malaysian former slaves, into the category "coloured." In the racial hierarchy of apartheid, whites sat at the top, followed by people from the Indian sub-continent, then coloureds, and finally black Africans. In the case of the San, however, their cultural heritage as supposedly "primitive" hunting and gathering peoples erased any privilege that their lighter skin colour might have afforded them among both whites and blacks.

We cannot always predict how we will respond when confronted with ethical challenges. As Sylvain notes, she had to figure out how to navigate the privileges that her different identities (such as white woman, foreigner, and adopted daughter) afforded her within a landscape so deeply shaped by racial apartheid. She had to consider whether to use the privilege afforded to her by her whiteness to help her San informants, or did invoking her white privilege to help individual San perpetuate racial inequality?

❖ About the Author ❖

Renée Sylvain studied anthropology at Wilfred Laurier University and then at the University of Toronto. She first travelled to Namibia as a doctoral student in 1996. Although this was two years after the end of apartheid in South Africa and six years after Namibian independence, she found that the effects of racism and colonialism continued. Sylvain, who teaches at the University of Guelph, continues to do research among San. She has recently been comparing the experiences of San in South Africa, Botswana, and Namibia as these people struggle to assert their human rights.

Loyalty and Treachery in the Kalahari

Renée Sylvain

The San (Bushmen) of the Omaheke Region in eastern Namibia are one of the most stigmatized and marginalized ethnic groups in southern Africa. Most live and work on cattle ranches owned by Afrikaner farmers, but an increasing number move between resettlement camps and the squatters' villages on the edges of urban areas, where they struggle to make ends meet by performing menial tasks for other ethnic groups and where they are the targets of racially and ethnically motivated violence. The situation of the Omaheke San is bleak, but not hopeless. They are remarkably adept at negotiating the extreme power asymmetries that structure their lives, and, even in the most marginal areas, they create and maintain a meaningful cultural life for themselves.

There is love and laughter in the lives of the San, and they are determined to improve their material conditions and "go forward."

My research focussed on one group of San, the Ju/'hoansi, who live and work on white-owned farms. My commitment to research that had social and economic justice as its primary goals meant that I had to be very careful not to exacerbate the already volatile relations between the San and other ethnic groups. I also had to determine how far to participate in the lives of people who must survive through banditry. The ethical codes and research contracts currently being elaborated are too aloof to help us navigate ethical problems that arise in particular field situations, and the good professionals they help us to be are not always the same as the good persons we hope to become. For the sources of an anthropologist's moral **agency**, we must look at how the anthropologist is variously defined as an agent. Specifically, we need to pay attention to the ways the anthropologist's own identity is shaped and played out in the process of conducting fieldwork.

The Ironic Advocate

Filling out forms and responding to the queries of ethics committees provides opportunities to reflect on the wisdom of imposing only one ethical vocabulary, a discourse of legal persons and professional responsibility, onto what most anthropologists insist is an unstable and contradictory moral engagement. Our compliance with codified and contract-based ethical frameworks often implies the betrayal of a deeper commitment to other moral vocabularies. This ironic conviction was what motivated many of us to do anthropology in the first place. . . .

It is widely recognized that fieldwork is a **rite of passage**: as neophyte anthropologists we go through the familiar phases of separation, **liminality**, and reintegration. However, in most tales from the field, this rite of passage is treated as something to be endured, survived, and surpassed in order to get down to the "real" business of gathering data and writing up one's research. "**Culture shock**," the dissonance that individuals often feel when first immersed in another culture, is often seen as an obstacle to knowledge, rather than an experience that can produce a more nuanced moral subjectivity. But as anthropologists who study rites of passage appreciate, these rites change the initiate's identity. The same is true for anthropologists. Our identities and our self-understanding change as we move through our initiation ritual of fieldwork.

The Hopeful Reformer

During my pre-fieldwork training in graduate school, I was duly humbled, diminished, and destabilized by the postmodern turn in anthropology. I was schooled in all the ways in which anthropology was implicated in colonial injustices, in its authoritarian predilection for silencing and then speaking for "the Other," and about how anthropology itself was suffering from an incurable identity crisis. While preparing for fieldwork among the San, I developed an appreciation for the extent to which they had been subject to racial stereotyping in the popular media and even in many early ethnographic works. So I saw myself as a reformer ready to study the intersections of gender, race, and class inequalities in a place where apartheid remained powerfully present, even after six years of independence from South African rule. My mission was to deconstruct colonial and neo-colonial stereotypes. So off I went to the Omaheke to do battle against the evils of bad discourse.

Before I could confront bad discourse, however, I had to get past the hostile Afrikaner farmers and onto their farms where the San are labourers. My anxiety only increased once I arrived in Namibia and was told by every local expert I met in the capital city that the farmers would shoot me. I decided to present myself to the farmers in very vague terms, as an "ivory-tower" ethnologist concerned primarily with a romantic prehistoric past. One of the first farmers to grant me permission to speak to his workers gave me a friendly warning: "If you interfere with my workers," he said, "I'll shoot you."

Despite the threats and the warnings, what I did not anticipate was the extent to which many farmers would enthusiastically support my research. Labour relations on the farms are based on the farmers' notions of "innate capacities" and levels of "cultural development" among different "nations." Since running a farm requires an intimate knowledge of the different "ethnic natures" of their various workers, farmers often see themselves as amateur ethnologists.

My first encounter with such a farmer taught me an important lesson about the difficulties of securing informed consent in a context marked by profound class, gender, and race inequalities. Immediately after I explained my project, the farmer turned to a Ju/'hoan woman working in his kitchen and demanded that she round up all the Ju/'hoan women on the farm and bring them to meet me at the farmhouse to answer my questions. Since the farmer insisted on observing, I had no choice but to conduct interviews with these women. I did my best to keep my questions harmless (asking if they remembered the "old time" ways), but the experience was almost as painful for me as I'm sure it was for the women.

After that encounter, I developed a coded introductory statement that my interpreter and I could present to Ju/'hoansi even if the farmer was present. In English or Afrikaans, I would explain that I was interested in learning about "old time ways." My interpreter would explain, in Ju/'hoan, that I wanted to talk to them about gender, race, and class issues. The farmer would hear the apolitical version of my project in a language he could understand, while the Ju/'hoansi heard the political version in a language he couldn't.

Upon arriving on a farm, I was usually obliged to visit with the farmer before I set off to the workers' compound. Since the Ju/'hoansi had just seen me sitting with their *baas* [boss], drinking tea and having a nice chat, I was initially treated with distrust. I would have to earn their trust and assure them that I would not disclose the content of our conversations to their employer, who, if he learned what we had discussed, would possibly fire them or, even worse, beat them.

Farmers were not the only obstacle to getting informed consent. Before we started interviewing farm workers, my interpreter warned me that almost every farm had a *witvoet* (white-foot), "a person who walks to the farmer with the black peoples' business." So first I had to become integrated into the social life on the farms in order for the San to tell me which of the workers could not be trusted. I ended up interviewing people about innocuous matters for months before I fully disclosed the true subject of my research. The issue of trust worked both ways: I had to find out who I could trust, and I had to prove myself trustworthy. To do this, I had to redefine myself as a white woman.

Neither a *Miessis*, nor a Missionary

When I first arrived in the Omaheke, I was addressed as *miessis*, the local term for madam, reserved for use by black and Bushman servants when they are speaking to a white farmer's wife. It is usually accompanied by a subservient posture, head bowed, hat in hands. I would reply, "I'm not a madam" (*Ek is nie'n miessis nie*). Upon hearing this, many Africans would fall back on the next likely identity for a white woman—if I was not a *miessis*, then I must be a missionary. Most abandoned this theory when they saw me smoking and heard me cursing at my truck.

The first farmer my husband and I met welcomed us warmly. He and his wife were excited to have visitors from so far away after years of isolation that came with the pariah status of their apartheid government. The farmer, a liberal thinker by local standards, explained how labour relations were shaped in the apartheid days: "When you first bring the blacks onto your farm, you take the biggest, strongest one down from the truck and beat him senseless with a *sjambok* [a leather whip]—from there you won't have any problems with the blacks on your farm." The farmer's wife asked about our experiences with the local black population. Since we were foreigners, they expected "the blacks" to get "cheeky" with us. The farmer advised us to get a deep tan (so that we would look like local whites) and to commit a few Afrikaans phrases to memory (these phrases had to be properly pronounced and preferably barked): "What do you want?" (*Wat soek julle?*) and "Are you looking for trouble?" (*Soek jy moelikheid?*). Safety, we learned, lies in being mistaken for Afrikaners, who the blacks "knew" to be capable of any form of barbarity. Initially my husband and I decided not to heed the well-intended advice, but there were episodes where we felt we had little choice.

One such occasion occurred in the squatters' village on the fringes of the black township of Epako, where many unemployed and impoverished San live. One young Ju/'hoan man, //Umte, was especially helpful as an informant, and he was one of the first San people to befriend us. One day, while my husband and I were conducting interviews and visiting //Umte's family, some young Damara men, local thugs who were constantly terrorizing and bullying the San, stole the family's donkey cart and donkeys. We heard the commotion when a group of San men set off in pursuit of the Damaras and the donkeys.

The San men caught up with the Damaras, and, just as my husband and I arrived, a fight was on the verge of breaking out. The chase had taken us into an area of the township dominated by Damaras, and the San were clearly outnumbered and were about to take a beating. When the Damara men caught sight of my husband, their combative posture intensified. At that point my husband barked, "*Soek jy moelikheid?*" Every non-San person within hearing range backed off several feet. The donkey-cart was immediately returned, with profuse apologies for the "misunderstanding," and a fight was avoided. The San had a good laugh when we returned to their shacks, but my husband and I had long conversations about the ramifications of our behaviour for the San after we left.

Now It's "N≠isa"

Firewood is a chronic problem in Epako. As the squatters' village expanded over the last decade, the surrounding veld [scrubland] has become denuded. Now San women must travel five to ten kilometres to gather firewood. While travelling through the veld, many are beaten, robbed, and raped by young men who belong to the township gangs. They must take this risk, though, since one cannot eat without firewood to cook the staple mealie [cornmeal] porridge.

As I got to know the San families in the squatters' village, I was eventually approached for assistance in gathering firewood. My truck would enable the San to gather a week's supply of firewood in only a few minutes if I could take them far enough from the denuded municipal lands. But gathering outside the municipal lands meant stealing from the vast farms in the surrounding area. My husband or I would drive several Ju/'hoan men 30 to 40 kilometres north of Epako. We would park the truck next to the fenceline of a farm owned by an absentee farmer, and while the Ju/'hoan men went into the bush we would deflate the truck tires. If we saw a dust cloud on the road indicating an approaching vehicle, we would give a shout to the Ju/'hoan men, who hid behind the bushes, while we pretended to pump the tires back up. We developed variations of

this method to avoid suspicion—for instance, opening the hood to check the fan belt or distributor cap.

As the veld around the squatters' village denudes, the Ju/'hoansi have no choice but to venture onto the white farms to poach firewood. In response, there are increasing episodes of violence against Ju/'hoansi, including beatings and electrocution. However, if the Ju/'hoansi got caught while they were with us, the chances they would be beaten were significantly reduced. Protected by our own whiteness, we would get little more than a scolding.

Our willingness to assist in their efforts to gather firewood was one way we were able [to] earn the trust of the Ju/'hoansi. Despite farmers' threats, we soon found ourselves "interfering" almost constantly with San farm workers. On the majority of farms we visited, we encountered very sick people, many of them children. Tuberculosis, malnutrition, and malaria were the primary ailments. The farmer was usually unwilling to drive them to town to get medical attention, or if he was willing, he would charge them more than they could afford for the petrol [gasoline]. Very often, we would smuggle these sick people off the farms to take them to the clinic or the hospital, and then, after they were treated, we would smuggle them back. This meant taking some risks, but, in the circumstances, it was the only way to behave morally.

Once the Ju/'hoansi had established that my husband and I could be trusted, they began to treat us differently. When I first arrived in the field, I was referred to by the Ju/'hoansi as "*/tun dima*" (little white woman). As I developed closer relationships with them, particularly with the family that adopted my husband and I, I was renamed "N≠isa." Many new responsibilities came with my status as **fictive kin**.

Once I was named, I became a relative of every woman named N≠isa and of anyone with a relative named N≠isa. In one village in the northern Omaheke, I was adopted by N!hunkxa. In accordance with Ju/'hoan practices, she would address me as "daughter," because her daughter and I shared the same name. I was expected to engage in the **generalized reciprocity** for which the Ju/'hoansi are famous. If I had a skirt I wasn't wearing often, I was expected to give it to my sister. An old pair of shoes I was

FIGURE 1.1   San Girls in Namibia.

ready to discard should be given to a relative who needed them. When I refused to provide assistance at an inappropriate time, or if I neglected to assist someone who had a legitimate claim on me, my Ju/'hoan family would chastise me by addressing me as *miessis*, implying thereby that I was behaving in an un-Ju/'hoan manner. I had to learn how to be less like a white person, whom the Ju/'hoansi characterize as "far-hearted," and more like a proper, if honorary, Ju/'hoan. I did my best to do my familial duties, but all the while, tugging at my conscience, was the knowledge that research contracts developed by the **non-governmental organizations** (NGOs) that work with the San contain an absolute prohibition against "hand-outs," with a special caution against gifts of clothing. Such gifts, it was believed, would instill a "dependency mentality" among the San.

White by Many Lights

As the Ju/'hoansi got to know me better, after I had transformed into what they called a "different" sort of white person, they occasionally manipulated my multidimensional whiteness. When I was on a farm, a Ju/'hoan man would approach me: "N≠isa, you must take my wife to the clinic, she is very sick. We'll hide her in the back of your truck under some blankets so the farmer won't know." On the farm, I was N≠isa, a co-conspirator, and a source of familial support and assistance. Once in town, however, I was to present myself to the clinic staff as "*die miessis*," and the Ju/'hoan patient was to be my "worker." This way we could count on the medical staff treating Ju/'hoan patients. The same applied in any government office. If the Ju/'hoansi arrived at a ministry office on their own, they would be passed over and ignored by the civil servants at the counter. However, if I came along and insisted that my "worker" needed his or her identity documents, the forms would be provided and processed.

So I learned about power not so much because I was studying it, but because I had it. I went to the front of every queue; I was given immediate attention in any government office; I was waited on promptly in any medical clinic or restaurant. I quickly saw that this kind of power and privilege can seriously warp an individual's character. One had to be careful and very self-aware.

In the offices of NGOs I heard a rumour (only that) about a young researcher who had gone into the north to work with the Ju/'hoansi. They told me that after only a few months in the bush, he had transformed the local Ju/'hoansi into his servants, who did his cooking and laundry, kept his house clean, and waited on him. I was unable to investigate this story myself. However, the complicated and occasionally antagonistic relations between NGO workers and anthropologists led me to take it with a grain of salt. But even rumour and myth can provide moral instruction, so I saw two interpretations. The NGO workers related it as a story about the assertion of racism and white privilege, but it might also be a story about a researcher "going native" and becoming the only sort of white person the San knew how to help him be.

When I heard this rumour, I remembered the constant pressure put on me by Ju/'hoan men to hire their wives to clean and cook for me and the scandal my husband and I caused by hand-washing our own laundry—a job that whites and non-whites alike consider a job for servants. I did eventually hire a particularly desperate but proud Ju/'hoan man to wash my truck on weekends, a pointless exercise in the Kalahari, but a way of enabling him to feed his family. To not do this, I thought, would have been morally callous. But, as I later came to see, to do so was also to risk moral peril.

There were other ways in which expectations of "white" behaviour imposed themselves. One Ju/'hoan man, Debe, with whom I had become very close, was struggling with an extreme addiction to

alcohol. He suffered from delirium tremens and was often on the verge of starvation and complete physical breakdown. Debe's drinking was the subject of many bitter and heated arguments between us. During one argument, he insisted that I must help him with his drinking problem, saying, "You must be like a white farmer and beat me if I drink." He accepted my vague explanations about why I couldn't administer a helpful beating, but at that moment I began to appreciate the trap that the local white people were in.

As I had more opportunities to interact with Afrikaners, I was reminded of George Orwell's essay "Shooting an Elephant," about a white police officer in colonial Lower Burma who is called upon to deal with a rogue elephant:

> I did not in the least want to shoot [the elephant]. . . . But at that moment I glanced around at the crowd that had followed me. . . . And suddenly I realized that I should have to shoot the elephant after all. The people expected it of me and I had got to do it. . . . And it was at this moment, as I stood there with the rifle in my hands, that I first grasped the hollowness, the futility of the white man's domination in the East. . . . I perceived in this moment that when the white man turns tyrant it is his own freedom that he destroys. . . . He wears a mask, and his face grows into it. ([1940] 1984: 22)

As I watched the Afrikaners struggle with their own power and privilege, I began to recognize that they, too, were not completely free—more comfortable for sure, but not entirely free. Their moral codes had to bend to scripts of which they were not the sole authors. The director of an NGO that began working with the San in 1998 told me that the San suffered from "internalized oppression." I doubt that all the oppression from which they suffer is internal, but I want to use her phrase, turned on its head: inside even the most liberal of whites, in the political and moral environment of southern Africa, grows an internal oppressor.

Even though the whites were also in their own kind of trap, my loyalties were to the Ju/'hoansi.

This usually required some form of treachery toward the farmers. I began to realize that much of my concern to demonstrate my trustworthiness to the Ju/'hoansi was not motivated by my desire to get them to open up to me so that I could gather data, but by my desire to be a different kind of white person, to distance myself from the whiteness of the Afrikaners. The abstract, disembodied expert on the construction of identity was under construction.

My Traitor's Heart

Afrikaners understood that I needed insight into the psychology of being white in southern Africa. One of the first books they suggested for my edification was Breyten Breytenbach's *The True Confessions of an Albino Terrorist* (1983), a story written by one of South Africa's most famous poets, who had spent 15 years in exile and was eventually arrested by the apartheid regime. The other was Rian Malan's *My Traitor's Heart* (1990), written by a descendant of D.F. Malan, South Africa's first nationalist prime minister and the founder of the formal system of apartheid. Were my white informants trying to tell me something? I already saw myself as an anti-racist feminist, strongly committed to class issues and social justice. But was I also a "race traitor"?

Alison Bailey defines "race traitors" as "privilege-cognizant whites who refuse to animate the scripts whites are expected to perform and who are unfaithful to **world views** whites are expected to hold" (1998: 28). On this definition, becoming a race traitor is a worthy goal. But it is clearly not as easy as this. There were many situations where animating "white-privilege scripts" was the only way to behave morally toward the Ju/'hoansi. By strategically playing the role of the white *miessis*, I was perpetuating a system of racial and class subordination; at the same time, I was securing medical care for a desperately ill individual. Ethics must negotiate with power, and one dubious act may be the necessary precondition for an ethical act. However, it is from such contradictory and ambiguous situations that a moral subjectivity evolves. . . .

Since I was conducting research on Ju/'hoan domestic servants on the farms, I was especially interested in the unique kind of class and racial consciousness they developed through their relationships with their white employers. Tchi!o, my main female informant and my closest friend in the field, confided to me many times that she sees her white *miessis* as lazy, stingy, and rather helpless, yet also trapped and desperate. She also told me that she knew that her *miessis* saw her as dull-witted and incompetent. What I had in common with Ju/'hoan domestic servants was not an essential womanhood and certainly not a shared perspective on the world derived from a similar position within the socioeconomic hierarchy. But we did share similar experiences of being "outsiders-within" (see Bailey 1998: 29 and Collins 1990). Tchi!o could see, from the outside, how whites lived and how whites saw and defined her. She could see herself through the eyes of whites. I could see, from the outside, how the Ju/'hoansi lived and how they saw and defined whites. However partial and myopic the view achieved, it was through their eyes that I had begun to catch glimpses of myself.

Alison Bailey claims that "World travel must put our privileged identities at risk by travelling to worlds where we often feel ill-at-ease or off-center" (Bailey 1998: 40). By travelling into the world of the Ju/'hoansi, I was also travelling into the world of racial inequality of which I was a part. Of course, anthropologists are professional world travellers, but it was only by putting my *professional* identity at risk that I could better appreciate my own position in the apartheid-coloured world of the Omaheke.

Conclusion

Just before he describes his arrest at Jan Smuts International Airport, Breyten Breytenbach poses the following question to his imagined interrogator:

> Will it be possible one day to know where you come from, and therefore where you are, and therefore where you are heading, and therefore what you are, in which case you should be able to attach a name to it?

He answers this question for himself: "if there is one thing that has become amply clear to me over the years, it is exactly that there is no one person that can be named and in the process of naming be fixed for all eternity" (1983: 13).

I was not limited to just one name or just one identity; I had to negotiate many. But it was very important that the Ju/'hoansi give me a name, and by manipulating my fictive Ju/'hoan identity and my multidimensional white identity, they gave me an invaluable source of moral subjectivity. By the moral codes under which I signed on to do fieldwork, I became a liar and a thief. But these codes were designed to regulate the behaviour of a person with a fixed identity: a professional researcher, an expert, a disembodied observer. They were never suited to regulate relations among friends and family (even fictive kin) for someone whose identity, by the very nature of fieldwork, is challenged, put at risk, and altered.

Of course, there are those for whom the processes that destabilize the self will appear as a loss of any centre of moral gravity. . . . And there are those who have raised doubts about the real depth of the doubling and decentredness that characterize anthropological fieldwork. That is, the rapport established by complicity with "natives" always has an element of insincerity and can only be sustained by ignoring the broader contexts of power that situate the ethnographer. However, that would only be so if there was a single unified self, a centre of moral agency to which the anthropologist fails to be true in the acts which express her complicity with her subjects and to which she can simply return when her ethnographic travels end. Those of us with a less abstract (and so less secure) view of the self will settle for, and even be consoled by, John Dewey's thoughts on such matters: "selfhood (except insofar as it has encased itself in a shell of routine) is in the process of making . . . [and] any self is capable of including within itself a number of inconsistent selves, of unharmonized dispositions" (cited in Rorty 1999: 78). Rorty explains Dewey's **pragmatist** view in terms that may suit many world travellers: "Moral development in the individual, and moral progress in the human species as a whole, is a matter of remaking human selves so as to enlarge the variety of the relationships which constitute those selves" (1999: 79).

By putting our own identities at risk, by "enlarging the variety of the relationships which constitute our selves," we develop new moral habits, not just new habits of behaviour, but also new habits of perception. By trying to see ourselves through other people's eyes, we expand the community of others to whom we must justify ourselves, and so to whom we belong. Except by the standards of the previous and narrower selves we have shed along the way, this does not sound like ethical collapse or moral decay, but the very substance of moral progress.

References Cited

Bailey, Alison. 1998. "Locating Traitorous Identities: Toward a View of Privilege-Cognizant White Character." *Hypatia* 13 (3) 27–52.

Breytenbach, Breyten. 1983. *The True Confessions of an Albino Terrorist*. San Diego: Harcourt Brace and Company.

Collins, Patricia Hill. 1990. *Black Feminist Thought: Knowledge, Consciousness, and the Politics of Empowerment*. New York: Routledge.

Malan, Rian. 1990. *My Traitor's Heart: A South African Exile Returns to Face His Country, His Tribe, and His Conscience*. New York: Grove Press.

Orwell, George. (1940) 1984. "Shooting an Elephant." In *George Orwell: Essays*. London: Penguin Books.

Rorty, Richard. 1999. "Ethics without Principles." In *Philosophy and Social Hope*. London: Penguin Books.

Note

1. Afrikaners are the descendants of Dutch settlers who colonized southern Africa beginning in 1652. (Stern's note)

Key Points to Consider

- Ju/'hoansi (or San) in the Omaheke area of Namibia are descended from formerly hunting and gathering peoples, but they lost their lands to German and Afrikaner colonists several generations ago.
- Racism and other legacies of apartheid contribute to the extreme poverty of the Omaheke San. Sylvain's fieldwork revealed that both whites and San held beliefs about the "nature" of members of the other group. These beliefs informed and constrained their interactions.
- Formal codes of research ethics are critical in designing and implementing research projects, but they do not provide a solution for every ethical dilemma anthropologists encounter in the field.
- In order to do ethnographic fieldwork, anthropologists develop relationships of trust with their informants.

Critical Thinking Questions

1. What did Sylvain set out to study in Namibia? Was she able to gather data on the topic? What are some examples of the data she collected?
2. What were the ethical dilemmas that Sylvain experienced while doing fieldwork? Would you resolve them in the same ways? Why or why not?
3. Informed consent—that is, participants' agreement to take part in a research project whose aims and parameters they understand—is one of the central principles of ethical research. What obstacles did Sylvain face in getting truly informed consent for her research? How did she handle the problem? What would you have done in the same situation?
4. Anthropologists sometimes experience "culture shock" or feelings of strangeness or disorientation when doing research away from their own cultures. By highlighting differences, moments of culture shock often help anthropologists recognize ideas that they or their informants take for granted. This can help them better understand their own and other cultures. Which of Sylvain's reactions to her experiences in Namibia would you explain as "culture shock"? Why? Have you experienced culture shock that led you to question something you previously took for granted?

Suggestions for Further Reading and Watching

Lee, Richard B., Robert Hitchcock, and Megan Biesele, eds. 2002. "The Kalahari San: Self-Determination in the Desert." Special issue, *Cultural Survival Quarterly* 26 (1): 8–61.

Marshall, John. 2002. *A Kalahari Family*. Watertown, MA: Documentary Educational Resources. Video recording, 360 min. (A five-part video series about a group of contemporary Ju/'hoansi living in another part of Namibia.)

Sylvain, Renée. 2002. "'Land, Water, and Truth': San Identity and Global Indigenism." *American Anthropologist* 104 (4): 1074–85.

———. 2007. "Structural Violence and Social Suffering among the San in Southern Africa." *Indigenous Affairs* 4: 16–21.

Chapter 2

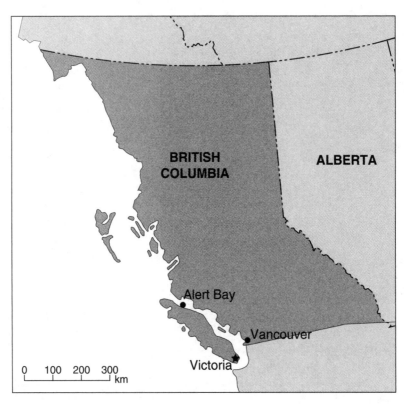

British Columbia

Introduction

Anthropology in Canada once concentrated on documenting the cultures of **Aboriginal peoples**, and on collecting tools, items of clothing, and religious objects connected to these peoples' cultures as they existed prior to European colonization. Initially, anthropologists focused on these tasks because they assumed that Aboriginal cultures would disappear as **First Nations** people interacted with non-Natives and adopted new religious practices and altered many of their **subsistence** activities. In fact, many early ethnographic reports include descriptions of practices that no longer exist, and Canadian museums contain objects that might have been destroyed if not collected. But this is not to say that **salvage anthropology**, as this kind of research was called, was always benign; sometimes anthropologists and others took cultural artifacts without permission, arrogantly believing that these items were better off preserved in a museum than kept and used by Aboriginal peoples.

In the late nineteenth and early twentieth centuries, anthropologists and others believed that **cultural assimilation** was inevitable. After all, until as recently as the middle of the twentieth century, the Canadian government actively enforced policies that were designed to make Aboriginal cultures disappear. Some of the government activities intended to undermine Aboriginal cultures include requiring Aboriginal children to attend residential schools, regulating and restricting subsistence work like hunting and trapping, and prohibiting Aboriginal religious and cultural ceremonies. The article below concerns the last of these. Rather than documenting loss, the author shows how an Aboriginal community coped with government demands by adapting, but not abandoning, a valued cultural practice.

In 1884 and again in 1895, the government of Canada amended the law governing Aboriginal peoples, known as the Indian Act, to criminalize two activities important to First Nations people in coastal British Columbia: the **potlatch** and the Hamat'sa dance. Despite vigorous efforts on the part of government administrators to control and transform the lives of First Nations peoples, neither the potlatch nor the Hamat'sa dance disappeared. The bans were eventually removed from the Indian Act in 1951, and both activities continue today.

In the article below, which has been shortened substantially, Aaron Glass describes some of the government's efforts to prevent Native people from potlatching and dancing as well as the efforts of Kwakwaka'wakw people in British Columbia to continue the two practices. Glass focuses especially on the Hamat'sa dance (also called the "cannibal dance") and looks at the ways Kwakwaka'wakw adapted their dances to fit their changing social and legal circumstances. He uses oral and written historical sources in addition to **ethnography** to uncover the multiple and overlapping meanings of the dance for its practitioners.

Kwakwaka'wakw are the First Nations bands whose historic language is Kwak'wala and whose traditional territories include the coastal areas of northeast Vancouver Island and the adjacent British Columbia mainland and small islands. There are several distinct bands, each with a specific name. Many older ethnographies and textbooks mistakenly label all Kwakwaka'wakw as Kwakiutl, but that name refers only to the band from Fort Rupert, British Columbia. The Fort Rupert Kwakwaka'wakw became well known, and the name Kwakiutl was popularized, through the writings of anthropologist Franz Boas (1858–1942) and the photography of Edward S. Curtis (1868–1952). The article below concentrates on the 'Namgis First Nation from Alert Bay.

Potlatches were not exclusive to Kwakwaka'wakw and are still practised by many First Nations groups in and along the Northwest Coast region of North America. In fact, the word *potlatch* comes from Chinook Jargon, a **pidgin language** spoken by various groups—mainly to facilitate trade—in the Pacific Northwest in the nineteenth and early twentieth centuries. Potlatches are sometimes described as "give-away feasts," but they were, and still are, complex social, political, economic, and religious events that were much more than give-away feasts. French anthropologist Marcel Mauss (1872–1950) named the potlatch as an example of a "total social phenomenon"—an institution or occurrence that is enmeshed in every facet of a culture. It is possible that Mauss overstated the all-encompassing nature of the potlatch, but there is no doubt that the government prohibition struck at an institution of great importance to Kwakwaka'wakw.

There were pronounced differences in status and power within traditional Kwakwaka'wakw society, and potlatches reaffirmed each person's position in the social hierarchy. Potlatches were hosted by chiefs to commemorate important events such as weddings and births, and to affirm the transfer of ritual names and roles from one person to another. Today they are also used to memorialize people who have recently died. As in the past, gifts, often of a substantial nature, are given by the host to the guests. The explicit purpose of the gifts is payment for witnessing important social events, but hosts also affirm and enhance their own status (and indebt their guests) through extravagant gifting and other displays of wealth. The dances performed during potlatches are also forms of religious or spiritual expression in that they are ritual presentations of Kwakwaka'wakw origin myths.

Kwakwaka'wakw today describe the Hamat'sa dance as one of the most important and most sacred of their traditional dances. The dancers enact mythological dramas depicting the acquisition, by ancestral heroes, of several sacred dances, songs, masks, and other ritual materials from a man-eating spirit. In the process, the hero becomes a cannibal and, as a result, he needs to be resocialized (initiated) before he can return to the world of humans.[1] Some of the dancers wear large bird masks to represent the attendants of the man-eating spirit. The initiate, while in his wild state, is "fed" bits of human flesh. While there is little direct evidence that the Hamat'sa dance ever involved the consumption of human flesh, it was an emotionally and symbolically powerful ritual event that greatly troubled missionaries and government administrators in the late nineteenth century.

Canadian officials had a variety of reasons and motives for prohibiting the potlatch and the Hamat'sa dance, and as Glass points out there was no unified, official position shared by all government officials. Some were motivated by a desire to convert First Nations peoples to Christianity and to stop any Aboriginal practices they perceived as pagan. Some who sought Aboriginal labour for the emerging lumber and fishing industries in British Columbia believed potlatches were extravagant and wasteful, perpetuated Indigenous economies, and distracted people from "productive" work. Others were embarrassed that Canada could be associated with the grotesque features of the Hamat'sa dance.[2] Finally, many officials assumed that Euro-Canadian ways of life were superior to those of First Nations, and even those who were not horrified by extravagant potlatches or simulations of cannibalism believed that Euro-Canadian values and practices would inevitably replace those of the First Nations.

Cultural traditions reinforce important social and emotional links to a people's past. We have a tendency to think of traditions as unchanging, but this is not the case for any people. The article below shows how Kwakwaka'wakw refused to abandon their potlatches and their dances, instead finding ways to continue their cultural practices in new contexts, such as celebrations of Canadian events and milestones. Dance is often treated as a form of **expressive culture**, appreciated mostly for its symbolic and emotional value to people rather than as a practice that has concrete effects. The historical and ethnographic evidence that Glass presents reveals, however, that expressive practices do have important real-life effects.

❧ *About the Author* ❦

Aaron Glass is an anthropologist, artist, and filmmaker at the Bard Graduate Center in New York. He has been conducting research on Kwakwa̲ka̲'wakw history, material culture, and expressive culture since the 1990s. His work is innovative in the way that it draws connections between visual and performing arts, historical processes, and contemporary social institutions. Recently, Glass has been working with the U'mista Cultural Society and others to document and recover historical materials about Kwakwa̲ka̲'wakw. One project involved restoration of the silent film In the Land of the Head Hunters, *made in 1914 by photographer Edward S. Curtis with Kwakwa̲ka̲'wakw in and around Fort Rupert.*

The Thin Edge of the Wedge: Dancing around the Potlatch Ban, 1921–1951

Aaron Glass

It was cold in the Alert Bay *gukw'dzi* [ceremonial big house] on the night of 25 February 2003, as the six members of the Indian Claims Commission filed into the house to witness a performance by the local G̲wa'wina Dancers. The Commission had come to British Columbia to hear testimony by elders in support of a Specific Claim, filed by the 'Na̲mgis First Nation on behalf of all Kwakwa̲ka̲'wakw bands, for reparations for social and cultural damage resulting from the Canadian government's prohibition of the potlatch from 1884 to 1951. After hearing the elders' personal stories of growing up in fear of provincial police and Indian agents, and their experiences of attending residential schools that attempted to eradicate the Kwak'wala language and customs, the singers invited the Commission to sit in the position of honour—at the back of the big house—as the G̲wa'winas shared their rich cultural heritage.

Dance is frequently mobilized by ethnic communities as a form of cultural heritage presentation. . . . The decision to perform dances for the visiting officials has local precedents in Alert Bay dating back to the early twentieth century, when 'Na̲mgis and other Kwakwa̲ka̲'wakw groups recognized royal birthdays, jubilees, coronations, and official visits, as well as certain provincial holidays. These earlier performances were almost certainly

part of efforts by First Nations to ingratiate themselves with colonial authorities. . . . The recent dance for the Indian Claims Commission, however, had a different focus and force. The G̲wa'wina Dancers were proving to the visitors—and . . . to the Canadian government—that those assimilation efforts failed. They were demonstrating that despite the potlatch prohibition, missionary conversion, and residential schools, there was a successful transmission of cultural knowledge . . . and the maintenance of a unique Kwakwa̲ka̲'wakw identity. This message was conveyed through both explicit statement and implicit demonstration. For instance, early in the performance the group leader, William Wasden Jr, introduced the Hamat'sa—commonly recognized as the most important dance of the Kwakwa̲ka̲'wakw—as follows:

> So the next dance that we're going to share with you tonight is what we call Hamat'sa. This is the most sacred of our winter dances, and . . . the dance that the early missionaries and the early Canadian government really didn't understand, and this is the dance that they were most against and wanted to put a stop to. So this is what really brought down potlatches and [the rest of?] our winter dances and ceremonies. And the Hamat'sa is about a cannibal danc-

er who is possessed by the man-eating spirit Baxwbakwalanuxwsiwe', and it's through song and dance and ritual that our people, our spiritual people, are able to do their work and drive this evil spirit out of the young initiate, and to enable him to become whole and one with himself, and through this great ordeal he'll become more spiritually grounded. The dancer that is going to dance tonight is Jonathan [Henderson] and he's been an initiated Hamat'sa for many years, and it's an honour to have him dance with us here tonight.

Wasden encapsulated themes of both colonial repression and survival of Aboriginal culture. He implied that due to governmental misunderstanding, deeply spiritual practices necessary to the well-being of Aboriginal society were outlawed. Yet initiation continues today. By authenticating Henderson's right to perform the dance, a restricted

FIGURE 2.1   A Hamat'sa dancer performs in a Kwakwa̱ka̱'wakw big house.

and inherited privilege,[3] Wasden was also suggesting that the performance was more than a simple display of cultural heritage; it was, in fact, a reflection of living Kwakwa̱ka̱'wakw social codes and norms.

Later in the evening, there was a short ceremony in which a dance blanket was given to a young woman by her grandmother, Pauline Alfred. It was transferred in public view of witnesses, as is the custom of the Kwakwa̱ka̱'wakw. Alfred accompanied the transfer with a speech addressed to the Commission, in which she stated that her granddaughter had taken it upon herself to both learn and teach the songs and dances of their people. This mixing of local "business" with dances otherwise directed at non-Aboriginals, be they tourists or government dignitaries, is common, and reveals the extent to which the presentation of dance is loaded with social meanings and obligations even when performed outside the ceremonial space of the potlatch (Ostrowitz 1991).

Of all the First Nations of the Northwest Coast, the Kwakwa̱ka̱'wakw have proved most successful at maintaining performative practices through the period of colonial infringement, and they currently wear this reputation as a badge of pride and identity (Ostrowitz 1991: 83–4). They have shown a remarkable resilience in the face of prohibition and a willingness to adapt dance display to non-ceremonial contexts, including tourist visits to the coast, residency in ethnographic villages at World's Fairs, celebration of provincial and federal holidays, and openings of art gallery and museum exhibitions.

This paper discusses specific strategies adopted by various Kwakwa̱ka̱'wakw bands to evade the potlatch prohibition and maintain dance practices under restrictive colonial policy between 1922 and 1951. Four general and related strategies are presented: sheer defiance, taking advantage of the language and loopholes of the law, altering the form and content of dance performances, and staging performances for colonial contexts and audiences.

Most of the evidence of such activities can be found in Aboriginal oral history, as well as in detailed correspondence within the Department of Indian Affairs (DIA). These remarkable documents reveal the extent to which colonial authorities in the government and Church struggled to understand and prevent Indigenous ceremony, and the creative efforts undertaken by First Nations peoples to both evade and alter the law itself. They allow to a certain degree the resuscitation of Aboriginal voice and **agency**, and they provide fascinating insight into a period of colonial dialogue and negotiation often overlooked when it comes to dance.

The potlatch and the law against it are among the most critically scrutinized aspects of Canadian colonial history. Yet most accounts collapse the performative features of the potlatch with the distribution of gifts, as did the law prohibiting both. In fact, the giving of gifts and the performing of dances have diverged and converged repeatedly over the past century, and while the significance of gift-giving has remained somewhat consistent (to validate displays of rank and hereditary privilege, and to pay witnesses), the meaning of dances has changed dramatically (from membership in secret societies based on spirit possession, to the enactment of cultural and familial heritage). In the mid- to late nineteenth century, the giving of gifts to validate **rites of passage** and displays of rank and privilege could be relatively independent of the seasonal cycles of ceremonial dance. By the turn of the twentieth century, the two came together, consolidated perhaps in an effort to more efficiently perform Aboriginal "business" under the watchful eye of colonial agents and missionaries. During the period in question here—1922 (the date of the largest prosecution of potlatch participants) to 1951 (the year the anti-potlatch law was dropped from the Indian Act)—the dances and gift-giving were separated, this time as a strategic measure to evade the letter of the law, as we shall see. Since the 1950s, public potlatches have increased in frequency but condensed further in form, and today represent a consolidation of what were in the nineteenth century very different ceremonial practices (Boas 1897; Codere 1950, 1966; Drucker and Heizer 1967; Rosman and Rubel 1971; Cole and Chaikin 1990; Jonaitis 1991). . . .

This essay focuses on efforts by Aboriginal peoples to retain performative knowledge and practice, even though these were intertwined with other concerns (including the maintenance of marriage and funeral customs as well as gift-giving). Most accounts of the history of Kwakwa̱ka̱'wakw ceremony either end in 1922, when the potlatch "went underground," or begin in the 1950s, when practices were "revived." The essay examines specific ways in which dance practice continued, even as that practice was negotiated within First Nations communities, and explores the legacy that these decisions left on different Kwakwa̱ka̱'wakw bands. . . . This history complicates our understanding of both colonial repression and Aboriginal response by illustrating specific ways in which both groups actively debated and articulated solutions to intercultural conflict. The fact that dance was a primary locus of contestation is a testament to its specific importance within First Nations societies, and to its general force as a form of **embodied knowledge** and cultural expression.

Dancing around the Potlatch Ban

Canada's colonial policy, like that of many settler states, sought to disrupt the cultural practice of its Indigenous people through assimilation and conversion, concomitant in part with the claiming of Aboriginal land and resources. In the late nineteenth century, British Columbia became a destination for significant numbers of gold seekers, settlers, and merchants. Around 1880, reserves and an Indian Agency office were established among the Kwakwa̱ka̱'wakw. . . . Partly in response to missionary and Agency appeals for federal assistance in assimilation efforts, the Canadian government amended the Indian Act in 1884. Consequently, "every Indian or other person who engages in or assists in celebrating the Indian festival known as the 'Potlatch' or the Indian dance known as the 'Tamanawas' [a Coast Salish term erroneously applied to the Hamat'sa]" would be guilty of a misdemeanour.

However, few convictions were made based on this statute, largely due to the vague wording of the law. . . . The Indian Act was amended further in 1895 in an effort to clarify the outlawed practices; the giving or receiving of gifts and the wounding or mutilation of living or dead bodies were explicitly mentioned. At no time was all dancing outlawed, though the prohibition did impose an end to all ceremony at which wealth was distributed, a common (if, at times, secondary) feature of most performative events on the coast. The law was further amended twice. In 1914, restrictions were placed on the unregulated wearing of First Nations' regalia and dancing off one's home reserve. Then in 1918, excess material accumulation and expenditure—what was perceived as "wasteful" in potlatch gifting—was outlawed in the context of wartime thrift. Potlatching was now elevated to a summary offence, and those convicted faced two to six months in prison.

. . . [I]t was not until a large potlatch hosted by 'Namgis chief Dan Cranmer, held at Village Island [east of Alert Bay] in the winter of 1921, that the force of the law bore down. When the Indian agent for the Kwakwaka'wakw, William Halliday, was informed about the potlatch, he arrested forty-five participants, twenty-two of whom were given suspended sentences in exchange for surrendering their masks and regalia. The rest were sent to prison in Vancouver (Cole and Chaikin 1990; LaViolette 1961; Sewid-Smith 1979).

After this, people in most communities were afraid to openly potlatch. But by this time, government and missionary agents were primarily concerned with non-Christian marriage practices, wasteful giveaways, and unhygienic conditions in ceremonial big houses. Dancing was now a subsidiary concern, especially since the violent and dramatic enactments of cannibalism and spirit possession had largely ceased. . . .

This shift in concern may have opened a space for First Nations peoples to seek out opportunities to dance in new contexts, which would nonetheless allow for the maintenance of some ceremonial practices, even at the expense of others. These "new dance performances utilized what non-Aboriginal Canadians were increasingly terming art . . ." (Hawker 2003: 120). But just as some sympathetic non-Aboriginals encouraged the performance of dance as folklore, others worried that any loosening of the potlatch ban would open the door to a full return to Indigenous

ceremony, and become "the thin edge of the wedge" into colonial assimilation policy.

Outright Defiance

Most histories of the Kwakwaka'wakw emphasize that potlatches continued (and even expanded in number and scale) during the early decades of the prohibition. . . . As if to rub their defiance in the face of the colonial government, many of these large potlatches were held outdoors, in full view of missionaries and Indian agents. . . .

In any case, most histories (both oral and written) mention that after 1922, the potlatch went underground. The most openly defiant chiefs simply continued potlatching at the remote villages—far from the prying eyes of agents—and during winter storms when travel was difficult (Cole and Chaikin 1990: 140). [DIA agent William] Halliday, in his 1935 memoir, acknowledged this practice but largely dismissed both its frequency and importance (Halliday 1935: 194). . . . Yet the DIA correspondences reveal the sheer number and variation of ceremonies held between 1922 and 1951. They are often specific as to village locations and hosting chiefs, and they provide an invaluable corrective to the often cursory accounts of the "sneak around" or "bootleg" potlatch.[4] . . .

When Halliday retired as Indian agent in 1933, he was replaced by Murray Todd the following year. While Todd initially suggested that the law be revised to allow the repayment of debts, he was soon confronted by an ever-increasing number of potlatches, and became stricter in his thinking (Todd to DIA, 10 March 1934). . . . In December 1937, Todd wrote letters of warning to prospective potlatch hosts, threatening to appoint replacement chiefs if they did not "discharge their duties as required." Yet potlatches continued. . . . In February 1943, Todd disrupted Winter Ceremonial dances in Kingcome [a settlement northeast of Alert Bay], and reported [the events] to D.M. Mackay, the Indian Commissioner for BC. . . . In both 1941 and 1944, Todd wrote to chiefs asking them not to potlatch under wartime conditions, urging thrift, loyalty, and cooperation. . . . Mackay finally urged Todd to threaten the bands with forced military service unless they stopped potlatching. Eventually, [in 1945,] a number of stalwart chiefs . . . formally agreed to cease potlatching until the law was amended. By that point, they would not have to wait long.

The Letter of the Law

. . . [T]he Indian Act, in conflating and confusing divergent practices among various First Nations, constructed "the potlatch" as an object and reflection of colonial society, thus revealing more about Canadian self-constitution than it does about Aboriginal cultures (Bracken 1997). At the same time, the law against the potlatch became a symbol of colonial repression for Indigenous people and a rallying point for their resistance efforts, especially among the Kwakwa̱ka̱'wakw (Loo 1992). While the law was never as effective as agents hoped, it did provide a visible structure against which First Nations peoples could push, in an attempt to maintain a modicum of self-determination (Cole and Chaikin 1990: 175). . . . [In fact, the] vague wording of the law itself was the greatest legal advantage for Aboriginal peoples. For the first decade of the prohibition, neither *potlatch* nor *Tamanawas* was defined at all. . . .

In addition to exploiting the fuzzy definitions of the statute, the Kwakwa̱ka̱'wakw stated their grievances in the form of petitions, and in the legal and ethical language of liberal European enlightenment, often fusing claims for Aboriginal rights with Christian ontology, perhaps to help win over missionaries. As early as 1886, chiefs at a village on or near Hope Island [northwest of Alert Bay] told the following to anthropologist Franz Boas, in what has become a standard refrain in the potlatch literature:

> We want to know whether you have come to stop our dances and feasts, as the missionaries and agents who live among our neighbors do. . . . We will dance when our laws command us to dance; we will feast when our hearts

desire to feast. Do we ask the white man, "Do as the Indian does"?! No, we do not. Why then do you ask us, "Do as the white man does"? It is a strict law that bids us dance. It is a strict law that bids us distribute our property among our friends and neighbors. It is a good law. Let the white man observe his law; we shall observe ours. And now, if you are come to forbid us to dance, be gone; if not, you will be welcome to us. (first reported in Boas 1888: 631)

They would continue to reiterate these themes [in petitions to the government, for instance] in 1918 (and again in 1925): "All we want is justice, and therefore we are not afraid to tell you that the law about the potlatch is not just" (in Cole and Chaikin 1990: 129, 137). . . .

The Kwakwa̱ka̱'wakw also took advantage of the discrepancies in personal attitude among agents. Two Cape Mudge chiefs responded to Halliday's announcement of the 1914 amendment by suggesting to him that Inspector Ditchburn approved of the potlatch and told them it was all right to practise it. In 1919, Aboriginals from Alert Bay invited their member of parliament H.S. Clements to hear their case and witness a performance, after which he wrote to Halliday saying that he saw nothing wrong with the "entertainment." Halliday berated Clements for trusting the Aboriginals, who told other villages that their government representative approved of the potlatch; Halliday added, "On the occasion of your visit, just after you left, the 'entertainment' was turned into a 'dance' where the wild man [Hamat'sa] appeared in an almost nude condition" (letters from Alert Bay Chiefs to Halliday, 21 September 1914; Clements to Halliday, 27 January 1919; and Halliday to Clements, 30 January 1919). . . .

Perhaps the most cunning and successful legal tactic was to separate the dancing and gifting portions of potlatch to avoid it being classed as a discrete "event" under the law (Cole and Chaikin 1990: 142–3; Loo 1992: 157). . . . What Halliday called the "camouflage" potlatch, Ditchburn dubbed the "disjointed" potlatch, and both found it nearly impossible to connect dances and gift-giving when separated in time. Furthermore, the payments owed to potlatch guests were increasingly made during the winter and cast as either Christmas presents or Christian charity. . . .

New Ways of Dancing

In addition to dancing at remote potlatches and separating dancing from gifting, the Kwakwa̲ka̲ʼwakw also sought new forms that would allow them to continue performative traditions. For example, Moses Alfred built a "gymnasium" in the upper floor of his house in Alert Bay, purportedly for the encouragement of health and hygiene, two central missionary and Agency concerns. Yet it was there that he accumulated his "Christmas gifts" to be distributed. Oral history records that this room was frequently used for potlatching, and Wayne Alfred, a contemporary carver and one of the founders of the G̲waʼwina Dancers, was taught by his elders to dance there in the early 1960s, when few young people had any context in which to perform (c.f. Sewid-Smith 1979: 54; Cole and Chaikin 1990: 143). Alfred suggested to me that by publicly criticizing the potlatch, his grandfather Moses was protecting his own clandestine activities (see below).

One of the by-products of anthropological collecting in colonial times was an increased interest among metropolitan audiences in things "primitive," both objects and people. As early as 1884, collector Johan Adrian Jacobsen took members of the Nuxalk (Bella Coola) Nation to Germany to carve objects and perform dances on a multi-city ethnographic tour. Anthropologist Franz Boas then coordinated a group of about fifteen Kwakwa̲ka̲ʼwakw, who performed at the 1893 World's Columbian Exposition in Chicago. A decade later, two Kwakwa̲ka̲ʼwakw men, Charley Nowell and Bob Harris, attended the 1904 Louisiana Purchase Exposition in St Louis under the auspice of collector Charles Newcombe. At both events in the United States, the dramatic dance displays made sensational headlines which . . . caused Canadian officials much concern (see Raibmon 2000; Cole 1985; Jacknis 2002). . . .

Even though the 1914 amendment expanded the reach of the law to include exhibitions and pageants,

Aboriginal people continued to seek alternative performance forms. They were not always successful. In 1929, for example, [DIA agent] Ditchburn denied requests to allow a performance in Victoria, worried that any sanctioned dancing would encourage a full return to potlatching. Halliday agreed with his decision: "I am very glad that you turned down the proposition of the Indians going to Victoria to give their exhibition dances, as I feel it would only be inserting the thin edge of the wedge" (letter from Halliday to Ditchburn, 31 January 1929).

As Indian agents struggled to maintain observance of the [potlatch] ban after 1922, the Kwakwa̲ka̲ʼwakw requested that they be allowed to award prizes to especially talented dancers. After all, the law allowed for the bestowal of prizes at competitive exhibitions, and in 1939 the Gitksan in northern BC were handing out cash "prizes" for successful speech making (Cole and Chaikin 1990: 153). In 1940, the people at Kingcome hosted a meeting with DIA and missionary officials, at which they presented a petition requesting permission to give prizes at "Indian dances" (Chiefs to Indian Commissioner for BC, 9 April 1940). . . .

In the end, the First Nations peoples requested the right to hold dances once a year (having given thirty days' notice and an invitation to the agent) and to award prizes for best dancing, acting in a mask or costume, singing or song composing, and acting as master of ceremonies. Winners would be determined by an appointed set of judges, and all prizes would be donated collectively. These measures ensured that the giving of valuables at dances could not be mistaken for a potlatch. They recast dancing as a competitive display of skill and as a form of employment—two highly valued aspects of any Protestant work ethic. . . .

A parallel strategy was to suggest that dancing was primarily—at least in the twentieth century—a secular form of entertainment, art, or cultural heritage. As early as 1897, Boas wrote an article for the Victoria *Province*, defending the potlatch as intrinsic to the economic and moral health of First Nations peoples, adding that the dances were "a harmless amusement that we should be slow to take away from the native who is struggling against the over-powerful influence of civilization" (reprinted in Keithahn 1945: 104–6). . . . Likewise, the Indian agent for the west coast of Vancouver Island suggested in 1914 that dances were for "pleasure and amusement" (Cole and Chaikin 1990: 128). In recasting Winter Ceremonials as secular entertainment, First Nations peoples compared their performances to non-Aboriginal dance and appealed to sympathetic anthropologists, lawyers, and missionaries, to help argue their case. The colonial authorities, for their part, debated the very possibility of integrating Indigenous custom into a Christian Canadian nation. . . .

Such issues were debated not solely within the non-Aboriginal, colonial community, but also among Kwakwa̱ka̱'wakw themselves. By the turn of the twentieth century, an increasing number of First Nations peoples—especially those converted to Christianity—came out strongly against the potlatch and Winter Ceremonials. On the occasion of a large petition to Ottawa in 1919, Jane Cook, a 'Na̱mgis woman and friend of the Church in Alert Bay, wrote to Duncan Campbell Scott, deputy superintendent general of Indian Affairs, informing him of the evils of the potlatch. She asserted that these included forced marriage, institutional poverty, and violent dances. She said "the Potlatchers" would never progress, become educated, or be loyal to Church or government, and that "there is no liberty in the Potlatch, No Choice whatever" (Cook to Scott, 1 February 1919; c.f. Loo 1992: 163; Robertson et. al 2012).

In 1922, two Kwakwa̱ka̱'wakw men, Dave Shaughnessy and Kenneth Hunt, acted as police informants and gave Halliday a list of the participants at the Village Island potlatch. By 1940, even Moses Alfred was publicly condemning the potlatch at a meeting in Alert Bay, following the big conference in Kingcome. He assured Inspector Coleman and Agent Todd, "You *must* give away and potlatch if you are to give a dance [and] there can be no potlatch without a dance." Fellow 'Na̱mgis George West echoed other Aboriginal people present when he said, "The Kingcome dances were put on for your show. Usually dances are put on for a purpose." All emphasized that "The Custom" and Christianity were fundamentally incompatible, and Aboriginal

people interested in progress were sure to give it up. Another Kwakwa̱ka̱'wakw, Joe Harris, added, "A lot of young people do not like the Indian dances, and they would rather practice the white man's dance."[5]

In fact, the overt integration of "the white man's dance" may have been a further tactic used by some to deflect attention from Indigenous ceremony. Charley Nowell (in Ford 1941: 224–5) tells of a 1921 marriage performed in the Alert Bay church and celebrated in the Day School hall with a feast and dance "in the white man's way"; later in the week, however, guests were paid surreptitiously. In 1922, after the big arrests of Village Island, the missionary at Cape Mudge assured Halliday that only small amounts of gifts were being distributed: "There have been none of the old time festivities here or at Campbell River. The young folks have done all the dancing, and they are doing it in the accredited white fashion, fox-trotting, waltzing, etc., etc." (letter from Cape Mudge missionary to Halliday, 26 December 1922). Despite the fact that Cape Mudge would soon gain a reputation for being the most progressive reserve in the Agency, rumours of potlatching would continue to circulate there. . . .

Like the use of guns to hunt, motorboats to catch fish, chainsaws to cut wood, and commercial paint to decorate masks and totem poles, the increasing fusion of Euro-Canadian practices with Indigenous ceremony throughout the twentieth century is not an easy index of assimilation or progress at the cost of tradition. It is rather a testament to Kwakwa̱ka̱'wakw adaptability in the face of increasingly invasive colonial control. It was difficult for missionaries and agents to forbid the giving of Christmas presents and displays of the foxtrot. It was even more difficult to deny First Nations peoples the right to dance at colonial celebrations.

Colonial Audiences for Outlawed Dances

As mentioned previously, some Kwakwa̱ka̱'wakw at the turn of the twentieth century showed a keen willingness to participate in American World's Fairs. Others danced for tourists en route via steamship to

Alaska (reported in Scidmore 1898: 22). There was also occasion to dance for anthropologists, such as Franz Boas (Glass 2009a); collectors, such as Johan Jacobsen and Charles Newcombe; and photographers, such as Edward Curtis (Glass 2009b; Evans and Glass 2014). It may be in part that these contexts allowed the sanctioned opportunity for performances that were otherwise frowned upon by missionaries and Indian agents. Aboriginal people today certainly explain the willingness of their forebears to dress up and "play Indian" for Edward Curtis's camera by pointing out that this non-Aboriginal man was paying them to dance rather than arresting them for it. However, there were also numerous efforts to perform dances for the very colonial powers bent on eradicating the potlatch.

In the hopes of demonstrating the harmlessness of their performances, the Kwakwa̱ka̱'wakw consistently invited members of the provincial and federal governments to witness their dance displays. In 1912, people from Alert Bay danced for the Duke and Duchess of Connaught, while the following year, Inspector Ditchburn reported, "His Royal Highness the Governor General was entertained by the ['Na̱mgis] Indians in a series of dances which were got up on the spur of the moment." . . . [I]n 1914, people gathered in regalia in Alert Bay to welcome the Royal Commission on Indian Affairs, and made a further gesture by donating money to the war effort. In March 1915, members of five bands formally requested that commissioners from Ottawa be sent to Fort Rupert to "look into the potlatch themselves," but none came. Planned dances were cancelled in 1922 when [the] Minister of Mines, Charles Stewart, failed to show up, and chiefs in regalia welcomed the Lieutenant Governor to Alert Bay in 1934 (DIA Annual Reports for 1913: 225–6 and 1914: xxviii; Chiefs to DIA, 2 March 1915; on Stewart's aborted visit, see Cole and Chaikin 1990: 134; see also Evans and Glass 2014: 17). . . .

In addition to pledging their loyalty to the State and Crown, many Kwakwa̱ka̱'wakw decorated their totem poles and canoe prows with British flags. Many photographs of potlatches around 1900 show Union Jacks flying over the proceedings, [and] First Nations peoples also marked events in the lives

of the Royal Family with performances. As early as 1887, people in Alert Bay celebrated the Queen's Jubilee with sports and canoe races (DIA Annual Report for 1887: 110), while troupe members at the Chicago World's Fair in 1893 danced in honour of the Queen's birthday in May. In 1937 there were much-photographed parades in regalia through Alert Bay to mark the coronation of King George VI. That same year a new totem pole was raised in Kingcome Inlet, dedicated as a memorial for King George V and celebrated with speeches and singing (Neill to Crerar, 5 January 1937). . . .

Another way the Kwakwa̱ka̱'wakw ingratiated themselves with the colonial administration was to perform for provincial holidays. . . . [T]his practice increased during the mid-twentieth century, as Canada (and BC specifically) attempted to differentiate themselves culturally from their English and continental origins. Indigenous art and performance became a sign of a [specifically] Canadian culture, and was showcased as one of Canada's unique contributions to the world (Nemiroff 1992; Hawker 2003). Here, the display of traditional culture may have served dual purposes, with the government appropriating what it believed were [dying] aspects of Indigenous folklore, while Aboriginal peoples asserted their cultural continuity and negotiated a place for themselves at the table of Canadian culture.

By the 1930s and 1940s, people in Alert Bay were marking May Day with parades and displays of British flags, but their attempts at performance displays in urban centres were continuously thwarted. . . . During the 1936 Vancouver Golden Jubilee, an Indian village was set up in Stanley Park, complete with local Coast Salish carvers and Salish and Kwakwa̱ka̱'wakw totem poles. There were "Indian pageants" overseen by the DIA, but these did not include Kwakwa̱ka̱'wakw dancers. A delegation of Kwakwa̱ka̱'wakw did paddle a dugout canoe through the waters around Vancouver to welcome King George VI and Queen Elizabeth in 1939; the paddlers included chiefs arrested in 1922 and those actively potlatching around the law. . . .

Finally, however, a group of Kwakwa̱ka̱'wakw from various villages spent a few weeks in 1946 performing dances at Vancouver's Diamond Jubilee.

A souvenir program recorded the names of dances (in English) and dancers (in Kwak'wala), including Moses Alfred and Dan Cranmer (host of the 1922 Village Island potlatch), along with many of the 1939 paddlers. The group also presented Viscount Alexander, the Governor General of Canada, with an honorary Kwak'wala title and a totem pole carved by Mungo Martin, soon to become famous through local museum activity. These performances organized not by the DIA but by the newly incorporated Native Brotherhood of British Columbia, a largely Christian political union of progressive members of Aboriginal communities, whose Kwakwaka'wakw president, William Scow, had acted as interpreter for the 1940 conference at Kingcome. . . .

This was the year that the new Canadian Citizenship Act was passed, which for the first time differentiated Canadian subjects from British. Three years later, in 1949, the government initiated the Massey Commission, which would investigate the state of culture in Canada and make specific recommendations on how best to encourage the emergence of a unique national culture through financial support to individuals and institutions across the country. Aboriginal art—visual and performative—would loom increasingly large in the federalist project.

Performing Culture and Culture as Performance

After World War Two, the Native Brotherhood increased its efforts to achieve social justice for Indigenous people. Though the potlatch was not a major concern for these progressive Christians, traditional dance was put to use as a public relations exercise. This strategy was increasingly adopted at home on the reserves too, and by more potlatch-minded people. In 1951, the year the potlatch ban was unceremoniously dropped from the Indian Act,[6] local chief councillor James Sewid organized a public Aboriginal dance as a fundraiser for the Alert Bay hospital. . . . There was much debate among chiefs as to the protocol involved, especially since it involved a

social principle antithetical to the potlatch—guests paid to watch dances rather than being paid to witness them. Even those formally opposed to potlatching, including the 1922 police informants, joined in to perform or instruct. Such dances were repeated almost every year for a decade, and also became part of Victoria Day and May Day celebrations in Alert Bay. In 1953, Chief Mungo Martin built a *gukw'dzi* in Victoria's Thunderbird Park, in which he hosted the first legal, public potlatch. In 1959, a delegation of Kwakwaka'wakw joined other BC First Nations to dance for Queen Elizabeth II in Nanaimo. Even today, many middle-aged Aboriginal people report these activities as the contexts in which they learned to dance and make regalia, having grown up in the late years of the potlatch ban (Cole and Chaikin 1990: 168–9; Sewid 1969: 158–63; 1979: 4; Jacknis 2002: 157).

The 1960s were characterized by increasing Aboriginal modernization and political mobilization, the growth of the tourist economy on the coast, and expansion in the display of a secular art and heritage. In 1965, James Sewid coordinated the building of a *gukw'dzi* in Alert Bay, the first new one built in Kwakwaka'wakw territory in decades. It became a headquarters for dancing for cruiseship tourists as well as reviving the potlatch, which is today proudly practised by all Kwakwaka'wakw bands. . . .

The history of adopting the strategies discussed above may have helped keep performative knowledge alive through the dark years of the potlatch ban. It has also resulted in the formation of a local concept of "culture" as performance. That is, people from Alert Bay [where public dance performance in a variety of venues is common] are more likely to say that "Kwakwaka'wakw culture" includes singing, dancing, art, and language, than are people who grew up in other villages. . . . There is a curious ambiguity to many cultural performances in Alert Bay, as in other Aboriginal communities today—a marked tension between discourses and practices tied to "sacred ritual" and those more closely related to "secular entertainment." On the one hand, the ambiguities challenge the very analytical utility of this distinction in the first place. But they are also debated locally, as people negotiate when it is appropriate to clap, to take photos, to stand and remove one's hat, or to distribute money, whether the audience is composed of locals, tourists, or visiting dignitaries. There is constant discussion on how to make non-ceremonial dance displays more commensurate with potlatch protocol and regulations about the hereditary ownership of dance rights (Glass 2014). While such specificities may be unique to the Northwest Coast, the issue of the adaptability of traditional dance is one shared—and vigorously negotiated locally—in Indigenous communities across Canada.

William Wasden Jr, speaker for the Gwa'wina Dancers, announces to his audiences, "We are not performing for you; we are sharing our culture." This sentiment is echoed by other groups among Northwest Coast First Nations. The "sharing of culture" seems to have emerged as a middle term between potlatch and show, sacred and profane, insider and outsider. It suggests the legacy of such negotiations, the strategic manoeuvres to adapt dance practices to meet changing ceremonial conditions and colonial encounters. The strength with which contemporary Kwakwaka'wakw communities cling to the potlatch and their performative heritage may reflect the degree to which they had to dance both around and against the law to ensure their survival. In the end, dancing did prove to be a thin end of the wedge, for it opened a space in oppressive colonial policy whereby Indigenous people could retain **embodied knowledge**, practise unique heritages, and support larger efforts toward self-determination.

References Cited

Boas, Franz. 1888. "The Indians of British Columbia." *Popular Science Monthly* 32 (5): 628–35.

———. 1897. *The Social Organization and Secret Societies of the Kwakiutl*. US National Museum Annual Report for 1895. Washington, DC: US National Museum.

Bracken, Christopher. 1997. *The Potlatch Papers: A Colonial Case History*. Chicago: University of Chicago Press.

Codere, Helen. 1950. *Fighting with Property: A Study of Kwakiutl Potlatching and Warfare 1792–1930*. Monographs of the American Ethnological Society #18. New York: J.J. Augustin Publishers.

———, ed. 1966. *Kwakiutl Ethnography*. Chicago: University of Chicago Press.

Cole, Douglas. 1985. *Captured Heritage: The Scramble for Northwest Coast Artifacts*. Seattle: University of Washington Press.

——— and Ira Chaikin. 1990. *An Iron Hand upon the People: The Law against the Potlatch on the Northwest Coast*. Vancouver: Douglas and McIntyre.

Department of Indian Affairs (DIA) Papers. RG10, Western (Black) Series. National Archives of Canada, Ottawa.

Drucker, Philip, and Robert Heizer. 1967. *To Make My Name Good: A Reexamination of the Southern Kwakiutl Potlatch*. Berkeley: University of California Press.

Evans, Brad and Aaron Glass, eds. 2014. *Return to the Land of the Head Hunters: Edward S. Curtis, the Kwakwaka'wakw, and the Making of Modern Cinema*. Seattle: University of Washington Press.

Ford, Clellan. 1941. *Smoke from Their Fires: The Life of a Kwakiutl Chief*. New Haven: Yale University Press.

Glass, Aaron. 2009a. "Frozen Poses: Hamat'sa Dioramas, Recursive Representation, and the Making of a Kwakwaka'wakw Icon." In *Photography, Anthropology, and History: Expanding the Frame*, edited by Christopher Morton and Elizabeth Edwards, 89–116. Farnham, UK: Ashgate Press.

———. 2009b. "A Cannibal in the Archive: Performance, Materiality, and (In)visibility in Unpublished Edward Curtis Photographs of the Hamat'sa." *Visual Anthropology Review* 25 (2): 128–49.

———. 2014. "The Kwakwaka'wakw Business of Showing: Tradition Meets Modernity on the Silver Screen and the World Stage." In *Return to* the Land of the Head Hunters: Edward S. Curtis, the Kwakwaka'wakw, and the Making of Modern Cinema, edited by Brad Evans and Aaron Glass, 315–57. Seattle: University of Washington Press.

Halliday, William. 1935. Potlatch and Totem: Reflections of an Indian Agent. London: J.M. Dent.

Hawker, Ronald. 2003. Tales of Ghosts: First Nations Art in British Columbia, 1922–1961. Vancouver: University of British Columbia Press.

Jacknis, Ira. 2002. The Storage Box of Tradition: Kwakiutl Art, Anthropologists, and Museums, 1881–1981. Washington, DC: Smithsonian Institution Press.

Jonaitis, Aldona, ed. 1991. Chiefly Feasts: The Enduring Kwakiutl Potlatch. New York: American Museum of Natural History.

Keithahn, Edward. 1945. Monuments in Cedar. Ketchican, AK: Roy Anderson.

LaViolette, Forrest. 1961. The Struggle for Survival: Indian Cultures and the Protestant Ethic in British Columbia. Toronto: University of Toronto Press.

Loo, Tina. 1992. "Dan Cranmer's Potlatch: Law as Coercion, Symbol, and Rhetoric in British Columbia." Canadian Historical Review 73 (2): 125–65.

Nemiroff, Diana. 1992. "Modernism, Nationalism, and Beyond: A Critical History of Exhibitions of First Nations Art." In Land Spirit Power: First Nations at the National Gallery of Canada, edited by Diana Nemiroff, Robert Houle, and Charlotte Townsend-Gault, 16–41. Ottawa: National Gallery of Canada.

Ostrowitz, Judith. 1991. Privileging the Past: Reconstructing History in Northwest Coast Art. Seattle: University of Washington Press.

Raibmon, Paige. 2000. "Theatres of Contact: the Kwakwaka'wakw Meet Colonialism in British Columbia and at the Chicago World's Fair." Canadian Historical Review 81 (2): 157–90.

Robertson, Leslie, with the Kwagu'l Gixsam Clan. 2012. Standing Up with Ga'axsta'las: Jane Constance Cook and the Politics of Memory, Church, and Custom. Vancouver: UBC Press.

Rosman, Abraham, and Paula Rubel. 1971. Feasting with Mine Enemy: Rank and Exchange among Northwest Coast Societies. New York: Praeger.

Scidmore, Eliza. 1898. Appleton's Guide-Book to Alaska and the Northwest Coast. New York: D. Appleton and Co.

Sewid, James. 1969. Autobiography of James Sewid, a Kwakitutl Indian. Edited by James P. Spradley. New Haven, CT: Yale University Press.

Sewid-Smith, Daisy. 1979. Prosecution or Persecution. Cape Mudge, BC: Nu-yum-balees Society.

Notes

1. In general, the Hamat'sa initiate, who performs the dance, is male. However, a small number of women have joined Hamat'sa societies. (Stern's note)

2. Franz Boas arranged for some Kwakwaka'wakw from Fort Rupert to perform at the 1893 World's Columbian Exposition in Chicago, and Glass reports that Canadian officials were troubled by news reports that Hamat'sa dances there included realistic depictions of mutilation and cannibalism. (Stern's note)

3. Kwakwaka'wakw and some other First Nations regard traditional dances and songs as property to be performed only by individuals who have inherited or been given the rights to do so. (Stern's note)

4. "Sneaking around" is how many Kwakwaka'wakw still refer to the underground activity of their ancestors. The term "bootleg potlatch" comes from Reverend John Antle of the Columbia Coast Mission (Halliday to Scott, 27 February 1931). (Glass's note)

5. [From n]otes taken at a meeting of the Indians at Alert Bay, 23 April 1940. Of course, it is nearly impossible to recover the individual motivations behind such discourse. For some, these sentiments may have been heartfelt, while for others their change of mind regarding potlatching may

have resulted from the scale of debts owed, rivalries with other families or villages, or more idiosyncratic circumstance. Others may have been concealing their own continued potlatching. (Glass's note)

6. The newly revised Act simply deleted the relevant section. Aboriginal people today still want a formal repeal and apology from the government for the policy and the arrests and confiscations that accompanied it. (Glass's note)

Key Points to Consider

- Cultural traditions reinforce important social and emotional links to a people's past.
- All cultural practices change as people adapt them to new circumstances. Kwakwa̱ka̱'wakw and other First Nations continue to adapt their traditions to meet changing social, economic, and political circumstances.
- Canadian colonial administration of First Nations forced drastic changes to Aboriginal practices, economies, and social life, but it did not succeed in eliminating distinct Native cultures.
- Expressive culture has symbolic and practical effects.

Critical Thinking Questions

1. What does Glass mean when he says that today some First Nations communities think about "'culture' as performance"? How did government assimilation efforts and Kwakwa̱ka̱'wakw resistance to assimilation contribute to this view?
2. Ask an older family member to tell you about a religious, family, or other tradition that she or he remembers from her or his childhood. Do you also participate in this tradition? Why or why not? If you do participate in it, how does your practice differ from that of your relative? To what do you attribute the changes?
3. Using the definition of "total social phenomenon" provided in the introduction to this chapter, discuss the Canadian institution of hockey. Do you think it fits the definition? Why or why not?
4. What things at your university are named for people or corporations? What did these people or groups do to earn this honour? How is this similar or different to the honour sought by a potlatch host?

Suggestions for Further Reading and Watching

Cranmer, Barb. 2000. *I'tusto: To Rise Again*. Vancouver: Moving Images. Video recording, 54 min.

Glass, Aaron. 2004. *In Search of the Hamat'sa: A Tale of Headhunting*. Watertown, MA: Documentary Educational Resources. Video recording, 33 min.

———. 2004. "The Intention of Tradition: Contemporary Contexts and Contests of the Hamat'sa Dance." In *Coming to Shore: Northwest Coast Ethnology, Traditions, and Visions*, edited by Marie Mauzé, Michael E. Harkin, and Sergei Kan, 279–303. Lincoln: University of Nebraska Press.

———. 2008. "Crests on Cotton: 'Souvenir' T-shirts and the Materiality of Remembrance among the Kwakwa̱ka̱'wakw of British Columbia." *Museum Anthropology* 31 (1): 1–18.

Mauss, Marcel. (1924) 2000. *The Gift: The Form and Reason for Exchange in Archaic Societies*. Translated by W.D. Halls. New York: W.W. Norton.

U'mista Cultural Society. 2003. "The Potlatch." In *The Story of the Masks*. Virtual Museum of Canada. www.umista.ca/masks_story/en/ht/potlatch01.html.

———. (1975) 2005. *Potlatch: A Strict Law Bids Us Dance*. Vancouver: Moving Images. Video recording, 54 min.

Chapter 3

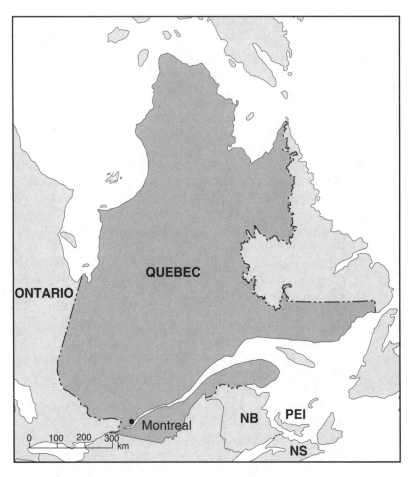

Quebec

Introduction

Language is intimately connected to culture; it is an important tool that people use to communicate, to make social connections, and to mark social differences between themselves and others. Thus, anthropologists are interested in language—both what people say and how they say it. Indeed, linguistic anthropology is one of the original subfields of the discipline. Over the years, anthropologists have found that no human language is more complex or more advanced than any other human language.

In the contemporary article below, linguistic anthropologist Monica Heller re-examines research that she conducted in the late 1970s during a period of intense struggle over language and political authority in Quebec, one that resulted in the election of the francophone **nationalist** Parti Québécois in 1976. While political struggles in Quebec are commonly expressed as conflict over language, at the time language was also a proxy for ethnic, religious, and class differences. Language had become an important marker of identity during the Quiet Revolution of the 1960s. The Quiet Revolution was a period of **modernization** and secularization in Quebec, during which the provincial government took over from the Catholic Church delivery of education, health care, and other public services. Part of the social process involved simultaneously valorizing the low-status vernacular (or everyday) French spoken by the vast majority of Québécois and establishing a standard Canadian French as the "good" and "proper" form of spoken and written expression.

Canada became officially bilingual only in 1969. Prior to that time, French had no formal status in the federal government and was actively discriminated against in most Canadian provinces. In much of Canada, francophones had no right to government services, including health care and schooling, in French. Ontario and Manitoba, both of which have large francophone populations, enacted laws to discourage the use of French and to discriminate against francophones. Even in Quebec, French was not the official language of work, and economic power was held by anglophones. Francophones had to learn English to advance politically, economically, and socially. Over time, many bilingual Canadian francophones left Quebec and became anglophones in a multigenerational effort toward socioeconomic advancement. Today, the majority of urban Quebeckers are bilingual, but this was not the case in the 1970s. At that time, the vast majority of francophones were stuck at the bottom of the socioeconomic ladder.

The issues Heller presents here are not unique to Canada or Quebec. **Language ideologies**—shared ideas about what constitutes "good" language as well as the relative prestige of a language and its speakers—exist in every society. The same struggles over the ways that different languages are evaluated, recognized, and supported have been documented in Belgium, Wales, Catalonia (in Spain), and elsewhere. Bilingualism (and multilingualism) is widespread and normal in many societies, but commonly it is people with lower statuses who learn the language of people with higher statuses. The **ethnographic** material that Heller presents in the article below is especially interesting because it reveals that although some brewery workers stood to benefit while others stood to lose from the new language regime, everyone was engaged in linguistic negotiation. Far from being linguistic bullies, the people Heller observed worked to accommodate the linguistic abilities and limitations of their co-workers and colleagues.

Anthropologists settle on fieldwork sites and research questions for many different reasons. Sometimes they are fascinated by a place or by a certain group of people; often they are driven by the desire to understand a particular social phenomenon. Frequently there is no single factor, and the selection of research questions and sites is the result of both interests and idiosyncratic personal histories. In the article below, Heller describes the combination of interests and circumstances that led her to study the ways that anglophone and francophone Canadians negotiate the language of their interactions. She discusses two related processes: "francophonization," which is the installation of French as the ordinary ("unmarked") language of work, and "francization," which is the establishment of a standardized formal French language supported and reinforced by private and public institutions, including news coverage, corporations, schools, and government services. Francization was part of a successful modernization strategy of Quebec nationalists. Curiously, this modernization also paved the way for Quebec to participate in **globalization**. In the period since Heller conducted the fieldwork she describes here, bilingualism has once again become the path to socioeconomic advancement in Quebec.

❖ About the Author ❖

Monica Heller is one of the foremost linguistic anthropologists working today. She is part of the Ontario Institute for Studies in Education at the University of Toronto. Heller grew up in Montreal in a multilingual Jewish family. Being neither Catholic nor Protestant, she felt somewhat immune from the passions and hostilities that surrounded the language and ethnic politics in Quebec in the 1960s and 1970s. Heller's work has focused on the ways language is embedded in social, economic, and political changes. In particular, she has studied the ways the speech habits of ordinary people inform and respond to official language policies and how language is connected to social difference and inequality. She conducted her earliest research in Quebec, followed by research in Franco-Ontario.

Brewing Trouble: Language, the State, and Modernity in Industrial Beer Production (Montreal, 1978–1980)

Monica Heller

Investigating Modernizing Nationalism: Sociolinguistics in the Brewery

The modernizing project of Quebec had many elements, and social sciences were involved in quite a few of them. **Demographers** correlated census questions about language with levels of education, revenue, and other important quality-of-life indicators. Anthropologists and historians undertook the construction of the story of Quebec's traditions. Sociologists and political scientists debated the best forms for the new social institutions (such as regional high schools and community health care centres) and political structures that were developed. Lin-

guists got involved in two things: demonstrating, through linguistic description, the regularity of the vernacular that served as an authenticating symbol of the Quiet Revolution, and the specificity of Québécois French; and developing standards and policies for the spread of French through all domains of Québécois life.

By 1978, I had already decided that social, economic, and political change in Quebec was going to be easiest to understand by looking at the relationship between language practices in everyday life and the **discourse** and practices of the institutions regulating ethnonational and ethnoclass organization. Since Canadian academics were not asking that question, I went to study in the United States. I reached a stage in the program in which

I was required to produce an empirical study in a subfield of linguistics different from my area of specialization.

This posed a problem, since I really didn't want to do anything different, until my mother suggested I look up her former graduate school classmate Pierre-Étienne Laporte. Laporte was then head of the research services of the Office de la langue française (OLF) and might be persuaded to let me do an internship. The OLF was set up in 1961, one year after the election of the Liberal government that ushered in the Quiet Revolution. Its role was (and still is) to help the **state** with the development and implementation of its language policy. This work was crucial, since the hallmark of the Quiet Revolution was a move away from religion and toward language as the key criterion of belonging to the Québécois nation, both because language was understood as democratic and because the political nationalist strategy required a break with the Catholic Church.

Not one to turn down an offer of free labour, Laporte agreed, and we worked out a plan for a study in the lexical semantics of automobile terminology. . . . I started my internship . . . by walking the streets of Montreal with blank line drawings of cars in my bag, asking mechanics, dealers, and service station attendants to add in the names of the parts indicated on the drawings.

Besides giving me an enormous appreciation of the numbers of different ways it is possible to say "hubcap" in Montreal (albeit without any explanation for why, of all the parts of a car, this one should be so particularly variable), this experience also raised some questions for me about what kinds of knowledge the OLF wanted, why, and what it might take to acquire it. Clearly, in order to effect a change in the way people talked about cars, the OLF needed to know what they said, but an overeducated young woman may not be the best person to find out what is going on in the nation's garages, and removing the terms from their context of use was unlikely to help. . . .

These questions were haunting me as I completed the other part of my internship, which mainly involved "helping" (that is, being taught by) two researchers in Laporte's department, André Martin and Denise Daoust (these are their real names, as is Laporte's). They had been assigned research aimed at facilitating what had become the major portion of the OLF's role, the implementation of La Loi 101 (Bill 101), the Charter of the French Language, which had been passed by the Quebec government the previous year. This law, which is still in effect (and still controversial), . . . [includes] the declaration of French as the official language of Quebec and also as the language of the workplace. This [latter] element was understood to be central to the possibility of finally gaining some power in the private sector, where the value of French as a linguistic resource was understood to lie.

The law spells out what applies to what kinds of workplaces, and, like any other law, leaves open for a certain amount of interpretation exactly what it might mean for the language of the workplace to be French. Nevertheless, companies of a certain size had to meet certain criteria in order to obtain the *certificat de francisation* they needed to have in order to do business in Quebec.

These measurement and evaluation problems were part of what Denise and André had to tackle, and they did so largely through the use of survey methods. Questionnaires were distributed to employees in the large companies considered the highest priority, surveying language choice in various domains of workplace activity and asking questions about the kinds of technical terminology issues I was trying to address with my car-part sketch (Daoust-Blais and Martin 1981). . . .

This bothered me. It seemed to me that to be asked those kinds of questions by the office at the same time that companies were being evaluated for their compliance with Bill 101 would incline people to be vigilant about how they filled out such questionnaires. I was also not sure how one might interpret the answers, given that, especially in large companies, people occupied different positions and were likely to have different opinions on the social changes occurring in their milieus. I discussed this with Denise one day after I had driven out of the city with her to collect completed questionnaires from a large US–owned automobile manufacturing plant situated in a predominantly francophone town.

She asked me how I might do it differently and ended up offering to help me write a grant proposal to the OLF's funding program. . . . The project proposal I developed with Denise's help focused on an in-depth ethnographic study of a single workplace, through which, I argued, I could grasp what "francization" meant to workers, what practices it was connected to, and why people did and said what they did.

When the project was funded, Denise and André helped me find a site. We wanted a workplace that was relevant both to the formal criteria of Bill 101's priorities (mainly that it had over one hundred employees) and to the spirit of its concerns (namely that its management had historically been English-speaking and that it was tied to a North American, or at least pan-Canadian, market). André narrowed the possibilities down to two: a branch of an American company that manufactured light bulbs, and an industrial brewery. In addition to the fact that, to be honest, I found beer more interesting than light bulbs (for no good reason other than sheer prejudice), the brewery was located on a subway line, which was important since I had no car, and in any event, they agreed. The company had been founded in late eighteenth century by a Briton whose family still owned and ran it. It had breweries across the country, and part of its head office was located in Montreal, with the other part in Toronto. The Montreal plant manufactured, bottled, and delivered beer in the Quebec market zone. . . .

In addition to simply observing every day, I learned what I could about the history of the company, about its current network and market, and about how it was regulated by the state. . . . In the latter half of my time there, I interviewed employees who, based on what I had seen and on what people told me, occupied revealing positions with respect to the francization process, and tape-recorded ongoing everyday interactions in some key sites. . . .

The Ethnolinguistic Organization of Expansion and Technologization

. . . [U]ntil the 1950s, even through the industrial transformation of brewing (and of this brewery) a decade or so earlier, the company thought of brewing as an art. Brewers thought of themselves as artisans, and they were trained on the job by "master brewers," that is, people who had mastered that art. In the 1950s, however, at least in Canada, the entire food-production and food-processing industry began to be reorganized on a larger scale, and understood through the lens of science rather than art. . . .

This shift had, of course, a major impact on hiring. First, the automatization involved in the process led to a hiring freeze in the Montreal plant from 1955 to 1970. Second, the mode of recruitment changed. Before the freeze, people were largely recruited through word of mouth, through family and neighbourhood connections. . . . Afterward, a human resources department was put in place, staffed largely by francophones with degrees in the field from the new francophone postsecondary institutions established in the 1960s and 1970s. They used their institutional networks to recruit employees with formal training in the natural sciences, engineering, or management. Thus the 1970s saw the arrival of a cohort of young francophones who had technical training . . . and whose personal histories usually revealed that they were in the first generation of their rural families to move to Montreal and to get a postsecondary education. Many of them filled management positions that older employees with more seniority would earlier have had access to. . . .

A second important shift, occurring at around the same time, was the company's expansion across Canada and even beyond its borders. . . . This expansion . . . fits an overall pattern related to the postwar economic boom. The brewery had long been based in Montreal, and served its expanding market from there until the improvement in the communications infrastructure and increased wealth made the opening of branch plants a more attractive option. Experienced managers were needed to oversee these operations; these were, of course, all anglophones based in the Montreal plant. . . . In addition, given the hiring freeze, many managers were reaching retirement age by the mid-1970s. Thus management positions were opening up through transfer and retirement at exactly the moment when the first generation of technically trained francophones were entering the labour market.

The final shift is linked to the context in which the westward expansion of the brewery was occurring: the financial centre of Canada was moving from Montreal to Toronto, in a long process that began in the postwar boom and accelerated rapidly in the 1970s. . . . This shift forced anglophone Montreal business to orient itself to a greater extent to Toronto and began drawing head offices there. . . .

The cumulative effect of these changes was to open up space in the brewery for francophone managers, to run the Montreal plant and serve the Quebec market. By 1978, while francophones were still overwhelmingly present at the lowest levels of the hierarchy in the production, distribution, and marketing sectors, they had made significant inroads at the two highest levels in those same sectors. . . .

Position and Interest in the Francization of the Brewery

I received a quick introduction to the politics of language and **ethnicity** in the brewery, as well as a confirmation of my assumptions about the social significance of the OLF, a few days after I started showing up for work. . . . I had been assigned to the quality control section of the lab. . . .

One day after lunch, [an older anglophone technician] asked me (in English) to come down to his end of the lab for a chat. . . . He said that I had been the subject of discussion among the people with whom he often had lunch, mostly men around his age, most of them English-speaking. They were

wondering what I was really doing there, whether perhaps my job was to secretly evaluate the extent to which the brewery was in conformity with Bill 101. They were more or less worried about whether I was a spy for the office.

I no longer recall exactly what I said, partly, I am sure, because I was concerned and upset and trying to stay calm and not make more of a mess of things; I know I told him about the fact that this work was for my PhD thesis, a public document; about my studies in the United States; about what I wanted to know; and about how the OLF figured in to the picture. . . . [T]hat encounter began a friendly relationship.

On the other hand, some francophones had expectations of me I was not able to fulfill, such as an active involvement in advancing efforts at francization, or direct intervention with the OLF on issues that concerned them. Exactly the things that reassured anglophones (my unclassifiable name, my studies in the United States, my ease with English) were sources of worry to them. . . . I had to work hard to gain credibility with both groups and to retain ease of access to relationships with members of both groups. But that experience also taught me exactly how the boundary worked and what the categorization was all about. Being enough of a Montrealer and enough of an outsider was both a problem and a resource. . . .

The workers on the production lines and in delivery . . . were almost all francophone men, with the exception of a few immigrants, mainly from Eastern Europe, who had been in Canada for about twenty years. Most of the francophones spoke only French. They paid little attention to the company's francization program, for the most part ignoring, for example, foremen's attempts to introduce new terminology into their work activities. In many ways, language had little to do with the core of the activities of the production line workers. They were also far removed from possibilities for promotion, which would have involved more than new terms in any case.

The foremen were also all francophone men. In contrast to the men working under them, they were active and invested in francization. They frequently asked for texts (such as forms they had to fill out) and terms to be translated, and sometimes worked on the translation themselves. They were as concerned about extending the ranges of use of French as they were about ensuring the "quality" of that French (in the form of finding the "right" term, for example). The younger ones among them were quite articulate about the political aspects of francization, associating it with the chances that people like them could hope for better lives. One of them told me:

In the beginning / the guys on the floor started laughing as soon as you talked about *soutireuses* / what's that a *soutireuse*? / they've been working on a filler for twenty-five years and then you tell them / it's not a filler it's a *soutireuse* / but it goes in / even if you don't want it to it changes [. . .] young people today are more ready to change it because we're all tied to the Quebec situation / we want to francisize / we want to be more free / but for that you have to make an effort.

[Au début / les gars sur le plancher partaient à rire dès que tu parlais de soutireuses / c'est quoi ça une soutireuse? / ça fait vingt-cinq ans qu'ils travaillent sur une filler pis tu leur dis / ce n'est pas une filler c'est une soutireuse / mais ça entre / même si on veut pas ça change [. . .] les jeunes d'aujourd'hui / ils sont plus prêts à le changer parce qu'on est tous reliés à la situation québécoise / on veut franciser / on veut être plus libre / mais pour ça il faut faire un effort.] (Interview with francophone foreman, 1978)

In fact, from what I could tell, none of the management positions were ever filled from the ranks of the foremen; at that level the company recruited only people who had had formal training in a technical field outside the brewery. But the prospect of "liberty" remained powerful. . . .

The small group of superintendents occupied, quite literally, a position of mediation between the workers and their foremen, on the one hand, and management, on the other, frequently visiting both types of spaces in the course of their work day, and having to interact with people at both levels. A small

group, they were all bilingual, and most of them of Irish origin. . . . They tended to keep apart from other employees, possibly as a way to minimize the risks that their role could entail.

The management level . . . was more complex. No sectors were exclusively or even mainly anglophone anymore, apart from the head office in the other building. The human resources department and the quality control lab were the two sectors now dominated by francophones, mostly young and including both men and women. Most of them were very actively involved in the francization of the company, scarcely surprising given that they had benefitted so directly from it and that their presence was legitimated by it. In many other departments there was a mix, including older male anglophones, usually with a great deal of seniority; older male francophones used to working under anglophone sector heads; and younger (also usually male) managers who had been hired recently. Administrative assistants (then still called "secretaries") were all female, and mainly francophone. Like the superintendents, they played an important role as linguistic mediators. They standardized their supervisors' texts and made sure they conformed to norms of written language, drawing on monolingual and bilingual dictionaries and grammar books when they needed to. They translated into French work produced by the older anglophones still around who had never needed to write in French before in their careers, and helped francophones in their efforts to francisize their own work practices. . . .

The embedding of ethnolinguistic categories in workplace stratification, the gendered nature of the work, and the different generational perspectives on those relationships all help us understand what francization meant to differently positioned employees in terms of the capital they could mobilize, the markets they had access to, and the risks and potential benefits involved in trying to acquire new capital or invest the capital they had in different markets.[1] As we will see further below, it was the francophones in upper management who had the highest, thinnest tightrope to walk. Anglophones had retreated to Ontario, the head office, or the basement (the basement excepted, these were not exactly hardship posts). Low-ranking workers were too far removed from the potential benefits of francization to get too excited about it, and the superintendents, most of whom had been around for a long time anyway, could draw little benefit. Foremen, especially the younger ones, had everything to gain and nothing to lose. Higher-ranking young managers had to balance the obvious benefits francization represented for them with their remaining dependence both on the older anglophones who were still around (and who, often, were in line for the jobs filled by the newly arrived francophones) and on the anglophone head office, in a national company that was still, at the end of the day, numerically dominated by English speakers and whose finances were run out of Toronto. . . .

The Interactional Accomplishment of Francophonization

Technical services included employees at a variety of levels. It included mechanics, electricians, and other tradespeople whose job was to maintain the physical infrastructure of the plant, whether on a routine or troubleshooting basis. They had dispatchers and supervisors. Upper management was involved not only in ensuring the quality of this basic function but also in longer-term planning. There was one secretary, Linda, who worked in the central office on an upper floor, with the department head, Albert, and his two assistants, Claude and Bob.

Linda was a young francophone with a strong mastery of English. Bob was an older Scot with a background in engineering who had been recruited directly from the United Kingdom twenty-five years before, precisely because of his technical training; he had chosen not to take opportunities for transfers to other provinces, saying simply that he wanted to stay in Montreal. Claude was a bilingual older francophone responsible for the maintenance work who had long been used to being the only francophone on the management team. His work, however, required him to move around the building a great deal and to interact with the francophone tradesmen

and dispatchers. Albert was a young francophone formally trained in engineering at a francophone postsecondary institution; he had very recently replaced the former head of the department, who had left to supervise the opening of a new plant in one of the western provinces. He had some working knowledge of English. A fourth member of the management team, Daniel, a young francophone with very limited knowledge of English, had also recently been promoted after his anglophone predecessor retired. He occupied a position under Claude and Bob and was based on the production floor, although, along with other people in the department, he often came by the office for a variety of reasons, including, in his case, attendance at the weekly management meeting in Albert's office. Together, they represented fairly well the range of trajectories of workers in the brewery.

How did they make things work in the office? Linda, of course, played a key role. She spoke mainly English with Bob, although she used a few fixed formulas from French, which Bob in turn picked up and used when addressing her and other francophones. She was his main mediator with the world of French, translating or editing his letters and memos. She was also a key linguistic resource for francophones invested in francization. In the following extract, we see her helping Simon, a young francophone supervisor, and his colleague Marc. They have come explicitly to ask Linda for help in translating the term "shopman," a designation for a low-ranking job in their area of work. Linda takes out her dictionary and leans on the counter to carry out the discussion.

LINDA:	I just looked for a dictionary oh (x)
SIMON:	Homme d'atelier [workshop man] makes a perfect literal translation
LINDA:	(x) What in English?
MARC:	Shopman
SIMON:	Shopman
MARC:	It's a guy who works in a [work]shop / an homme d'atelier well no
LINDA:	A journalier [day labourer]
MARC:	A journalier I've seen that somewhere
SIMON:	No journalier doesn't work for me

LINDA: No a manutentionnaire [handler, packer]

SIMON: A manutentionnaire doesn't work for me either / an homme d'atelier works for me

(they laugh)

MARC: But what does it mean?

SIMON: Well it's the it's

MARC: That's why the [pl.] (x)

SIMON: Well it's for

MARC: It's the [pl.] the [sing.] the [pl.] the guys from the factory [floor]

SIMON: It's that's going to be a mechanic who'll be employed as a "gofer" / "gofer this gofer that"

(they laugh, and shortly afterward Simon and Marc go back to work)

[LINDA: J'ai juste cherché un dictionnaire oh (x)

SIMON: Homme d'atelier fait une traduction littérale parfaite

LINDA: (x) Quoi en anglais?

MARC: *Shopman*

SIMON: *Shopman*

MARC: C'est un gars qui travaille dans un atelier / un homme d'atelier ben non

LINDA: Un journalier

MARC: Un journalier j'ai vu ça quelque part

SIMON: Non journalier ça fait pas mon affaire

LINDA: Non un manutentionnaire

SIMON: Un manutentionnaire ça fait pas mon affaire non plus / un homme d'atelier ça fait mon affaire

(Ils rient)

MARC: Mais qu'est-ce que ça veut dire?

SIMON: Là c'est le c'est

MARC: Ça c'est pourquoi les (x)

SIMON: Ben c'est pour

MARC: C'est les le les gars de l'usine

SIMON: C'est ça va être un mécanicien qui va être employé comme gofer / gofer this gofer that

(Ils rient)

Simon and Marc are already well into their conversation about what constitutes a good French term for the English "shopman" (a worker in the "[work] shop") by the time they arrive at Linda's desk. Linda proceeds by hauling out her French–English dictionary and asking for the English term they are trying to translate. Neither Simon nor Marc is particularly seduced by the dictionary, however; whether it is opaque to them (Marc's "But what does it mean?"), or somehow just doesn't feel right (Simon's "It doesn't work for me"), the term is rejected, and they proceed by trying to go closer to what they understand the core meaning to be, for them ("the guys from the factory [floor]," "a mechanic who'll be employed as a gofer"—this last triggers Simon's association with a well-known play on words (go for—go fer—gopher) understood to be at the origins of the term "gofer" to designate an employee whose job is to supply materials to his superiors in a workshop or other workplace involving materials, at their orders: "go for this, go for that"). It may be an old joke, but it serves to defuse the tension around the terminological—and sociopolitical—impasse the three have found themselves in: the men are not prepared to alienate themselves entirely from the referential realities and social register they need to operate in (*homme d'atelier* works for Simon; *journalier* and *manutentionnaire* have no resonance in their repertoires, they do not actually mean the same thing, and they sound, well, they sound like they come out of the dictionary, not out of a foreman's mouth). The joke also serves as a reminder of the English work world with which Marc and Simon are familiar; they know exactly where the term "gofer" comes from, but no idea what *manutentionnaire* might mean.

Linda, her counter, and her dictionaries are important spaces for negotiation of francization among some of its interested parties—foremen and superintendents like Marc and Simon. In that conversational space, they can move back and forth between French and English, and between sanctioned linguistic authorities on the standard language and what people actually say in situated practices, in an attempt to create something sayable that is also recognizably French. Francization is thus exposed as not simply a matter of substituting the objectively constituted "francophone" way of talking about things for the existing "anglophone" way but, rather, as a complex constitution of a social voice that does not yet exist. Simon is not quite prepared to assume the authority for creating that voice (and going ahead and using *homme d'atelier*); he would rather be able to draw on the authority of sanctioned sources like the dictionary. He is caught ideologically between language as neutral and autonomous object, and language as social practice. Really, the only way out is a good laugh. This example also displays the hidden work of people like Linda. Translation and corpus planning are not in her job description, but they occupied a significant portion of her time and allowed many members of her department to achieve their linguistic goals.

With her and the younger francophones, Bob used a few fixed phrases and formulas in French (usually "Bonjour, comment ça va?"—Hello, how are you?), a kind of symbolic recognition of the new place of French and francophones in the department. He did not invest much more time and energy in learning French than that, but he didn't really need to. He was soon going to retire, so there were few consequences for him if he failed to understand everything that people were saying around him. . . . [I]f his colleagues needed his expertise or his approval, they spoke to him in English.

Bob continued to speak English with Claude, as they had always done, although Claude spoke French with other francophones. For people like Claude, francization was complicated. He had built his career around being able to function in both French with those under him, and English with his colleagues and supervisor in the office. . . . In particular, this had always meant that Claude read materials and wrote his reports in English. Now . . . he was expected somehow, magically, to read these texts and produce these reports in French, and the latter especially proved extremely difficult.

Daniel was the newest on the scene, a unilingual francophone (and direct beneficiary of francization, like Albert). His recent promotion put him for the first time in contact with anglophones like Bob. In those instances, Linda and Albert helped out.

Like everyone else, Albert had competing pressures to juggle. His relationship with Bob required constant facework, since in terms of seniority Bob should have been promoted to Albert's position, and everyone knew that. Albert, the newcomer, also needed to be able to rely on Bob's knowledge, not only in terms of his technical expertise, but also in terms of the knowledge built up in twenty-five years of service to the brewery. At the same time, Albert needed to construct his legitimacy in relation to the francophones under him, both as their sector head and as the representative of the processes that were opening up possibilities and changing their status in the workplace. Not surprisingly, Albert often switched between French and English, a clear index of his position on the cusp of the wave of social change flowing through the brewery.

Let me illustrate the ways in which the different positions of Bob, Claude, Daniel, and Albert played out in the workplace. Below I provide some extracts from their regular team meetings, usually held once a week in Albert's office. Most of the time, Bob spoke only when explicitly invited to by Albert, and most of the time he did so in English, with some transition routines in French like those I show below. Everyone else spoke French. . . .

The meeting usually followed the following format: Bob, Claude, and Daniel delivered an oral version of their weekly written report (a text they normally brought with them into the meeting), and any member of the team could comment on it or ask questions about it. Albert transmitted information from the higher ranks of management and ensured that his team members made the necessary decisions and achieved a consensus on any forms of action that needed to be undertaken.

At the beginning of the following extract, we pick up (that is, I start the recorder) as people are coming in and standing around. Albert is having a side conversation with Bob in English. After a pause, everyone moves to a place around the table. While I had already met everyone but Daniel, this extract is from my first visit to a department meeting. It is possible that my association with francization added pressure on Albert to establish a French framework for the meeting, but his French opening routines are followed quickly by a repetition in English of the same utterance, specifically addressed to Bob.

ALBERT: He would have got

BOB: He's twenty-one years of age

ALBERT: Yeah twenty-one years of age
(pause)

ALBERT: *Bon mais vous pouvez fermer la porte c'est tout ce qu'on va avoir aujourd'hui/ tout le monde connaît Monica?* (okay but you can close the door that's all we're going to have today / everyone knows Monica?) Bob, have you met Monica?

Although Albert addresses Bob in English, Bob does his best to include a little French in his response.

ALBERT: On Monday afternoon we have a meeting with Daniel Vincent?

BOB: What time is it?

ALBERT: Uh

CLAUDE: Right signs

ALBERT: *Douze heures* [12 o'clock] signs

BOB: *Quelle place?* [What place?]

ALBERT: I think it's in my office

Bob continues to do his best to include French in his responses to Albert; below, his French is part of a series of strategies both Albert and Bob use to mitigate the face-threat of Albert's request, a request that would normally be issued from senior to junior.

ALBERT: Uh it's like passing the buck to somebody but uh (*he laughs*) can you spend some time some time with Pierre (x) Monday / it could be a good thing

BOB: *Avec plaisir* [with pleasure] [. . .] okay I'll do that uh / I charge Anne *rien* [nothing] / but *spécial pour toi* [special for you] forty-five dollars an hour

While Albert is doing the discursive work of including Bob, Bob is doing the discursive work, within the limits of his proficiency in French, of recognizing the new regime and Albert's legitimate occupation of a position that might otherwise have been his. He could simply have stuck to English, but here and quite systematically in every conversa-tion involving a francophone, he engages in similar practices.

In the following extract, we see how Claude copes. He has on the table in front of him the writ-ten text of his report, in English. He navigates back and forth between that text and an oral summary in French. His hesitations and pauses can be read as markers of the tension this causes in him.

CLAUDE: *Oui* [Yes] / uh vacation staff/Roland Masse George Kovacs *cette semaine / la semaine prochaine* [this week / next week] Roland Masse George Kovacs again / uh uh temp Denis Blais he's on the lubrication survey Léo Charrette uh working on the expense budget but he's going off for two weeks *hein*? *il prend deux semaines de vacances ça je l'avais donné ça y a un bout de temps* [eh? he's taking two weeks' vacation that I gave him that a while ago]

The team (with the largely invisible contribu-tion from Linda) is constructing francization in the "language of work" sense, as a process. Implicitly and consensually, they move toward a new con-vention of language choice, in which French is the unmarked [ordinary] language. Each one draws on the linguistic resources at his or her disposal, as a function of their life trajectories and their structural position in the organization of the company. Those who profit the most from the change provide scaf-folding and safe zones backstage for those who do not have the capital they need. . . . As long as people like Bob (and to a lesser extent Claude) do not re-sist, they are offered the means to continue to func-tion without losing face. Albert is not cut off from their expertise and can construct his legitimacy as a trained francophone manager. Daniel is a legitimate participant, which would have been impossible ear-lier given his lack of English. And while Linda's salary may not take her contribution into account, she does accumulate **symbolic capital**, and makes herself indispensable.

The discursive strategies adopted are a way to keep the company going, avoiding open conflict or loss of employee time that might otherwise have had to go to expensive recruitment and training efforts. None of the brewery's employees has an interest in hobbling his or her employer. Their strategies allow for the peaceable introduction of francophones into new positions of power and the concomitant establishment of their language as the language of work (which legitimates their presence and their exercise of control). Francization is centrally about francophonization; and while the state uses clumsy, awkward means to push the process along, on the ground, actors draw on their resources to appropriate the process in ways that make sense to them. Notably, these are ways that allow for the company to slowly carve out the space of a regional Quebec market, and continue to make a profit while doing so.

Discursive Shift and Political Economic Change

The transition from traditionalist to modernizing discourses happened under particular political economic conditions. Along with growing wealth and consumption, the reorganization and expansion of markets during the postwar boom years, the ethnonational mobilization that succeeded in asserting control over the apparatus of the state (of Quebec), and the increasing importance of science and technology all help to explain what happened in this workplace and many others. . . .

In the end, the investment in unilingual spaces didn't make bilingualism less valuable; it simply reorganized it. It made bilingualism less the privileged domain of the francophone male working class, and more that of the emergent middle class involved in national and international markets whether they belonged to the ethnonational category of "francophone" or "anglophone." It forced anglophones to choose between involvement in a wider English-speaking

market outside Quebec (commonly known as "taking the 401," for the highway connecting Montreal and Toronto) or learning French to capitalize on new opportunities as bilingual brokers between the Quebec market . . . and the national and increasingly globalized market dominated by English. Francophones were able to remain monolingual while profiting from the expanded opportunities of the regional market, until they bumped up against the need for English at higher corporate levels. Sooner or later they had somehow to invest in English. . . .

This had yet to become an issue in the late 1970s. Then, francophones were just beginning to get a generalized experience of modern, technologized, credentialized life. But that tension began to emerge around the contradiction between the focus on language skills (as opposed to ethnonational group membership) in official discourse (as in Bill 101), and the real-life salience of ethnicity in organizing access to advantageous positions in reshaped markets. This tension . . . calls into question who counts as a francophone, what counts as bilingualism, what role the state should play in the reproduction of the nation, and, indeed, whether we should be talking about nations at all. . . .

I have showed here some of the ways in which a critical ethnographic sociolinguistic approach can be applied to what looks like a simple policy problem: is a company adopting French as the language of work? By asking how language is related to the resources at stake in the company (from information, to promotion, to jobs), and to legitimate access to them, I ask how language functions in struggles over power, and how it is embedded in the reproduction or production of various social categories.

I have tried to show that the OLF's question cannot be answered in simple, categorical terms. The question, and how to answer it, can only make sense once the political economic conditions that underlie the ideologies of language and identity we use to organize ourselves are apprehended. . . .

. . . [It is] important to capture how things work out for different categories of social actors, and to explain why it works out well for some,

[but] maybe not so well for others. . . . If the brewery was indeed moving more and more toward adopting French as the language of work . . ., this depended on some change in personnel and in organizational structure that had begun to come into existence prior to [the enactment of Bill 101.] [I]ndeed one could say [the changes] made [Bill 101] possible. . . .

Reference Cited

Daoust-Blais, Denise, and André Martin. 1981. "La planification linguistique au Québec: Aménagement du corpus linguistique et promotion du statut du française." In *L'État et la planification linguistique*, edited by André Martin, 43–99. Quebec: Office de langue française.

Note

1. The "capital" and "markets" that Heller references here are not financial capital or markets, but rather personal skills, connections, and resources that may confer socioeconomic advantages. (Stern's note)

Key Points to Consider

- Language ideologies reflect status differences among people as well as peoples' ideas about what constitutes the "proper" way of speaking.
- Francization was part of the successful modernization strategy of Quebec nationalists.
- Modernization paved the way for Quebec to participate in globalization, and, in the period since Heller conducted the fieldwork described here, bilingualism has once again become the path to socioeconomic advancement in Quebec.

Critical Thinking Questions

1. Do you speak more than one language? How and why did you acquire fluency in your second language? Is one of your languages generally considered to be more prestigious than the other? Why or why not? What are the contexts in which you use each of your languages?
2. How did Heller's status as an outsider help or hinder her research at the brewery?
3. Which types of employees of the brewery found bilingualism to be valuable to their work? For whom did bilingualism lead to promotion or advancement in the company? Who was not helped? Why?

Suggestions for Further Reading

Heller, Monica. 1994. *Crosswords: Language, Education, and Ethnicity in French Ontario*. Berlin: Mouton De Gruyter.

————. 1999. "Heated Language in a Cold Climate." In *Language Ideological Debates*, edited by Jan Blommaert, 143–70. Berlin: Mouton De Gruyter.

———— and Lindsay Bell. 2012. "Frontiers and Frenchness: Pride and Profit in the Production of Canada." In *Language in Late Capitalism: Pride and Profit*, edited by Alexandre Duchêne and Monica Heller, 161–82. New York: Routledge.

Hill, Jane H. 1998. "Language, Race, and White Public Space." *American Anthropologist* 100 (3): 680–9.

Chapter 4

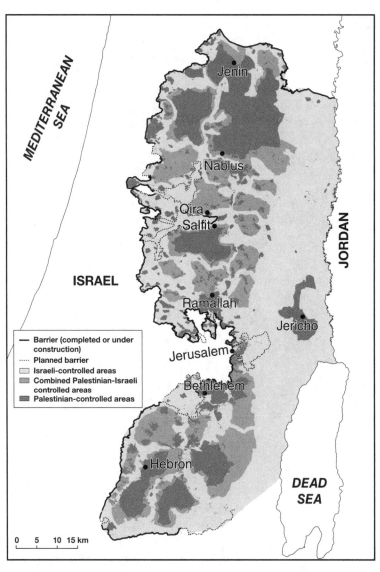

Palestine (West Bank)

Introduction

The opening scenes of Charlie Chaplin's 1936 film *Modern Times* are set in a factory. While the assembly-line workers are engaged in physically repetitive and mentally dulling tasks, the company president sits in his office alternately piecing together a jigsaw puzzle and monitoring the factory floor via a video screen. Seemingly at random, the company president appears on the video screen to order a speed-up on the assembly line. In a telling scene, several assembly-line workers get into a physical altercation. Someone stops the production line, but to avoid being struck, Chaplin's character starts the belt moving again. Immediately his antagonists drop their fists, pick up their tools, return to their workstations, and resume their never-changing assembly tasks.

The film uses satire to depict the dehumanization that can result when individuals' **agency** to determine how to use their time is restricted. Chaplin's is a comic representation, but the film's success and endurance come from the fact that it addresses an issue that concerns real people—how and by whom **temporal regimes** are organized and enforced. The article below concerns a controversial subject that many people have strong feelings about—competing Israeli and Palestinian claims to govern the West Bank, a region of land lying to the west of the Jordan River. The author, Anne Meneley, describes the way temporal regimes are implicated in Israelis' and Palestinians' competing claims. The ability to make demands on other people's time is a form of power. The powerful can exert their authority by speeding things up or slowing them down. Meneley is supportive of ordinary Palestinians who find their day-to-day activities and their short- and long-term security threatened by a variety of external forces including regulations established by the Israeli **state**.

A temporal regime is a culturally determined way of regulating time. It is reinforced through institutions or repetitive actions that often hide the relations of power involved. People come to think of a temporal regime as ordinary common sense, forgetting that it was invented to suit some particular purpose and may benefit some interests at the expense of others. When a temporal regime or other cultural practice is considered common sense, anthropologists may describe it as **naturalized**. In North America, for example, we are accustomed to thinking of the school year as beginning in early fall and concluding in the spring, with summer "off." We might, in fact, become distressed if the academic calendar was changed to eliminate summer vacation. Our nine or ten month "school year" dates from a time when many children were needed to help on their families' farms. This is no longer the case, but we have retained the school calendar and created new institutions—the family vacation, summer camp, swimming lessons, and the luxury of sleeping late—and new rationales about child development that support retention of the existing regime. Yet families without the financial means to organize costly recreational activities or supervision for their children may experience the summer "vacation" from school as added stress rather than a time of relaxation.

Each temporal regime encourages a particular **time discipline**, a culturally distinct way of viewing the use of time as correct, even moral. Individuals who do not share the temporal norms of those around them are sometimes disparaged as lazy, weird, or obsessive. Different economic adaptations are associated with different temporal regimes and expectations for time discipline. For example, among groups who make their living from farming, people think about and organize their time around climate and crop cycles. This may mean working very long hours in certain seasons and facing few demands in others. People who raise dairy cattle have their schedules tied to the feeding, milking, and calving demands of the animals. The kind of time discipline that is required for farming is very different from that of an office worker or a sales clerk, who may travel an hour to work, spend eight hours on the job, and then travel another hour home. English historian E.P. Thompson distinguished between the time discipline of farming and fishing, which he called "task orientation," and the time discipline of wage labour, which he called "clock orientation." Like Charlie Chaplin, Thompson saw clock orientation as dehumanizing. In reality, today, most people's lives combine elements of both clock and task orientation, and we are subject to several different temporal regimes that likely require different forms of time discipline. Universities, for example, are organized into academic terms, each with a particular rhythm of classes, papers, and exams. Some employers offer part-time jobs with "flexible hours," jobs in which employees often do not know from one week to the next when they will be scheduled to work. In addition to school and work, family life, religious activities, and sports all involve different calendars, and it can be quite difficult to balance the conflicting demands of different temporal regimes.

The geographic region referred to as the West Bank is, today, home to approximately 2.7 million Palestinians. The region has been under military occupation by the Israeli army since 1967. Some Israelis believe that this land should be part of Israel and have established "settlements" on land previously owned and still claimed by Palestinians. According to the CIA *World Factbook*, more than 340,000 Israeli settlers currently live in the West Bank (CIA 2013). While many of their settlements were authorized by the Israeli government, others were not, and the Israeli government has only rarely removed settlements that encroach on land owned by Palestinians. In 2002, the Israeli government began erecting a border fence, referred to as a "security barrier," between Israel and the West Bank. While many portions are constructed of electrified wire, in some places the barrier is a concrete wall up to eight metres high. The security barrier has been routed to incorporate many Israeli West Bank settlements on the Israeli side of the fence. In places, as well, the barrier separates Palestinians from their fields and orchards which are now on the Israeli side. And according to the Israeli peace activist group B'Tselem (2012), as many as a quarter of a million Palestinians live in towns that are fully or partially encircled by the barrier.

Meneley makes reference to the Palestinian ***intifadas***. The Arabic word *intifada* is usually translated as "uprising" and can be used to refer to any kind of rebellion or resistance movement. The Palestinian *intifadas*—there have been two—were protests against Israeli occupation of East Jerusalem, the West Bank, and the Gaza Strip. The first *intifada* (1987–1993) largely consisted of economic boycotts of Israel and Israeli businesses and stone throwing. Palestinian actions against Israel during the second *intifada* (2000–2005) were more violent and many more Israelis and Palestinians were injured and killed. It is important to note that only a small percentage of Palestinians engaged in violent acts, and many opposed the use of violence as a form of protest. Israel mounted a military response to both uprisings. The security barrier and increased number of checkpoints described in the article were also a response to the second *intifada*.

The stated purpose of the security barrier is to stop terrorists from entering Israel, and it may do that. It also prevents mundane interactions between Israelis and Palestinians that could serve as a basis for mutual understanding. And as Meneley and many other authors point out, it also impedes Palestinians from visiting relatives, going to work or school, attending medical appointments, and engaging in other routine, peaceful activities. It assumes that every Palestinian is a potential terrorist. Israeli peace activist and MacArthur ("genius") fellow David Shulman has written that the security barrier perpetuates "a regime of terror inside the [occupied] territories, leaving most Palestinian villages encircled, isolated, essentially ghettoized, and at the mercy of bands of marauding settlers" (Shulman 2007: 144).

The article below concerns the way that Israeli regulation of Palestinians' movement produces a temporal regime in conflict with the temporal regime associated with olive oil production. Each regime requires a different kind of time discipline, and each contains uncertainties. But, as Meneley points out, the uncertainties of agriculture—will the rains be sufficient but not too plentiful?, will they occur at the "right" time?, and will insects and other pests be manageable?—are compounded for all Palestinians on the West Bank by the uncertainties of living under Israeli military occupation. Of particular concern for the development of commerce are fixed and temporary (or "flying") checkpoints and other Israeli regulations that prevent or slow the movement of Palestinian people and goods.

The temporal regulation Meneley describes is extreme, but even so it is not unique. Similar sorts of social control through the regulation of time were documented for the communist era in Romania (Verdery 1996). Classic anthropological studies also looked at how temporal regimes figure into the real lives of people, especially in the context of ritual. Edmund Leach (1910–1989), for example, theorized that rituals enable people to mark the passage of time, causing us to consider some periods as sacred and others as non-sacred (Leach 2000). Leach did not confine his theorizing to a single cultural group but rather proposed a general theory of the relationship between time and ritual. For Palestinian olive producers, as Meneley reports, harvest periods were ritual periods for family celebration, but these have been disrupted by Israeli occupation. During harvest and at other times, Palestinians' lack of control over time serves as a constant reminder of the lack of control over other aspects of their lives.

❖ *About the Author* ❖

Anne Meneley teaches anthropology at Trent University. She studied at McGill University and then at New York University, where she earned her PhD. Meneley's earliest research concerned the lives of women in Yemen. She then began researching the production of olive oil in Tuscany and Umbria, Italy. The following reading represents a blending of her interest in olive oil and her continuing interest in the peoples and cultures of the Middle East.

Time in a Bottle: The Uneasy Circulation of Palestinian Olive Oil

Anne Meneley

Olive oil has been a central element of Palestinian agriculture for centuries. It is a relatively durable food **commodity**, unlike fresh produce such as strawberries or tomatoes, which rot quickly in the sun. Unlike wine, however, olive oil does not improve with age, and is best consumed within a year or two of its production. It is extremely sensitive to exposure to heat, air, and light, which cause the quality of the oil to deteriorate rapidly. It is also expensive to store and ship; the days of the Roman terracotta amphorae are gone, and now olive oil is often stored in glass bottles, heavy and easily breakable. These particular qualities of olive oil plague all producers who wish to sell their surplus, but

Palestinian olive oil producers face additional challenges when trying to produce and export their oil because of the Israeli occupation.

As Palestinians produce more olive oil than they consume, they need to find markets for the excess. Two important markets were lost in the last two decades: the Palestinian workers in the Gulf states who were evicted after the Iraqi invasion of Kuwait in 1990, and Jordan, because around the same time, King Hussein closed the border to Palestinian oil to encourage Jordan's own olive oil production. Palestinian producers and marketers are often reluctant to sell to large Israeli firms, who buy olive oil from poor farmers for less than it costs to produce it. (There is also considerable resentment at the fact that the fruit of Palestinian labour is then sold as a "Product of Israel," extending the occupation into the culinary realm.) Palestinian olive oil producers now aim at markets in Great Britain, France, the United States, Japan, Australia, New Zealand, and Canada. Consumers abroad often buy Palestinian olive oil out of a desire to help the Palestinian cause, but are unwilling, even for the sake of solidarity, to do so if the oil is not graded as "extra virgin," a relatively recent designation of quality established by the International Olive Oil Council. The designation means that a chemical analysis of the oil affirms an acidity level of at least 0.8 per cent and that the oil passes a . . . taste test where its flavour is determined to have no flaws.

"Extra virgin" is a term with little currency in everyday Palestinian life. Traditionally produced Palestinian olive oil, with its thick consistency, heady fragrance, and dark green colour, is beloved of Palestinians in the West Bank and Gaza; of Palestinians forced from their land and homes in 1948; and of Israeli peace activists and leftists. Yet it cannot be graded as extra virgin by international standards because of its high acidity level; it also diverges quite markedly in taste from the international **hegemonic** standard. Palestinian olive oil traditionally had a much higher acidity level of 2.5 to 4 per cent (Rosenblum 1996: 64), and the taste of the "new" oil seems but a pale reflection of the oil Palestinians recall with such affection. Olive oil

plays a significant role in what Nadia Serematakis calls "secondary **commensality**," connecting displaced Palestinians with a lost homeland. References to this role for olives abound in Palestinian cultural production. In Najwa Qa'war Farah's short story, for instance, the protagonist Abu Ibrahim, his heart broken by his forced exile to Lebanon, has only olives to connect him to Palestine. "He lived in dread that the jars of oil and olives he'd brought with him should all be consumed, for it was only when he tasted them that his misery would leave him briefly" (Farah 1992: 440).

In the last two decades, there have been several initiatives to transform Palestinian olive oil production, funded by the US Agency for International Development, the European Union [EU], and individual EU countries, primarily Italy and Spain, in order to bring Palestinian oil up to the standard where it can be graded as "extra virgin." The EU in particular has very particular customs requirements about the chemical content of foreign-produced olive oil. This reorientation of the Palestinian olive oil market toward international consumers has required dramatic transformations in the cultivation, harvesting, and pressing of olives—in turn rendering the olive oil industry ever more sensitive to time.

Time on Their Hands

The cumulative loss of labour opportunities in Israel after the 1987–1993 *intifada*, and in the Gulf after the Iraqi invasion of Kuwait, left many Palestinians unemployed and with time on their hands. The enforced idleness deepened in late 2000 with the second *intifada* when the Israeli military imposed a lockdown on entire districts like Salfit and Jenin, blocking people and goods from entry or exit. In the words of one olive oil producer, these closures led to a kind of involuntary "reruralization" of the West Bank. The revitalization of the olive oil industry was a way of providing meaningful work to Palestinian farmers, and therefore enough income to encourage them to stay on their land, and a way of alleviating the boredom produced by checkpoints, curfews, and closures, the flip side of the terrifying incursions of the Israeli army. It is ironic indeed that the agricultural labour undervalued when the more lucrative Gulf and Israel were open is revalued now that the Palestinian population has been bottled up by intensified Israeli occupation.

Advisers from France, Spain, and Italy recommended changes in the Palestinian olive oil industry, in accordance with the latest European techniques for producing high-quality extra virgin oil. These foreign experts pushed for a **holistic** approach to olive production, "from tree to table," seeking to reshape every aspect of cultivation, harvesting, processing, bottling, and shipping. For instance, foreign experts recommended that Palestinian farmers give up plowing with a tractor directly under the trees canopy, as this disrupts the shallow root system of the native olive trees, adapted as they are to Palestine's dry climate. Olive cultivation, like any other kind of agriculture, is governed by seasonal time. October is the month for spreading organic fertilizer (sheep, cow, or chicken manure), then tilling the soil (foreign experts have recommended horizontal instead of vertical tilling on the terraces, in order to preserve water). In Palestine, olive production has a biannual cycle of poor and plentiful harvests, and pruning practices shift accordingly. In February and March the trees are pruned with scissors in the year of a good harvest, but with saws before a bad year. June is the month where traps must be put out for the olive fly: infected olives rot on the branch. In August and September, the foreign experts encourage frequent irrigation but do not press the point because many farmers do not have access to wells, as Israel will not allow Palestinians to dig wells without a permit that is difficult to obtain. All of these cultivation activities need to be carried out according to the seasonal cycle, yet for many Palestinian farmers seasonal agricultural time is disrupted by what one might call "occupation time." This concept is closely related to what anthropologist Jeff Halper has defined as the Israeli "matrix of control": the military bases, outposts, and checkpoints in the West Bank; the Israeli-built "separation barrier" that encloses [Israeli] settlements, along with a good deal of Palestinian

agricultural land, on the "Israeli" side; and the bewildering thicket of residence and travel permits that hinders the movement of Palestinians and the few commodities they have available for global circulation. In addition, . . . Israeli settlements, protected by the Israeli army, have expanded apace, often next to, or obliterating, Palestinian olive groves. These elements combine to distort the time horizon of olive oil production, irrespective of the requirements of the seasons.

The many farmers whose land is close to a military outpost or a bypass road connecting settlements to Israel proper, or whose land is walled off from the village by the "separation barrier," are required to get special permission to gain access to their own land. Egress is through small "agricultural gates" in the wall, which may or may not be open when the farmer needs to pass. Those Palestinians whose land lies close to an [Israeli] settlement or outpost are in particular danger. Settlers are apt arbitrarily to declare a "security zone"; Palestinians who come close, even if they own the land, are at risk of being beaten or shot.

By far the most sensitive time, in both the seasonal and bureaucratic-military senses, is the olive harvest. For high-quality, low-acidity oil, it is best to pick olives when they are half green and half black; they should be harvested by hand, not by beating the branch with a stick, which is faster, but can damage the fruit, raising the acidity level. The olives should be collected and stored in a ventilated plastic box, and taken directly to a mill that uses cold processing. All of these processes should be undertaken with the utmost speed. A friend told me of his memories of picking olives as a child, when children were given time off school to help with the harvest. His family would pack food, cooking implements, and drums, and then after a hard day's picking, they would have a celebratory meal. The extended family would camp out in the olive groves. Polyphonic songs were common, when men in the trees would sing one humorous refrain and women would answer with another. But for those whose land lies close to a settlement or army encampment, the fear of being shot has taken the joy out of olive picking.

FIGURE 4.1   Palestinian women harvest olives in October 2004 after being granted permission from the Israeli Defense Forces to cross the separation barrier to reach their olive orchard.

The olive harvest has gone from being a time of communal hard work and celebration to being one of isolation, tension, and fear.

The problem is the direct interference in the olive harvest by Israeli settlers, who harass the pickers, and by the army, which seldom intervenes to stop the settlers' attacks, and administers the bureaucratic restrictions upon the number of family members who will be given access to the land. Harvesting is the most labour-intensive phase of the agricultural cycle, but in areas near settlements or military bases, permission is only given to the nuclear family members, who cannot possibly pick all their olives quickly enough by themselves. If the olives are left to sit, they begin to rot, and the acidity level of the oil produced from them rises. Of late, groups of international volunteers have come to help pick the olives of vulnerable farmers and also provide a human shield against army or settler harassment.

Though Palestinians' agricultural labour has been revalued when bottled as extra virgin olive oil, it can also be cheapened by "occupation time," as Palestinians attempt to distribute their oil to global consumers. E.P. Thompson's chapter "Time, Work-Discipline, and Industrial Capitalism," from *The Making of the English Working Class*, notes the transformation from agricultural time, structured by seasons associated with varied tasks, to "clock time," which organized the working hours of industry to extract maximum surplus value from the workers. "Clock time" grew faster and faster as capitalism developed, with advances in communication and transportation eventually making it possible for agricultural products susceptible to spoilage, like extra virgin olive oil, to be exported intact around the world in a timely fashion. Such late capitalist, "just in time" production is the mode to which Palestinian olive growers aspire, but the occupation has effectively obstructed them from realizing the benefits that their economy desperately needs. "Occupation time" works to prevent Palestinians from realizing the value of their labour, as embedded in the product of extra virgin olive oil, at the same time as it interferes with the seasonal rhythms of old. It is its own temporal category.

Time–Space Distortion

Olive oil travels on the same roads as Palestinians do, and suffers the same delays. It takes far longer to traverse the tiny territory of the West Bank than it should. The newly constructed bypass highways provide efficient transport for settlers who work in Israel, but Palestinians are forbidden to use them. The highways that serve the Palestinian population are not only poorly maintained by comparison, but they are interrupted by frequent Israeli checkpoints, some of them massive, permanent structures where people are often forced to make long, boring, thirsty, and humiliating waits. The fact that a Palestinian woman felt compelled to invent "queuing socks" to alleviate the stress on the feet produced by hours of standing is a testimony to how long these waits can be (BBC News 2007). Temporary roadblocks known as "flying checkpoints," in an unintentional oxymoron, also appear without warning. And then there is the unsightly "separation barrier," multiple barbed-wire fences, or, in many spots, 25 feet of concrete rising to cut off roads and dirt tracks from top to bottom of the West Bank.

"Here in this country you cannot plan!" exclaimed the head of the olive oil division of the Palestinian Agricultural Relief Committee (PARC), an NGO [**non-governmental organization**] founded in 1983 and designed to help farmers stay on their land, upon encountering a flying checkpoint on the road to Jericho. He said he had learned, in his time with PARC, every back road that might provide an escape from the monotony of waiting and the potential harassment by the Israeli soldiers at a checkpoint. For olive oil fares no better than people's feet:

its quality and market value deteriorate rapidly in the heat and the sun. The unpredictability of the flying checkpoints severely distorts the ability of olive oil professionals to predict how much time it will take for them and their oil to get from one part of the West Bank to another. Since the second *intifada* erupted, said the head of Zaytoona, an olive oil company based in Ramallah, he no longer fixes the time of business appointments, because there is no way to know whether there will be new flying checkpoints or lines at the permanent checkpoints.

Along with chemical analysis to determine acidity and sterol count, a test that can be performed at universities in Nablus, Ramallah, and Bethlehem, or at the Ministry of Agriculture, high-quality extra virgin olive oil needs to be anointed as "without defects" by a certified olive tasting board. As part of the transformation of the industry to serve global markets, European tasting experts now train Palestinians to be professional tasters. There are three tasting panels, one for the south of the West Bank, one for the central part, and one for the north. Each batch of oil needs to be judged by seven or eight professional tasters, but the combination of unpredictability of travel and the restrictive nature of many Palestinians' permits has necessitated the superfluous triplication. . . .

My first visit to a Palestinian olive oil co-operative was in Qira, in the Salfit district. The day before, on my way north from Jerusalem, I had navigated the Qalandiya checkpoint, with its crowds of buses and taxis, for the first time. Once in Ramallah, I had to wait for a man who had the correct permit to accompany me to Salfit. The bus in which we rode was stopped twice at flying checkpoints, where all the young male passengers had to disembark. Yet deep into my interview with Hamid, head of the olive oil co-operative, he had not mentioned these obvious obstacles to his work. With deliberate naïveté, I asked: "How does all this permit and roadblock stuff affect your capacity to export your oil?" Laughing and looking at me as if I were from Mars, he answered: "Oh, in every single way, every single second!" As the Palestinians have no airport or seaport, the facilities built in Gaza in the 1990s having been destroyed and cut off from the West Bank by Israel, their oil has to depart through the Israeli port at Haifa. (Oil from the southern West Bank commonly goes through the southern Israeli port of Ashdod.) Before it goes to Haifa, the oil is sold to PARC. When the *intifada*-era curfews started in Qira, a PARC volunteer moved from house to house to collect olive oil from each farmer. And then there were the travel permits. PARC needed a courier with an East Jerusalem ID card, whose bearers have Israeli residency and travel documents (but not citizenship), and hence can move more freely than other Palestinians from one city to another, or, in the cases of Nablus and Hebron, from one part of the same city to another. Even when the oil arrives in Haifa, there is no guarantee that it will be shipped with any speed. In fact, said Hamid wearily, "They [the Israelis] always try to stop the oil." PARC therefore packs it very well, insulating the bottles in anticipation that the shipment may sit for several months in port. Hamid suspected that oil destined for an Italian Palestine solidarity group was sent to a fair trade distributor in Britain out of deliberate malevolence.

Another olive professional, head of a group of olive oil co-operatives in Bethlehem, spoke of an occasion when a shipment languished in Ashdod "for 25 days in the sun." The olive oil was completely ruined. Another time their oil sat in Haifa's port for six months, and yet another time, the Israelis broke so many of the bottles that the oil could not be shipped. This professional said his organization always insures the oil before it is shipped, to guard against delays. In the past, PARC was able to fill shipping containers with pallets of carefully packed olive oil directly from its bottling facility in al-Ram, a suburb of East Jerusalem. But Israel abruptly changed the procedures, requiring that the pallets be shipped to the Beitunia checkpoint near Ramallah where there is no storage facility. There the olive oil sits in the sun until it is searched and waved on to Ashdod, where it undergoes another search before it is packed in containers and shipped. PARC also needs to obtain permission from the military to ship the oil, a process that can take from 24 hours to three weeks. PARC has clients of long standing in the US and Japan, but the conditions of circulation (or lack thereof) of Palestinian

olive oil mean that long-term marketing plans and reliability of delivery, essential for establishing consumer trust, are severely hampered. I met one PARC client (or "partner," as they called her) in Ramallah. She is a Jewish American woman who expressed her opposition to Israeli policies in the West Bank by starting a non-profit olive oil company to sell Palestinian oil to private customers, at small fair trade shops and fundraising events. She runs her organization on a shoestring budget, often paying for shipments out of pocket, so any delay in her olive oil shipment is nerve-racking. If she does not receive the bill of lading on time, she is still charged storage fees in the US.

It is not only the Israeli state that can hold up olive oil deliveries: the shipment of a man who sold Palestinian oil through his Presbyterian Church network was stopped at the US border because the label said "Product of Palestine" and the US does not recognize "Palestine" as a state. Every year, the annual work party for Zatoun, a Canadian non-profit that depends on volunteers to pack the olive oil into 12-bottle boxes and stuff brochures into envelopes, is postponed because Canada Customs has stopped the shipment to search it, without explanation, but with a charge of Cdn $1,200, a significant sum for this small operation.

Sending olive oil through the port of Aqaba in Jordan is no solution to the problems of going through Israeli ports, because the road to Aqaba, with delays at the Israeli-controlled border bridges, takes two days. So Palestinians only use the Aqaba facility when shipping to Arab states like Saudi Arabia that will not accept goods from an Israeli port. Since the majority of their exports now go to the US, EU, Canada, and Japan, the Palestinians continue to ship through Haifa or Ashdod, because "occupation time" notwithstanding, the ports themselves are only an hour away. They can only insure the oil and hope the shipments will proceed smoothly.

Trees and Time

He had gone to his olive trees. They consoled him, but they also gave him pain. He felt personally related to each of them. He loved their

graceful beauty and faithful generosity. The grove was a holy place for him. He was intimately acquainted with each breeze that rustled the shimmering leaves. Weren't they the children of last summer's winds? . . . These olive trees had witnessed the era of the Turkish sultans. They had survived the British Mandate. They remained now, unperturbed and strong, combating time itself with their silent endurance and devotion. Why couldn't he be like them? Why must he desert them? Why could he not endure steadfastly, as they endured?
—*Najwa Qa'war Farah, "The Worst of Two Choices: or, The Forsaken Olive Trees" (1992: 438)*

The above passage captures, and the short story's title suggests, the terrible choice facing families torn apart during the mass displacement of Palestinians during the 1948 war, a choice between the land and the trees and reunification with relatives who had fled or been driven from their homes. The protagonist, Abu Ibrahim, notes the capacity of the olive tree to "combat time" with its endurance. The olive tree is a widely recognized symbol of Palestinians' steadfastness in the face of the appropriation and/or occupation of their land. The longevity of olive trees contests Israeli claims that the land was barren before the Zionist settlers arrived. The terraces on which many of the olive trees are planted attest to the ancientness of cultivation, since terraces do not occur naturally but rather require much hewing of stone and hauling of infill earth. Since the terraces require maintenance lest they be washed out, they are signs of long-standing Palestinian investment in the land and its productivity. The trees and the terraces serve as a means of transference of the properties of time into the properties of space; the age of the olive trees is a material manifestation of Palestinians' connection to their land. Mature olive trees are supposed to remain rooted, to remain entwined with the land and the people who own them and tend them.

One of the more shocking practices of the Israeli occupation has been the uprooting of these supposedly immovable objects, symbolically and materially breaking the long-lived and seemingly inalienable connection between person, olive tree, and land. Israel here transgresses an ethical precept enshrined in the Old Testament: "Even if you are at war with a city . . . you must not destroy its trees for the tree of the field is man's life" (Deuteronomy 20:19–20). It is particularly egregious to see the ancient olive trees dug up from Palestinian land adorning the entrance to new [Israeli] settlements like Ma'ale Adumim and Pisgat Ze'ev.

. . . [O]live trees are an important element of the Palestinian nationalist imagery, in direct confrontation with Israeli nationalist imagery claiming that the land Israel now occupies was empty of people. Yet olive trees and olive oil are not only images; they are an integral part of the efforts to keep land in Palestinian hands. While Fischer (2006) notes that much contemporary Palestinian olive oil cannot be sold, in contrast to the vibrant long-distance trade in olive oil and olive oil soap centred in nineteenth-century Nablus (Doumani 1995), he does not mention the obvious reasons why not: the infrastructure of containment imposed by the Israeli occupation, which distorts time as much as space. If olive trees are "icons of ecology," icons of rootedness, then olive oil is an icon of arrested circulation, as the movement of bottles of oil, bottled Palestinian labour time, is itself bottled up within the occupation time of the Israeli state.

References Cited

BBC News. 2007. "Palestinian Invents Queuing Socks." *BBC News*, March 19. http://news.bbc.co.uk/2/hi/middle_east/6466057.stm.

Doumani, Beshara. 1995. *Rediscovering Palestine: Merchants and Peasants in Jabal Nablus, 1700–1900.* Berkeley: University of California Press.

Farah, Najwa Qa'war. 1992. "The Worst of Two Choices: or, The Forsaken Olive Trees." In *Anthology of Modern Palestinian Literature*, edited by Salma Khadra Jayyusi, 113–16. New York: Columbia University Press.

Fischer, Michael. 2006. "Changing Palestinian–Israel Ecologies: Narratives of Water, Land, Conflict, and Political Economy, Then and Now, and Life to Come." *Cultural Politics* 2 (2): 159–91.

Rosenblum, Mort. 1996. *Olives: The Life and Lore of Noble Fruit*. New York: North Point Press.

Key Points to Consider

- All people are subject to temporal regimes and various forms of time discipline that are expressed culturally.
- Time regulation is a form of social control that may arise in the context of the social control of other domains of life. Frequently the power relations are hidden.
- Israeli military occupation of the West Bank has produced a temporal regime in which the power relations are visible. International standards for extra virgin olive oil also have a temporal regime, but the power relations are less visible.
- Olive oil is economically important to Palestinians who have few other economic opportunities. Its symbolic importance has been elevated by Israeli activities that impede Palestinian efforts to produce and market olive oil and to engage in other economic activities.

Critical Thinking Questions

1. What temporal adjustments did Palestinian olive oil producers have to make in order to sell olive oil into global markets? What does Meneley describe as the drivers of those changes?
2. Why does Meneley entitle this article "Time in a Bottle"? What are the different ways that time is invoked for the production of Palestinian olive oil?
3. What is the connection between time and space described in the article? Can you think of other situations in which time and space are tied together? What are some of the consequences of conflating time and space?
4. Meneley also conducted research on the production of Italian olive oil. In comparing the production and marketing of Italian and Palestinian olive oils, she observed that supposedly neutral judgements about the quality of an olive oil are tied up with attitudes about the people who produced it. Can you think of some other examples of products in which quality is tied to attitudes about the producers? Why do you think this is so?
5. Make a list of verbal expressions that convey cultural ideas about time. Pick one and identify the context(s) in which you are likely to hear the expression. Who uses this expression? Why? What ideas are being conveyed?

Suggestions for Further Reading and Watching

Braverman, Irus. 2009. "Uprooting Identities: The Regulation of Olive Trees in the Occupied West Bank." *PoLAR: Political and Legal Anthropology Review* 32 (2): 237–64.

Chaplin, Charlie. (1936) 2003. *Modern Times*. Burbank, CA: MK2 Productions and Warner Home Video. Video recording, 87 min.

Meneley, Anne. 2005. "Oil." In *Fat: The Anthropology of an Obsession*, edited by Don Kulick and Anne Meneley, 29–43. New York: Penguin.

Shulman, David. 2007. *Dark Hope: Working for Peace in Israel and Palestine*. Chicago: University of Chicago Press.

Stern, Pamela. 2003. "Upside-Down and Backwards: Time Discipline in a Canadian Inuit Town." *Anthropologica* 45 (1): 147–61.

Verdery, Katherine. 1996. "The 'Etatization' of Time in Ceauşescu's Romania." In *What Was Socialism, and What Comes Next?*, 39–58. Princeton, NJ: Princeton University Press.

Chapter 5

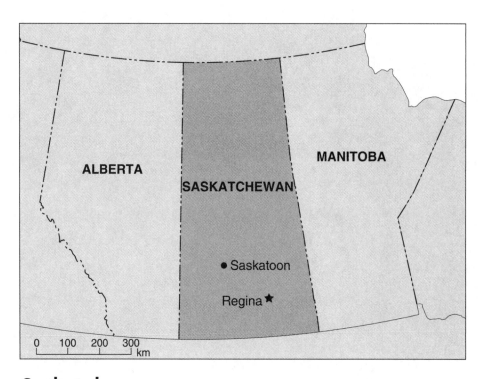

Saskatchewan

Introduction

When people think about the job of the anthropologist, they usually picture a university professor who teaches classes, writes books and academic journal articles, and does research in a distant part of the world. While this may have been true in the past, most contemporary anthropologists actually work not for universities, but for hospitals, governments, non-profit agencies, and, sometimes, private corporations. Often their job titles do not include the word *anthropologist*, but they are anthropologists nonetheless, using their skills in **ethnographic** observation and analysis to assess the needs of a population, to design culturally and socially appropriate programs, to aid **development**, or to help a group advocate for itself. These **applied** or **practising anthropologists** often work close to home, though some work for international development agencies and for multilateral organizations such as the World Bank. The reports they write are usually for their employer or a client rather than for academic journals. Some university-based anthropologists also do applied work alongside their academic activities.

Anthropologists are citizens as a well as teachers and researchers, and, thus, sometimes they use their anthropological training to support their activities as citizens, just as lawyers or other skilled professionals might use their training to advance a cause they feel is important. When anthropologists apply ethnographic methods to analyze an aspect of their own lives (to advance theory or for practical purposes), they are engaged in something called **autoethnography**. In the article below, Alexander Ervin presents an example of applied anthropology and autoethnography, describing and analyzing a successful protest movement he participated in. The movement succeeded in preventing a massive expansion of uranium mining and processing in Saskatchewan.

Saskatchewan is a world leader in uranium mining and milling, in recent years accounting for up to a quarter of the annual global production. Much of the current uranium extraction is for nuclear power generation, but initially Canadian uranium ore supplied the weapons industry. Uranium was mined in the Northwest Territories and Ontario, and there are known deposits of uranium in Quebec, Nunavut, and Labrador. At present, all of the operating uranium mines in Canada are located in northern Saskatchewan.

Mining is a substantial economic activity in Canada. It constitutes 4 per cent of Canada's economic output, and it accounts for more than 20 per cent of our exported goods. There are mines in every province and territory, and Canadian mining firms—some of the largest in the world—operate in more than one hundred countries. While there are environmentally better and worse ways to remove minerals from the earth, mining is always physically destructive, massively reshaping landscapes and watersheds and frequently leaving a toxic legacy. In Canada, and elsewhere in the world, mining proposals often generate opposition from people whose experience with mining companies has led them to fear that their communities and livelihoods will be disrupted without the promised benefits of employment or economic development.

In the original, unabridged version of the article, Ervin notes that his data come from many sources. In addition to engaging in **participant observation** of protest events and organizational activities, he reviewed thousands of pages of documents in the form of email and social media postings written by participants in the protest movement, transcripts of public hearings, and news reports. In describing his methods, Ervin uses the term *praxis*. By this he means that he employs theory not for its own sake, but integrated with social action. Like most others who use this term, Ervin identifies himself as someone who has a social justice agenda and not only expects his research to make practical contributions to improving lives, but involves the people being studied in all aspects of the research process. No research is apolitical or without prior assumptions, but not all researchers acknowledge their biases as clearly as Ervin does.

One of Ervin's biases is his opposition to what he regards as overly close relationships between corporations and government. He makes this clear in the very first sentence when he writes that the "article is intended as encouragement for activists in struggles with transnational corporations in partnership with the neoliberal **state**." The term *neoliberal* is not used much outside of academic circles; nonetheless, **neoliberalism** is a now widespread form of governance in Canada and around the world. Neoliberal governments prioritize capitalist forms of competition rather than collective action among organizations and individuals, claiming that the former is more efficient. One of the ways neoliberal states do this is by cutting taxes, reducing regulation, and privatizing public services and assets.

The article below describes an unusual event—a grassroots protest movement that successfully opposed a corporate megaproject that had the enthusiastic support of the Saskatchewan government and other powerful actors. Ervin uses the metaphor of a rhizome to explain why the Coalition for a Clean Green Saskatchewan was successful. In botany, a rhizome is a plant stem that spreads underground, sending out new roots and shoots at various nodes, some quite far from the original plant. Saskatchewan has a relatively small population, just over one million people, dispersed across a very large territory. Ervin's analysis suggests a number of reasons why a coalition of ordinary citizens achieved their goals.

❖ About the Author ❖

Alexander M. (Sandy) Ervin is an applied anthropologist within the University of Saskatchewan. Sandy Ervin began his career in anthropology studying the multi-ethnic Canadian community of Inuvik, a government-created town in the Northwest Territories. He was hired by the Department of Indian Affairs and Northern Development (now Aboriginal Affairs and Northern Development Canada) to help it understand the social and economic divisions between the Inuit, First Nations, Métis, and non-Aboriginal residents of the town. In subsequent years, Ervin has applied his anthropological training to social issues and public policy questions in Saskatchewan. His research has helped non-profit agencies involved in refugee resettlement, disability services, and community development. He is currently working with First Nations and settler communities in Saskatchewan to oppose the siting of a high-level radioactive waste dump near their homes.

A Green Coalition versus Big Uranium: Rhizomal Networks of Advocacy and Environmental Action

Alexander M. Ervin

Introduction

This article is intended as encouragement for activists in struggles with transnational corporations in partnership with the neoliberal state. I present a case study where rapidly emerging circumstances generated a movement in resistance to nuclear expansion in a Canadian province. This movement effectively joined a public debate that questioned the expansions of the uranium and nuclear industries while also advocating for renewable energy.

My analysis frames the movement implicitly within **political ecology**, more directly the study of social movements and, to a lesser extent, social networks. . . . My focus is most directly on the remarkable case study rather than offering a unique theoretical contribution. I suggest, given the right contexts, that non-hierarchical, emergent movements may work exceptionally well at mobilizing environmental resistance—especially so when their members are well informed, highly motivated with extreme urgency, and [confident] in their civic capacity. Imposing top-down hierarchical, strategic planning with external, visible leader/spokespersons (e.g., Greenpeace or Sierra Club campaigns) may not always be productive and may instead generate internal conflicts that stymie the tasks at hand and inhibit the flow of local, grassroots spontaneity, and moral authority.

Methodological and Ethical Issues: Towards a "Militant Ethnography"

. . . Praxis, especially as an applied anthropologist, is as important to me as understandings of social process. "Militant ethnography" as described by Jeffrey Juris in his analysis of movements against corporate **globalization** is relevant.

> To grasp the concrete logic generating specific practices, one has to become an active participant . . . one has to build long-term relationships of commitment and trust, become entangled with complex relationships of power, and live the emotions associated with direct-action. . . . *Militant ethnography thus refers to ethnographic research that is not only politically engaged but also collaborative thus breaking down the divide between researcher and object* (Juris 2008, 20, my emphasis).

This resonates with my experience—and I was already engaged in this struggle before it occurred to me to conduct research on it. . . .

[My] motivation for writing about [the recent anti-nuclear movement in Saskatchewan] comes from the fact that the success exceeded expectations. Our opponents' positions of influence, power, and advantage seemed overwhelming. My focus here is on the details of emergence and action that account for success. . . .

Ethical questions need a reply—one question is whether this article provides the means for

opponents to co-opt our resistance by providing too much information about our strategies. When I was approached to write an article on this topic, the first question that occurred to me was, would I be revealing too much? So I took it to one of our last meetings to discuss the invitation. The consensus . . . was that I should write the paper. One person, who has been a community activist/developer over the last twenty years, told us that it was because of inspiration from a similar paper while a graduate student that she decided to do community development work. . . .

The Situation

Many policy-makers and capitalists aspire to make Western Canada an energy corridor with massive exports going to the United States as well as meeting domestic need. This energy-producing regime involves conventional oil, tar sands bitumen, heavy oil, gas, coal, and uranium. . . . Regarding uranium, Saskatchewan is currently the world's largest producer of high-grade (up to 20 per cent) uranium ore, and the largest transnational uranium mining company, Cameco, is headquartered in Saskatoon. Other powerful entities include Areva, the French national uranium and nuclear power producer; Bruce Power, a major operator of nuclear power stations in Eastern Canada; and Atomic Energy of Canada Limited (AECL), a designer and builder of reactors. The Saskatchewan Chamber of Commerce and its city branches see opportunities for spin-off benefits. The University of Saskatchewan has entered into partnerships with this corporate sector and looks to expand its nuclear research facilities.

Above all, the provincial government elected in 2007 and formed by the Saskatchewan Party has strong aspirations of creating **value-added [economic] opportunities** beyond mining uranium. Saskatchewan premier Brad Wall boasted after coming to office that Saskatchewan was to become the "Saudi Arabia of uranium," including nuclear power production and possibly the upgrading and refining of the mineral. These players imagine that such developments would bring major boosts to the economy in exports and domestic growth and provide cheap, "clean" energy for the synthesizing of tar sands oil in Alberta. Much of the flow of information and the manipulation of **symbols** [was] fed to the public by a compliant print media through editorials, pundit commentary, business section stories, and advertising.

The Emergence of the Coalition for a Clean Green Saskatchewan

Movements of resistance to uranium and nuclear production in Saskatchewan go back to the 1970s. . . . There were a few successes—community and movement resistance stopped a proposed uranium refinery in 1981, and some other campaigns prevented proposals for nuclear reactors. The principal organization [resisting uranium development] had been the Inter-Church Uranium Committee Educational Co-operative (ICUCEC) formed through Catholic and mainstream Protestant churches, though it also included many non-believers. However, ICUCEC started to take a less conspicuous role after a lengthy legal battle in the 1990s and early 2000s.

. . . [T]he Coalition for a Clean Green Saskatchewan (henceforth referred to as the Coalition, Clean Green, or CCGS) was formed in 2006 in Saskatoon with the idea of providing resistance if there was a necessity to mobilize against nuclear development beyond mining. Clean Green had an explicit dual mandate beyond opposition to nuclear development—*to promote the adoption of a renewable energy regime.*

The Uranium Development Partnership (UDP)

In the fall of 2008, the new Saskatchewan government created a commission of uranium and nuclear experts to advise on value-added benefits. The commission chair was a nuclear physicist at the University of Saskatchewan. Other members included representatives of the Saskatchewan Chamber of Commerce, Cameco, Areva, Bruce Power, a gas and pipeline company, TransCanada, urban and rural municipality organizations, an electrical workers union, another nuclear physicist, a First Nations chief, and an environmentalist—the controversial Patrick Moore, an early member of Greenpeace (but repudiated by Greenpeace itself) who now supports and is a paid lobbyist for nuclear power. The provincial government released the Uranium Development Partnership (UDP) report in March 2009.

There were five broad areas of recommendation with many specifics. The first involved mining and exploration with all recommendations directed towards easing current regulatory and royalty regimes to allow expansion. The second was that of upgrading and refining of uranium. The report suggested that facilities in Ontario were sufficient to meet current Canadian needs. However, with the supposed "Nuclear Renaissance," there could be future opportunities for Saskatchewan when second-generation technologies come into being. Power generation was the third domain. The report recommended the establishment of two or three nuclear plants with 1,000 to 1,200 megawatt capacities each to provide 45 per cent of Saskatchewan's future electricity needs and export surpluses. Area four favoured establishing Canada's "high level, used fuel, deep repository" in Saskatchewan. The safety of the current technology and the billions of dollars that would be poured into the Saskatchewan economy were touted as reasons to feel secure about this proposal. The fifth recommendation area called for the establishment of a major university research and development centre. Besides conducting research and training for the uranium mining industry, a new nuclear reactor was proposed for training reactor personnel, conducting research, and possibly producing medical isotopes (Uranium Development Partnership 2009).

Bruce Power and Its Search for a Reactor Site

In the fall of 2008, Bruce Power, a manager of Candu reactors in Ontario, began a search for reactor sites on the North Saskatchewan River. This campaign came into prominence in the spring of 2009, coincidental with the release of the UDP report, of which Bruce Power was a participant. While promoting the advantages for meeting the future energy needs of the western provinces and helping to assist in "reducing carbon emissions," the idea was to also provide energy for the processing of oil from bitumen in Northern Alberta. Any reactors would have to be near large water bodies since they are dependent on massive quantities of water for cooling, especially for the high-level radioactive fuel waste that has to be kept in water for at least a decade before it can be moved into long-term, dry storage. Bruce Power made pitches to residents along the river near large towns.

A former politician closely allied to the current government operated as Bruce Power's agent. Using a very aggressive sales technique, this individual approached farmers and ranchers in the region of the village of Paradise Hill. A group of rural people organized and held public meetings to express their alarm and to protest reactors being situated there. Almost five hundred residents showed up to a meeting in March to express their anger and fears concerning health risks. . . . [In this and other nearby regions,] grassroots coalitions involved hundreds of farmers, ranchers, and townspeople, and during the spring and summer of 2009, they met virtually every week.

Despite the upwelling of opposition to the government's plans, the situation looked grim for people in the North Saskatchewan Valley and those who were part of CCGS or veterans of previous campaigns in other communities. There had been no opportunity for a "level-playing field" debate, and our adversaries had held all the advantages with full support from powerful entities including the corporate media.

The Emergence of a Wider Coalition

Because of the urgency of the issue, using existing networks, two meetings were rapidly organized in Saskatoon. The first was held in the winter of 2009, the second the following spring. Saskatoon was

chosen because it was the most central location and was also where both ICUCEC and CCGS were located. Approximately sixty people attended each meeting, representing many more in their home regions. Each meeting lasted about six hours; organized under the light control of a moderator, all voices were heard. Joining these meetings were activists in the Saskatchewan Environmental Society; some members of ICUCEC; Clean Green; the Sierra Club of Canada; various church activist or social justice wings involving Catholics, Unitarians, [the] United Church of Canada, Lutherans, Anglicans, and Mennonites; Kairos, Saskatchewan (an ecumenical social justice group); plus scattered and overlapping networks of "free radicals" who had participated in previous movements.

It was proposed to take the original Coalition for a Clean Green Saskatchewan and broaden it to be the umbrella for the province-wide movement. This new set of networks was to prepare for action in anti-nuclear/pro-renewable campaigns and maintain continuous support and mutual information-sharing as individuals and as autonomous groupings. [Several regional anti-nuclear grassroots organizations] signed on. . . .

A steering committee was established and occasionally communicated by conference calls, but it had no governing authority. A web page with many attachments was created by the Saskatoon group that took on a clearing house role. Some of the functions included maintaining the web page, extending the networks, producing pamphlets, billboards, YouTube videos, posters, and buttons, and alerting people to events and meetings. [Some of the regional groups] also created their own web pages. Several Facebook sites were formed that created larger networks—one of the Facebook sites had over two thousand "friends." . . .

By mid-spring 2009, the Coalition was established and daily preparing for the biggest and most important policy debate that the province had faced in the last forty years. Yet, this must be underscored—there was absolutely no central organization, no executive, and no hierarchy. Each group operated entirely independently but in loose coordination and affinity with the principles of CCGS. Decision-making was purely horizontal or even anarchistic (in the positive sense of that term) and based completely on networks and participatory democracy. Everything depended on the intentions, knowledge, research capabilities, networks, and actions of the people involved. They were not at all dependent on links or directions (including funding) from outside sources such as political parties, national environmental groups, or special economic interests. It was an entirely homegrown, grassroots, emergent, and self-generating, self-organizing, and constantly expanding concerned citizens' movement.

The Future of Uranium Consultation Process

In the late spring of 2009, the provincial government announced that it had created a one-man task force to assess the public response to the Uranium Development Partnership's recommendations. It probably expected at least tacit support for its agenda. . . . The hearings, called the "Future of Uranium," were given support staff and chaired by the retired, most senior civil servant in the province, Dan Perrins. The hearings were held in May and June of 2009. A report was to be written in August, presented in September, and the government was to respond by December on how it would implement the findings from both the UDP and the Future of Uranium hearings. The government was fast-tracking the process during Saskatchewan's brief summer when people were thinking of other things or farming.

Four days of stakeholder presentations were held in Saskatoon and Regina with organizations providing oral briefs with written transcriptions and recordings put on the Future of Uranium website. Thirteen public meetings were held in communities across the province on evenings in June. The format involved two video presentations—one that summarized the UDP position, then a second documented the province's present power facilities and future electric energy needs. These videos were followed by presentations involving advocates of alternative positions and opposition to the UDP proposals. Then people were divided into breakout groups with facilitators. Everybody was given

a chance to speak—everything was voice recorded, and flip charts displayed the points. All statements were placed on the Future of Uranium website.

During stakeholder presentations, there were 61 briefs. Persons or organizations affiliated with or having parallel positions to the Coalition made 45 of those. Those in support of the UDP report made 16. While coming primarily from ordinary citizens, the presentations [opposing uranium development] were well researched and articulate.

For the Coalition, the most significant task was to mobilize attendance through notices, distributed pamphlets, Facebook events, and word of mouth. We were well-organized regarding the southern half of the province with established networks and organizations in place [in] most of the larger regional centres. . . . Given the long distances and lack of existing networks [in] the six northern communities, we were not able to make many contacts there. However, judging from the transcripts, similar dissent arose in those communities. Altogether, 2,637 people participated in the community consultations, with the largest being in Saskatoon (805), Regina (413), and Prince Albert (435).

At the Saskatoon meeting, I along with several other activists scanned the large crowd of over eight hundred and realized that we collectively knew [fewer] than one hundred of those present. This suggests that while our efforts to encourage people to attend the meeting were crucial, most of the attendees were not immediate, direct participants in our networks. Though the emergent grassroots response derived from our promotional efforts, it was largely independent of our collective solidarity and was ultimately a reflection of the public mood. . . .

After each meeting, some [Coalition members] wrote reports on what happened and what to expect, and these [reports] made their way through our email networks where they were discussed. Among the suggestions was to call for straw votes in each breakout session to see how many supported nuclear development and how many opposed. [Our side] approximated 80 per cent in each case. Another suggestion was to provide very specific answers to recommendations made in the UDP report. At an earlier meeting, it was noticed that many of the anti-nuclear people were speaking passionately about such issues as Hiroshima, Chernobyl, and the military-industrial complex, but not to the specifics of the UDP report about which Perrins was mandated to evaluate the public's opinions. Statements became more focused on the recommendations, because it was realized that if it did not hear otherwise, the government could interpret that there was little or no opposition to the specific policy directions it proposed. . . .

The pro-nuclear/pro-uranium side included provincial and city chambers of commerce, mining companies, an electrical workers' union, Bruce Power, Areva, and Cameco. The following points summarize their arguments:

- We mine uranium and sell it, why not do more?
- Developing nuclear plants, a used-fuel deep waste [r]epository, and increased mining would have beneficial economic multiplier effects.
- Saskatchewan is in a strategic position to become a world leader at the forefront of a Nuclear Renaissance.
- Nuclear power will provide for growing energy needs because it ensures base-load capacity for energy production while eliminating coal plants.
- Excess energy production provides export opportunities.
- The proposed nuclear expansion would provide jobs and development opportunities for impoverished Native people.
- The technology is safe now and nuclear waste is minimal.
- We must not miss opportunities when they arise—the Chamber of Commerce claimed that $13 billion was lost to the local economy when a uranium refinery was rejected.
- Nuclear power provides a solution to global warming.

The anti-nuclear position was represented by the Saskatchewan Environmental Society; groups affiliated with the Coalition; those involved in the alternative energy business; Christian, Jewish, Unitarian, and ecumenical groups; the Green Party of Saskatchewan; the National Farmers Union; and several thousand citizens who voiced their opinions.

Their collective arguments can be roughly summarized this way:

- Nuclear energy is ultimately always tied to military dimensions—Canada was involved in the Manhattan Project, supplied uranium for Cold War nuclear weapons, and sold technologies that enabled the Indian and Pakistani nuclear weapons programs, right through to the current use of depleted uranium in military operations.
- Enormous public subsidies have already been bestowed upon the nuclear industry with little benefit to the public except huge public expenditures and debt.
- There [have] been enormous costs and overruns, delays, breakdowns, and eventual decommissioning costs of power plants, all costing many billions of dollars, ultimately again at taxpayers' and ratepayers' expense.
- The costs of nuclear power per kilowatt-hour are more expensive than any alternatives and are getting higher.
- Financial planning companies never recommend investments in nuclear power.
- Private companies never insure nuclear projects—government has to insure liability.
- There are extreme health and environmental dangers [in] all aspects of the nuclear fuel chain.
- Nuclear waste is extremely dangerous even in small quantities—no country has found a provable solution for its disposal, and it is extremely dangerous for thousands of years.
- The nuclear industry is a failed 1950s industry that falsely claimed it would produce "energy too cheap to meter." The claim of a "Nuclear Renaissance" is false. The proportion and amount of energy being created worldwide by nuclear plants is actually declining.
- We have many lessons illustrating the ultimate dangers of nuclear energy from Hiroshima, through Three Mile Island and Chernobyl to many other accidents at nuclear plants.
- Nuclear power is not "clean and green"—it too has a heavy carbon footprint and emits other carcinogenic and toxic pollutants in mining, construction, and many other associated activities.

- Nuclear [power generation] provides uncertainty for future generations left with enormous financial debts and decommissioning costs. They would also be stuck with managing the toxic, carcinogenic wastes while not benefitting from the energy itself and would have lost out on the opportunity to have investment in renewable energy.
- It is time to invest in cheaper renewable energy sources such as wind, sun, geothermal, biomass and biogas, and co-generation, following the examples of Denmark, Germany, and Spain.

Events after the Future of Uranium Hearings, July through December 2009

The issue continued to be in the news with setbacks for the nuclear industry. The government of Ontario cancelled a $26 billion contract with Atomic Energy of Canada, Limited to build two new reactors because of higher-than-expected costs. Shortly thereafter, Ontario passed an energy act considered the most progressive alternative energy policy in Canada.

The Canadian Nuclear Waste Management Organization, an industry group charged with finding a location for a "deep underground repository" for 45,000 metric tons of "high-level spent nuclear fuel," held a meeting in Saskatoon in September 2009 that had not been announced to the public or to the press. Only invited stakeholders could attend. Saskatchewan, because of its relatively low population and its granite formation in the Northern Canadian Shield, has been targeted as a site for this waste dump, which would have to be protected and monitored for many thousands of years and has all sorts of potentials for leakages and accidents, including during the transportation of the material to the repository site. Clean Green "outed" the meeting and exposed the intention of the organization with a clever and humorous media stunt with actors in hazard suits "sweeping nuclear waste" under a carpet shaped like Saskatchewan. The stunt and a press conference were held in front of the meeting site, and it was widely reported by the media.

FIGURE 5.1   Members of Clean Green Saskatchewan sweep mock spent fuel-rods under the carpet to protest a proposal to locate a nuclear waste storage facility in the province.

Anticipating the government's response to the Perrins report and announcing its intention to go ahead with the UDP recommendations, the Coalition organized a "No Nukes—Go Renewables" parade and rally for 4 October from the university campus to a bandshell in a downtown park. Over five hundred supporters of the Coalition from all over the province came to the event, which took on a community-enhancing tone with entertainment and speakers. . . .

Perrins had already released his report in early September, although the government had not yet replied to it. To us, the report was a gratifying surprise. As a reflection of what he heard from citizens across the whole province, he wrote that 84 percent of the respondents were opposed to nuclear power and the establishment of the nuclear waste repository. Majorities were also opposed to increased mining, the building of a university reactor, and a waste dump. He proposed a study on all alternatives including renewable energy and suggested that the government would need to move slowly, if at all, with regard to nuclear expansion (Perrins 2009). This placed the government in a difficult position, putting the brakes on its aspirations for a rapid value-added nuclear expansion.

In the fall of 2009, Bruce Power disappeared from the Saskatchewan scene, and there were occasional statements from government officials and in the corporate media that nuclear power may now be too expensive for the province. Then in December, the provincial government announced it would not pursue nuclear power as an option, although that decision would be reviewed again in 2020. It is, nonetheless, looking for ways to expand uranium mining and facilitate a university nuclear research centre. Its position on nuclear waste remains a mystery. Still, most of these events would suggest that Clean Green Saskatchewan made notable progress with regard to its objectives.

What Accounts for the Coalition's Impact?

There were several hundred people in the various communities and about thirty in Saskatoon that were the most active. [Hundreds more] were engaged as direct participants in the organizational and action aspects of the movement, and thousands were indirect or casual supporters of the Coalition. . . . Some were consistently involved, but others popped in and out for specific tasks. . . . As one person put it, we were "organic like a mushroom with a huge underground base and dropping spores all over the place." . . .

So there were no hierarchies, no superstars, no designated leaders, no organizational executives, and no formal memberships. Among the well informed and active, though, there was passion and extraordinary diligence in voluntary effort. The provincial meetings developed the solidarity that was constantly reinforced by Internet communication

through emails, the Clean Green web page, and Facebook communication. The use of the Internet was dense in its frequency; there was daily discussion and much iteration regarding positions, strategies, statements, and events. People worked to achieve consensus on each detail through various levels of working groups focused on media strategies, organizing events, and getting turnouts to hearings. Especially important during the thirteen community public hearings was the sending of messages giving summaries and providing tips so that the next groups were prepared. . . .

People met every week during the spring and summer of 2009. Meetings were long, loosely chaired, and a lot of secondary, off-track chatter was permitted; yet, inclusion was achieved. Clean Green in Saskatoon operated on consensus, and no votes were ever needed to resolve a dispute. . . .

One noteworthy dimension was the capacity of citizens in the scattered regions to effectively do their own research from a proliferation of reliable online resources that had been shared. . . . The presentation of factual, rational positions tended to prevail over emotional ones. Although nuclear energy is complicated, a kind of "people power" through information was expressed through a great deal of cogent variety in the presentations of stakeholders and in the five-or-so-minute arguments individuals used at the community public forums. . . .

There was a remarkable amount of ingenuity and organizational ability within the Coalition; rallies and media stunts were well designed and organized; and the 13 community consultations were venues where informed populist voices were heard. A clear vision of what we wanted was presented—"no nukes, go renewable," an alternative energy future of wind, solar, co-generation, biomass, "negawatts," smart-metering, run-of-the-river hydro, and decentralized, multiple-optioned community-based energy production. The Coalition started to effectively insert new symbols, information, and alternative discourses into the public sphere—the media no longer ignored us. Billboards, pamphlets, buttons, logos, web pages, and videos started to shape alternative visions. The Coalition always showed a great deal of adaptability with constant feedback capable of adjusting to new situations. There was a sense of urgency that we had to act now and with all the effort that was possible.

What emerged was a rural–urban coalition—never before seen in my forty years in the province. There were certainly elements that were politically leftist and environmentally activist at the beginning. But with the inclusion of the rural networks, the political tone of the movement became more centrist but still adamant in its opposition to nuclear expansion. The government got the message that Clean Green will resist all the way; that it includes many people from its vital rural voting public; and that it has superb mobilizing skills. . . .

Still, any claim to success must be tempered with the reality of certain circumstances external to the movement, such as revelations about the costs of nuclear energy. Ontario's decision to cancel a potential $26 billion contract for reactor construction was a major blow to Bruce Power and AECL, which have had some difficulty marketing new reactors. Another dimension likely playing a role to our benefit was the province's revenue predicament. It had taken a major hit recently in royalties because of a sharp decline in potash sales, a major source of Saskatchewan's wealth. In the face of substantial deficits, people seriously considered whether the province could afford the risks and financial burdens of expensive nuclear partnerships.

We had a consistent forum through the summer of 2009 in the Future of Uranium consultations and its press coverage. The author [of the resulting report], Dan Perrins (2009), did a diligent job reporting what he heard, and his public recommendations made it extremely difficult for the government to proceed as originally planned. He was committed to being unbiased and was respected by both sides of the issue. Going against the findings and recommendations of a report that the government itself had commissioned to gauge community and public opinion would give fodder to the press and [the] opposition party in the legislature. The government understood the political risks. There will always be opposition from movements such as CCGS and local community groups. Financially too, the huge debt implications, as well as liability issues, play an

enormous role now in any government decision to have nuclear power in its energy mix.

Conclusions Theoretically Framed

Our central question has been, what accounts for the Coalition for a Clean Green Saskatchewan's success as an environmental movement? Loosely within a range of post-1960s social movements, Clean Green Saskatchewan could be considered as among those labelled New Social Movements. These are movements that are not as oriented to class and economic issues as those rooted in the earlier history of industrialism. . . . Post-1960s movements can include youth, gender, religious, ethnocultural, neo-anarchistic, anti-economic globalization, and environmental movements, in addition to movements in reaction to these trends. Mellucci [1996] points to the cultural dimensions of power as expressed by the generation, manipulation, and flow of symbols and information. Movements must respond or confront these with effective alternatives. . . .

As a further cultural manifestation, there seemed to be some significant similarities in movement-relevant values and orientations among the several hundred activists affiliated with CCGS. Beliefs in participatory democracy, complete gender and age equity, equality even regarding expertise, lack of any hierarchy or formal organization, consensus in decision-making, and as much emphasis on the process as the outcome were all eased into implicitly and expressed through action. There was no need for any discussion on anything resembling organizational matters—people just plunged in with their efforts. . . . The reality is that most of the active participants were already veterans of other movements focused on feminism, peace, social justice, anti-neoliberal globalization, or similar environmental issues. . . . This made solidarity, common goals, and strategies more easily achievable while also reinforced by the shared recognition of urgency.

While not necessarily the explicit values of the majority of its activists, the Coalition did exhibit a general kind of anarchism. The organization lacked a head or any designated leadership, was amorphous in structure, and entirely voluntary in affiliation. All decisions were reached by consensus, often after considerable discussion. . . . It did this largely without the colourful terminologies, costumes, and street theatre that had sometimes come to be associated with affinity groups since the 1999 World Trade Organization protests in Seattle. Yet, the rally in the park and the carpet-sweeping street theatre skit (in response to the secret meeting of the Nuclear Waste Management Organization) contained occasional elements of that approach. . . .

[The use of digital information technologies] was a hallmark of Clean Green Saskatchewan. During the height of the campaign, I found myself the recipient of and occasional originator of messages or information sharing in no less than seven, frequently overlapping, digital networks. . . . The networks were used to prepare pamphlets, videos, and media statements for the public, to organize events such as rallies, and to inform and prepare people for meetings. Through the networks flowed substantial and relatively comprehensive information of a nature that could potentially bring people up to roughly equivalent capacity. This information even included extremely complex topics such as reactor types, radioactivity, health hazards, alternative energy technology, medical isotopes, comparative histories and policies relevant to nuclear power, and the economics of electricity production. There is an encyclopedic wealth of information available online. This meant that an activist even at a relatively remote farm or ranch had roughly the same access to information as someone operating out of a university library. It is hard to imagine anything similar in information power and flow operating even ten years ago.

These networks were essential to any success the movement could claim. The density, concentration, overlap, and content of such messaging and reflection would be quite profound if it were retrieved, documented, and analyzed. What emerged out of the many networking nodes and its links was a kind of super-organism of information and advocacy. This affinity and capacity-building was reinforced in the old-fashioned face-to-face way through meetings, public hearings, and rallies.

Among those discussing New Social Movements and networks in a neo-anarchistic vein, there is repeated reference to the concept of "rhizome," originated by Deleuze and Guattari (1987, 13–26). This playful and enigmatic notion was largely meant to metaphorically describe systems of thought or analysis that are not linear or hierarchical. In addition, rhizomes are subversive to dominant ways of thinking that are considered more tree-like (arboreal) with hierarchically oriented, descending taproots and ascending trunks, branches, and stems. Implicitly anarchistic, rhizome systems of thought, with their above and below "runners," criss-crossing and randomly connecting strings of thought, logic, subject matter, metaphor, and example, have no central point, no clear entry point, no midpoints or precisely identifiable cohesion. . . . Yet, they all work in their own peculiar ways towards generating understanding, creativity, and action. They are grounded and lateral; at the same time, rhizomes do take root in places where more noticeably interconnected ideas can arise or events can occur. . . . And . . . "rhizomes" extend their thoughts to [other people], who in turn connect them in their thoughts, words, and actions with others [with] whom they communicate. . . .

Thus, I see the expression, organization, communication, and direction of the Coalition—as highlighted by its organic, rhizome-like nature—impossible to now root out. The real and virtual networks are the multitude of effectively linked rhizomes taking root and emerging from the ground occasionally in the form of local groupings or chapters of CCGS. . . . The rhizomes took root and arose in other forms, some temporary and others potentially more lasting. . . . Herein lies the real strength of CCGS and how the efforts of several thousand people were mobilized by a hundred or so activists through 2009 to successfully register opposition to the expansion of the nuclear industry in Saskatchewan.

. . . . It cannot be overemphasized how much the government and its corporate allies wanted the value-added uranium and nuclear facilities and had assumed public agreement. An eight-month frame for consultations and decision-making was set from the release of the UDP report to December 2009. The community-based organizations in the Coalition organized, lobbied, and demonstrated with the maximum of fervour and urgency. Because of our clear unity, we displayed to the government the adamant community opposition that would occur if any particular decisions for the location of nuclear reactors or waste dumps were made. Then, the government's own commissioned report displayed 84 per cent opposition to nuclear reactors. . . . The political risks were too high, and the province took the prudent, precautionary route—for now.

References Cited

Deleuze, Gilles, and Felix Guattari. 1987. *A Thousand Plateaus: Capitalism and Schizophrenia*. Minneapolis: University of Minnesota Press.

Juris, Jeffrey S. 2008. *Networking Futures: The Movements against Corporate Globalization*. Durham, NC: Duke University Press.

Mellucci, Alberto. 1996. *Challenging Codes: Collective Action in the Information Age*. Cambridge: Cambridge University Press.

Perrins, Dan. 2009. *Future of Uranium Consultation Process*. Report for the Saskatchewan government, Regina, SK.

Uranium Development Partnership. 2009. *Capturing the Full Potential of the Uranium Value Chain in Saskatchewan*. Report for the Saskatchewan government, Regina, SK.

Key Points to Consider

- The Coalition for a Clean Green Saskatchewan was made up of an ethnically, economically, and politically diverse set of citizens.
- The Coalition for a Clean Green Saskatchewan was organized in a non-hierarchical manner, and yet it was able to effectively organize a coherent response to a government and industry plan to promote uranium mining and processing and nuclear power generation in the province.
- Digital and social media were critical to sharing information and strategies among Coalition participants, but meetings, rallies, and other "old fashioned" forms of political organizing were also essential to getting the anti-nuclear message heard.
- The Government of Saskatchewan may have backed away from the plan to expand uranium mining and processing and nuclear power generation for economic reasons unrelated to the citizen protests.

Critical Thinking Questions

1. What are the explanations that Ervin offers for the Coalition's success in stopping expanded uranium development in Saskatchewan? How are the organizational and protest tactics described here similar to or different from those described by Anna Willow in Chapter 15 of this reader? Are there any common lessons that activists might take from these two very different environmental protests?
2. Thinking about participant observation as an ethnographic research technique, would you describe Ervin's methodology as participant observation? Why or why not? How is the research that Ervin describes here similar to or different from classic participant observation?
3. Write a brief autoethnography about an event from your life. Does the process of careful description lead you to any new insights about the event? What are they?

Suggestions for Further Reading

Bernauer, Warren. 2012. "The Uranium Controversy in Baker Lake." *Canadian Dimension* 46 (1): 35–9. http://canadiandimension.com/articles/4470.

Ervin, Alexander M. 1991. "Roles for Applied and Practising Anthropologists Working with Immigrants and Refugee Settlement Agencies." In *Immigrants and Refugees in Canada: A National Perspective on Ethnicity, Multiculturalism, and Cross-cultural Adjustment*, edited by Satya P. Sharma, Alexander M. Ervin, and Deirdre Meintel. Saskatoon: University of Saskatchewan.

———. 2005. *Applied Anthropology: Tools and Perspectives for Contemporary Practice*. 2nd ed. Boston: Pearson.

Graeber, David. 2002. "The New Anarchists." *New Left Review* 13: 61–73.

Harper, Janice. 2007. "Secrets Revealed, Revelations Concealed: A Secret City Confronts Its Environmental Legacy of Weapons Production." *Anthropological Quarterly* 80 (1): 39–64.

World Nuclear Association. 2013. "Brief History of Uranium Mining in Canada." Appendix 1 to *Uranium in Canada*. London: World Nuclear Association. www.world-nuclear.org/info/Country-Profiles/Countries-A-F/Appendices/Uranium-in-Canada-Appendix-1--Brief-History-of-Uranium-Mining-in-Canada.

PART II
Gender/Embodiment

Chapter 6

Indonesia

Introduction

Speakers of English often make a distinction between **sex** and **gender** that does not exist in every language and culture. Sex we treat as natural, something that arises from biology and that can be recognized physically, whereas gender is understood to be presented (performed, even) as qualities and roles associated with one's sex. An individual's **sexuality**—his or her erotic desires and practices—is independent of both sex and gender. **Ethnographic** research shows that gender, sex, and sexuality are distinct domains that, when examined cross-culturally, do not occur together in any consistent patterns.

Although our bodies are part of our natural or biological endowments, we recognize and use our bodies in ways that are defined by culture. In other words, human bodies do not exist as abstract, culture-free entities; rather, it is through cultural practices and social institutions that we come to understand our bodies and the bodies of others in particular ways. Like all other aspects of culture, these understandings vary over time and cross-culturally. Like **language**, **embodiment** is learned along with culture, and from infancy we are **enculturated** to hold our bodies in particular ways, to wear clothes (or not) in particular ways, and to interpret sensations as pain or pleasure in particular ways—ways that fit with our culture's ideas about sexual difference, **race**, social **class**, age, and so on. We can think of the human body is a "social skin" through which we define and announce which groups or categories of individuals we belong to (Turner 2012: 503).

The article below concerns the intersection of gender, sex, and sexuality among a group of Minangkabau from West Sumatra, Indonesia, who are known as *tombois* (pronounced like the English word *tomboys*). These individuals were recognized as female at birth, but they dress and act as men. Anthropologist Evelyn Blackwood, who self-identifies as lesbian, initially assumed that tombois were lesbians who took on "butch" or masculine characteristics. Eventually, as she reports here, she realized that she had misunderstood tombois' gender identity.

Transgender and genderqueer individuals have not been widely recognized in the West until quite recently. Some individuals who today consider themselves transgender and/or queer might have identified as butch (masculine women) or queens (effeminate men) in the recent past. This situation contrasts with other, mostly non-Western, societies that have long recognized what anthropologists call a "third sex" or a "third gender" in addition to male and female. (*Third* is the term used, even though a culture may recognize more than three sex/gender categories.) In the full version of the article, Blackwood describes third genders from the Middle East, Albania, and Native North America. There is no single "third gender." Members of a third gender can be biological males, biological females, or intersexed. Some cultures associate third-gendered individuals with same-sex erotic desires; in other cultures, third-gendered persons are assumed to be sexually abstinent. In some places, third-gendered individuals play a spiritual role; in others, they are considered deviant or "transgressive." Blackwood reports that among the Minangkabau, tombois are generally seen as transgressive.

Blackwood makes a distinction between "gender as cultural category" and "gender as subjective experience." By "gender as cultural category," she refers to culturally created and shared understandings about gendered distinctions and about the characteristics of each gender. These characteristics include things like personality, physical appearance, and practices that members of a culture associate with a particular gender. By "gender as subjective experience," Blackwood means how actual individuals understand themselves as gendered human beings, and how they embody this identity in their practices.

A few words about gender and pronouns: English grammar forces speakers to select a gendered pronoun—*he/she/him/her*—to reference an individual in the third person. For many years, it has been common among English speakers to violate this grammatical rule by using a plural third-person pronoun—*they/their*—if the person's gender is unknown or unspecified. Many people believe this approach is preferable to assuming a person's gender based on clues such as occupation, appearance, or name. This is sometimes also the current practice when writing or speaking about transgender individuals.

Many transgender people prefer to be referenced by the gendered pronouns that conform to their identity as male or female. But this is not true for all, and some transgender individuals prefer pronouns that do not make a binary distinction between male and female. A number of ungendered or ambiguously gendered pronouns have been coined to refer to individuals who identify as queer and/or transgender. Currently, there is no widespread agreement as to which of the newly created pronouns to use. In 2014, the Vancouver School Board, for example, adopted the gender-neutral pronouns *xe*, *xyr*, and *xem* (rhyming with *they*, *their*, *them*; the *x* is pronounced like a *z*). More common are *ze* in place of *he* and *she*, and *hir* as a combination of *him* and *her*. The article below was published several years ago when gender-neutral pronouns were used much less commonly. Thus, Blackwood opts to combine *she* and *he* as *s/he* and *him* and *her* as *hir*, which was the approach preferred by transgender activists in North America at the time.

❖ About the Author ❖

Evelyn Blackwood teaches anthropology at Purdue University in Indiana. She earned an undergraduate degree in psychology before studying anthropology at San Francisco State University and Stanford University. Her research concerns the intersection of matrilineal kinship, gender roles, Islam, and the state in Indonesia. She has also published extensively on transgender and lesbian identities outside the West.

Tombois in West Sumatra: Constructing Masculinity and Erotic Desire

Evelyn Blackwood

During anthropological fieldwork on gender and agricultural development in West Sumatra, Indonesia, in 1989–1990, I pursued a secondary research goal of investigating the situation of "lesbians" in the area. I met a small number of "women" who seemed butch in the way that term was used in the United States at the time.[1] In West Sumatra these individuals are called *lesbi* or *tomboi* (derived from the English words *lesbian* and *tomboy*). Although there are similarities, a *tomboi* in West Sumatra is different from a butch in the United States. . . . The term *tomboi* is used for a female acting in the manner of men (*gaya laki-laki*). Through my relationship with a tomboi in West Sumatra, I learned some of the ways in which my concept of "lesbian" was not the same as my partner's, even though we were both, I thought, women-loving women.

This article explores how tombois in West Sumatra both shape their identities from and resist local, national, and transnational narratives of gender and sexuality. By focusing on West Sumatra, I provide an in-depth analysis of the complexities of tomboi identity for individuals from one ethnic group in Indonesia, the Minangkabau. . . .

Theories concerning the intersection of genders and sexualities provide considerable insights into, and a variety of labels for, gendered practices cross-culturally. In opposition to biological determinism, social constructionists argue that gender is not an essence preceding social expression but an identity that is constructed and fluid. The multiplication of "gender" categories in cross-cultural studies, however, suggests that gender remains a problematic concept. Part of the problem, I would argue, comes from the conflation of two distinct but interacting processes, gender as cultural category and gender as subjective experience.

. . . Studying gender as a cultural category highlights normative representations of gender and the ways they are legitimated, privileged, and hegemonic. It allows one to identify so-called traditional gender systems, or "everyday categories of gender" (Poole 1996), . . . and to establish which gender representations are dominant or acceptable, and thereby which are transgressive. . . .

[In contrast, v]iewing gender as subjective experience exposes all the processes of negotiation, resistance, manipulation, and displacement possible by human subjects. Gender in this sense constitutes a set of social identities. . . . Learning, piecing together, adopting, or shaping identities (such as race, class, gender, or sexuality) is an ongoing social process through which individuals negotiate, produce, and stabilize a sense of who they are. These identities are shaped and redefined in relation to dominant gender **ideologies**. . . .

. . . [In this article,] I show how the gender and **kinship** ideologies of the Minangkabau, the dominant ethnic group in West Sumatra, construct a system of oppositional genders ("man"–"woman") that persuades tombois to see themselves as masculine. The **discourses** of a modernizing Minangkabau society, the Indonesian state, and Islam reinforce this system through their representations of femininity and "female" nature. At another level, tomboi identity incorporates new models of sexuality and gender made available by the transnational flow of lesbian and gay discourse from Europe and North America.

This essay also explores the relation between gender ideology and the production of gender transgression. *Webster's College Dictionary* (1991) defines *transgression* as a violation of a law, command, or moral code; an offence or sin; or more neutrally, passing over or going beyond (a limit, boundary, et cetera). . . . I include within [the term *gender transgression*] any gender identities . . . that go beyond, or violate, gender-"appropriate" norms enshrined in dominant cultural ideologies. By defining gender transgression in this way, I want to highlight the way that various social structures and cultural ideologies interconnect to produce gender transgression.

Central to this analysis is the concept of **hegemony**. . . . Hegemonic or dominant gender ideologies define what is permissible, even thinkable; they serve as the standard against which actions are measured, producing codes, regulations, and laws that perpetuate a particular ideology. Dominant ideologies generate discourses that stabilize, normalize, and **naturalize** gender (Yanagisako and Delaney 1995); yet within any dominant ideology there are emergent meanings, processes, and identities vying for legitimacy, authority, and recognition.

. . . The growing literature on "female-bodied" gender transgressors tends to cast the transgression as resistance to . . . male dominance or patriarchy. For instance, US gender ideology has produced at various [times and places] butch-femme (Kennedy and Davis 1993), camp and drag (Newton 1972, 1993), and transgendered people (Bolin 1994; Garber 1991; Stone 1991). Some scholars argue that these identities result from a hierarchical gender system of compulsory heterosexuality and oppositional genders.

Evidence from Island Southeast Asia raises questions about the relationship between oppressive gender ideology and gender transgression. In her overview of gender in Island Southeast Asia, Errington (1990) suggested that gender is less [important] than other categories, such as rank and age, in determining access to status or power. According to Errington, in the central islands of Southeast Asia "male and female are viewed as complementary or even identical beings in many respects" (1990: 39). . . . [Nonetheless], gender transgressors are well known throughout the islands.

The Minangkabau tomboi poses a further challenge concerning the relationship between oppressive gender ideology and gender transgression. The Minangkabau are a hierarchical, kin-based society in which both women and men lineage elders have access to power. . . . A closer reading of cultural processes circulating in West Sumatra suggests the interrelation of kinship, capitalism, religion, and the **state** in producing gender transgressions.

Misreading Identities

. . . West Sumatra is the home of the Minangkabau people, one of the many ethnic groups that have been incorporated into the state of Indonesia. The Minangkabau, with a population over four million people, are rural agriculturalists, urban merchants, traders, migrants, and wage labourers. They are also Muslim and **matrilineal**. Being matrilineal means that, despite the fact that they are devout Muslims, inheritance and property pass from mother to daughter. I conducted research in the province of Lima Puluh Kota near the district capital of Payakumbuh. In 1990, the province had a population of 86,000; the large majority were Minangkabau.

Far from being an isolated region, the province is well integrated into global trade networks. Rice and other agricultural products produced in the region are traded well beyond Sumatra. Many Minangkabau men and women work for years in cities outside West Sumatra, providing further connections to the national and international scene. Villages have anywhere from 15 per cent to 25 per cent of their residents on temporary out-migration. Despite out-migration, many villages maintain a rich cultural life based on kinship ties; most social and economic activities are centred in and organized by matrilineally related groups. Other villages are more urban oriented, particularly where migration has led to reliance on outside sources of income.

I had no trouble locating males in West Sumatra who were *bancis*, a term that is defined in Echols and Shadily's Indonesian–English dictionary (1989) as "effeminate or transvestite homosexual[s]."

This definition links bancis' gender identity (effeminate or transvestite) and sexuality (homosexual). In the district capital I met several bancis or *bencong*, as they are referred to in West Sumatra. Bancis are obvious to local people, who comment on their appearance or taunt them when they walk down the street. Although bancis do not carry themselves as men do, they do not carry themselves exactly like women, either; rather, they behave in the exaggerated style of fashion models, a style that in itself is a caricature of femininity, one they have been exposed to through fashion magazines and televised beauty pageants. Their sexual partners are indistinguishable from other men and are generally thought to be bisexual, or *biseks* in local parlance, as these men might also have relationships with women.

My search for "lesbians" was more difficult. I asked some high school–aged acquaintances . . . who had friends who were bancis, whether they knew any lesbis . . . in the area. I was told that there were several but that those women were worried about being found out. I was given the impression that such women were very coarse and tough, more like men than women. After several months in West Sumatra, one of my young friends introduced me to Dayan.[2] S/he, however, did not fit the stereotype. In hir midtwenties, s/he appeared to me to be boyish-looking in hir T-shirt, shorts, and short hair, but s/he did not seem masculine or tough in any way that I could perceive. I consequently felt quite certain that I had met another "lesbian." The term *lesbi* that my friends used also offered familiar footing to an outsider from the United States.

Negotiating our identities was a perplexing process in which we each tried to position the other within different cultural categories: butch–femme and *cowok–cewek*. *Butch–femme* is [a North] American term that refers to a masculine-acting woman and her feminine partner. *Cowok–cewek* are Indonesian words that mean "man" and "woman" but have the connotation of "guy" and "girl." It is the practice of female couples to refer to a tomboi and hir feminine partner as cowok and cewek. . . . In both the United States and West Sumatra, female couples rely on and draw from dominant cultural images of masculinity and femininity to make sense of their relationships. These similarities were enough to cause both my partner and myself to assume that we fell within each other's cultural model, an assumption I was forced to give up.

Dayan operated under the assumption that I was cewek, despite the inconsistencies of my behaviour, because that fit with hir understanding of hirself in relation to hir lovers, who had all been cewek. For instance, my failure to cook for hir or organize hir birthday party were quite disappointing to Dayan. On another occasion, when I visited an American friend of mine at his hotel, s/he accused me of sleeping with him. In hir experience, ceweks are attracted to men and also like sex better with men. Yet, as the one with the cash in the relationship, I was allowed to pay for things despite it not being proper cewek behaviour. In rural Minangkabau households, men are expected to give their wives their cash earnings. Expectations about the husband's responsibility to provide income are even greater for middle-class Indonesians, for men are represented as the sole breadwinners. Perhaps Dayan justified my actions on the grounds that I was an American with considerably more income than s/he. Certainly s/he was willing to entertain the possibility of my difference from hir understanding of ceweks.

One day I overheard the following exchange between Dayan and a tomboi friend. Dayan's friend asked if I was cewek, to which Dayan replied, "Of course."

"Can she cook?"

"Well, not really."

The friend exclaimed, "How can that be, a woman who can't cook? What are you going to do?"

I was surprised to find that my gender identity was so critical to this (macho) tomboi. The fact that I had a relationship with Dayan said very little to me about what kind of woman I was. I interpreted my relationship with Dayan as reflective of my **sexual identity** (a desire for other women).

For my part, I assumed that Dayan was a butch, more or less in congruence with the way I understood butches to be in the United States in the 1980s, that is, as masculine-acting women who desired feminine partners. S/he always dressed in jeans or shorts and T- or polo shirts, a style that was not at odds with the casual wear of many lesbians in the United States. One day, however, I heard a friend call hir "co," short for cowok. I knew what *cowok* meant in that context; it meant s/he was seen as a "guy" by hir close friends, which did not fit my notion of butch. I heard another female couple use the terms *mami* (mom) and *papi* (pop) for each other, so I started calling Dayan papi in private, which made hir very pleased. But when I told Dayan s/he was pretty, s/he looked hurt. Then I realized my mistake: "pretty" (*cantik*) is what a woman is called, not a man. Dayan wanted to be called "handsome" (*gagah*), as befits a masculine self.

Dayan's personal history underscored hir feelings that s/he was a man. S/he said s/he felt extremely isolated and "deviant" when s/he was growing up and acted more like a boy. People in hir town called hir *bujang gadis*, an Indonesian term meaning boy-girl (*bujang* means bachelor or unmarried young man, and *gadis* means unmarried young woman) that used to refer to an effeminate male or a masculine female. . . . As a teenager, s/he only had desire for girls. S/he bound hir breasts because s/he did not want them to be noticeable. They did not fit with hir self-image. As a young adult, s/he hung out with young men, smoking and drinking with them. S/he said s/he felt like a man and wanted to be one. I finally had to admit to myself that tombois were not the Indonesian version of butches. They were men.

Cowok-Cewek

I met two other tombois in West Sumatra, Agus and Bujang, who were both friends of Dayan. The first time I met Agus, s/he was wearing a big khaki shirt and jeans; even I could not mistake the masculine attitude s/he projected. S/he wore short hair that was swept back on the sides. S/he carried hirself like a "man," smoked cigarettes all the time, played cards, and made crude jokes. S/he struck me as coarse and tough like cowoks were said to be. Dayan admired Agus and thought hir the more handsome of the two.

Dayan told me that Agus, who was approximately thirty years old, had only been with women, never with a man. S/he had had several lovers, all beautiful and very feminine, according to Dayan. . . . Agus spent much of hir time with hir lover, Yul, who lived in a large house only a few minutes by bus outside of Payakumbuh. Yul, who was in her early fifties, was a widow with grown children, some of whom were still living at home. After Agus started living with her, Yul wanted her children to call Agus papi. She said she did not care if her children disapproved of her relationship. If her children did not act respectfully toward Agus, Yul would get angry with them and not give them spending money when they asked for it. But one of Yul's daughters argued that because Agus is not married to her mother, s/he should not be part of the family and be treated better than her own father had been. . . .

The other tomboi I met, Bujang, was at that time living at hir mother's in a rural village. Bujang seemed quiet and sombre. Boyish features and oversized clothes that hid hir breasts made it impossible for me to tell if s/he was male or female. We talked very little because hir mother was there. Later Dayan told me Bujang's story. Hir mother had forced hir to marry; s/he had had a son but then left hir husband. S/he had a lover (who, Dayan said, was feminine) and moved with her to Jakarta, where they lived for some time to avoid the prying eyes of relatives. Under continued pressure from hir family, however, and lacking adequate income, Bujang finally returned home with hir son, leaving hir lover temporarily in hopes of finding a better way to support hir family. Hir cewek lover, however, eventually married a man.

Partners of tombois fit within the norms of femininity and maintain a "feminine" gender identity. Their sexual relationships with tombois do not mark them as different; their gender is not in question. . . . Yul, Agus's lover, was feminine in appearance. She had shoulder-length permed hair, wore makeup and lipstick, and had long fingernails. Yul had never been with a tomboi before she met Agus.

She had not even thought about sleeping with one before. Although she sometimes wore slacks and smoked, even hung out at the local coffee shop with Agus to play cards, she was called *ibu* (mother) by men and mami by Agus. No one would think she was a tomboi just because she was partners with one; she was cewek. As a cewek, she adhered to the hegemonic standards of femininity in her appearance and behaviour.

Although the fact that they sleep with tombois makes them "bad" women in the eyes of local people, for premarital sex and adultery are disapproved of for women, ceweks are still women. Even tombois expect ceweks to have greater desire for men because that is seen as natural for their sex. Dayan once said, "Unfortunately, they will leave you for a man if one comes along they like. It's our fate that we love women who leave us." No one seems to consider a cewek's desire for tombois problematic; she remains a woman who desires men.

Performing Masculinity

Tombois model masculinity in their behaviour, attitudes, interests, and desires. Dayan often spoke of being *berani* (brave), a trait commonly associated with men, as an important part of who s/he was. S/he attributed the ability to be a tomboi to being berani; it meant, among other things, that one could withstand family pressures to get married. S/he said the ones that are berani become cowok. In talking about Agus's situation with hir lover Yul, Dayan commented that Agus was not brave enough to sleep at Yul's house anymore. S/he thought that Agus should not let Yul's children force hir to move out. Agus was not being as brave as Dayan thought a person should be in order to live up to the cowok identity.

Tombois pride themselves on doing things like men. . . . They smoke as men do; rural women rarely take up smoking. They go out alone, especially at night, which is a prerogative of men. Like men, they drive motorcycles; women ride behind (women do drive motorcycles, but in mixed couples men always drive). Dayan arrived at my house on a motorcycle one time with a man friend riding behind.

Like Minangkabau husbands, they move into and out of their partners' houses. Dayan said s/he often gets taken for a man if someone only sees hir walking from behind. Sometimes in public spaces, particularly in urban areas, s/he is called *mas*, a contemporary Indonesian term of address for a man. The thought that a tomboi might marry a man or bear a child like a woman seemed unconscionable to Dayan. S/he had little sympathy for Bujang, who was forced to marry, saying, "This person is cowok! How could s/he have done that, especially having a baby. That's wrong."

The taunting and joking between Agus and Dayan reflect one way in which their masculinity is negotiated. Agus's teasing questions to Dayan about whether I was a proper cewek is one example. . . . Another time Agus heard me call Dayan by hir first name. S/he gave Dayan a disparaging look, letting Dayan know that s/he was not demanding enough respect from me as hir cewek. Minangkabau usually do not call their spouses by their first names. Women generally use the term of address for older brother (*udah*), while *papi* is more common in urban areas or among those who live elsewhere in Indonesia.

Dayan also commented to me about a story circulating in West Sumatra concerning a female who passed as a man. This individual was rumored to have married his partner by going to another district where no one knew he was female. He (the cowok) runs a store, it was related; he wears loose clothes and straps his breasts down so they are not apparent. His wife (the cewek) is said to be very pretty. Dayan's response to this story was, "Oh, that cowok must really be a cowok," signifying that he had become the ultimate tomboi, one who passes as a man.

The sparring and comparing of masculine selves reveal one of the ways tombois create, confirm, and naturalize their identities as men. The teasing helps to reinforce . . . the masculine code of behaviour. Their actions suggest that being cowok is an identity one can be better or worse at, more or less of; it is something that must be practised and claimed. . . . As any man does, they are negotiating their culture's ideology of masculinity.

Tombois construct their desire for and relationships with women on the model of masculinity. The oft-repeated statement that their lovers are all feminine underscores their position as men who attract the "opposite sex." Because I was Dayan's partner, hir friend assumed that I was a particular gender, in this case the feminine woman. Their use of gendered terms of endearment, *mami* and *papi*, and the terms *cowok* and *cewek* reflect tombois' understanding of themselves as situated within the category "men" (*laki-laki*). Tombois' adherence to the model of masculinity and their insistence on replicating the heterosexuality of a man–woman couple [reveal] the dominance of the normative model of gender and heterosexuality.

Gender Ideology and Gender Transgression

In constructing themselves as masculine and their relationships as heterosexual, tombois are gender transgressors who nevertheless reflect the dominant ideology. . . . As Dayan's story indicates, it was not sexual desire for women that "drove" hir to produce a masculine identity. . . . S/he had already established a masculine identity before s/he was aware of hir sexual desires for women. Having identified hirself as masculine, s/he also laid claim to a desire for women. . . .

What social conditions produce the tomboi identity? . . . I turn now to social processes . . . in West Sumatra and the Indonesian state, looking first at the interrelations of Minangkabau kinship, gender, and economics in the production of oppositional genders.

Minangkabau Ideology and Oppositional Genders

Although the Minangkabau people are considered a single ethnic group, there are many Minangkabaus— [with] many . . . identities. . . . Minangkabau people are urban, rural, educated, and devout; they are civil servants, migrants, and farmers. Their identities vary according to their exposure to media, state ideology, Western-oriented education, and religious fundamentalism. The multiplicity of identities attests to the complex processes at work in contemporary Indonesia as individuals and ethnic groups situate themselves within the postcolonial state.

The construction of gender in West Sumatra is equally complex. There are marked gender differences attached to male and female bodies, but these differences are produced within a matrilineal system that privileges women. . . . The Minangkabau gender ideology I describe here has its basis in rural, rather than urban or non-farming, life in West Sumatra.

Through its very commonness, something as simple as the segregation of girls and boys enculturates and reinforces ideas about sex difference. As is typical of many Islamic cultures, there is lifelong physical segregation of the sexes in most public spaces and events. Girls and boys socialize in predominantly single-sex groups. Teenaged girls and women are expected to stay in at night; going out alone after dark is frowned on. In contrast, adolescent boys and men can be outside in the evenings and often hang out in predominantly male-only spaces, such as coffee shops. These gender differences reflect the Minangkabau (and Islamic) view that men and women have different natures. Men are said to be more aggressive and brave than women. Boys are admonished not to cry—crying is what girls do. Women are expected to be modest, respectful, and humble . . ., especially young unmarried women.

. . . Women lineage elders are powerful figures who, if they are wealthy, control land, labour, and kin. Economically, women control the distribution of land and its produce. Men figure peripherally in their wives' houses, but they maintain important relations with both **natal** and **affinal** houses. . . . Elite men and women carry out kinship affairs in democratic fashion, with neither women nor men able to enforce decisions without the agreement of the other side. Although gender ideology signifies differences in rights and privileges, it does not encode men's hegemonic superiority.

Minangkabau kinship and marriage practices provide deeper insights into the construction of gender and sexuality. Individuals, whether male or female, are not considered adult until they have married heterosexually. Everyone is expected and strongly encouraged (in some cases forced) to marry. . . . While this expectation is commonplace in most cultures, its significance goes beyond the mere requirement to reproduce. Marriage constructs an extended network of kin and affines that forms the basis of social life in the village. For Minangkabau women, the continuation of the matrilineal kinship network through marriage and children is critical to their own standing and influence both in the kin group and in the community. An unmarried or childless daughter denies the lineage any offspring through her and risks the future status of the lineage.[3] . . . A man's marriage does not produce lineage heirs, making men peripheral to lineage reproduction. . . . Women lineage heads exert control over young women to avoid the risk of a bad marriage or no marriage at all. Thus, in this matrilineal system, men are not the primary ones controlling women through marriage; senior elite women control young women through their desires to maintain and strengthen their own lineage standing (Blackwood 1993).

In the context of this rural kin-based society, heterosexual marriage is a paramount feature of Minangkabau kinship ideology. Within the terms of the kinship ideology, women are producers and reproducers of the lineage. There are no acceptable fantasies of femininity or female bodies in rural villages that do not include marriage and motherhood. This ideology remains hegemonic at the same time that emerging discourses of modernity and capitalism have opened up possibilities of resistance to marriage restrictions (Blackwood 1993).

Minangkabau culture produces gender transgression, I argue, because of restrictive definitions and expectations of masculinity and femininity attached to male and female bodies. In this case, male dominance is not an adequate reason for gender transgression because the Minangkabau do not fit any standard criteria for male dominance. It is not "men" (patriarchy) or their oppressive gender hierarchy that creates transgressions but, rather, a gender and kinship ideology that privileges women and men, yet insists on oppositional genders.

How does this sex/gender system induce the tomboi to claim a masculine identity? Why is (or was) this the form that transgression took? . . . To answer these questions, one needs to look at the way tombois are treated within the dominant culture. Tombois imagine themselves masculine, and as such are tolerated to a certain extent, but there is a contradiction between the way tombois define themselves and the way others define them. Tombois are under great pressure to carry out family obligations, to marry a man and be reproductive. Dayan said that every time s/he saw hir mother, she asked when s/he was getting married. Hir mother worried that a woman could not support herself alone; she needs a husband. Hir mother's statement was a clear refusal of Dayan's self-definition as a man, a refusal that typifies the attitude of others within the local community.

The constant pressure to get married and the threat of forcible marriage reveal the way a person's body determines a person's gender. In this system the hegemonic, legitimate gender is based on one's sex; gender is not considered an "identity," performed or otherwise. . . . A tomboi, according to the Minangkabau sex/gender system, is a "woman" even though s/he enacts a masculine gender, hence the refusal to legitimate that enactment and the insistence on the fulfillment of hir reproductive duties. Denying the female body is impermissible. Although tombois insist on being treated as men by their partners, their masculinity lacks cultural validation. Society insists on the priority of the body in determining gender.

Dayan said s/he played too rough and enjoyed boys' activities when s/he was little, so people called hir *bujang gadis*, a label that meant others perceived hir as masculine. At that time s/he had no other recourse but to assume s/he was a boy. Without other options available, and seeing that hir behaviour falls outside the bounds of proper femininity, the tomboi denies hir female body, binding hir breasts so that the physical evidence will not betray hir. S/he produces the only other gender recognizable in the sex/gender system, the masculine gender. . . .

The Promotion of Motherhood and Heterosexuality

. . . [W]hat messages about gender at the national level lead to the production of tomboi identity? The Indonesian state, particularly since the inception of the New Order in 1965, has avidly pursued a policy promoting nuclear families and motherhood.[4] This state ideology emphasizes the importance of women's role as mothers and consciously purveys the idea that women are primarily responsible for their children and their family's health, care, and education. . . . All state family policies are oriented around a nuclear family defined as a husband, wife, and children in disregard of the many forms of family found within the borders of Indonesia. . . .

Television and magazines are replete with images of soft, pretty, domestic women. Advertisements bombard women with the most fashionable clothes, skin care, and health care products necessary to make them successful women. . . . Women characters on popular television series are primarily domestic, irrational, emotional, and obedient—and incapable of solving their own problems (Aripurnami 1996). . . . The message for women is that it is a national and religious duty to marry heterosexually and be feminine. . . .

Other representations of motherhood come from fundamentalist Islam, which claims that motherhood is the natural role for women and their destiny because they are female. Islamic fundamentalists idealize women as mothers and wives under the supervision of husbands (Blackwood 1995). In regard to sexual practices, many Muslims believe same-sex sexuality is immoral, and this was Dayan's understanding of hir faith. . . .

The emphasis on heterosexual marriage and the nuclear family suggests that compulsory heterosexuality and women's subordination are actively being produced at the national level by religion, the state, media, and multinational corporations. . . . For those ["women"] who do not fit the normative model of gender, or find it limiting and oppressive, such a model persuades them of their masculinity, producing gender transgression.

Despite the dominance of the ideology of femininity and motherhood at the state level, there are cracks within it—unintended consequences that ironically open a space for imagining other gender and sexual possibilities. In its efforts to create modern nuclear families, state discourse undermines the influence of lineage elders in several ways. First, whereas rural life in many areas of Indonesia customarily centres around kin, state discourse emphasizes the priority of the nuclear (male-headed) family over the larger kin group. State support for nuclear families allows a daughter to contest her mother's authority. Second, the discourse of modernity, with its emphasis on individualism and consumerism, provides a model of self-earned income for the earner's use alone. Finally, the availability of non-agricultural labour for women in a global economy also models alternatives to life in a rural household. All these processes undermine extended families and their power to require a daughter's marriage and support of the lineage (Blackwood 1995). These imaginable alternatives help to question the ideology of oppositional genders, creating the possibility of gender and sexual identities not predicated on sexed bodies. For tombois these alternatives raise the possibility that their masculinity does not have to make them men.

Cewek Resistance to Marriage and Heterosexuality

The hegemonic heterosexuality of the state and the Minangkabau kinship system produce not only the tomboi as gender transgressor but also a different form of transgression. Some women participate in compulsory heterosexuality, marrying men and bearing children, but then quietly claim the right to choose a tomboi partner. For some women, the pressure to marry a man makes refusal nearly unthinkable and marriage inevitable. For other women who marry heterosexually, their action fulfills a sense of duty to their mothers, their lineage, and themselves. Whatever the reason, women who have married and borne children are in a better position to resist both state dictates and local sanctions concerning women's sexuality. As there are few private spaces where young unmarried women can safely pursue erotic relationships, marriage allows them to establish their own households apart from their mothers'. . . .

A "normative" woman, that is, one who has the appearance of fitting gender norms, can pursue her desire for and sexual relations with a tomboi without becoming marked as a gender transgressor. This fact points to the privilege associated with the dominant gender ideology. Enacting the gender that is appropriate for one's sex fits with the heterosexual **paradigm** and is less problematic than enacting the "wrong" gender.

Transnational Lesbian and Gay Discourse

In addition to local and state discourses, tomboi identity is situated within a transnational lesbian and gay discourse circulating in Indonesia primarily through national gay organizations and their newsletters. First organized in the early 1980s, these groups have nurtured a small but growing nationwide community of gays and lesbians, thereby developing a consciously new gay identity for Indonesians. . . .

The new lesbian and gay movement in Indonesia is creating an identity distinct from the gender-marked banci and tomboi identities. . . . [G]ay and lesbian activists in Indonesia distinguish themselves from both bancis and tombois. Gay and lesbian identity is associated with a "modern," educated middle class, while banci is a "lower-class construction" distinct from the gay and lesbian community, although the distinction between the two is not that neat (Oetomo 1996: 263). Similarly, cowok–cewek are thought to be predominantly from the working class and not like lesbians of the middle and upper-middle classes (Gayatri 1994). . . .

. . . Media attention to an increasingly international gay and lesbian movement has brought into common use the terms *lesbi* and *tomboi*, transformations of the English terms *lesbian* and *tomboy*. . . . The terms *tomboi* and *lesbi* are now synonymous for many people. . . . This usage is inconsistent, however, with the term as used by activists, who define a lesbi as a woman who is sexually active with another woman. . . .

The transnational discourse on gender and sexuality is complicated by media coverage of transgendered individuals in Indonesia and other parts of the world. Indonesians know of both American and Indonesian transgendered people who have had sex-congruence surgery (bringing their sex into congruence with their gender). In fact Dayan's sister was so worried that s/he might want surgery that she specifically warned hir against it, at the same time pleading with hir to get married. Consequently, transnational narratives produce yet another possibility, that of surgically bringing one's body into conformity with one's gender, a model that fits with older indigenous notions of the primacy of bodies in determining gender. . . .

Plural Identities

I want to pull together the various threads of my argument to reveal how one particular tomboi is situated within these narratives of gender, sexuality, and culture. Many representations of femininity circulate in Indonesia (Sears 1996). In like manner, female subjects who are masculine, erotically attracted to women, or both are represented in many different ways. They are seen as "deviants" from the model of mother and wife so central to Indonesian state ideology, as the stereotypically masculine lesbian portrayed by the media, as women who love each other (the model favoured by some activists), and as men (the identity claimed by tombois).

Dayan is positioned within all these possibilities. A product of the postcolonial Indonesian school system, s/he graduated from a technical high school with ambitions for a career. But, like many others in the working class, s/he struggles to find work. S/he is a member of hir mother's lineage but lives with hir older sister on their deceased father's land in a community that is only 15 minutes from the district capital, where some of hir brothers work. . . .

Dayan's location on the fringes of urban culture helps to explain hir rejection of Minangkabau womanhood. Raised in a family with little matrilineal money or land and thus dependent on the father's family to provide land and house, s/he, hir mother, and hir sister have lost some of the crucial connections that authorize women's power. . . . [T]he family's marginal position between rural and urban means that their desires are directed toward urban opportunities, not village and matrilineal relations. The Minangkabau world Dayan knows is that of a struggling, urban-oriented family.

Like many youth growing up, Dayan has been influenced by divergent ideologies of womanhood. Educated in the "modern" school system, Minangkabau youth have received little state validation for the importance of Minangkabau women. . . . Schoolgirls learn "proper" gender roles and are indoctrinated in the importance of becoming wives who serve their husbands' needs. They are inundated through media with representations of urban, middle-class, docile women. Yet with the increased availability of education, civil service, and other wage-labour jobs in the last thirty years, young women now have the right to choose their spouses or to pursue higher education and careers in urban areas. Many villagers believe that the potential economic benefits of higher education or urban careers may enhance lineage status, especially when successful educated daughters use their income to remodel or build new lineage houses. Many young women grow up believing that they are better off today under the patriarchal New Order because they can seek their own jobs and choose their own husbands. To these young women, the Minangkabau world of powerful elite women . . . seems distant and old fashioned. . . .

The masculinities that tombois construct reflect their different locations in the global market as well as the local community. Hegemonic masculinity is represented and enacted differently in the village, in urban areas, and on movie screens. It also is a hybrid of local, national, and transnational representations. In rural villages a young man may smoke, drink, gamble, and use coarse language, but he is also admonished to be strong, industrious, respectful of his elders, and responsible to his lineage and his wife's family. The bravado and coarseness of young urban (poor, working-class) men in Indonesia is far from the politeness and respectfulness of rural men. While Dayan's masculinity reflects more of the village, Agus's interpretation reflects a combination of the coarse masculinity and male privilege of urban areas. Dayan told me that when Agus is at Yul's house, "s/he expects to be served and won't do anything for hir wife except give her money." . . .

Dayan's experience of lesbian and gay discourse creates another distinction between hirself and Agus. Dayan described Agus as an old-fashioned tomboi, one who "is like a man and won't be any other way." Hir statement implies that s/he sees Agus as holding onto certain normative ideas of gender that contemporary Indonesian lesbians no longer find satisfying. S/he said further that "Agus has never been out of the *kampung* [village]," implying that had s/he been, Agus might see other models of lesbian relations and quit trying to be so much like a man.

In the past few years, Dayan has lived in Jakarta for one to two years at a time. Both at home and in Jakarta hir friends are cowok–cewek, but these friends also know about the Euro-American model of lesbian identity. At different times Dayan claimed both a masculine identity and a lesbi identity. . . . Hir statements imply that despite feeling like a man, the availability of other models makes it possible to [integrate] the tomboi identity with a lesbian identity. . . .

Conclusion

Identity for tombois in West Sumatra at this point in time is a bricolage, a mix of local, national, and transnational identities. If their identity growing up was shaped by local cultural forces that emphasized oppositional genders, their movement between cities and rural areas means that they have been exposed to other models of sexuality and gender identity that they have used to construct a new sense of themselves. The complexities of their gender identity make it impossible to align tombois with any one category, whether "woman," "lesbian," or "transgendered person."

Tomboi identity refracts and transgresses normative gender constructs. While some theorists identify gender transgression as resistance to male-dominant hegemonic order, tombois in West Sumatra suggest a more complicated cultural production of gender transgression. They cannot be [understood] simply as the product of male dominance. The tomboi identity in Minangkabau culture speaks to the significance of a hegemonic kinship ideology—in which each gender is rigidly distinct and based on two sexes but not male dominant—in producing particular forms of gender transgression. For the tomboi, processes of postcolonialism, capitalism, and modernity also converge to produce and reinforce gender transgression.

. . . Although the Indonesian state enforces heterosexuality, wage labour and capitalism create a space for the tomboi to live as a single female. The discourse of modernity—the importance of education, careers, and middle-class status— legitimates models other than motherhood and femininity for females. Though the tomboi remains a deviant, s/he is also finding more room to negotiate a future.

At the same time, other models of sexuality and gender are becoming visible in a globalized world, multiplying, collapsing, and refracting social identities in new ways. Where sexuality was embedded in the ideology of oppositional genders (*man–woman*, *cowok–cewek, banci–laki asli* [real man]), sexual "identity" and the possibility of sexuality between two women or two men are emergent cultural practices. Desiring women is being rewritten for some as a product of the variability of human sexuality rather than the "natural" urge of the male body and the prerogative of "men."

References Cited

Aripurnami, Sita. 1996. "A Feminist Comment on the Sinetron Presentation of Indonesian Women." In *Fantasizing the Feminine in Indonesia*, edited by Laurie Sears, 249–58. Durham, NC: Duke University Press.

Blackwood, Evelyn. 1993. *The Politics of Daily Life: Gender, Kinship and Identity in a Minangkabau Village, West Sumatra, Indonesia*. PhD diss., Stanford University.

———. (1995) "Senior Women, Model Mothers, and Dutiful Wives: Managing Gender Contradictions in a Minangkabau Village." In *Bewitching Women, Pious Men: Gender and Body Politics in Southeast Asia*, edited by Aihwa Ong and Michael Peletz, 124–58. Berkeley: University of California Press.

Bolin, Anne. 1994. "Transcending and Transgendering: Male-to-Female Transsexuals, Dichotomy, and Diversity." In *Third Sex, Third Gender: Beyond Sexual Dimorphism in Culture and History*, edited by Gilbert Herdt, 447–85. New York: Zone Books.

Echols, John M., and Hassan Shadily. 1989. *Kamus Indonesia Inggris: An Indonesian–English Dictionary*. 3rd ed. Jakarta, ID: PT Gramedia.

Errington, Shelly. 1990. "Recasting Sex, Gender, and Power: A Theoretical and Regional Overview." In *Power and Difference: Gender in Island Southeast Asia*, edited by Jane M. Atkinson and Shelly Errington, 1–58. Stanford, CA: Stanford University Press.

Garber, Marjorie. 1991. "The Chic of Araby: Transvestism, Transsexualism and the Erotics of Cultural Appropriation." In *Body/Guards: The Cultural Politics of Gender Ambiguity*, edited by Julia Epstein and Kristina Straub, 223–47. New York: Routledge.

Gayatri, B.J.D. 1994. "Sentul-Kantil, Not Just another Term." Unpublished manuscript.

Kennedy, Elizabeth, and Madeline Davis. 1993 *Boots of Leather, Slippers of Gold: The History of a Lesbian Community*. New York: Penguin Books.

Newton, Esther. 1972 *Mother Camp: Female Impersonators in America*. Chicago: University of Chicago Press.

———. 1993. *Cherry Grove, Fire Island: Sixty Years in America's First Gay and Lesbian Town*. Boston: Beacon.

Oetomo, Dede. 1996. "Gender and Sexual Orientation in Indonesia." In *Fantasizing the Feminine in Indonesia*, edited by Laurie Sears, 259–69. Durham, NC: Duke University Press.

Poole, John Fitz Porter. 1996. "The Procreative and Ritual Constitution of Female, Male, and Other: Androgynous Beings in the Cultural Imagination of the Bimin-Kuskusmin of Papua New Guinea." In *Gender Reversals and Gender Cultures: Anthropological and Historical Perspectives*, edited by Sabrina Ramet, 197–218. London: Routledge.

Sears, Laurie J. 1996. "Fragile Identities: Deconstructing Women and Indonesia." In *Fantasizing the Feminine in Indonesia*, edited by Laurie Sears, 1–44. Durham, NC: Duke University Press.

Yanagisako, Sylvia, and Carol Delaney. 1995. "Naturalizing Power." In *Naturalizing Power: Essays in Feminist Cultural Analysis*, edited by Sylvia Yanagisako and Carol Delaney, 1–22. New York: Routledge.

Notes

1. I use "women" in [quotes] because at the time of first meeting, I assumed these individuals were women. (Blackwood's note)
2. I use fictitious names for the individuals mentioned in this article. Dayan (pronounced "Daiyon") lived with an older married sister in a small town about an hour from where I lived. I visited Dayan mostly on weekends at the sister's house. (Blackwood's note)
3. This is not an insignificant concern because prestige, status, and property are all at risk. One young married woman I knew was in turmoil over whether to have another child because her only daughter is not strong. Although she already

has two children, a number that the Indonesian state says is sufficient for a family, she thinks that she should have another daughter to ensure the perpetuation of her lineage. (Blackwood's note)

4. The New Order refers to the postwar regime of General Suharto, who became acting head of state in 1966 and remained president until 1998. (Blackwood's note)

Key Points to Consider

- Many of the world's cultures provide "third-sex" or "third-gender" categories in addition to male and female. Sometimes these categories reflect sexuality. Sometimes transgender individuals are understood to abstain from sexual activity.
- Minangkabau culture provides for third-gender/third-sex categories. Biological males who identify as women are called *bancis*. Biological females who identify as men are called *tombois*.
- Minangkabau tombois do not necessarily think of themselves as lesbians. Tombois are sexually attracted to women because they see themselves as men.
- International gay and lesbian rights discourses about same-sex desire circulate in Indonesia and counter the indigenous transgender categories of banci and tomboi. According to Blackwood, gay and lesbian are globalized, urban, and middle-class identities, while banci and tomboi are rural and working-class identities.

Critical Thinking Questions

1. How did Blackwood's culturally informed conception of gender affect the way she interpreted Dayan's subjective sense of gender?
2. Based on the information Blackwood provides about Dayan, how do you think Dayan would feel about Blackwood's use of genderless or gender-ambiguous pronouns? Do you think Blackwood made the correct choice? Why or why not?
3. How do tombois' identities as men intersect with Minangkabau practices of kinship, descent, and inheritance?
4. Increasingly over the last several years, English speakers have used *sex* and *gender* as synonyms, with *gender* tending to replace *sex* as a way to refer to a biological state. This is especially common when discussing animals. What social significance do you see in the attribution of *gender* rather than *sex* when describing a dog as male or female? Explain your reasoning.

Suggestions for Further Reading and Watching

Blackwood, Evelyn. 2000. *Webs of Power: Women, Kin, and Community in a Sumatran Village*. Lanham, MD: Rowman and Littlefield.
———. 2010. *Falling into the Lesbi World: Desire and Difference in Indonesia*. Honolulu: University of Hawaii Press.
Herdt, Gilbert, ed. 1994. *Third Sex, Third Gender: Beyond Sexual Dimorphism in Culture and History*. New York: Zone Books.

Littlewood, Roland. 2002. "Three into Two: The Third Sex in Northern Albania." *Anthropology and Medicine* 9 (1): 37–49.

Longinotto, Kim, and Jano Williams. 1995. *Shinjuku Boys*. New York: Women Make Movies. Video recording, 53 min.

Padawer, Ruth. 2014. "When Women become Men at Wellesley." *New York Times*, 19 October. www.nytimes.com/2014/10/19/magazine/when-women-become-men-at-wellesley-college.html.

Peterson, Britt. 2014. "The Quickly Shifting Language of the Transgender Community." *Boston Globe*, 9 March. www.bostonglobe.com/ideas/2014/03/09/the-quickly-shifting-language-transgender-community/J0yimos7SoZmVy8mm1Q9LL/story.html.

Chapter 7

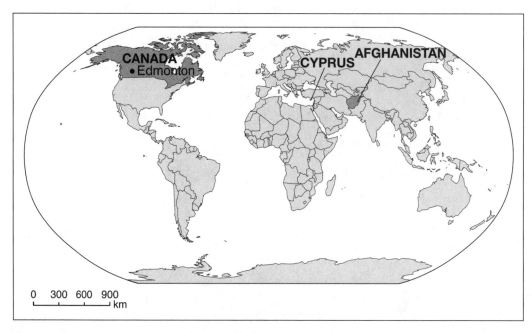

Canada, Cyprus, and Afghanistan

Introduction

Canadians have complicated and ambiguous views of the projection and use of Canadian military power in the world. On the one hand, many Canadians (and others around the world) associate the Canadian Armed Forces with humanitarian work such as peacekeeping. Indeed, most Canadian schoolchildren learn that Lester B. Pearson, prime minister from 1963 to 1968, was awarded the Nobel Peace Prize in 1957 for his role in creating the peacekeeping agency of the United Nations. At the same time, Canadians engage in practices that celebrate the Canadian Forces as warriors. At the national level, there is the Canadian War Museum, which opened in 2005, as well as the image of the Vimy Ridge memorial adorning our new polymer $20 bills. Many individual Canadians voice special reverence for veterans of World War II, and each November nearly every public official and a substantial percentage of ordinary citizens don red poppies to remember Canadians' military service in the First World War and beyond.

Despite these personal and public celebrations of military prowess, international peacekeeping continues to be an important aspect of Canadians' image of the country as a peacemaker, often contrasted with a widely held image of the United States as a war maker. Since the 1980s, however, Canada has been stepping back from international peacekeeping and has not engaged in strictly peacekeeping (non-combat) operations since the end of the **Cold War** (1945–1991). At the end of 2014, only about one hundred members of the Canadian Armed Forces were seconded to the UN for peacekeeping purposes, and of those, only about twenty were serving as troops in UN peacekeeping missions (UN 2014). In contrast, between 2001 and 2011, almost 40,000 men and women served with the Canadian Armed Forces in the war in Afghanistan.

The article in this chapter concerns the effects of combat in Afghanistan on one company of Canadian infantry. Anne Irwin takes up the rarely questioned claim that military service in general, and military combat in particular, works as a **rite of passage** that turns boys into men. She observes that "the military and the infantry in particular are frequently considered sites where **hegemonic** masculinity is produced and reproduced." By *hegemonic masculinity* she references traits widely, though not universally, associated with manliness.

Rites of passage are cultural means for facilitating the sometimes stressful movement of individuals through the **life course**. As Irwin notes, military deployments in general, and trips into possible combat situations in particular, display the three-stage structure anthropologists recognize as characteristic of rites of passage: separation from the familiar, **liminality**, and reintegration into society. At both the beginning and the end stages, participants' preparations include dressing in distinctive clothes, eating particular foods, physically separating themselves from certain people and familiar surroundings, and following special instructions—all actions undertaken by young people serving in the Canadian Forces. As well, trips into possible combat situations are liminal periods characterized, in part, by **communitas**. Anthropologist Victor Turner (1920–1983) introduced the term *communitas* for periods during rituals and other communal events distinguished by shared intense emotions and the temporary abandonment of status and other differences. But Irwin also finds that military combat is a poor example of a rite of passage because it prematurely ages the young combat veterans. Thus, rather than facilitating passage through the life course, combat interrupts and disorganizes young men's and women's life courses.

In the full version of this article, Irwin notes that the literature on masculinity rarely even acknowledges the existence of aging men, as if masculinity is age specific as well as **gender** specific. In her references to premature aging, Irwin suggests a novel way to interpret soldiers' physical and psychological response to warfare. It is noteworthy that she makes only oblique references to post-traumatic stress disorder (PTSD), which seems to dominate the news coverage about current and former members of the Canadian Forces.

PTSD was first recognized as a mental illness in 1980 following the activism of veterans of the US–Vietnam War. In media and popular culture, PTSD is now often treated as the expected outcome of many stressful events, including combat. It is important not to discount the problem of PTSD; studies suggest that it affects approximately 8 per cent of Canadian veterans of the war in Afghanistan. But as Irwin argues, warfare has other social and physical consequences for soldiers that are not readily classified as mental illness.

✹ About the Author ✹

Anne Irwin studied anthropology at the University of Calgary and then at the University of Manchester (UK), where she earned her PhD before returning to Calgary to teach. Irwin retired from academia in 2010 and changed career directions. Since 2013, she has worked as a doula in British Columbia; prior to becoming an anthropologist, she was an officer in Canadian Armed Forces reserves.

"There Will Be a Lot of Old Young Men Going Home": Combat and Becoming a Man in Afghanistan

Anne Irwin

Introduction

The title of this [article] was inspired by a comment made to me by a key **informant** during the course of field research with a Canadian infantry rifle company engaged in combat operations in southern Afghanistan during the summer months of 2006. He was an experienced soldier, a sergeant whom I had known since 1996 when I had studied the same unit during peacetime training in Canada. The company had been "outside the wire," that is, outside the protective confines of the coalition base at Kandahar Air Field, for several weeks, but had returned to the base for two days of preparation for a major offensive operation. We were sitting in the shade of the big tent where we slept while on base, watching some young soldiers as we talked about his fears that he would not be able to accomplish his personal goal for this tour of duty in Afghanistan, "to bring all my boys home." Our conversation veered to the topic of the end of the tour and of adjusting to life at home and he commented, "there will be a lot of old young men going home from this tour." I dutifully recorded the comment in my field

notes that evening and forgot it until I began thinking about the notion of combat service as a rite of passage into manhood. I believe his comment captures very eloquently the paradoxes and complexities of the idea of war service as a transition into male adulthood.

There is a widely held perception in popular culture, within the military as well as within academic studies of the military, that military service in general and combat service in particular constitute rites of passage into manhood. This is expressed in recruiting slogans such as "the Marine Corps builds men" and "we'll make a man of you," and it is also prevalent in motion pictures. One of the most common **tropes** in war films is the transition from boy to man effected by the experience of combat. The academic literature likewise is replete with metaphors of coming of age through military service (see for example Ben-Ari 1998: 115; Hockey 1986; Kaplan 2000; Samuels 2006; Sinclair-Webb 2000; Winslow 1999). One scholar expresses the opinion of many when she writes, "war has been accepted as the great touchstone of manliness since time immemorial" (Oldfield 1989: 237). . . .

A case can certainly be made that combat service bears the characteristics of a rite of passage, but I argue in this [article] that combat service, although transformative, is not a rite of passage for it does not permanently or completely alter participants' statuses from youth to adult manhood. War service does not turn boys into men, but rather, it turns them into old men without passing through adulthood, and even that transformation is not complete, as they retain many of the characteristics of youth.

I begin . . . by presenting the context of the research on which the argument is based, followed by an **ethnographic** account of the tour of Afghanistan in which I participated as a researcher. I subsequently problematize the idea that there is a one-to-one correspondence between the infantry and a unitary masculinity. I then apply van Gennep's tripartite model of the *rite de passage* (1977) to the combat tour, focusing primarily on the liminal and re-integration phases of the tour to make the argument that soldiers returning from the tour have not been transformed into adult men but are in some respects stuck in youth and in other respects prematurely old, so that their statuses are indeed a hybrid that could be termed "old young men."

Research Context

In February 2006, the First Battalion of the Princess Patricia's Canadian Light Infantry, an infantry battalion of the regular Canadian Forces (CF), deployed to southern Afghanistan as part of Canada's contribution to the US–led "Operation Enduring Freedom." The battalion constituted the core of Task Force Orion, the battle group that was responsible for security in the province of Kandahar. Task Force Orion was only a small part of the Canadian contingent, which totalled more than 2500 military personnel. As the Canadian combat unit, the Task Force, numbering approximately 450 personnel, was specifically tasked with "conducting aggressive interdiction operations" (Lt Col Ian Hope, personal communication).

I had been studying the First Battalion of the Princess Patricia's Canadian Light Infantry since 1991 when I spent several months in the field with the unit in Alberta, Canada, as it trained for conventional warfare and for peacekeeping (Irwin 1993). In 1995/1996, I spent almost a year with the unit as I tried to understand how soldiers in this peacetime and peacekeeping army made sense of and negotiated their roles as warriors and soldiers (Irwin 2002). In 2006, the unit's role changed dramatically when it deployed to southern Afghanistan, where there was no peace to keep, but where the unit was expected to undertake what the military calls "full-spectrum operations," including combat (Lt Col Hope, personal communication). Because of my longstanding research relationship with the unit, I had no trouble gaining access when I proposed to accompany them for the second half of their tour. I went to Afghanistan in March 2006 for two weeks . . . to determine the feasibility of a longer study. . . . I returned to Afghanistan at the end of May and spent the remainder of the tour with the unit, returning with the soldiers to Canada at the end of August. . . .

During the period of my research, the battalion's role did not change, but the public in Canada did become more aware of the true nature of the unit's activities as the death toll rose, and by the end of the tour, there was open acknowledgement in the media and among the public that the Canadian Forces were involved in fighting counter-insurgency warfare. Because I was interested in how soldiers negotiated their identity as warriors in the context of their changing roles from peacekeepers to warfighters, I used traditional anthropological methods, primarily **participant observation**, living in close intimacy with the troops and participating in their experiences, short of combat, as fully as possible.

Ethnographic Account of the Tour

My research was conducted almost exclusively with one of the rifle companies, Charlie Company, which consisted of about 85 soldiers of all ranks, ranging from private to major and from eighteen years of age to the late forties, among whom only three were women.[1] . . .

The primary focus of my research was 8 Platoon, one of the three platoons that along with the headquarters made up the company. Each platoon was commanded by a lieutenant, who was assisted by his second in command, a warrant officer. The platoon was divided into three sections and a headquarters. Each section of the platoon consisted of five to eight infantrymen commanded by a sergeant with a master corporal as his second in command. . . . I was the only woman in [this] group. Each of the sections and the platoon headquarters was assigned during operations to one light armoured vehicle (LAV), which was the soldier's home during operations outside the wire. . . .

Any analysis of the tour in Afghanistan must take into account the spatial organization of the experience of the soldiers. The central organizing principle, the notion of "the wire" was used to categorize people and to structure all the routine features of social life, including time, social interaction, and experience. The wire referred to the concertina wire surrounding the coalition base at Kandahar Air Field (KAF), and the term "outside the wire" was applied to any activity that took place outside of those protective confines. The most basic distinction between categories of people was that between the people who never left the wire, or the base, and those whose duties regularly and routinely took them outside.

For the troops at KAF, life in Afghanistan was uncomfortably hot (averaging in the mid-fifties Celsius in July), involved long hours of work, and entailed facing the risks presented by the occasional rocket and mortar attack on the camp. . . . Soldiers were also subject to certain deprivations: alcohol was not permitted, and sexual relations, even between spouses serving a tour together, were forbidden. Soldiers were also armed at all times except during physical training and going to the showers, although their weapons were not loaded. . . . I remember feeling very strongly on arriving in Kandahar Air Field that this base was an operational base in a war zone, in part because of the constant dust and noise of helicopters coming and going, and the fact that all military personnel were armed at all times. . . . However, after spending a number of weeks outside the wire, when I returned to KAF I found the differences between KAF and any other peacetime military base to be superficial.

Task Force Orion's tactical headquarters were at KAF. . . . Each company was assigned an enormous tent that slept 200 soldiers in double bunk beds. All members of the company, including the company commander and the company sergeant major and all the other company officers, shared the same accommodations. Most soldiers screened off their beds with tarps and blankets to achieve a modicum of privacy, but the resulting privacy was at best illusory and was paid for by a decrease in air ventilation. . . .

The unit rarely spent more than a few days at KAF at any one time, spending most of their time "outside the wire," living a nomadic life, traveling by day and night in the LAVs, sleeping when the opportunity presented itself in the sand next to their vehicles. . . . In [the riskiest] spaces, weapons were kept loaded at all times, and soldiers usually wore body armour and helmets unless they were very close to their vehicles. . . . But in all cases the threat of enemy action, although not always in the forefront of one's mind, was like a constant background hum. . . .

What was most apparent about daily life outside the wire was that there was very little that was routine about it. . . . There was no day-to-day routine for sleeping and eating, not even predictable shifts. Moving by convoy and other missions were often conducted during nighttime, whether intentionally or because of unexpected delays and changes of plans, of which there were many. Because of the intensity of the operational tempo, sleep was a rare commodity. Soldiers became adept at sleeping whenever and wherever they had a chance. Often the chance to sleep only came during daylight hours, for a few hours at a time, but even this sleep was constantly interrupted by the bangs of artillery and mortars, the noise of vehicles starting up, and the sound of small arms fire. . . .

Outside the wire, the daily menu of hard rations or individual meal packs . . . became tedious. There was quite a range of different meals, but after a while they all came to taste the same. Soldiers went to great lengths to structure meals in as "normal" a fashion as possible. For example, despite temperatures soaring into the sixties Celsius . . . , if at all possible meals would be heated before being eaten. . . . Wherever feasible, meals would be eaten as close as possible to the "normal" time of day: breakfasts in the morning, lunches near midday, and suppers in the evening. Sections would almost always eat together, and while each soldier would have his or her individual meal pack, the accessories, such as coffee, tea, and gum, were usually pooled and shared afterwards, and the desserts and main meals often traded. . . . Frequently, meals would be heated and ready to eat when an order to move would come over the radio and the meals were set aside to be eaten hours later, or sometimes not at all if the delay pushed into the next meal period. Issued meals were supplemented with treats received from family and friends back home, and there were very strong social norms enforcing an ethic of sharing. If anyone were to eat a treat that he had received from home without offering to share with section mates, someone would be sure to ask pointedly, "What does that taste like?" . . .

As I have suggested with respect to meals, another stress factor outside the wire was the fact that plans and orders were constantly changing, and it was therefore impossible to plan ahead or to pace oneself. On one occasion 8 Platoon was sent on what was to be a three-day operation, but the platoon was warned to pack for a week because there was a chance that the mission would be extended. In fact the operation lasted twenty-one days, and on any given day the soldiers had no idea how much longer the mission would last, although rumours about imminent return to KAF abounded. Soldiers were therefore always faced with mundane decisions such as whether to change into that one last clean T-shirt, or pair of socks, or to make them last one more day in case they stayed out longer. . . .

Military Masculinity Problematized

. . . The military and the infantry in particular are frequently considered sites where hegemonic masculinity is produced and reproduced (Anonymous 1974; Dunivin 1994; Gill 1997; Helman 1997; Sinclair-Webb 2000). Some scholars have added nuance to these analyses by pointing out that even in the military, the supposedly quintessential site of monolithic masculinity, there are pluralities of forms of masculinity that are called forth in

different contexts. . . . [Yet,] what sort of adult masculinity is the end product of the rite of passage that so many consider combat service to be[?] Acker argues that "currently, [adult] hegemonic masculinity is typified by the image of the strong, technically competent authoritative leader who is sexually potent and attractive, has a family, and has his emotions under control" (Acker 1990: 153). If this is indeed the model of masculinity into which combat is supposed to transform young men, then as we will see, the experience of combat cannot be considered the rite of passage that accomplishes this.

The Tour as a Rite of Passage

Even as we reject the experience of combat as a rite of passage, however, a tour of duty in Afghanistan can be analyzed in terms of the tripartite structure of a rite of passage (Turner 1974, 1977; van Gennep 1977), with the deployment phase (the departure from Canada) representing the rite of separation, operations in the country representing the liminal phase, and the redeployment (the return to Canada) representing the reintegration phase. During the deployment phase, soldiers are confronted with many of the classic characteristics of a rite of separation, including the most obvious: the physical separation from pre-existing statuses by means of geographic removal from the country. In preparation for this removal, soldiers participate in mission-specific training and are tested to ensure that there are no medical, psychological, or personal reasons for them to be left behind. Immediately before the deployment they are issued new uniforms because in Afghanistan they wear the "arid Can pat," or Canadian camouflage pattern designed for desert environments, whereas in Canada they wear a green camouflage uniform. They get their hair cut very short and some even shave their heads, and there are official farewell ceremonies as well as unofficial parties. They update their wills and make arrangements in case of being killed or wounded, ensuring that their next of kin notification forms are up to date and correct.

One last activity is a formal picture-taking event, organized by the battalion, when each soldier has his or her photograph taken in "full fighting order," wearing a beret with the unit cap-badge rather than a helmet as would be normal during operations. These photos, which soldiers call their "death photos," are filed for use in the press release in the event of the soldier's death. There are some superstitions around these photos. One soldier who was sick on the day the photographs were taken had never had a "death photo" shot and took this to mean that he would survive the tour. . . . All of these activities carried out in preparation for leaving the country and the possibility of death seem to be symbolic of the stripping away of pre-existing statuses. It would appear, then, that the deployment phase looks very much like the separation phase of a rite of passage, but the liminal phase is more difficult to delineate.

Considering the tour itself a liminal phase would suggest that the tour takes place in one undifferentiated realm, but, as mentioned above, the central organizing principle of the tour is the **phenomenological** difference between life at KAF and life "outside the wire." For the soldiers who spend the entire tour in Kandahar Air Field, the period in Afghanistan certainly has aspects of liminality: physical separation, deprivation, and . . . a certain amount of communitas (Turner 1974, 1977). But for the combat soldiers

who spent little time at KAF, the times inside the wire and outside the wire were so fundamentally different from each other that it is difficult to consider the tour as all one phase. It is probably more accurate to consider the periods outside the wire as liminal episodes, so that each trip outside the wire was itself a rite of passage consisting of the three phases nested within a longer liminal phase. . . .

In this [article] I am not evaluating just any tour as a rite of passage, but specifically the experience of combat. In addressing the question of whether combat transforms youth into men, one of the first steps must surely be to define what I mean by *combat*, a task that is not as straightforward as one might expect, especially in the Afghan context of counterinsurgency warfare. A minimalist definition would limit the notion of combat to the **emic** concept of the TIC, the acronym soldiers use to refer to "troops in contact." A TIC refers to a discreet event, bounded in time and space, during which soldiers are engaged violently with the enemy. This minimalist definition however would not include a range of activities that are nonetheless experienced as combat or combat-like. An example would be when a vehicle full of troops triggers the explosion of an IED (improvised explosive device) without the immediate presence of the enemy. These occasions, which are far more frequent than actual fire fights, pose a danger to life and limb and usually include the threat of a subsequent ambush and actual combat. . . .

. . . TICs were very rare occurrences. And yet, every member of the Company who served outside the wire during the 2006 tour considers him or herself to have "done a combat tour." If we are to respect the soldiers' existential reality, we might define combat as any time outside the wire during which the potential for and threat of combat were ever

FIGURE 7.1　Canadian soldiers from Princess Patricia's Canadian Light Infantry outside "the wire" in Afghanistan in July 2002.

present (as was a constant need to prepare), and occasionally manifest. Using this definition, there are certainly some very strong indications that the episodes outside the wire could be considered combat and were also liminal experiences.

The Liminal Experience of Combat

Leaving the wire always entailed much preparation: checking maps, issuing orders, loading equipment into the LAVs, and loading extra ammunition in the LAVs. On a personal level, almost every soldier took the opportunity while at KAF to get his or her hair cut extremely short, and many chose to shave their heads in the interests of hygiene because of the lack of opportunity outside the wire to wash. On the boundary of KAF there was a buffer zone between rows of concertina wire where convoys leaving the camp would stop; soldiers would dismount from the vehicles, load the magazines onto their personal weapons, and arm the big cannon on the LAV. . . . Soldiers would climb back into the vehicles once more, post air sentries to stand in the open hatches of the vehicles, and head out for anywhere from three days to three weeks of operations.

The combat soldiers experienced each of these episodes outside the wire as an ordeal to endure and survive and as a period of deprivation, both of which are among the characteristics of the liminal phase. These periods were also understood and experienced as tests of skill and ability, both at the personal and the group level, during which soldiers struggled to maintain alertness despite fatigue and boredom. The constant fear of injury or death and the necessity to be ready for any eventuality competed with the need for sleep. Of all the deprivations—freshly cooked food, sex, alcohol, washing—lack of sleep was the most debilitating and the most salient feature of life outside the wire.

Along with intense sleep deprivation, life outside the wire was characterized by uncertainty and unpredictability, in part due to the actions of the enemy and in part due to the commands of higher authority. Soldiers were constantly aware that a routine patrol or convoy might lead to walking or driving into an ambush. . . . [C]ommanders would issue orders, only to change them hours later. On one occasion, the company received four changes of mission in as many hours. Although plans were made in response to enemy activity or a threat of enemy activity, or requests for assistance from allied forces, to the soldiers these constantly changing plans appeared capricious. . . . [I]n short, these soldiers found themselves at the mercy of those in command, another feature of the liminal phase.

In some respects, and at some moments, normative masculinity was turned upside down.

Certainly, one of the features of adult masculinity is control over one's bodily functions, yet soldiers spoke unashamedly among themselves and in front of me of losing control over their bladders and bowels before, during, and after firefights. A number of them confided in me that they vomited before combat operations, or even operations that might lead to combat. Incontinence can be thought of as a marker of extreme old age and infancy, yet none of these young men was the least bit embarrassed or ashamed to acknowledge this loss of control over bodily functions. . . .

Soldiers were also not ashamed to display signs of affection with each other, and . . . [they were] very open and expressive of their grief in the context of the death of comrades. . . . On one occasion, 8 Platoon was supposed to have been sent to an area of high risk, the Panjwaii District. This was a notorious district where the platoon had been involved in fire fights on multiple occasions. . . . At the last moment, . . . 9 Platoon was sent instead, and 8 Platoon remained behind in the relative safety and comfort of a forward operating base. . . . The next morning, the sergeant major spread the word that there was to be a company parade in the centre of the FOB. The soldiers formed up in a hollow square and the company commander addressed them, telling them that Corporal Chris Reid had been killed in an improvised explosive attack, and that the platoon was still engaged in a TIC. The expressions of grief and dismay were open and genuine, and many soldiers wept openly. Only a few hours later, at around midday, the sergeant major called everyone together for another parade and again the company formed up in a hollow square. This time the company commander began with the words, "there's no easy way to tell you this. This morning I told you that 9 Platoon was still involved in a TIC in Panjwaii. There have been three KIA [killed in action]" and as he announced their names, "Sergeant Vaughn Ingram, Corporal Bryce Keller, and Private Kevin Dallaire," I heard moans behind me, and, glancing over my shoulder, saw a number of soldiers dropping to their knees, sobbing. . . .

. . . There were myriad ways that soldiers learned from each other to make sense of and express their experiences. One of the most striking and humorous was the day after a firefight when a spontaneous discussion arose about how "our TIC" would be portrayed in a Hollywood movie. Unfortunately I did not have my audio recorder near at hand, but to this day I remember vividly the animated way in which they discussed which Hollywood stars would play which soldier in the company, how rather than walk to the village, they would rappel out of helicopters, they would never run out of ammunition, and every hand grenade would explode with the force of a five hundred pound bomb.

Coming Home: Reintegration

. . . [T]he real test of whether the tour of Afghanistan can be considered a rite of passage into manhood is the reintegration phase during which initiands are reintegrated into society in new statuses with new responsibilities and privileges. I want to consider now how soldiers are reintegrated into society and, especially, in what statuses they are reincorporated. The return to Canada from combat duty in Afghanistan was a protracted process, involving first a return to KAF from outside the wire. Several days were spent at KAF returning some equipment, attending briefings, sleeping as much as possible, doing laundry, and passing on "soldier-level tips" for survival to the incoming soldiers who were to replace them. Subsequently there was an air journey to the Canadian

Forces support base in the Persian Gulf where soldiers turned in their weapons, ammunition, and body armour. For most of the soldiers this was a moment full of meaning: shedding the more than twenty pounds of ballistic plates encased in Kevlar and handing over the weapon that had been within reach for the entire tour were powerful **symbols** that the tour was over and that they had survived it.

From the Persian Gulf they flew, unarmed and dressed now in civilian clothes, to Cyprus for the "decompression" which consisted of a few briefings but which was mostly devoted to relaxation in the form of sleep, binge drinking, and sightseeing. After five days in Cyprus they boarded an aircraft yet again, now dressed in clean uniforms, wearing berets instead of helmets, for the final leg home. Fighter planes escorted the returning aircraft into the Edmonton International Airport and, once the soldiers deplaned, motorcycle police escorted their buses to the base. . . . At the base a lecture building had been set aside for the reunion with their families. It was a very emotionally charged moment, with mothers and fathers, wives, husbands, and children running to greet the returned soldiers. Many tears were shed on the part of family members and soldiers. . . .

This moment was the ultimate reintegration, the moment when soldiers returned to their families and to their homes. What was particularly striking to me was how many mothers . . . told me that they hardly recognized their own sons because of the dramatic physical changes that had taken place during the tour. Because I had been with them constantly during the second half of the tour, I had not noticed the changes myself, but when I was shown photographs of soldiers taken before the tour, I was immediately struck by how much they had aged. They did not seem to have aged into adults, however, but into old men.

. . . In their ethnography of aging dancers, [Wainwright and Turner] suggest that the rigours of the dancer's life lead to premature aging of the body so that dancers can be considered to be too old for their work well before middle age (2004: 111). The same phenomenon is true of infantry soldiers, and a forty-year-old infantry corporal is certainly considered "over the hill" by his peers and superiors. . . . At the start of the redeployment phase, as we were about to return to KAF, a number of soldiers complained to me that they had lost from 25 to 35 pounds of muscle, and that they were worried that they would look like "scrawny old men" in front of their replacements who would look like they did at the beginning of the tour: fit, strong, "buff." Many of the returning soldiers were also marked by scars and permanent disabilities, some severe enough for them to have to leave the service. . . .

Others returned with less visible scars, with psychological wounds which made sleep difficult. Several soldiers and I commiserated with each other over the irony of not being able to sleep in the safety of one's own bed whereas we had slept soundly (albeit for only short periods at any one time) lying in the sand next to a light armoured vehicle. All the returning members of 8 Platoon had experienced far more dramatic events than most young adults experience: they had suffered bereavement, having had friends killed beside them; some of them had administered first aid to badly wounded comrades; they had been called upon to make life-or-death decisions in split seconds; and some of them had killed in the heat of battle.

Thomson and Whearty have suggested that, as men age, they tend to downsize their networks of friends and kin (2004: 4). This was evident among the returning soldiers, who tended to limit their closeness to those who had shared with them the intense experience of combat. Most of them told me that none of their friends, family members, or even other soldiers who had not served in Afghanistan would ever be able to understand what the tour was like. All of these factors combined to give the impression of old age, both physically and emotionally, yet in many ways the returning soldiers also seemed mired in a perpetual adolescence.

This perpetual adolescence was evident in the way their section commanders referred to them always as "the boys." Indeed, they constantly referred to themselves and each other as "the boys." And in many respects, they were still boys. Although on the tour they had experienced an array of dramatic and even traumatic events, many of them had never lived anywhere but with their parents or in barracks, and I was constantly surprised by their naïveté especially with respect to financial matters. Most of them had never held a mortgage or taken out a bank loan or, indeed, signed a lease. Living at home or in an institutional setting had in some ways infantilized them; being told what to wear, when to eat, and when to wash had resulted in the tendency to diminish their sense of autonomy and **agency**, and this was exacerbated by the uncertainty and unpredictability of life during the tour.

. . . [T]hese soldiers made up for the deprivations of the tour immediately on arrival in Cyprus through drinking and casual sex. During the decompression in Cyprus, no one was permitted to rent or drive any type of motor vehicle. . . . The explanation offered by commanders for this policy included the fact that Cypriots drove on the left, so adjustment to driving would be difficult, as well as the risks associated with drinking and driving. . . . There were, however, many recreational packages available in Cyprus, and among the most popular was the go-kart track with a bar. During the two evenings I spent at the track with some of the soldiers I was reminded again and again how very young they were as they drank beer and played boisterously, racing go-karts around the track and bumping into the rubber tires that formed the perimeter of the track, only days after being involved in a deadly firefight. . . .

Conclusion

. . . I have argued against the popular image of combat service as a rite of passage into manhood. I have tried to show that the traditional form of masculinity that is deemed to be the product of military **socialization** is more complex and pluralistic than the prevailing stereotypes allow. Although I agree that combat service has some of the features of a rite of passage—specifically, a tripartite structure of separation, liminality, and reintegration—I question the simplistic notion that this rite of passage . . . transforms boys into men. I have tried to demonstrate that although combat may be experienced as a transformative liminal phase, young men who go to war return not magically transformed into adult men but rather changed into old young men who are perhaps still liminal or marginal in the sense that they are neither old nor young, neither youth nor adult, but boys with some of the attributes of extreme old age. . . .

References Cited

Acker, Joan. 1990. "Hierarchies, Jobs, Bodies: A Theory of Gendered Organizations." *Gender and Society* 4 (2): 139–58.

Anonymous. 1974. "Life in the Military." In *Men and Masculinity*, edited by Joseph H. Pleck and Jack Sawyer, 127–9. Englewood Cliffs: Prentice-Hall.

Ben-Ari, Eyal. 1998. *Mastering Soldiers: Conflict, Emotions, and the Enemy in an Israeli Military Unit*. New York: Berghahn Books.

Dunivin, Karen O. 1994. "Military Change and Continuity." *Armed Forces and Society* 20 (4): 531–47.

Gill, Leslie. 1997. "Creating Citizens, Making Men: The Military and Masculinity in Bolivia." *Cultural Anthropology* 12 (4): 527–50.

Helman, S. 1997. "Militarism and the Construction of Community." *Journal of Political and Military Sociology* 25 (2): 305–32.

Hockey, John. 1986. *Squaddies: Portrait of a Subculture*. Exeter: University of Exeter Press.

Irwin, Anne. 1993. *Canadian Infantry Platoon Commanders and the Emergence of Leadership*. MA thesis, University of Calgary.

———. 2002. *The Social Organization of Soldiering: A Canadian Infantry Company in the Field*. PhD diss., Manchester University.

Kaplan, Danny. 2000. "The Military as a Second Bar Mitzvah: Combat Service as Initiation to Zionist Masculinity." In *Imagined Masculinities: Male Identity and Culture in the Modern Middle East*, edited by Mai Ghoussoub and Emma Sinclair-Webb, 127–44. London: Saqi Books.

Oldfield, Sybil. 1989. *Women against the Iron Fist: Alternatives to Militarism 1900–1989*. London: Blackwell.

Samuels, Karen. 2006. "Post-traumatic Stress Disorder as a State of Liminality." *Journal of Military and Strategic Studies* 8 (3): 1–24.

Sinclair-Webb, Emma. 2000. "'Our Bülent Is Now a Commando': Military Service and Manhood in Turkey." In *Imagined Masculinities: Male Identity and Culture in the Modern Middle East*, edited by Mai Ghoussoub and Emma Sinclair-Webb. London: Saqi Books.

Thomson, E.H., Jr, and P.M. Whearty. 2004. "Older Men's Social Participation: The Importance of Masculinity Ideology." *The Journal of Men's Studies* 13 (1): 5–24.

Turner, Victor. 1974. *Dramas, Fields, and Metaphors: Symbolic Action in Human Society*. Ithaca: Cornell University Press.

———. 1977. *The Ritual Process: Structure and Anti-Structure*. Ithaca: Cornell University Press.

van Gennep, Arnold. 1977. *The Rites of Passage*. London: Routledge Press.

Wainwright, Steven P., and Bryan S. Turner. 2004. "Narratives of Embodiment: Body, Aging, and Career in Royal Ballet Dancers." In *Cultural Bodies: Ethnography and Theory*, edited by Helen Thomas and Jamilah Ahmed. Malden, MA: Blackwell Publishing.

Winslow, Donna. 1999. "Rites of Passage and Group Bonding in the Canadian Airborne." *Armed Forces and Society*, 25 (3): 429–57.

Note

1. I use the male gender throughout the paper . . . in order to ensure anonymity for the women soldiers who were so few in number. (Irwin's note)

Key Points to Consider

- Cultures develop a number of responses to stressful situations. Rites of passage are one type of response. Diagnosis and treatment of mental disorders are another.
- Military combat service displays several of the structural features of rites of passage.
- The actual forms that masculinity takes in every culture are broader than those associated with idealized masculinity, or what the author refers to as "hegemonic masculinity." Few people would claim that combat veterans are not manly, yet many of the traits and behaviours Irwin observed contrast with idealized male characteristics.
- Many people associate the Canadian Armed Forces with United Nations Peacekeeping, but in the last decade many more Canadian soldiers have been involved in warfare than in peacekeeping.

Critical Thinking Questions

1. What traits do you associate with masculinity? With aging? Can you think of any cultural practices or products that reinforce these perceptions? How does Irwin see the combat tour as promoting or inhibiting manhood?
2. Does Irwin consider the combat tour as a rite of passage? In what ways does it fit the definition of a rite of passage? In what ways does it fail to fit this definition? Give specific examples.
3. Consider the ways that a combat tour (a trip outside "the wire") is a liminal period. What are some of the specific things that make it a distinctive time separate from ordinary military life and from time spent at Kandahar Air Field?
4. Like Irwin, Vered Amit (Chapter 18) considers life-course transitions of contemporary young Canadians. In what ways does the transition from youth to adulthood differ for military combat veterans and university students? In what ways is it similar? Explain your reasoning.
5. Why do you think that Irwin chooses to avoid mentioning post-traumatic stress disorder?

Suggestions for Further Reading and Listening

CBC (Canadian Broadcasting Corporation). 2009. *Ideas: How to Think about Science*, Episode 22, Allan Young. Toronto: CBC. Online podcast, 54 min. www.cbc.ca/radio/ideas/how-to-think-about-science-part-1-24-1.2953274#episode22.

Gardiner, Steven. 2013. "In the Shadow of Service: Veteran Masculinity and Civil-Military Disjuncture in the United States." *North American Dialogue* 16 (2): 69–79.

Irwin, Anne. 2008. "Redeployment as a Rite of Passage." Report for the Canadian Defence and Foreign Affairs Institute.

———. 2009. "Diversity in the Canadian Forces: Lessons from Afghanistan," *Commonwealth and Comparative Politics* 47 (4): 494–505.

Maloney, Sean M. 2005. "From Myth to Reality Check; From Peacekeeping to Stabilization." *Policy Options* (September): 40–6.

Chapter 8

North America

Introduction

Eating disorders are not modern diseases that, in some cases ironically, arose amidst our contemporary cultures of abundance. In actuality, some of these disorders have been known for a long time, and there is good evidence that something similar to many contemporary eating disorders existed in Europe in the Middle Ages and perhaps even earlier. In 1873, British physician William Gull published a description of a disease whose symptoms, he said, included a loss of appetite, extreme emaciation, and physical restlessness. He called the disease *anorexia nervosa*.

The diagnostic criteria have changed a bit since Gull's enumeration of anorexia's symptoms. The most recent edition of the World Health Organization's *International Classification of Diseases* (ICD-10) lists the following criteria:

1. "deliberate and sustained weight loss through purposeful dieting, excessive exercise, induced vomiting, and/or the use of diuretics and"
2. "a dread or fear of fatness (WHO 2015)".

The recent fifth edition of the American Psychiatric Association's *Diagnostic and Statistical Manual of Mental Disorders* (DSM-5), widely used in North America to diagnose mental illness, adds one other attribute of anorexia: a distorted body image that the sufferer does not recognize as thin (APA 2013).

As with most mental illnesses, the cause of anorexia is unknown. Many patients diagnosed as anorexic are girls or young women, and early psychiatric theories considered anorexia to be a primarily female disease caused by women's emotional imbalances (sometimes labelled *hysteria*), bad mothering, or sexual abuse. The idea that anorexia derives from women's unique emotional distresses persists in contemporary medical circles. For example, the well-respected Mayo Clinic's (2015) guide to diseases and conditions explains anorexia as an unhealthy way to cope with emotional problems and suggests that young women in particular "may have obsessive-compulsive personality traits" and tendencies to "equate thinness with self-worth" that may contribute to the development of this illness.

Anorexia is most commonly diagnosed in white middle-class girls and young women living in wealthy countries, leading some to label it a **culture-specific syndrome** and to look for cultural causes. Rejecting theories that blame anorexia on women's supposed emotional frailty, some feminist scholars, such as Susan Bordo (2013), have described the disease as a symptom of a patriarchal and commercial culture that idealizes thinness and focuses excessive, often negative, attention on women's bodies.

Many anthropologists feel that culture-specific syndromes are better understood as culture-specific sets of symptoms rather than as distinct illnesses that arise primarily in certain cultures. After all, illness and health are experienced differently among different cultural groups, to the extent that the same underlying medical condition might be expressed through different symptoms among disparate peoples. This fact helps remind us that health and illness derive from interactions of biological, environmental, cultural, and social factors. As well, it helps us avoid mind–body dualisms. Finally, it reminds us that we should examine health and illness in the social contexts in which they occur in order find effective treatments. With respect to anorexia, it may be that white middle-class girls in wealthy countries are more likely to be diagnosed with anorexia because we expect this to be the case. Some recent anthropological work has shown that anorexia affects males and females, wealthy and poor, of many different countries and cultures.

Anorexia is a serious illness, diagnosed in just less than 1 in 100 North American girls and women and in approximately 1 in 300 North American men and boys. Significantly, it is the mental disorder most likely to lead to the sufferer's death. The high mortality rate—between 5 and 20 per cent, according to Statistics Canada (Langlois et al. 2011)—is a reflection of the fact that the existing treatments are often ineffective.

In the article below, Richard O'Connor and Penny Van Esterik argue that the absence of effective treatment for anorexia comes from the mistaken belief, shared among physicians and feminist cultural critics, that anorexics fear fatness. The authors single out for special criticism what they identify as a **Cartesian dualism** among medical practitioners. Based on the writings of French philosopher René Descartes (1596–1650), *Cartesian dualism* refers to a separation of phenomena into two distinct and independent entities such mind and body, physical and mental, or individual and society. The authors, like the feminist critics, regard culture as the source of the beliefs and practices of anorexics that contribute to their illness.

One of the great strengths of the article below is the way the authors show the value of **ethnography** for understanding the world of individuals with a particular mental disorder. By listening closely to the ways that anorexics explain their actions, the authors develop an interpretation of the aetiology or cause of the disease that is very different from that developed by either physicians or feminist critics. The Canadian and American former anorexics that O'Connor and Van Esterik studied did not have a "fat phobia" or even misrecognize the thinness of their bodies. Nor were the young people "atypical" of anorexics, as a strict application of the diagnostic tools would suggest. In becoming anorexic, the **informants** drew on **hegemonic** cultural values of North Americans—not the value of feminine beauty, but rather the valorization of athleticism, self-discipline, and **asceticism**.

Ascetics are individuals who give up or restrict physical pleasures such as alcohol, sex, or rich foods in order to achieve spiritual or moral benefit. Ascetics and others who endure great pain are lauded as heroes in our literature and popular culture. Furthermore, many of the religions practised in North America encourage at least temporary asceticism in the form of fast days, avoidance of alcohol, and sexual abstinence. The ethnography reported here reveals that many anorexics draw on these cultural **tropes**, but they take them to extremes. O'Connor and Van Esterik argue that effective medical treatment for anorexia must recognize the cultural forces at work. The authors believe that anthropological forms of analysis can point the way to effective treatments for anorexia and other disorders by identifying and translating the cultural factors that cause or compound biological processes.

❖ About the Authors ❖

Richard O'Connor studied anthropology at the College of William and Mary and at Cornell University, and he now teaches at Sewanee: The University of the South in Tennessee. His long-term ethnographic research has concerned the intersection of politics, economy, and environment in Southeast Asia, especially Thailand. Recently, he and co-author Penny Van Esterik have been collaborating on two health and nutrition projects, one on anorexia and one on breastfeeding. His interest in anorexia stems, in part, from the personal experiences of his daughter who was anorexic during part of her teen years.

Penny Van Esterik was born and raised in Toronto. She earned her BA at the University of Toronto and her PhD at the University of Illinois. She recently retired from her position as a professor of anthropology at York University, where she had taught since 1984. Like O'Connor, she has conducted much of her research in Thailand. A medical and sociocultural anthropologist, Van Esterik has written extensively on the relationships between economic development, nutrition, gender, and food policy.

De-medicalizing Anorexia: A New Cultural Brokering

Richard A. O'Connor and Penny Van Esterik

Anorexia mystified Becca:

> To this day, I really don't know why, all of a sudden, I decided to have these weird eating patterns and not eat at all. Exercise so much. I think that I was just a perfectionist, just wanting to make my body even more perfect. But the thing is, a skeleton as a body really isn't perfect. So I don't know exactly what my train of thinking was.

The usual explanations didn't work: she had no weight to lose ("people would always tell me how skinny I was"), no festering trauma, no troubled psyche. On the contrary, an upbeat person ("I'm very energetic and very bubbly"), she got along well at home ("I have really loving and supportive parents") and school. A top athlete who made excellent grades and had good friends, life was going well when anorexia suddenly came out of nowhere. Neither Becca nor her therapists could explain how it all happened. Becca's story isn't exceptional. Although a clinician would rightly diagnose "atypical anorexia nervosa," her type-denying case is anything but atypical. Through in-depth interviews with 22 recovered anorexics (20 female, 2 male) in Tennessee and Toronto, we repeatedly heard type-denying cases. So did Garrett (1998) who, in interviewing 34 Australian anorexics, found vanity did not explain the disease, and Warin (2005), whose 46 anorexic subjects at three sites (Australia, Scotland, Canada) repeatedly told her "anorexia was not solely concerned with food and weight." Clinicians in Asia report similar findings (Khandelwal, Sharan, and Saxena 1995; Lee, Ho, and Hsu 1993), as do those in the US (Katzman and Lee 1997; Palmer 1993), who find many patients neither fear fat nor crave thinness as a "typical" anorexic should. Indeed, what the public and many professionals have come to expect—women dieting madly for

appearance—does not adequately explain cases on either side of the globe.

Instead of adolescent girls literally dying for looks, we found youthful ascetics—male as well as female—obsessing over virtue, not beauty. Their restricted food intake was never just instrumental (the means to weight loss) but always also expressive or adventurous or even accidental. Most had an experience of transcendence or grace, echoing the "distorted form of spirituality" that Garrett (1998: 110) found in Australia. That said, today's pathology is neither specifically religious, as anorexia once was (Bynum 1987), nor the performance of tradition, as monastic asceticism still is (Flood 2004). Indeed, precisely because our interviewees' self-imposed asceticism developed outside established religious institutions, it had no community or tradition to regulate it, to reign in excess. Initially exhilarating, their virtuous eating and exercising eventually became addictive. That, anyway, was what our interviewees described—the anorexic's anorexia.

Shockingly, that isn't the disease that many institutions are treating. Although most professionals know it's not as simple as a desperate striving for beauty, research has yet to capture the complexity that practitioners actually face. Take distorted body image: this is still an official diagnostic criterion, but that cliché had collapsed under contradictory evidence by the early 1990s (Hsu and Sobkiewicz 1991). Categorizing anorexia as an *eating* disorder is also problematic: many cases might more readily be called *exercise* disorders, and every case is an ascetic disorder. The pressures and challenges of adolescence have similarly been ignored, as has the unsettled issue of **gender**: while most sociocultural explanations treat anorexia as a women's disease (e.g., Bordo 1997), men make up from one-fifth (full syndrome) to one-third (full or partial syndrome) of sufferers (Woodside et al. 2001). Over the years the putative cause has changed—from hysteria or pituitary dysfunction a century ago to malignant mothering or sexual abuse today—but the one constant is the way in which these explanations look *through* rather than *at* the anorexic as a whole person. The discourse on anorexia thereby detaches from that anorexic's experience and values. No wonder treatment programs are so unsuccessful (Agras et al. 2004; Ben-Tovim et al. 2001)!

Medicalizing—and Mystifying—Anorexia

How has health care moved so far away from the anorexic's anorexia? The larger intellectual answer is Cartesian dualism: in dividing mind from body and individual from society, modern thought fights any realistic social and cultural understanding of disease. The more immediate institutional answer is **medicalization**: over two centuries, by isolating the sick and sickness from their surroundings, biomedicine has complicated diseases like anorexia and obscured their causes. An emerging literature shows how treatment programs can exercise a **Foucauldian** power over anorexics (Eckermann 1997), replicate conditions that support and possibly cause the disease (Gremillion 2003, Warin 2005), and, by labelling the person an anorexic, inspire efforts to live up to that diagnosis (Warin 2005, 2006). Our interviewees supported these findings, testifying to how treatment sometimes aggravated their affliction and inspired resistance. While medicalization can save lives, in this regard its hegemony hurts patients.

Our findings stress how medicalization detracts from research, by obscuring the causes of anorexia. We set out to contextualize anorexia, only to end up de-medicalizing the syndrome. When we look at the mind/body split, for example, we find that in imposing this arbitrary Cartesian distinction, medicalization makes anorexia into a mental illness—the mind's war on the body. That sounds reasonable—and if we ignore the "mindful body" (Scheper-Hughes and Lock 1987) and neuroscience, it might be—but how and why this happens becomes a total mystery. Yet all we had to do was erase this Cartesian division to see how an intense mind-with-body activity (restrictive eating and rigorous exercise) bootstrapped anorexics into anorexia much as boot camp makes civilians into soldiers. And if we examine the individual/society distinction, we see that in isolating anorexics as abnormal, medicalization takes them out of the environment that gives them social and moral reasons to restrict. Suddenly their actions look completely senseless, inviting arbitrary psychological and biological guesswork. Yet all we had to do was put the person back in context for the obvious evidence to suggest that anorexics were misguided moralists, not cognitive cripples. Warin (2003) makes a similar point: seen in context, anorexics are following cultural rules for hygiene, not obsessing randomly or venting secret traumas. Again and again, contextualizing anorexia challenges the way medicalization constructs the condition by isolating it.

One disease, two approaches: who has it right? We don't deny that anorexics need medical attention—indeed, it's the most directly deadly mental illness—but medicalizing anorexics and pathologizing their asceticism and other cultural practices have a miserable record of repeated failure. Today, over 130 years after physicians first isolated self-starvation as a disease, biomedicine can neither adequately explain nor reliably cure, nor even rigorously define anorexia (Agras et al. 2004). As medicine's isolating has failed so spectacularly, perhaps anthropology's contextualizing can do better?

Contextualizing Anorexia

What is striking about reconnecting anorexia to its context is just how much the obvious evidence can explain. Once our interviews had given us life-course and life-world details, anorexia was anything but exotic. Its extraordinary asceticism had ordinary roots: schooling, sports, work, and healthy eating all taught self-denial that these overachievers took to heart. Anorexics simply exaggerated—and eventually incarnated—the deferred gratification that is so widely preached to the young. Anorexia, then, did not come out of the blue. It came out of perfectly obvious surrounding values and local bodily practices.

In Becca's case, for example, although anorexia is unexpected for her, it develops out of obvious life-course patterns that she readily describes. In her words, "I'm a real big perfectionist." In growing up,

> I kind of had this image of Becca. When people referred to me it was because of something that had been done quite well. That's what perfection came to. I wanted every little thing about me to just—I guess—be an example. That people would look at me and, like, "Wow, there goes Becca! Oh, that's the perfect child!"

What Becca describes is a virtuous identity, not a mental pathology. What goes wrong is that she applies this to eating. Her diet thereby takes on a moral character where fat is evil and she chooses good relentlessly.

> In third grade I almost had an eating disorder. For some reason I just got scared of fat. I would look at nutrition panels and I would observe the fat, what it said, and I really got scared of fat. I would only eat Kellogg's cereal. Mom was like, "I just cooked dinner and you're eating Kellogg's cereal!" "I like Kellogg's!" My mom got to the point where like, "Rebecca, if you don't stop eating just Kellogg's corn flakes I'm going to take you to see a doctor." And that scared me. I didn't want anyone to think that there was something the matter with me. So how my mom and I approached the problem was we started going to this health food grocery store called Whole Foods. They have a lot of organic products. We would go every Sunday. It was quite a distance. I would get really upset when we didn't get food from Whole Foods.

Was Becca idealizing supermodels? No—and neither was Jim. He reports the same third-grade aversion to fat ("I remember I stopped drinking whole milk and eating red meat in third grade. . . . That was back when the big health trend was fat. We didn't eat anything fat. No fat at all. Never. None."). Only much later, as a high-school runner, did this health-obsessed athlete train himself into anorexia.

Anorexia's Cultural Connection

Becca's restricted eating copies her mother directly ("I look up to my mom a lot and my mom eats really small portions because she gets full easily"), whereas Jim's regimen develops mutually with his mother ("we pushed each other into having these athletic, healthy lifestyles"). That familial link was typical: nearly three-quarters of our interviewees (16 of 22) grew up valuing healthy eating and living. Then, as anorexics, all obsessively exaggerated the restrictions inherent in healthy eating. And now, in recovery, all of them watch what they eat, a reasonable yet distant echo of their earlier obsession.

Are these fringe attitudes, the delusions of a few health fanatics? On the contrary, our informants echo how contemporary culture moralizes eating. Witness the popular prejudice whereby fat people, seen as "letting themselves go," are stigmatized as weak or even bad, while slim people, perceived as strict with themselves, exemplify strength and goodness. Or consider how people readily judge their own eating, speaking of "sinning" with dessert, "being good" with veggies, or "confessing" a late-night binge. What is at stake here is virtue, not beauty. Over the last century or so, as the body has increasingly become a moral arena, eating and exercise have come to test our moral fibre (Brumberg 1997, Stearns 1999).

Anything but marginal, this discourse of individual responsibility is heavily promoted by health agencies and widely accepted by the public. It urges the good person to eat sparely and nutritiously, exercise regularly, avoid all health risks, and—as a matter of self-respect—keep a slim and attractive body. True, few people live up to this demanding discipline, but fewer still contest that it is "right," the proper way to live. So it's a bit like a Sunday sermon where the lifestyle urgings are scientific rather than religious—or are they? The discourse of healthy eating cherry-picks science. A more realistic perspective would recognize that health is broadly social, not narrowly individual, and that the "domain of personal health over which the individual has direct control is *very* small when compared to heredity, culture, environment, and chance," in the words of Marshall Becker (1986: 20), dean of a public-health school. Becker goes on to characterize today's faith in healthy living as "a new religion, in which we worship ourselves, attribute good health to our devoutness, and view illness as just punishment for those who have not yet seen the Way" (ibid.: 21). Well, it is religious—evangelical even—but it's not very new. Early nineteenth-century health and fitness movements developed this moralizing discourse (Green 1988), but it was not until the turn of the twentieth century that it became mainstream (Stearns 1999).

What draws people into this discourse? Our interviewees gave us two answers: a bodily predisposition and identity politics. Here's Becca on identity:

> My best friend's family—whenever I would come to their lake house or something—they would always, "Goodness gracious, we gotta have fruit for this child! We have to have carrots. Here we have all the other little girls that are having cookies and this kid's eating carrots and fruits and healthy peanut butter snacks."

Becca restricts her food intake and, against the background of today's cultural concerns, others notice. Their feedback makes this a point of pride, an arena for further achievement. This isn't exceptional. Most of our informants described how a slim body, strict eating, rigorous exercise, or even being anorexic became an identity that they began to value and build into their youthful sense of self. Here age matters: our informants all developed anorexia during adolescence, a transitional time that intensifies the need to find and express one's identity.

The Anorexic's Constitution

A further factor explaining anorexia appeared when we looked at our informants historically rather than just situationally. Here, in shifting from a life-world to a life-course context, we found a biocultural "flywheel" carried them into anorexia. To make sense of this evidence, we had to revive the old-fashioned and

decidedly non-Cartesian idea that each person has a distinctive constitution. Our update is biocultural.

Anorexics are not culturally but bioculturally constructed. To starve oneself draws on capacities and inclinations that develop only over years. From conception to adolescence, each person's initially wide possibilities progressively narrow as the organism grows and adapts to a particular environment. Day by day, the interaction[s] of biology, culture, and chance fix points that shape later interactions, and bit by bit the guiding force of this biocultural hybrid—a constitution—grows. Our informants had developed constitutions as children that later predisposed them to anorexia as adolescents. Three dispositions stood out:

- *A performative disposition*: Although most children perform for the admiration of parents and teachers, our informants had long built their sense of who they were, and how they thought, felt, and acted, around sustained superior performance. All had records of high achievement and roughly a third called themselves perfectionists. Almost all excelled academically; four-fifths grew up not just with but through dance, athletics, or both, and out of that subset, over half were so good that they competed regionally or nationally.

- *An ascetic disposition*: As determined achievers, our interviewees had mastered deferred gratification long before they took up restrictive eating in adolescence. Some developed self-denial as a bodily mode through sports. Molly, for example, says: "Athletics actually taught me self-discipline. So I knew how to push myself and I knew how to be mentally tough. I learned you can always push yourself further. What you think you can do, you can do more." That attitude got her into anorexia as well as state tournaments.

- *A virtuous disposition*: A major figure in the study of anorexia, Hilde Bruch characterized her anorexic patients as "outstandingly good and quiet children, obedient, clean, eager to please, helpful at home, precociously dependable, and excelling in school work" (1962: 192). That fit how our interviewees saw themselves. Although we had no way to confirm that they were as good as they said, a virtuous disposition is the single most consistent explanation for their remarkable success as children, students, and athletes.

Were someone to take up dieting, healthy eating, or training for any reason, these dispositions would intensify their practice. In this sense our informants were primed for anorexia. All of this was quite obvious once we looked at life-course.

Reviving Empiricism

None of what we have attributed to constitution, identity, and ideas about healthy living is guesswork. It's what our informants reported, each speaking independently. With remarkable consistency they describe paths into anorexia that are obvious and rather ordinary—at least until the last step. That final exceptional step—becoming anorexic—is mysterious. None of our informants could say how or even when it happened. So perhaps here, as the change comes invisibly, clinical inference might reasonably replace everyday evidence. And yet, when we pieced together what our informants said separately, we discovered that even the final move into anorexia had left empirical tracks. We found eight recurring features that, taken together, suggested how intense restriction of food intake and exercising integrated into a self-sustaining system. . . .

Empiricism has answers that medicalization dismisses. Instead of making the most of what is obvious, specialists assume anorexia has an underlying pathology, that the cause is deeper than what the surface suggests. And that might eventually prove to be the case—we certainly can't rule out what is yet to be discovered—but for now it is more helpful to reason with the obvious rather than guessing at the obscure. That is better science: by the law of Occam's razor (the principle of parsimony), simple and direct explanations should take precedence over the complex inferences that now "explain" anorexia. It is also better medicine: addressing the obvious—by showing anorexia's everyday dimensions—would allow anorexics to participate in their own recovery, quite unlike some treatment programs where specialists take control (cf. Gremillion 2003).

A New Cultural Brokering

Anorexia falls into a culturally constructed black hole. Here medicalization is less about establishing hegemony than coping with anomaly. Certainly clinicians are not silencing patients—the anorexic has no story to tell. As Becca says, what happens makes no sense. That would explain why British schoolgirl anorexics make "'chaotic,' 'regressive,' and 'rebellious'" statements, refusing to "package their illness narratives" in an appropriate story (Rich, Holroyd, and Evans 2004: 185–6). Their "chaos narrative" (Frank 1995: 97) is no story at all. How do you explain what your culture hides or imagines wrongly? That puts anorexics, their families, and caregivers all in the same boat, lost in culturally uncharted waters.

Applying anthropology can help. Although medical anthropologists often act as cultural brokers (Helman 2006), it is usually *between* cultures, translating Western medicine and non-Western patients for each other. But the brokering we propose, in translating a biocultural disease for today's biology-or-culture thinking, is *within* our own culture. Here the real challenge is not explaining this particular eating disorder, but establishing how sickness and health are social, and not just individual, matters. Like it or not, we fall ill and recover as social and moral beings, not solitary bodies. Anorexics, in living a truth that Cartesian dualism denies, become patients that modern medicine doesn't know how to cure.

Can cultural brokering suggest cures? Crossing cultures and healing illness take different skills. Although some exceptional individuals do both in fields like cultural psychiatry (Kleinman 1987), cultural brokering can serve medicine precisely because it comes from outside the rigorous standards, narrow focus, and quick decisions that most health care rightly requires. Here, taking the role of outsider, the anthropologist can broker an appreciation of context, diversity, and holism that few health-care professionals have the time, training, or detachment to provide for themselves. At least for anorexia, that is desperately needed. Now that medicalization has lost the anorexic's anorexia, even the brightest anorexics and best clinicians labour under a handicap that cultural brokering could relieve.

References Cited

Agras, W. Stewart, et al. 2004. "Report of the National Institutes of Health Workshop on Overcoming Barriers to Treatment Research in Anorexia Nervosa." *International Journal of Eating Disorders* 35: 509–21.

Becker, Marshall H. 1986. "The Tyranny of Health Promotion." *Public Health Review* 14: 15–25.

Ben-Tovim, D.I., K. Walker, P. Gilchrist, R. Freeman, R. Kalucy, and A. Esterman. (2001) "Outcome in Patients with Eating Disorders: A Five-Year Study." *The Lancet* 357: 1254–7.

Bordo, Susan. 1997. "Anorexia Nervosa: Psychopathology as the Crystallization of Culture." In *Food and Culture, A Reader*, edited by Carole Counihan and Penny Van Esterik, 226–50. New York: Routledge.

Bruch, Hilde. 1962. "Perceptual and Conceptual Disturbances in Anorexia Nervosa." *Psychosomatic Medicine* 24 (2): 187–94.

Brumberg, Joan Jacobs. 1997. *The Body Project: An Intimate History of American Girls*. New York: Random House.

Bynum, Caroline Walker. 1987. *Holy Feast and Holy Fast: The Religious Significance of Food to Medieval Women*. Berkeley: University of California Press.

Eckermann, Liz. 1997. "Foucault, Embodiment, and gendered subjectivities: The Case of Voluntary Self-Starvation." In *Foucault, Health, and Medicine*, edited by A. Petersen and R. Bunton, 151–70. London: Routledge.

Flood, Gavin. 2004. *The Ascetic Self: Subjectivity, Memory, and Tradition*. Cambridge: Cambridge University Press.

Frank, Arthur W. 1995. *The Wounded Storyteller: Body, Illness, and Ethics*. Chicago: University of Chicago Press.

Garrett, Catherine. 1998. *Beyond Anorexia: Narrative, Spirituality, and Recovery*. Cambridge: Cambridge University Press.

Green, Harvey. 1988. *Fit for America: Health, Fitness, Sport, and American Society*. Baltimore: Johns Hopkins University Press.

Gremillion, Helen. 2003. *Feeding Anorexia: Gender and Power at a Treatment Center*. Durham: Duke University Press.

Helman, Cecil. 2006. "Why Medical Anthropology Matters." *Anthropology Today* 22 (1): 3–4.

Hsu, L.K. George, and Theresa A. Sobkiewicz. 1991. "Body Image Disturbance: Time to Abandon the Concept for Eating Disorders?" *International Journal of Eating Disorders* 10: 15–30.

Katzman, Melanie A., and Sing Lee. 1997. "Beyond Body Image: The Integration of Feminist and Transcultural Theories in the Understanding of Self-Starvation." *International Journal of Eating Disorders* 22: 385–94.

Khandelwal, Sudhir Kumar, Pratap Sharan, and S. Saxena. 1995. "Eating Disorders: An Indian Perspective." *International Journal of Social Psychiatry* 41 (2): 132–46.

Kleinman, Arthur. 1987. "Anthropology and Psychiatry: The Role of Culture in Cross-cultural Research on Illness." *British Journal of Psychiatry* 151: 447–54.

Lee, Sing, T.P. Ho, and L.K. George Hsu. 1993. "Fat Phobic and Non–Fat Phobic Anorexia Nervosa: A Comparative Study of 70 Chinese Patients in Hong Kong." *Psychological Medicine* 23: 999–1017.

Palmer, R.L. 1993. "Weight Concern Should Not Be a Necessary Criterion for Eating Disorders: A Polemic." *International Journal of Eating Disorders* 14: 459–65.

Rich, Emma, Rachel Holroyd, and John Evans. 2004. "Hungry to Be Noticed: Young Women, Anorexia, and Schooling." In *Body Knowledge and Control: Studies in the Sociology of Physical Education and Health*, edited by John Evans, Brian Davies, and Jan Wright, 173–90. London: Routledge.

Scheper-Hughes, Nancy, and Margaret M. Lock. 1987. "The Mindful Body: A Prolegomenon to Future Work in Medical Anthropology." *Medical Anthropology Quarterly* 1: 6–41.

Stearns, Peter N. 1999. *Battleground of Desire: The Struggle for Self-Control in Modern America*. New York: New York University Press.

Warin, Megan J. 2003. "Becoming Clean: The Logic of Hygiene in Anorexia." *Sites: Journal of Social Anthropology and Cultural Studies*, n.s., 1 (1): 109–32.

———. 2005. "Transformations of Intimacy and Sociality in Anorexia: Bedrooms in Public Institutions." *Body and Society* 11 (3): 97–113.

———. 2006. "Reconfiguring Relatedness in Anorexia." *Anthropology and Medicine* 13 (1): 41–54.

Woodside, D. Blake, Paul E. Garfinkel, Elizabeth Lin, Paula Goering, Allan S. Kaplan, David S. Goldbloom, and Sidney H. Kennedy. 2001. "Comparisons of Men with Full or Partial Eating Disorders, Men without Eating Disorders, and Women with Eating Disorders in the Community." *American Journal of Psychiatry* 158 (4): 570–4.

Key Points to Consider

- Anorexia and other eating disorders are often associated with white middle-class girls and young women in contemporary wealthy countries. However, anorexia is not a new disease; nor is it experienced only by relatively affluent females. Anorexia is extremely difficult to treat and leads to death more commonly than does any other mental illness.
- Existing treatments rely on assumptions that anorexics have a fat phobia and misrecognize the thinness of their bodies. These assumptions are not borne out by ethnographic research, which instead suggests that many anorexics restrict their food intake as a form of self-discipline.
- Cultural beliefs affect the ways that health and illness are understood in all cultures. It is a mistake to assume that diseases have purely biological causes. By paying attention to cultural beliefs, anthropologists can often help find effective treatments. O'Connor and Van Esterik refer to this work as "cultural brokering."

Critical Thinking Questions

1. What do O'Connor and Van Esterik mean when they refer to the body as a "moral arena"? Do you agree with this characterization of the human body? What sorts of bodily practices support your position?
2. Do O'Connor and Van Esterik regard anorexia as a mental illness? A problem of cultural distortion or misinterpretation? A social effect of consumer culture? What evidence supports your response?
3. Some athletes ingest steroids and other potentially dangerous substances in order to improve their athletic performance. Similarly, some students use Adderall or other restricted stimulants without medical supervision to improve their academic performance. Do you think that using "performance enhancing drugs" is analogous to anorexia? Why or why not?

Suggestions for Further Reading

Bordo, Susan. 2013. "Not Just 'a White Girl's Thing': The Change Face of Food and Body Image Problems." In *Food and Culture: A Reader*, 3rd ed., edited by Carole Counihan and Penny Van Esterik, 265–75. New York: Routledge.

Gooldin, Sigal. 2008. "Being Anorexic: Hunger, Subjectivity, and Embodied Morality." *Medical Anthropology Quarterly* 22 (3): 274–96.

Lindford-Steinfeld, Joshua. 2003. "Weight Control and Physical Readiness among Naval Personnel." In *Anthropology and the United States Military*, edited by Pamela R Frese and Margaret C. Harrell, 95–112. Gordonsville, VA: Palgrave McMillan.

Van Esterik, Penny. 1989. *Beyond the Breast–Bottle Controversy*. New Brunswick, NJ: Rutgers University Press.

———. 2008. *Food Culture in Southeast Asia*. Westport, CT: Greenwood Press.

Chapter 9

Ontario

Introduction

The accelerated movement of money, corporations, consumer goods, media, technologies, and ideas across international borders has characterized the current era of **globalization**. There have been accelerated flows of people between countries as well, but with less ease than with other types of flows. Importantly, transnational movements of people require different public policy responses than do the transnational movements of capital, media, or consumer goods. For example, governments must determine which people to admit, under what circumstances, and for how long, and whether and how to incorporate newcomers as citizens.

Historically and until the 1960s, Canada had a **race**-based immigration policy that favoured immigrants of European heritage and actively excluded would-be Canadians from Asia. This changed in 1967 with the introduction of a "points system" that scored aspiring immigrants on attributes such as educational attainment, work experience, age, and the ability to speak French and/or English. While the introduction of the points system is not the only factor that has contributed to changes in Canadian immigration trends, the ethnic composition of Canada's immigrant population has clearly shifted over the past half century. In 1966, just before the implementation of the points system, the top seven sending countries were the United Kingdom, Italy, the United States, Germany, Portugal, France, and Greece (Department of Manpower and Immigration 1966). In contrast, in 2012, the top seven sending countries were China, the Philippines, India, Pakistan, the United States, France, and Iran. As well, the foreign-born portion of the Canadian population has grown somewhat, from around 15 per cent in the 1960s to approximately 20 per cent today. In the largest metropolitan areas, though, the percentage of the population composed of immigrants is as high as 40 per cent (Citizenship and Immigration Canada 2013).

Canada is widely regarded as a country that is welcoming to immigrants and that does a good job integrating immigrants as citizens. Social scientists regard citizenship as not only the formal legal membership status accorded to a person by the laws of a **state**, but also a social position that comes with substantive rights and obligations associated with fitting in. Thus, **substantive citizenship** involves a sense of belonging achieved through being able to participate economically, socially, and culturally on the same basis as others in the society. It is possible to feel a sense of belonging without being a **legal citizen**, and in some cases legal citizens find it difficult to exercise substantive citizenship rights.

Beginning in the late 1990s and continuing to the present, people who study immigration have observed that as a group, recent immigrants have not fared as well economically as earlier cohorts of newcomers to Canada. Particularly troubling is evidence that recent immigrants, especially those from places other than Europe and the United States, have substantially lower earnings and much higher levels of unemployment than do Canadian-born citizens with similar levels of education and work experience. Despite having been admitted to Canada based on their employment profiles, many skilled immigrants end up taking "survival jobs" that do not require advanced education. Because of their economic insecurity, some recent immigrants have found it difficult to fully integrate and enjoy the benefits (substantive citizenship) of living in Canada. The various explanations offered for this situation include **racism** on the part of employers, non-recognition of foreign credentials and experience, and immigrants' unfamiliarity with Canadian workplace culture and norms. The phenomenon is probably not attributable to any single cause, and sociologists Gillian Creese and Brandy Wiebe (2009) have found that in addition to the barriers just listed, immigrant services agencies push immigrants into low-skilled, low-paid jobs because the agencies are under pressure to show that they are helping their clients find work.

The article by Lalaie Ameeriar presented below examines the situation of highly educated Pakistani women living in Toronto as they attempt to establish their substantive citizenship as Canadians. Many of the women have had trouble finding professional employment commensurate with the work they did before immigrating. Just as translations from one language to another are always imperfect, translations from one cultural context to another are also imperfect. Ameeriar contrasts the ways that the Pakistani and other South Asian women and their cultures are received in two different contexts: employment support provided by immigrant settlement agencies and cultural festivals. Referencing an insight by anthropologist Mary Douglas (1921–2007), Ameeriar notes that the aspects of South Asian cultures most often celebrated at government-funded cultural festivals—food and clothing—are the aspects of South Asian identity that women are told to erase in their search for professional employment. In her classic work *Purity and Danger* (1966), Douglas defined "dirt" as "matter out of place." For the women Ameeriar studied, food smells and ethnic clothing were exotic and interesting in the anonymous and impersonal setting of a cultural festival, but these cultural indicators were taken to be out of place, offensive, and potentially frightening when associated with individual job seekers. In employment contexts, the immigrant women are pushed to become invisible by "sanitizing" the work environment of their scents and sights. The title of the article, "The Sanitized Sensorium," refers to this demand. A sensorium is the portions of the brain that receive and process sights, sounds, smells, and other sensory inputs. Ameeriar also employs the phrase "radical alterity" to describe the way the women are received by potential employers—meaning that their cultural differences from "ordinary Canadians" are regarded as too enormous to be bridged (see Mackey 2002).

The challenges of immigrant integration—for both immigrants and the state—are not new. As Ameeriar observes, however, Canada's practices of immigrant integration changed as Canada shifted away from post–World War II **Keynesianism** in the 1980s. Keynesianism, named for British economist John Maynard Keynes (1883–1946), aimed to prevent wild economic swings while also reducing economic inequality. In ideal situations, national governments managed monetary and fiscal policy in order to stabilize the environment for business. In return, businesses paid workers wages sufficient to support a family and contributed to other benefits such as pensions and unemployment and health insurance, and they submitted to controls like workplace safety monitoring, all of which enhanced the physical and economic security of workers and their families. Governments used tax revenues to provide other social benefits like public education, public health programs, old age pensions, and social security. The safety net programs were universally available, but they were administered in a one-size-fits-all way that aimed at assimilating immigrants and ethnic minorities to Euro-Canadian (often Anglo-British) norms.

Keynesianism gave way to **neoliberal** forms of governance for a number of reasons (Harvey 2005). One of the effects of neoliberalism in Canada has been the transfer of many social programs—such as immigrant integration—from government to non-profit organizations like the settlement agencies described in the article. The laudable goal of greater cultural sensitivity, unfortunately, also reinforces distinctions among groups and encourages competition between them. Immigrants, like the ones described by Ameeriar, must navigate the simultaneous calls to both assert and erase their difference.

⁂ *About the Author* ⁂

Lalaie Ameeriar earned her BA in anthropology at the University of Toronto and her PhD in anthro-pology at Stanford University. She now teaches in the Department of Asian American Studies at the University of California, Santa Barbara. The article presented here discusses part of her dissertation research, in which she examined the experiences of professional women who had immigrated to Canada from Pakistan and were living in Toronto. This research also looked at the government policies and programs that contributed to the ways these women made their lives in Canada. Her current work concerns racial profiling of women at the Canada–US border.

The Sanitized Sensorium

Lalaie Ameeriar

"Don't show up smelling like foods that are foreign to us." This was the core curriculum (and moral imperative) delivered to a room full of Pakistani, Indian, and Bangladeshi women seeking work in the Greater Toronto Area. As the 15 participants in this government-funded workshop stared back at their instructor, I wondered what these women were supposed to be learning. Each had sat for hours in the back of a local government-funded immigration office—a tired, windowless room set aside to support immigrant integration. The lesson plan the instructor delivered seemed surprisingly off key for a workshop intended for foreign-trained professionals—women with advanced levels of education and undeniably valuable skill sets. Smelly bodies? Really? . . . And yet, during this **pedagogical** effort at facilitating immigrant women's entrance into the workforce, each participant had been subjected to intimate instructions: "make sure your clothes are clean," "don't wear the shalwar cameeze,"[1] and "don't wear headscarves." It was a barrage of regulatory proscriptions aimed at the immigrant body.

Political leaders and citizens alike in the United States, Britain, France, Germany, and Canada (to name a few) are currently undergoing struggles to understand the place of minority culture within the politics of **multiculturalism**, identity, and difference. In 2009 French president Nicholas Sarkozy declared that the Islamic burqa is "not welcome," while in October 2010, German chancellor Angela Merkel said that the attempt to build a multicultural society in Germany "has utterly failed." In contrast, Canada has long been hailed as the premier success story of multicultural inclusion. . . . In Toronto, the urban centre of Canada, half the population is foreign born (45.7 per cent), and it is thus an important site for understanding the daily practice and the intimate spaces in which multicultural **ideologies** are negotiated. The contemporary Canadian experience can be a representative moment from which to understand the politics of multicultural states.

I conducted **ethnographic** research over 24 months in Lahore and Karachi, Pakistan, and Toronto, Canada, between 2001 and 2010 on the politics and practice of multiculturalism in Toronto. I found two contradictory strains of multicultural practice in Canada: on the one hand, the denial of "difference" with regard to immigrant bodies, on the other, the simultaneous recognition of that very difference. Contemporary **discourse** in Canada on multiculturalism . . . describes a relinquishing of cultural imperialism and a celebration of "mult-iness" as demonstrated by cultural festivals or other public celebrations, yet I found an imposition of a dominant culture through government-funded settlement services that institute new ideals of bodily comportment on immigrants by teaching them how to dress and act. This dual mode of **interpellation** puts immigrants in an impossible situation in which they must sometimes suitably display their

Otherness and at other times [hide] their cultural difference.

To analyze this dual mode of interpellation, I develop the concept of "the sanitized sensorium" as a means to understand forms of **embodiment**, such as smell, appearance, and bodily comportment, presumed necessary for inclusion in the public sphere of multicultural Toronto. The daily practices in agencies such as the one described above serve to construct a sanitized body, and the senses become a crucial means by which the sanitized body is created. As I will demonstrate, the practice of multiculturalism as it pertains to the integration of foreign labour is ultimately not about getting employers not to discriminate. Rather, it is about making yourself into someone who will not be discriminated against. . . .

. . . The role of smell in excluding immigrant bodies has been well examined (e.g., Manalansan 2006; Ong 2003; Walcott 2003), focusing on the smells of cooking both being a tie to one's heritage but also a means of exclusion. Food smells become signifiers of difference and . . . ultimately become representative of immigrant communities' inability to assimilate. . . . What I seek to contribute . . . is an examination of the ways such sensorial phenomena are managed by the . . . state as an important part of the process of "immigrant integration."[2] . . . The job market and the cultural festival are two different [sites] in which the smell of food on the body is understood in two diametrically opposing ways. While on the job market, the smell of South Asian food on the body suggests that these foreign women cook foreign food at home, however during cultural festivals, the smell of generic South Asian food reminds Canadian consumers of exotic lands where exotic foods originate. . . . Between these differen[t] contexts, the smell of citizenship changes. . . .

Multiculturalism in Canada

. . . The federal policy of multiculturalism was implemented in Canada in 1971, accompanying the introduction of the points system.[3] Multicultural policy broadened the definition of Canadian citizenship at the policy level: federal institutions and agencies were encouraged to promote "the development of a Canadian identity, the reinforcement of Canadian unity, and the improvement of citizenship participation" (Department of Canadian Heritage 2007). . . . [M]ulticultural policy in Canada certainly at the federal level has always ultimately been an integration-based "population management tool." . . . However, in the context of public debate in Canada, multiculturalism refers not only to the policy of the federal government but also to the lived experience of ethnic diversity and the philosophical ideal of cultural and ethnic pluralism (Kallen 1982).

Since its implementation as federal policy, multiculturalism has been subject to critique. Its early supporters, and canonical writers in the field, Charles Taylor (1994) and Will Kymlicka (1995), wrote within the context of Canada and described multiculturalism as a progressive form of liberalism. Others writing on multiculturalism in Canada have addressed whether or not liberalism as a doctrine is compatible with multiculturalism. . . .

Scholarly writing about multiculturalism in Canada (outside of Quebec) can broadly be divided into three categories: multiculturalism seen as serving assimilationist goals, multiculturalism as a tool that co-opts the real interests of Canada's minority groups, and multicultural policy as meeting the needs of the recognition of minority groups (Abu Laban and Stasiulis 1992). The second category is crucial for my analysis here, in suggesting that multicultural policy focuses on culture while ignoring the real material interests of minority groups. . . .

Contextualizing "Settlement" in Toronto

To examine the intimate spaces in which multiculturalism is negotiated, I've been conducting ethnographic **fieldwork** in Toronto since 2001. During that time I conducted participant-observation in immigration consulting offices, government offices, settlement services agencies, mosques, cultural festivals, and women's homes, and [I've] conducted

interviews with 120 Pakistani immigrants, governmental workers, non-profit workers, mullahs,
government-funded cultural translators, and immigrant women. Toronto is a compelling site to
examine multiculturalism because it is the premier
urban destination of migrant groups to Canada. In
1961, "non-whites" composed 3 per cent of the population of Toronto (Siemiatycki and Isin 1997); in
2006, half of Toronto's population was "non-white."
Toronto went from being known as "the Belfast of
the North" to adopting the motto "Diversity Is Our
Strength" in 1998, to reflect the racial and ethnic
diversity of the city. In 2008, nearly half the population of Toronto was foreign born at 45.7 per cent,
compared to 23 per cent in New York.

Despite accounts that stress the promises of
globalization . . ., the story of the South Asian **diaspora** in Toronto is intimately tied to decline. In
contrast to images of the highly mobile South Asian
tech worker that often underpin these accounts,
36.5 per cent of the Pakistani population of Toronto lives in poverty in housing projects peripheral
to the city (Ornstein 2006). When I asked various
community representatives, including the Pakistani
embassy, the Pakistani business council, and local
community workers and members, they each (and
independently of one another) reported rates of
poverty at 80 per cent. This statistic is interesting
because it varies dramatically from perceptions of
the state; Statistics Canada puts the rate of poverty at closer to 40 per cent. A rate of 40 per cent
is [dramatic] on its own; the perception among the
community that it is double that figure indicates
an even more overwhelming sense of social decline
within the community. Regardless of this discrepancy, it is indisputable that the economic and political conditions of Pakistani immigrants in Toronto
belie the rhetoric of equality within a model of difference. Many become deskilled, working in what
are known as "survival jobs," such as cashiering,
and living in pockets of poverty in marginal parts
of the city.

While in Toronto, I spent time with Pakistani
immigrant women as they navigated the intri-
cate system of "settlement services," which are
government-funded, privately run organizations in

place to facilitate immigrant women's entrance into
the public sphere, indicative of the neoliberal shift
in immigrant care taking place since the 1990s.
These agencies dealt with issues pertaining to "settlement" such as employment and health care. The
South Asian organizations all played a role, some
in lesser degrees than others, in organizing social
activities around South Asian heritage month. Academic accounts of neoliberalism have focused on
the emergence of new forms of rule and a growing
number of institutionalized forms that take on the
function[s] of governance that were formerly within
the purview of the state (Sharma 2008). This has
resulted in the increasing scope and power of voluntary organizations located between the state and its
citizens. . . . Such organizations have proliferated to
take over numerous governmental activities [includ-
ing] the "settlement" of new immigrants. . . .

The story of settlement is folded into a broader
history of both political-economic reforms and the
turn to multicultural policy. Historically, Toronto
had a number of voluntary self-help organizations
for new immigrants based on local immigrant, ethnic, and religious organizations. After World War
II, with the turn toward a Keynesian welfare state in
Canada, the government began to assume a principal role in building programs and services involving
education, public health care, and social services in
the care of its citizens. The period between 1940 and
1970 was marked by the rise of the welfare state in
Canada, when high levels of employment and rapid economic growth were complemented by extensive social assistance. However, during the 1990s,
the postwar Keynesian welfare state came undone.
Governmental deficits and Canada's economic integration within a global economy instigated accel-
erating economic and social restructuring in which
individual responsibility became intensified, leaving
the governance of settlement to settlement services
agencies.

In Toronto there are more than 100 settlement service agencies organized around ethnic
identities. . . . Many centres are organized around
a common ethnic or religious identity (e.g., family
services for South Asians or the Portuguese community women's centre). I visited all of these small

agencies during the course of fieldwork. In general, I went to the most popular workshops for new immigrants and attended a total of 50 unemployment workshops over the course of 18 months. I attended workshops that were profession specific, such as those for nursing and engineering, as well as some that were organized around particular ethnic identities. There was a serious discrepancy between the mandates of the centres, the expectations of participants, and what actually happens in the space of the workshops, as many participants had understood them to be placement centres. . . .

To explore these issues, I conducted [in depth] fieldwork at [the] South Asian Women's Centre in the west end of Toronto. . . . From 1999 to 2000, it provided services to nearly five thousand women and children in the form of information, counselling, and advocacy. Founded in 1982, the centre catered to South Asian women immigrants at their first level of what non-profits term *integration*; therefore, many of [its] clients are very new immigrants. The centre was housed in a small converted storefront located in a new "Little India" or "Little Pakistan," depending on whom one asked. The neighbourhood was economically marginal and populated by a large immigrant community because of the availability of difficult-to-find, low-cost housing. The main street was filled with small Indian and Pakistani restaurants, grocery stores, dollar stores, and a storefront mosque. Many of the city's "settlement services" were located nearby, but the centre of the social world of many Indian and Pakistani women was the South Asian Women's Centre.

The Smell of Citizenship

To explore the relationship between smell and citizenship, I examine the production of "South Asia" and the "South Asian" cultural festival in diaspora. Multicultural practice in this context specifically *calls for* foreignness, exoticness, of smelling "different." "Foods that are foreign," marked "bad" in the context of the job search where difference is to be mitigated, are marked delicious in the context of multicultural celebrations. The meaning of

the purported "difference"—food or smell—varies radically according to context. Rather than the *production* of a "radical alterity" (Povinelli 2002) in this context, there is a containment of it, in pursuit of recognizable difference. But the management of difference does not go undisputed. Below, I focus on the **agency** of the Pakistani women I interviewed as they fashion alternative models of the self by resisting norms, values, and constructions of appropriate citizenship around the category "South Asian." . . .

. . . On 14 December 2001, the government of Ontario declared May as South Asian Heritage Month under the South Asian Heritage Act 2001. Since then, celebrations have been held throughout the country that are launched by the federal government in Ottawa, which hosts the largest celebration on Parliament Hill. Members of all levels of government have participated in South Asian Heritage Month. For instance, in recent years representatives including Minister of Citizenship, Immigration, and Multiculturalism Jason Kenney attended. They made public appearances and gave speeches encouraging diversity. In a speech at [the South Asian music festival] DesiFest, during the event that closed the South Asian Heritage Month activities in 2008, Jason Kenney said,

> Our core Canadian values are democracy, freedom, human rights, and the rule of law. The more than 200,000 people who come to Canada annually from every corner of the world embrace these values, adding an often indefinable element to our sense of who we are . . . it's great to witness such a committed and dedicated group of people who clearly see links between their Canadian citizenship, their civic participation, and their commitment to maintaining a connection with their cultural heritage. . . . Canada has an enviable record of integrating newcomers by encouraging their full participation in our society. One of the cornerstones of our pluralistic society is that all citizens benefit from equality under the law, regardless of their cultural or religious background.

As this quote demonstrates, the government is deeply invested, not only financially but also ideologically, in the promotion of "diversity" and more specifically [in] South Asian Heritage Month.

The flagship event of the South Asian community in Toronto takes place in August in the form of a cultural festival called "Masala! Mehndi! Masti!" that official materials translate as "Spices, Henna, and Fun." (A number of my interviewees stressed that they thought it was peculiar to use the term *masti* as they understood it to be a derogatory term for girls who do "bad things.")[4] As I walked through MMM in 2003, I noticed a smaller section of tables for non-profit groups—eclipsed by stages of South Asian dance performances, tables of Indian food, and stalls selling jewellery. I walked over to the table for the South Asian women's collective with which I was volunteering and sat down next to Madiha, my friend in the field. Madiha was a Pakistani woman who had been living in Canada for approximately three years before we met. She was a settlement counsellor who had migrated with her engineer husband and their two small children. All around us, **tropes** of "India" stood in for an imagined "South Asia." . . .

MMM prominently featured two commoditized elements always associated with "South Asia" in these festivals—food and clothing. The food section was under a tent away from the main building and adjacent to the outdoor marketplace. Many popular restaurants from "Little India" set up stalls to sell food. Mango lassi was sold everywhere as a popular "authentic" South Asian drink, as were butter chicken and samosas. It is not just the fact of Indian food being sold but also the type of Indian food sold, with each stand specializing in generic Indian food that could be purchased at any food court restaurant in any mall.

The other major area of consumption at the festival was of clothing. There were numerous stalls that featured Indian sari fabrics, heavy gold and silver jewellery, lighter cotton fabric tunics, and leather slippers—garments representing a popular notion of South Asia, one that arises out of film, television, and media representations of India. In conversations with the vendors, I learned that the buyers here were most often tourists . . . who wanted to purchase an authentic piece of India, thus revealing that these particular commodities also signify very different meanings depending on who was wearing them.

During the last day of MMM I had volunteered to sit at one of the tables with Lubna, a 40-year-old single woman who had migrated from Karachi on her own. I had met Lubna at an unemployment workshop. It was pouring rain that day, coming down so hard that it looked like the rain was shooting up from the streets. There were still hundreds of celebrants, brightly coloured signs and streamers decorating the tents set up in the streets—although all were drooping with the weight of the water. The numerous stalls were still serving barbecued corn, tandoori chicken, dosa,[5] and brightly coloured matai [sweets]. As Lubna and I enjoyed our refuge from the rain, she described to me how she felt that the entire festival suggested a mainstream *Indian* population that was very different from a mainstream Pakistani population, "We're poorer, not well organized, and don't do Bollywood or dancing," she said, "so who is this for?" Many Pakistanis felt they were not part of the larger South Asian community, a division that was highlighted during South Asian Heritage Month. . . .

Sitting in many non-profit centres, I found myself participating in conversations leading up to South Asian Heritage Month, which took an unexpected form. I repeatedly heard the sentiment expressed by Amina, "I refer to myself as Pakistani and don't agree that all Indians, Pakistanis, et cetera can be called South Asians. We might come from similar geographic regions but have individual characteristics."

As this case demonstrates, Pakistani women are actively redefining the terms of belonging through resisting available multicultural categories. Although the Pakistani women I spoke with were being interpellated as Canadian citizens in job settings, with particular demands on bodily comportment, they were simultaneously being interpellated as multicultural ethnic minorities in reference to discourses of the South Asian diaspora. . . .

Cultural festivals also emerge as a type of sensorium, in which subjects are supposed to distinguish between appropriate and inappropriate moments to display their Otherness. In the context of the cultural festival they are admired and appreciated as signs of an authentic South Asia. During South Asian Heritage Month activities take place throughout the city that consist of dance performances, arts exhibits, and predominantly food festivals selling Indian food. . . . The goal of these festivals is outreach to the larger community, and so there is often a large percentage of non–South Asians in attendance. Over the years, I overheard a number of conversations as I waited patiently in line at various South Asian festivals for my mango lassi by non–South Asians remarking on how delicious the food smelled and how exotic it all was.

These kinds of phenomena signal the ways the smells of an imagined South Asia are only situationally repugnant. . . . The exotic smells of South Asian food are simultaneously a barrier to employability and even citizenship in certain contexts. Yet how can this be reconciled with the fact that in the context of the cultural festival, which is also situated squarely within the state and within the practice and logic of multiculturalism, these same people are encouraged to highlight their difference? Here, the smell of citizenship changes. Rendered in terms of the sensory pleasures of an exotic South Asia, foreign smells become part of an acceptable model of difference. "I am tolerant, that food smells really good." In the cultural festival, such smells become cultural commodities rather than liabilities. The broader implication here pertains to the contradiction at the heart of multiculturalism: be different, but only in certain contexts. . . .

Sanitizing the Other

Job training workshops are a crucial site to witness the implementation of the sanitized sensorium. They allow one to observe how immigrant bodies have become central to the making—not the undermining—of national identity. Settlement services workshops assumed a particular kind of

unemployed **subjectivity**. Because the women were both skilled *and* unemployed, workshop organizers assumed there must be some other problem. This problem was located not in labour markets or the regulation of professional labour but in the body. In this section I focus on the erasure of bodily difference in terms of sight and smell. . . .

The workshop I detail below was part of a one-day event called "Business Etiquette." Although I focus on the details of this workshop, these were pedagogies I heard repeatedly in a number of different workshops. On this particular occasion 20 women were in attendance. The speaker on this day, Dana, was from a large, well-established international association that conducts non-profit work internationally. Dana was a woman of European descent in her mid-forties. When I later interviewed Dana about how she came to give these workshops, she described a trajectory that was common among all but one of the workshop coordinators that I interviewed. The workshop leaders were older white women who were born and raised in Canada, most of whom had entered the workforce after their children had gone away to college. When I asked her about instructions and how she decided on the content of the workshops, she said she would gauge her audiences' needs after meeting them. Although there was uniformity generally in the content across the workshops, she made changes depending on who was in the audience. I focus on smell here because it was a direction repeatedly given to women from the subcontinent. I conducted contrasting fieldwork in settlement agencies for diverse groups of newcomers, as well as participated in workshops in which the participants were primarily from Europe and the instructions were markedly different. They did focus on bodily comportment involving gestures but never on smell or "ethnic" dress.

Dana began with a remark that signalled her assumptions about class and education. She recommended that all participants at some point go to another local agency that offers English as a second language classes, as well as academic tutoring that takes people through to grade 12. . . . Dana had not realized that her audience was composed mainly of fluent English speakers who were highly skilled in specialized professions in Pakistan.

The class began with a video called *First Impressions* which was used widely in these workshops. In making a successful impression in a job interview, it suggested 45 per cent is packaging, 35 per cent is responsiveness, and 10 per cent is experience. Many of the participants expressed shock and horror when the video also revealed that interviewers will decide whether they like you within the first seven seconds. The video describes two characters, an Asian businessman, Chang, and a Latina working-class woman, Rita, who both struggle in their job search because they do not have the appropriate bodily comportment required to make it past their first interview. The video provides a highly gendered account of what the two did wrong. Rita mistakenly takes her children to job interviews [and] wears makeup that is too bright and clothing that is too revealing—the emphasis is on her clothing and sexuality. Chang's instructions are also directed toward his comportment. He fails to have a firm handshake; he bows when he is not supposed to; he offers his business card with both hands, rather than with one hand by one corner. Both are illustrated as haphazard and clumsy. The entire class burst into laughter when the video described Chang as "successful" after he managed to acquire a six-month contract rather than a long-term, full-time job. When the video was over, Dana went over some key elements emphasizing behaviour. "During an interview," she said, "you need to be confident, make eye contact," but "don't be too over confident—you need to have a good attitude, don't be too pushy."

Much of the hour-long lecture that followed had to do with bodily comportment. "It doesn't matter what you did in your home country. You're in Canada now," she emphasized. When discussing the issue of clothing, Dana suggested they consider their surroundings. "Don't wear a shalwar or a headscarf," she suggested. She added that she had a coworker who kept her "traditional" dress at home. "You need to consider how they perceive you. You need to fit." Dana offered an example of a woman who was wearing a hijab and who was being interviewed at a home for the developmentally disabled. Her interviewers asked her what she would do about the scarf because they argued one of the patients could pull at it and potentially hurt her. This example demonstrates a series of entrapments. First, the woman in question wearing the hijab is confined to the realm of unskilled, servile labour. Second, the hijab becomes inappropriate even in the privatized labour space of the home-care attendant. Dana happily illustrated that the woman decided not to wear it to work. She added that "10 per cent of what interviewers consider is 'fit' in the workplace," effectively suggesting, "if you wear the hijab, you are never going to get work."

Dana stressed that "you always need to look good, even if you're just dropping off a resume." She suggested "dressing plainly, so you don't distract the employer from what we're saying, yet dress formally, don't wear sunglasses, and do not take your children to your job interview." Of note here is Dana's use of "we," referencing a racial and national community that excluded her audience. She continued by saying that on job applications, "we can't always understand your names, so please print clearly, or if you can, change your name, get a nickname if it's hard to pronounce." On being questioned about dressing formally, she suggested they "go out and see what people are wearing, dress plainly, be up-to-date, but dress modern." She continued, "Always be sure to shower first, you want to smell clean and not like Indian food, or masala or foods that are foreign to us. You want to present yourself as clean and professional." Her emphases suggested to her audience that, at present, they were neither clean nor professional. . . .

When I later had the opportunity to speak to Zeba about her experience in the workshop, she highlighted the issue of smell. "Why do they think I smell bad? It is just food. They eat Indian food at the shopping centre!" . . . Smell is implicated in a social and moral order tied to the prevailing ideology of multiculturalism in Toronto. Classen, Howes, and Synnott (1994) have argued that the sense of smell has been excluded from the realm of reason, associated instead with savagery. In the context of Toronto, Rinaldo Walcott (2003) has examined the ways that the "food odours" of Somali residents in a primarily white condominium in Toronto were imagined to be an "affront to 'Canadian ways of living'" (126) and [were] used to mark them as outsiders. . . .

That Dana instructed the women not to smell like South Asian *food* demonstrates that the concern is not with the women smelling of garbage or body odour but, rather, of "foreignness." Smell is also particularly gendered in this context because the smell of cooking reminds people that these "foreign-trained professionals" also cook, invoking images of the domestic area, or cooking, and women's unpaid work. . . . The instructions in workshops were directed toward their "South Asian-ness" such that smell and appearance become intertwined with cultural and bodily difference.

Inclusion and exclusion of Pakistani women in Canada's public sphere, while mediated by the senses, is about being, in the words of Mary Douglas ([1966] 2002), out of place. It is not only about "smelly bodies" but also about the *idea* of "smelly bodies." The issue of smell defines how a Canadian (or national) body should be; the national body does not smell—or, more accurately, smells in such a way that the very odour disappears. It is not an issue of not smelling, but smelling "like us," with its attending assumption that "we" have no smell. We are neutral.

The example above was not unique, and smell is not the only marker of difference implicated in these sanitizing processes. Bodily actions were also deeply implicated in the making of "modern" citizens. I participated in a range of workshops that all mirrored one another and were all geared toward bodily difference. A second example is from another course I attended at a larger settlement services agency in downtown Toronto for a range of highly skilled workers. . . . [T]he presenter, Susan, was teaching a group of seven women from diverse backgrounds: two engineers, three teachers, a doctor, and a lawyer all from Pakistan and India. . . .

. . . Susan began session two of the workshop by playing the *First Impressions* video and commenting

on Chang and Rita as they faltered. Susan suggested that in their "self-selling" techniques, they should shorten their names or chose Canadian nicknames to make it easier for employers. Susan gestured toward Zainab and Tania, the Pakistani women in attendance, and said "it's important to keep your traditional clothes at home, don't wear headscarves, 90 per cent of how they are judging you is fit in the workplace." Zainab and Tania were not wearing headscarves or shalwar cameeze suits, but the spectre of "traditional culture" had again appeared.

The marking of immigrant bodies was made particularly evident in the case of Razia, a participant in a workshop geared toward foreign-trained professionals from diverse fields. Razia had been living in Toronto for a year and a half and had been a practising lawyer in Pakistan for five years before immigrating. To be reaccredited as a lawyer, she learned she would have to begin her education again. While holding several survival jobs, such as making kebabs at an Indian restaurant and cashiering at Walmart, she too attended a range of unemployment workshops that did not teach her how to become employed as a lawyer. She regularly wore a scarf around her neck, and while some employers in various survival jobs were accepting of it, unemployment workshop leaders suggested she stop wearing it. Razia was not wearing anything resembling Pakistani clothing or representing "the Muslim veil." "I got it at the Dufferin Mall. Why do they think it's Pakistani? Because I'm Pakistani?" . . . Even though she did what was required of her and erased traces of minority culture from her body, what she wears and how she smells will always be marked Other because of the colour of her skin. . . .

Conclusion

In this analysis, I have sought to examine emergent contradictions in Canadian multicultural policies. . . . As the example of settlement services demonstrates, neoliberal forms of governance aimed at immigrant integration result in the disciplining of immigrant bodies by illustrating obstacles to their successful transition to full participation via the **formal economy**. However, as the example of the South Asian festival suggests, other practices within the Canadian regime of multiculturalism tend to reinforce those same differences. Thus, these various attempts at "inclusion," produced by different modalities of state governance, have unintended, contradictory effects. Here, these contradictory forms of interpellation, the attempts to simultaneously erase and celebrate . . . differences, result in the further marginalization and alienation of immigrant[s]. . . .

Debates around multiculturalism since the 1970s, at least in Canada, have focused on a perceived tension between giving newcomers a "sense of belonging" versus emphasizing differences between communities and, therefore, promoting the development of ethnic enclaves ("Strike Multiculturalism" 2010). . . . The contemporary "crisis of multiculturalism" is not owing to the presence of unassimilated minorities but, rather, owing to the ways that "difference" is controlled, managed, and contained [in ways that create] competing narratives of citizenship. . . .

References Cited

Abu-Laban, Yasmeen, and Daiva Stasiulis. 1992. "Ethnic Pluralism under Siege: Popular and Partisan Opposition to Multiculturalism." *Canadian Public Policy* 18 (4): 365–86.

Classen, Constance, David Howes, and Anthony Synnott. 1994. *Aroma: The Cultural History of Smell.* London: Routledge.

Department of Canadian Heritage. 2007. *Canadian Multiculturalism: An Inclusive Citizenship.* Ottawa: Government of Canada. www.pch.gc.ca.proxy.lib.sfu.ca/progs/multi/inclusive_e.cfm.

Douglas, Mary. (1966) 2002. *Purity and Danger: An Analysis of Concepts of Pollution and Taboo.* New York: Routledge.

"Strike Multiculturalism from the National Vocabulary." 2010. *Globe and Mail,* 9 October. www.theglobeandmail.com/news/national/time-to-lead/multiculturalism/part-6-editorial-strike-multicultural-ism-from-the-national-vocabulary/article1748958.

Kallen, Evelyn. 1982. "Multiculturalism: Ideology, Policy and Reality?" *Journal of Canadian Studies* 17: 51–63.

Kymlicka, Will. 1995. *Multicultural Citizenship: A Liberal Theory of Minority Rights.* Oxford: Oxford University Press.

Manalansan, Martin. 2006. "Immigrant Lives and the Politics of Olfaction in the Global City." In *The Smell Culture Reader,* edited by Jim Drobnick, 41–52. New York: Berg Publishers.

Ong, Aihwa. 2003. *Buddha is Hiding: Refugees, Citizenship, The New America.* Berkeley: University of California Press.

Ornstein, Michael. 2006. *Ethno-Racial Groups in Toronto, 1971–2001: A Demographic and Socio-Economic Profile.* Toronto: Institute for Social Research, York University.

Povinelli, Elizabeth. 2002. *The Cunning of Recognition: Indigenous Alterities and the Making of Australian Multiculturalism.* Durham, NC: Duke University Press.

Siemiatycki, Myer, and Engin Isin. 1997. "Immigration, Diversity, and Urban Citizenship in Toronto." *Canadian Journal of Regional Science* 20 (1): 73–102.

Sharma, Aradhana. 2008. *Logics of Empowerment: Development, Gender, and Governance in Neoliberal India.* Minneapolis: University of Minnesota Press.

Taylor, Charles. 1994. "The Politics of Recognition." In *Multiculturalism,* edited by Amy Gutmann, 25–74. Princeton, NJ: Princeton University Press.

Walcott, Rinaldo. 2003. *Black Like Who? Writing Black Canada.* Toronto: Insomniac Press.

Notes

1. Loose cotton pants (*shalwar*) and a tunic-style blouse (*cameeze*) worn by both men and women in parts of South and Central Asia. (Stern's note)
2. "Integration" predates the government of Jean Chretien, but it became a crucial hallmark of his government as a new agenda for the management of immigration. (Ameeriar's note)
3. The women I interviewed migrated under the "points system" of migration in which points are afforded according to one's skills and abilities. Many were the primary applicants in their immigration cases, while some migrated as secondary applicants to their husbands. The majority applied under the "skilled worker" category, while some applied under the family class category. (Ameeriar's note)
4. *Masti* is also a term used in India by men who have sex with men to refer to casual sexual encounters—although this definition never arose in my ethnographic fieldwork. (Ameeriar's note)
5. A south Indian dish of curried meat or vegetables served in a rice-and-lentil pancake. (Stern's note)

Key Points to Consider

- Public policies are not uniform in their goals or their practices, and they often push in contradictory directions. In Canada today, immigrants and ethnic minorities are simultaneously encouraged to present and to hide their ethnic differences.
- Recent cohorts of skilled immigrants to Canada have found it difficult to find work commensurate with their education and work experience. Experts have offered various explanations, each of which suggests different policy solutions.
- Women who immigrate to Canada from South Asia and the Middle East are often assumed to be oppressed by their male relatives, yet immigrant services agencies often push them into low-skill, low-wage employment that makes it extremely difficult for them to survive on their own.
- Ethnographies of the senses—what people hear, smell, taste, touch, and see—provide useful ways to understand the world from the perspectives of the people studied.

Critical Thinking Questions

1. What do the immigrant women described by Ameeriar learn in the employment workshops? What do the presenters appear to think are the obstacles to immigrants' successful integration into the workforce? Who bears the responsibility for immigrant integration?
2. Ameeriar refers to a "barrage of regulatory proscriptions aimed at the immigrant body." Based on the evidence she presents, do you think that the women she studied would succeed in finding employment if they followed the advice about food smells and clothing?
3. Consider Mary Douglas's assertion that people think of things that are out of place as dirty and as potential sources of contamination. Can you identify some objects that are categorized differently depending on the setting? Chose one and describe how your view of the object changes in different contexts.

Suggestions for Further Reading

Ameeriar, Lalaie. 2012. "The Gendered Suspect: Women at the Canada–US Border after September 11." *Journal of Asian American Studies* 15 (2): 171–95.

Mackey, Eva. 2002. *The House of Difference: Cultural Politics and National Identity in Canada.* Toronto: University of Toronto Press.

Sharma, Nandita. 2005. "Canadian Nationalism and the Making of a Global Apartheid." *Women and Environments International Magazine* 68/69: 9–11.

PART III

Kinship/Marriage/Family

Chapter 10

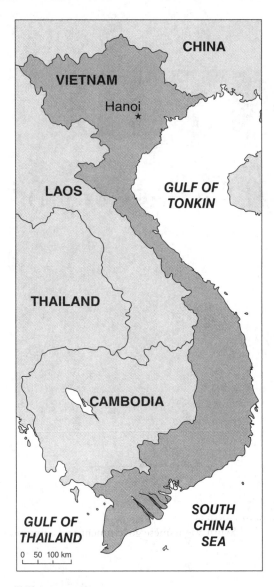

Vietnam

Introduction

Where do ideas about what constitutes a normal family come from? How do these ideas change? Who is eligible to become a parent? Who is not?

Canadians generally think of **marriage** and childbearing as intensely personal decisions that have nothing to do with government. The intimate world of family is an area in which we exercise a substantial degree of **agency**, but our decisions about who and when to marry, how many children to have, how to space those children, and if and when to move out of our parents' house are outcomes not of individual choice, but rather of cultural norms and attitudes. Laws and other government policies and programs—integral to culture—are especially relevant for reinforcing or changing the forms families take and ideas about what a family should look like. Nonetheless, actual changes may be unintended consequences of other policy decisions.

In many parts of the world it is considered problematic (even morally or socially dangerous) for women to become pregnant outside of marriage. Andrew Ryan, a columnist for *The Globe and Mail*, reported that the British were shocked and alarmed to learn that almost half of all British babies born in 2012 were born to unmarried mothers. He also noted that "in North America, the percentage of children born to unmarried couples stands at 41 per cent in the United States and a *respectable* 25 per cent in Canada. We are Canadian!" (Ryan 2013, *italics added*). However, in assuming that national culture somehow explains these differences, the columnist did not consider that, unlike either the United States or Great Britain, Canada officially recognizes common-law marriage. Thus the comparative statistics, based on censuses and surveys, do not distinguish which parents were in marriage-like relationships and which were formally married. Indeed, some Canadian parents in common-law relationships likely reported their status as "married," while parents in similar relationships in the US and the UK did not. It would be surprising if Canadian marriage trends diverged that dramatically from those of either the US or the UK. More likely, the legal distinction allowed a measurement error.

The article below concerns the relatively new phenomenon in Vietnam of unmarried women purposefully becoming pregnant, intending to raise their child without a spouse. Anthropologist Harriet Phinney's **ethnography** reveals that some older single women chose motherhood as a form of old-age security. But old-age security is not the only, and probably not the most important, reason the women had for becoming mothers. Rather, they were responding to government campaigns that valorized motherhood. Many of the single mothers Phinney met had previously heeded wartime calls to put off marriage as patriotic duty. In the postwar period, the government initiated programs to promote childrearing and family-building as the patriotic duties of women.

Phinney conducted the ethnographic **fieldwork** reported in this article in two rural districts of northern Vietnam and in and around Hanoi from 1995 to 1996 and again in 2004. This was a period of political and social stability following more than four decades of war beginning with World War II. World War II was followed by the First Indochina War (1946–1954), a war to end French colonization. Next came the Second Indochina War (1955–1975), known in Vietnam as "the American War" and in North America as "the Vietnam War." This war was initially a conflict between the US-backed South Vietnamese government and communist forces in North and South Vietnam. The North Vietnamese consolidated control over the entire country in 1975, but this did not bring peace. What followed was war with the communist Khmer Rouge in Cambodia, which lasted until 1989.

The women who were Phinney's primary **informants** were born between 1946 and 1969, with most born in the 1950s. As Phinney explains, most had not married because of the wars, and by the time there was peace they were in their 30s and believed that they were "too old" to find a husband. In the complete version of the article, Phinney reports that she learned a number of Vietnamese expressions that labelled a single woman in her late twenties or early thirties as too old to get married. Other cultural beliefs including that a husband should be older than his wife and that each person has only one true love also discouraged many women from pursuing marriage.

As Phinney explains in the unabridged version of the article, non-marital pregnancy and childrearing is acceptable for only some women. The Vietnamese she studied made a moral distinction between younger and older single women who become pregnant. Pregnancy was considered problematic for young unmarried women—they were encouraged to have abortions. In contrast, a woman considered too old to get married was encouraged to have a child so that she would not be lonely. Becoming pregnant, for these older women, was desexualized and divorced from ideas about romantic love; the goal was a child, not marriage. In most cases, the fathers were married, but the act of impregnating an older single woman was often not considered a threat to the "**conjugal bond**" of existing marriages. In fact, Phinney was not able to interview any men who had impregnated older single women because the women kept those men's identities secret.

Older single mothers were not socially isolated. Quite the opposite; parenting helped them avoid isolation and enabled them to get out and meet other mothers, to build a network of female friends, and to cultivate relationships for the benefit of their child.

In her analysis, Phinney draws on ideas from several theorists often cited by contemporary anthropologists. Political scientist Benedict Anderson described the **nation** as an "imagined community" of people who think of themselves as sharing a common history, culture, and language, and even the same physical/biological substance. According to Anderson, nations are modern inventions created through practices and artifacts like map-making, censuses, history books, and newspapers that help groups of people learn to think of themselves as being like each other, sharing a "horizontal comradeship," and distinct from other groups of people.

Laws and other government policies are reflections of the culturally shared norms and attitudes in particular places; at the same time, they help to shape citizens' norms and attitudes. In the article, Phinney writes of "shifts in **governmentality**," by which she means changes in government activities that alter the ways that people act in order to be good citizens. The term *governmentality* comes from the writings of French social theorist Michel Foucault (1926–1984), who noted that, for the most part, government activities are not directly coercive; rather, people monitor themselves to act in ways that they believe are good and moral, and their understanding of what is good and moral is shaped, in part, by government activities. The "Happy Family" program described by Phinney represented a shift in governmentality in Vietnam. In wartime, North Vietnamese government programs encouraged women to defer marriage and romantic love and, instead, to direct their love to the nation by supporting the war effort. In peacetime, women were told that they could best support the nation by creating strong families. A similar shift occurred in North America in the 1940s and 1950s. American and Canadian women were encouraged to work in factories during World War II and then to embrace marriage and motherhood after the war.

Finally, Phinney uses the term *interpellated*, borrowed from French Marxist philosopher Louis Althusser (1918–1990), to describe how individuals learn to recognize themselves as the targets of particular programs. The "Happy Family" program, for example, was directed to married women, but the older single women Phinney met also saw themselves as capable of creating happy families as a way to continue to contribute to the nation. As a result, they were interpellated into the modern, happy Vietnamese family.

In most countries, there are governmental and non-governmental programs that build people's sense of belonging and contribute to their expectations and understanding of what it means to be a good citizen. Some of these policies and programs also help to define the ideal family. Ideas about ideal families may be conveyed through things like schoolbooks that depict families in certain ways, but not others, or that show men and women engaged in certain tasks, but not others. Government actions such as providing child care, offering tax deductions related to raising children or for enrolling children in after-school sports programs, and requiring that birth certificates request "mother's and father's names" rather than the names of parents without specifying gender also reinforce certain ideas about how families contribute to the nation. No single program or practice is powerful enough to transform cultural norms, but in combination these "micro-technologies," as Phinney calls them, work to create shared norms around the happy, healthy family.

❧ *About the Author* ❧

Harriet Phinney teaches anthropology at Seattle University in Washington. After attending Grinnell College, she earned a master's degree in international public health from the University of Michigan and then a PhD in anthropology from the University of Washington. Her long-term ethnographic research on love, marriage, sexuality, reproductive health, and HIV in postwar Vietnam concerns the ways that government policies and practices surrounding health-care delivery contribute to unintended outcomes.

Asking for a Child: The Refashioning of Reproductive Space in Postwar Northern Vietnam

Harriet M. Phinney

Introduction

Quynh did not think about having a child until she was in her early thirties, an age too old to find a good husband. Having spent her youth taking care of her younger siblings after her parents died, Quynh never had time to consider marriage. Had her parents been alive they might have hired a *ba moi* (a traditional matchmaker) to arrange a suitable marriage for Quynh when she was still young enough to be a desirable wife. But, since arranged marriages were no longer considered acceptable and Quynh was too shy to meet a potential husband through her work friends (a modern route to marriage), she remained single. Instead she devoted her time to the Women's Union's war and postwar efforts. When she was 40 she finally agreed to meet a man her age from

Hanoi, whose wife had been sent by the government to Germany for work. He and Quynh developed a close relationship; she got pregnant in 1992. "My friends had advised me to *xin con* [ask for a child] and when they found out I was pregnant they congratulated me for having a *cho nuong tua* [someone to lean on]," she said. "I decided to have a child because of the 1986 law which grants me the right to do so. Had there been no law, I would not have dared go ahead and have a child on my own."

Quynh's account of her decision to *kiem con/xin con* (ask for a child)[1] speaks to the everyday realities older single women faced in postwar Vietnamese society and the manner in which they sought to obtain what they considered to be rightfully theirs—a child. Quynh was not alone; throughout northern Vietnam, a number of older single women had their opportunities to marry thwarted as a result of the war. Beginning in the mid-1980s, some of these women, like Quynh, broke with existing marital and childbearing conventions to decide it was not necessary to marry in order to have a child. They asked men they would not or could not marry to get them pregnant.

This paper elucidates the women's postwar experiences that prompted them to "ask for a child," **state** policies that provided a different dynamic for bearing children out of wedlock, and the manner in which the Women's Union sought to confer social acceptance on . . . "asking for a child." On a broader level, the paper brings into focus the effects of war on family formation . . . [within] a postwar society largely lacking able-bodied young men. I argue that, as a result of the women's agency and the state's decision to incorporate single mothers and their children into society rather than condemning or ostracizing them, a new reproductive space was forged in which **ideologies** of motherhood, family, and reproduction took on new meaning in postwar northern Vietnam. That the women managed to obtain male compliance and familial, social, and state support is, in many ways, truly remarkable. Yet, the women's agency and the state and society's acceptance of older single women who "asked for a child" represent a highly pragmatic solution to addressing the needs of unmarried women in a postwar society faced with large numbers of single mothers.

Absent Men, Age, and Loneliness

The experiences of women who "asked for a child" in postwar Vietnamese society varied depending on a number of factors including their wartime experiences, whether they had loved a man, what they had sacrificed during the war, and how larger **structural factors** associated with the war and the state's efforts to create a modern socialist society affected them. Nonetheless, all of the women with whom I spoke shared at least three common experiences: there were few if any men for them to marry, they considered themselves unmarriageable, and they were lonely.

Demographers Hirschman, Preston, and Vu have estimated that from 1965 to 1975, "the risk of dying for young men aged 15–29 was more than seven times higher than the 'normal level' of non-war mortality. . . . [M]ortality among all Vietnamese men above age 15 was twice as great as would have been expected in the absence of war" (1995: 805). Results of other **demographic** surveys conducted between 1983 and 1987 indicate that "in many rural areas, males accounted for only 42 to 44 per cent of the population[, while] the percentage of women [aged 20 to 29] . . . was as high as 65–67 per cent in some areas" (Khuat 1998: 35). This [un]balanced sex ratio still existed 15 years after the end of the Second Indochina War (Khuat 1998). Although American bombing had stopped by 1973, many Vietnamese soldiers remained away from home until 1990 due to the Cambodian–Vietnamese border conflict and to the Chinese invasion of Vietnam. Nam (born in 1945) described the situation thus:

After the war with the French there were still a lot of men, but after the American war there were only a few men scattered about. Before the American war, we did not have this situation of single women asking for a child; there were many many young men, but after the war they were all gone, all of them.

The second experience the women shared was the realization that they were unlikely to marry. Most of the women with whom I spoke attribute their lost marital opportunities to the American War. Their boyfriends had died in the war, their parents wanted them to postpone marriage until after the war when their brothers would hopefully come home, the women never had a chance to fall in love because the men their age were off fighting, or the women had devoted their marriageable years to helping with the war effort. During the mid- to late 1960s Ho Chi Minh [then president of North Vietnam] called upon the Vietnamese youth to set their personal lives aside and help with the Democratic Republic of Vietnam's (DRV) final push to liberate the South. The Lao Dong [Vietnam Workers'] Party devised a new slogan called Ba Khoan (the Three

Delays) (Chanoff and Doan 1996: 61). If you don't have a child, delay having one. If you aren't married, delay getting married. If you aren't in love, delay love. The Party promoted the idea that in order to be fully committed to the war effort soldiers should have little or no romantic involvement or emotional ties "to the rear." The nation was to be the principal if not sole object of one's affection (Phinney 2003). Many young people heeded Ho Chi Minh's appeal.

The women I interviewed were 25 years or older when the war was over. They were either too old to find suitable spouses or were unwilling to marry the men who were available. The women's unmarried male age mates who did survive the war returned home to marry women five to seven years younger than they were. Ha (born in 1957) said, "I was old already, I was 25. At that age we should have been wives, had children already. . . . My friends and I, we knew our chances of marrying had been thwarted."

The third shared experience was feelings of loneliness. When the war was over, the women I spoke with who had postponed (or never had the opportunity) to bear a child, marry, or love found themselves alone in a way they had not been during the war. The "horizontal comradeship" (Anderson 1991: 7) they had felt with fellow Vietnamese during the war began to dissipate now that it had been won and the realities of a society devastated by a horrendous war prompted people to refocus their attention. Single women not only had to confront the reality that it would be extremely difficult to find a man to marry should they wish to do so, but they had to live in a society that no longer valorized the efforts of single women.

Many of the women with whom I spoke recalled the loneliness they felt after the war; a loneliness they explained as a result of being childless, not because they were single. Loneliness was discussed in terms of having to *di choi* (play, go out, and have fun) by yourself, coming home after visiting friends and relatives who had children and a family of their own, not being able to talk with other women about the childbearing experience, listening to other women talk about their children, and not knowing what it was like to have a child of your own to love and nurture and who can love you back. The women

were also worried about having to face old age alone, with no one to take care of them.

Drawing upon socially accepted ideas of what constitutes a desirable husband and having not found what they desired, the women I interviewed decided not to accept a fate of being lonely childless women, but actively to change their fate. No longer needing to fit into socially sanctioned behaviour for marriageable women (because they were considered—or considered themselves—unmarriageable anyway), the women were free to bear children outside the confines of marriage. In doing so they helped open a space for what many women get married for—to have a child, a decision buttressed by the state's recognition of older single women's need for children.

Shifts in Governmentality: State Policy and Maternal Identity

Compounding older single women's loneliness were feelings of inadequacy and the discomfort they experienced moving about in a society increasingly structured around marital and familial relations. By the mid-1980s, with the war over, the Vietnamese state was no longer able to call on the "community of sentiment" (Anderson 1991) that had bound many people together in their love for the nation and devotion to its liberation. In 1986, in order to regain its political and moral authority, the state formally embarked upon *doi moi* (renovation), a new form of governmentality. In doing so, it [elevated the importance of] the household as the primary economic unit, making the family the focus of state-building efforts. An important component of the intensified focus on the family was its attention to the social and personal value of biological motherhood. The 1986 Law on Marriage and the Family and the "Happy Family Planning Campaign" . . . stressed the importance of biological motherhood and . . . provided a different social context for single motherhood than had previously existed.

In 1986 the state [introduced a new] Law on Marriage and the Family which is widely recognized to give all women the right to have a child. Article 3, Chapter 1, states: "The state and society shall protect the mothers as well as their children, and shall assist the mothers in fulfilling their noble tasks of motherhood" (*Fundamental Laws*, 1993). It is notable that nothing is said here about single mothers. And yet, the law is broadly construed as providing older single women the right to have a child. A senior lawyer at the Ministry of Justice with whom I spoke said Article 3 is the first law enacted specifically to recognize the right of all women to have a child. Article 3, by providing legal sanction for older unmarried women who want to bear a child is also state recognition of a postwar society in which vast numbers of single women were unlikely to marry but would need a child to take care of them in their old age. It is not insignificant that the state chose to recognize such a reproductive strategy at a time (the beginning of *doi moi*) when it sought to withdraw its welfare responsibilities.

Three other [sections] of the 1986 law [also offer] legal recognition for older unmarried women's maternal desires. These [sections] focus on children born out of wedlock, giving them the same rights as other children. The 1986 law links the rights of a mother to those of her children; in doing so, it opens up a new legal space for reproducing. This is because a woman's rights derive from the child whether or not the father is present. As Silva points out, "the recognition that an illegitimate child is not an unwanted child allows for a reconstruction of unmarried motherhood" (1996: 4). . . . The 1986 Law on Marriage and the Family, in turn, gave married men implicit approval for helping older single women exercise their right to become mothers. Providing legal recognition of the women's reproductive agency, the state enabled older single women to get pregnant without fear of [negative repercussions from the] state. . . . The women with whom I spoke who "asked for a child" cited the 1986 law either as making their lives as single mothers more socially bearable or as one of the deciding factors in deciding to go ahead and bear a child out of wedlock.

The second aspect of the focus on biological motherhood was the state's promotion of the idea of a "Happy Family." "The Happy Family," also a component of the state's new governmentality, represents an intensified focus on the population as the means for producing a modern Vietnamese citizenry. A "Happy Family" is orderly, has an adequate income, two children, and stable conjugal relations. Family planning billboards in towns and cities portrayed a "Happy Family" of well-dressed mother, father, a boy, and a girl. The slogans read "Stable population, wealthy society, happy family." . . . Replacing the old revolutionary slogans designed to mobilize women for the war, the "Happy Family" posters instead were designed to encourage women to focus on their domestic lives—to create happy families.

It is under the guise of helping people create and maintain happy families that the state seeks to maintain its authority through the micro-technologies of the family planning program, as well as through other programs implemented by the Women's Union. This would not be a new tactic for the DRV, but one geared to a different goal, that of revalorizing the private family sphere by relocating the individual back within the family. . . .

Women are the principal targets of the family planning campaigns, the focal point for the state's efforts to produce a modern **subjectivity**. Family planning programs "encourage . . . women to adopt an intensified focus on their bodies as the locus of their 'femaleness'" (Rofel 1999: 246). In the process, women come to feel "that their most important goal is fulfilling a biological desire for motherhood" (ibid.). It is within the context of the state's intensified focus on family planning and promotion of "The Happy Family" that some older single women decided to "ask for a child." Older single women, despite being unmarried and not a target of the Vietnamese state's family planning program, nonetheless were "interpellated" (Althusser 1971) by this call for a happy family, the centre of which was children. Rather than adopting a niece or nephew, as unmarried women had commonly done in the past, the women I met were adamant about the importance of having a biological child.

"The Happy Family" campaign operated similarly to the 1986 Law on Marriage and the Family in that it also redefined the social context for bearing children. The campaign, by providing a social identification for women based on their maternal bodies, enabled those who did not marry to participate in society on the same basis as married women—that of reproducing and becoming a mother. Older single women, who earlier responded to the state's call for patriotic love to free the nation or who were forced to stay at home because their brothers and fathers had left to join the war effort, now responded to the portrayal of feminine responsibility and maternal desire produced by the state's new focus on the household and family planning to build a wealthy nation. . . . The combined effects of war and socialist policies contributed to the women's ability to transform themselves from childless women to mothers. And yet, women who "asked for a child" clearly exceeded the bounds the state had envisioned in its imaginings of a "Happy Family."

Neo-traditionalist Discourses: Reconciling Ideological Contradictions

In this section, I tease out the manner in which the Women's Union, an organ of the state, drew upon conventional **gender** identities to provide justification for married men's willingness to comply with older single women's requests for a child. In doing so, the process by which **tropes** of gendered **sexuality** were picked up, reiterated, and transformed to produce social support for a new female subjectivity becomes evident. This process is visible in the Women's Union's responses to letters written to the state newspapers by men who had complied with women's wishes to become pregnant. Most significant is the way the column seeks to reconcile society's

obligation to women who deferred childbearing and marriage due to the war with the state's postwar attempt to create "Happy Families" in which, ideally, the conjugal bond has social primacy.

In 1990, Vo Xuan Phong (1990) wrote a letter to Chi Thanh Tam,[2] the advice columnist for *Bao Phu Nu Viet Nam* (*Vietnamese Women's Newspaper*), explaining that his wife had recently learned that he had agreed to get a single woman pregnant. He had met the woman a long time ago in the Truong Son Mountains; she loved him then and still did, so she "asked him for a child." Hesitant at first, Vo Xuan Phong eventually agreed because the woman was lonely and only living with her mother. Then his wife found out. He now regrets his action and wants to know how he should explain himself to his wife. Chi Thanh Tam suggests that if his wife is a good person, if she has "heartfelt sympathy," then she will understand the other woman's "eager need to become a mother." Chi Thanh Tam reminded Vo Xuan Phong that "women's need/requirement to be a mother is an 'instinct' (*thien ban*) and therefore, it is natural that, now after years of dedicating their youth to strengthening the country," many single women feel "sorrow, self-pity, and misery because they cannot build a family and become a mother." Chi Thanh Tam then advises [him] to explain the situation to his wife and to his children. He should stress that his relationship with the woman is not a love affair and remind them that they "have many riches and the single woman has few." Finally, Chi Thanh Tam suggests that [he] decide how he wants to help the child he begat and then tell everyone his plan so it is out in the open.

In 1992, Hoang Van (1992) similarly wrote to Chi Thanh Tam for advice. Hoang Van begins his letter stressing that he married for love and that he very much loves his wife and four girls. But, his parents want a son to pass down the lineage. Upon hearing of a single woman in his village who was too ugly to get married, but wanted a child, he approached her. She gave birth to a boy. Now, everyone in the village, including his wife, claims that the child must be his because it looks just like him. What should he do? Chi Thanh Tam replied that it is clear Hoang Van is a good husband and a responsible father. He should therefore tell his wife the truth; by being open and honest with her he will develop *tinh cam* (sentiment, deep emotional bond). She will trust him more. "You need to make her realize that the other woman does not want to steal you away. Tell your wife the situation so she can understand. She will have sympathy with the other woman. Later you can decide if you want to recognize the child," writes Chi Thanh Tam.

In these two responses, Chi Thanh Tam weaves together three **essentialist** notions of Vietnamese women in order to provide support for the older women who had "asked for a child" and the men who helped them. The first is the idea that all Vietnamese women are inherently maternal. Though presented as a given and stated to remind men and their wives of women's innate nature, its reiteration further stitches maternal desire into Vietnamese female subjectivity such that maternal desire becomes embedded in the female body and inseparable from it. The second idea is that women share a common understanding with one another, a community of sentiment, one based on women's knowledge that all women are inherently maternal and that real happiness for a woman derives from bearing and raising children. The third belief is that Vietnamese women will willingly sacrifice their own feelings for the benefit of others.

Chi Thanh Tam contends that once wives understand the situation of older single women "asking for a child," the wives will be sympathetic to these women's lonely realities. Thus, Chi Thanh Tam tries to dispel the worries of wives who are concerned that an emotional attachment will develop between their husbands and the other women, threatening or weakening their marital bonds. The story by Hong Lien (1989) titled "*Hai nguoi phu nu*" ("Two women") serves to boost this assertion. It is a story of a wife who discovers that her husband helped another woman get pregnant. Curious, the wife arranges to meet the other woman to learn more about her. When she does, she realizes that the woman is a good person and develops admiration for her. It is not insignificant that the other woman had

requested to be transferred to another work place so as to be away from the man and his family.

There the story ends. The wife is not jealous, she ceases to worry, and she sympathizes with the other woman. Like many such stories printed in [*Vietnamese Women's Newspaper*] . . . the story draws on the essentialist tropes of Vietnamese women stated above. Ironically, wives are asked to sacrifice their desire for the ideal socialist marriage, one that unites love, marriage, and reproduction in a monogamous relationship, for the benefit of another woman who was said to have lost her youth fighting for the nation. It is unfortunate, as Ngoc Van (1989), a journalist sympathetic to the plight of older single women, wrote, "one family's happiness is another's unhappiness."

What assumptions make Chi Thanh Tam confident that marriage can withstand the turmoil a husband may bring to his family should he engage in sexual relations with a woman who "asked for a child"? Her confidence is based on common notions of gendered sexuality in which men and women are portrayed as having divergent sexual inclinations. . . . The difference between male and female sexuality was described to me in terms of a proverb that compares men to sticks and women to sand. "Men go from place to place poking holes in the sand, leaving a trace behind them but forgetting where they have been." Men like to experiment with sex and like novel things. Gammeltoft encountered similar beliefs in her research:

Even though men should ideally be faithful to their wives as well, it is widely recognized that men like "something different" (*cua la*) and that men—in contrast to women—cannot control their sexual urges when they are away from their wives. . . . While women are said to be able to live without it easily, sex is usually considered to be a necessity for men. (Gammeltoft 1999: 181)

Women are said to engage in sexual intercourse principally for the purposes of demonstrating their love and for having children. This attitude is consistent with Khuat Thu Hong's (1998) finding in her study on sexuality that women are rarely portrayed as desiring or enjoying sex, but are instead portrayed as passive victims of male desire.

Nguyen Cu (1989), a participant in a *dien dan* (forum discussion in newspapers) around the issue of male compliance, suggests that it is beneficial to differentiate between two different kinds of children born out of wedlock. . . . Nguyen Cu distinguishes between two different kinds of extramarital sex: sex engaged in to satisfy the "spiritual need" of a woman who cannot have a husband and sex engaged in as an act of love. The former is acceptable because the man's family can remain intact, the latter impermissible because it leads directly to family ruin. According to this logic, because a man is capable of engaging in sexual intercourse without loving a woman, his decision to get an older single woman pregnant is permissible. He can engage in sex without risking his relationship with his wife, which is supposed to be based on love. Thus, a child born outside a love relation is in no danger either of bringing a man and woman together or of causing a family to split up.

What about older single women? Did they engage in sex to demonstrate their love too? No. The women I interviewed made it quite clear that they had established relations with the men in order to "ask for a child." . . . [M]ost of the women I interviewed had once loved a man. But, their love was thwarted; they were unable to marry the man they loved. Having previously loved a man, they were not interested in loving another. They wanted to save all their love for their child. The women also knew that acceptance of their "asking for a child" is based on the belief that the sex they engage in is for the purposes of procreating only. This is not to be a love relationship. It cannot be a love relationship, because "as everyone knows" Vietnamese women only really love one man in their life. According to this logic then, older single women, having loved, are capable of engaging in sexual intercourse for the sole purpose of procreating. This is their standard narrative, and it is socially acceptable because everyone [also accepts] the need for older single

women to satisfy their maternal desires and their right to do so.

Recognizing the pragmatics of the situation, we might ask how extraordinary the strategy "asking for a child" is. It turns out that it is linked to past reproductive strategies as well as to established notions of gendered sexual identities.

When I arrived in Hanoi in 1995 and was looking for people to talk to about older single women "asking for a child," I was introduced to a gynecologist who worked for the Ministry of Health. In the course of our conversation she told me that it was not uncommon for a married woman whose husband was infertile to go to the hospital to get inseminated. Because I had thought there were no sperm banks in Hanoi, I was puzzled. The doctor laughed. "You in the West," she said, "with all your technology you make everything so complicated."[3] The doctor proceeded to explain. A woman will go into a room, lie down on a bed, and cover herself from head to toe with a sheet. Then an "unremarkable" (*binh thuong*) looking man will come in the room and inseminate her. "Unremarkable" so that the father will not be easily identifiable. The woman and the sperm donor remain anonymous to one another.

. . . A traditional doctor I went to in Hanoi said that in the old days an infertile man might bring a stranger into his home at night to get his wife pregnant. Acquaintances in Hanoi told me that men who had become infertile as a result of being exposed to chemicals during the war would take their wives to a hospital to be impregnated. In all of these cases, the identity of the man remained unknown or hidden and no one revealed that the child was not biologically related to its father. . . .

Looked at from within Vietnamese logic of reproduction and family formation, the stories reveal a highly pragmatic solution for achieving a couple's desire for creating a family ostensibly linked by blood. They also indicate that the strategy of asking a man to impregnate a woman other than his own wife, a woman with whom he would not maintain an ongoing relationship, was not necessarily new. Nonetheless, although single women's reproductive strategy has many parallels to the strategies of infertile couples in the past, "asking for a child" represents a significant departure from it. In the past, couples sought to procreate within the context of marriage and to carry on the ancestral lineage. "Asking for a child" is fundamentally different because it does not continue the Confucian-influenced patriarchal convention of bearing children to continue a male's ancestral heritage, but instead serves solely to create a new reproductive space for "unmarriageable" older single women.

Conclusion

Quynh made the decision to "ask for a child" after the promulgation of the 1986 Law on Marriage and the Family. As a Women's Union official, she had been unwilling to break with marital and childbearing convention prior to the law. The law and the efforts of the Women's Union to provide social support for this new maternal subjectivity enabled

her to respond to the state's call for a new feminine identity—one that no longer focused on devoting oneself to the war effort but to the raising of the nation's children.

Many of the other women whom I interviewed, however, decided to "ask for a child" prior to the 1986 law. Having dedicated their youth to the nation, and been subject to a succession of ideological campaigns (during and after the war), these women took it upon themselves to change their fate from being childless women to single mothers, regardless of any social or legal ramifications. These women spoke of the importance of bearing a child in order to feel like and be recognized as a "real" woman and of the need to have a child to take care of them in their old age. In many ways the "Happy Family" campaign and the justifications provided for the 1986 law draw upon the same concerns. Yet, it was only when the state came to recognize the need to switch to a new form of government, one in which the individual and the family (not the state)

FIGURE 10.1 Mothers and babies in the northern province of Bac Ninh, Vietnam.

took responsibility for its citizens, that it became feasible for the state to acknowledge older single women's proactive reproductive strategy. The focus on biological reproduction promoted by the "Happy Family" campaign arose concurrently with the 1986 Law on the Family and Marriage. The result was to improve the social and psychological conditions for all single mothers and their children. The state's wartime policies, after all, had been partially responsible for creating the demographic situation leading to single women's dilemmas in the first place. Together, the 1986 law and the "Happy Family" campaign created additional incentive for older single women to "ask for a child" and provided them with a greater ability to do so within the bounds of socially acceptable behaviour. The state's postwar redefinition of women's identity in terms of motherhood is designed to encourage women to participate in society in terms of their maternal identity. Women who are not married and yet do respond to the state's call are in effect placing themselves within the state's modern mode of governmentality.

The actions of the state and the Women's Union can be read as engaging in a pragmatic solution to dealing with a large population of single women who would need welfare assistance as they aged and as a humanitarian act compensating single women for having lost their youth to the war. The women I interviewed also demonstrated their pragmatism and reproductive agency; men and the state responded.

References Cited

Althusser, Louis. 1971. *"Lenin and Philosophy" and Other Essays*. Translated by Ben Brewster. New York: Monthly Review Press.

Anderson, Benedict. 1991. *Imagined Communities: Reflections on the Origin and Spread of Nationalism*. London: Verso.

Chanoff, David and Doan Van Toai. 1996. *"Vietnam": A Portrait of Its People at War*. New York: I.B. Tauris.

Fundamental Laws and Regulations of Vietnam. 1993. Hanoi: Gioi Publishers.

Gammeltoft, Tine. 1999. *Women's Bodies, Women's Worries: Health and Family Planning in a Vietnamese Rural Community*. Surrey, UK: Curzon.

Hirschman, Charles, Samuel Preston, and Vu Manh Loi. 1995. "Vietnamese Casualties during the American War: A New Estimate." *Population and Development Review* 21: 782–812.

Hoang Van. 1992. "Chi Thanh Tam kinh men" ["Dear Sister Thanh Tam"]. *Bao Phu Nu Viet Nam*, 14 September, 6.

Hong Lien. 1989. "Hai nguoi phu nu" ["Two women"]. *Bao Phu Nu Viet Nam*, 9 August, 6.

Khuat Thu Hong. 1998. *Study on Sexuality in Vietnam: The Known and the Unknown Issues*. Hanoi: Population Council South and East Asia Regional Working Paper.

Ngoc Van. 1989. "Ban ve van de con ngoai gia thu" ["Discussion Regarding Children Born out of Wedlock"]. *Bao Phu Nu Viet Nam*, 28 June, 6.

Nguyen Cu. 1989. "Chi Thanh Tam than men" ["Dear Sister Thanh Tam"]. *Bao Phu Nu Viet Nam*, 7 June, 6.

Phinney, Harriet. 2003. *Asking for the Essential Child: Revolutionary Transformations in Reproductive Space in Northern Viet Nam*. PhD thesis, University of Washington.

Rofel, Lisa. 1999. *Other Modernities: Gendered Yearnings in China after Socialism*. Berkeley: University of California Press.

Silva, Elizabeth Bortolaia. 1996. "Introduction." In *Good Enough Mothering? Feminist Perspectives on Lone Mothering*, edited by Elizabeth Bortolaia Silva, 1–9. London: Routledge.

Vo Xuan Phong. 1990. "Chi Thanh Tam kinh men" ["Dear Sister Thanh Tam"]. *Bao Phu Nu Viet Nam*, 12 February, 6.

Notes

1. The women and those who speak about them use one of two phrases to refer to their reproductive agency: "*kiem con*" (finding a child) and "*xin con*" (asking for a child). I have chosen to use the English phrase "asking for a child" throughout the paper. (Phinney's note)
2. Chi Thanh Tam is the pseudonym for a group of women who read and respond to personal letters asking for advice that are sent to *Bao Phu Nu Viet Nam* (Vietnamese Women's Newspaper). (Phinney's note)
3. In vitro fertilization has been available in Vietnam since 1997. (Stern's note)

Key Points to Consider

- Cultural beliefs and demographic factors affect people's decisions about whether and when to marry and have children.
- Government policies and practices also have a strong influence on seemingly personal and intimate matters such as the timing and spacing of pregnancies.
- In Vietnam, some older unmarried women "ask for a child" as a way to enhance their immediate lives and long-term security. They are "agents" who have chosen to see themselves as targets of the "Happy Family" campaign.
- In the past, out-of-wedlock pregnancy might have been a problem in Vietnam, but this is no longer the case for women perceived to be "too old" to get married. Many single mothers regard "asking for a child" as a way to continue to be a good citizen.

Critical Thinking Questions

1. According to Phinney, how do children enhance the lives of single women in Vietnam? Are there any negative repercussions to becoming pregnant outside of marriage? What evidence does the author provide?
2. What was the "Happy Family Planning Campaign"? Who were the messages aimed at? How were unmarried women affected? What does Phinney mean when she asserts that the "Happy Family" campaign and the 1986 Law on Marriage and the Family "redefined the social context for bearing children" and created "a new reproductive space" for older single women?
3. Phinney states that the Vietnamese government relied on "micro-technologies of the family planning program" to encourage women to refocus their energies on their individual households. Think about your own experiences with health care in Canada or in another country. What micro-technologies did you encounter that were meant to produce happy, healthy citizens?
4. How is raising a child connected to Vietnamese women's sense of themselves as good citizens? In what ways do Canadians connect citizenship to having children? How are ideas and messages about the welfare of children and the welfare of the country transmitted here? Try to be specific.

Suggestions for Further Reading

Dölling, Irene, Daphne Hahn, and Sylka Scholz. 2000. "Birth Strike in the New Federal States: Is Sterilization an Act of Resistance?" In *Reproducing Gender: Politics, Publics, and Everyday Life after Socialism*, edited by Susan Gal and Gail Kligman, 118–47. Princeton, NJ: Princeton University Press.

Kanaaneh, Rhoda Ann. 2002. *Birthing the Nation: Strategies of Palestinian Women in Israel*. Berkeley: University of California Press.

Phinney, Harriet M. 2008. "Objects of Affection: Vietnamese Discourses on Love and Emancipation." *Positions: East Asia Cultures Critique* 16 (2): 329–58.

———. 2008. "'Rice Is Essential but Tiresome; You Should Get Some Noodles': *Doi Moi* and the Political Economy of Men's Extramarital Sexual Relations and Marital HIV Risk in Hanoi, Vietnam." *American Journal of Public Health* 98 (4): 650–60.

Chapter 11

Russia

Introduction

How do people choose a marriage partner? What characteristics do they look for in a spouse? What characteristics are deal-breakers?

Marriage is an important **life-course** event found in almost every culture, but there is significant cross-cultural variation in the forms that marriage takes and in the expectations that people have about married life. Though many Canadians and others in the West idealize the choice to marry as an autonomous decision made by lovers, cultural norms and practices strongly influence this choice. Individuals draw on cultural norms and expectations when assessing whether someone possesses characteristics that would make him or her a good husband or wife and even whether a particular match is appropriate. Personal characteristics that can affect this assessment include age, marital status, education, income, social **class**, religion, **ethnicity**, individual and family reputation, personality, and physical appearance.

Marriage is a cultural institution that connects individuals as well as families, and it is widely regarded as essential for the reproduction of the society. Even in places like Canada where marriage is often treated as a source of personal fulfillment, marriage trends play a significant role in defining the character of the nation as a whole. In the article below, Sonja Luehrmann discusses changes in marriage trends in a remote area of Russia along the Volga River. Specifically, Luehrmann examines local attitudes about well-educated women who use the Internet to find husbands in Europe, North America, and Australia.

Cross-border marriage is not a new phenomenon, but it has likely become more widespread in recent decades with the creation of the Internet. In the article, Luehrmann pays a great deal of attention to Virginia, an agency that provides Internet-mediated introductions and other matchmaking services to women in Yoshkar-Ola (the capital of Russia's Marii El Republic) and to men living outside of Russia. According to Nicole Constable (2004: 170–1), who has done extended **ethnographic** research on cross-border marriage, the number of Internet-based services providing international introductions to potential spouses jumped from approximately 150 in 1998 to at least 400 just two years later, around the time Luehrmann began her **fieldwork** in Yoshkar-Ola.

Despite the apparent increase in the number of people participating in Internet-mediated introductions to potential spouses, cross-border marriages and the people who seek them are frequently disparaged. Sometimes, especially in wealthy countries, this disdain becomes so widespread that it contributes to a **moral panic**. The common stereotype of cross-border marriages is that they are between white men from wealthy countries and poor Asian or Eastern European women. The men are often believed to have flaws that make them poor marriage material, while the women tend to be thought of as either dangerously naïve or overly calculating. Stereotypes also affect the type of information exchanged through international matchmaking agencies—these agencies often encourage men's and women's idealized images of **gender roles**, and they frequently emphasize attributes of their female clients that appeal to Western men's erotic fantasies. Still, research by Constable, Luehrmann, and others indicates that Internet courtships are no more fraught or unrealistic than those conducted through more conventional means.

Globally, women are more likely than men to emigrate in order to marry. As well, marriage migration tends to follow the same pathways as labour migration and occurs for many of the same reasons. But not all international marriages are cross-cultural. In fact, it is common for **transnational migrants** to seek marriage partners from their countries of origin. This preference may have a secondary effect of encouraging additional migration. Canada, for the most part, encourages marriage-driven immigration; other countries are less enthusiastic. In the Netherlands, for example, Muslim men who look abroad for marriage partners are frequently accused of being unwilling to integrate into Dutch society (Schinkel 2011). Such accusations are also evidence of moral panic.

As Luehrmann describes, women in Yoshkar-Ola pursue international marriage for a variety of reasons. Life in post-socialist Russia is quite difficult for people living in remote and rural regions such as the Marii El Republic, and many women and men see outmigration as their only hope. As people move away from a rural area, that area and its remaining residents can appear even less attractive to those who remain. Importantly, migrants are likely to be people of reproductive age and their children, further contributing to the decline in that area. Since the collapse of the Soviet Union, birthrates in Russia have fallen and death rates have risen. The reproductive behaviour of women in particular tends to engender moral panic in many cultures. In the modern Russian context, this concern was recently made clear by Russian president Vladimir Putin when he reportedly told a female speaker at a meeting of his political party that his only wish was that she "not forget about fulfilling [her] obligations with regard to solving [Russia's] **demographic** issues" (quoted in Gessen 2014: 61). However, while women's reproductive behaviour is central to demographic concerns in many parts of post-socialist Europe, Luehrmann reports that it is not part of the **discourse** about cross-border marriages in Marii El. Residents there do not blame women who migrate for being selfish or unpatriotic, as happens elsewhere; instead, they offer other explanations.

❖ *About the Author* ❖

Sonja Luehrmann grew up in Germany and learned Russian in high school. She first visited Yoshkar-Ola in 2000 to teach German. She later returned to conduct her dissertation research on atheism as state religion in the Soviet Union. She also conducted ethnohistorical research in Alutiiq (Inuit) communities in Alaska. Luehrmann earned advanced degrees in history and anthropology at Johann Wolfgang Goethe University in Germany and at the University of Michigan. She teaches anthropology at Simon Fraser University.

Mediated Marriage: Internet Matchmaking in Provincial Russia

Sonja Luehrmann

Devushki, ne khodite zamuzh za inostrantsev— podderzhite otechestvennogo proizvoditelya!
(Girls, don't marry foreigners—support a domestic producer!)
—Slogan on a mug bought at a department store in Yoshkar-Ola, summer 2003

Susan Gal and Gail Kligman have argued that concerns over the reproduction of the nation have placed women's behaviour at the centre of political debates in many post-socialist **states** (Gal and Kligman

2000: 15). During a year as a teaching fellow at Mari State University in Yoshkar-Ola, the capital of one of the autonomous republics in Russia's Volga region, I found that women's reproductive labour was one of the few commodities which the republic was bringing to an international market, while anxieties about national reproduction centred on men as endangered and rejected "domestic producers." Many of my female students and other acquaintances were corresponding with American, Western European, and Australian men who had obtained their addresses through Internet matchmaking agencies. Sometimes they asked me to translate difficult passages, such as one in which an American man wrote that he had walked by "Victoria's Secret" in the "mall" and wanted to know his friend's "measurements" in order to buy her a present there.

Another acquaintance, the 20-year-old son of one of my colleagues, showed me photographs taken on a summer trip to the US, which included several pictures of suburban couples in their kitchens or in front of their cars. After working at a summer camp, he had been able to travel around the Midwest by visiting several female relatives and friends of his family who had married Americans, and was obviously very favourably impressed with the conditions in which he found them living.

. . . In Yoshkar-Ola Internet matchmaking agencies were a ubiquitous presence, and many women considered the possibility of looking for a husband abroad as one potential way of coping with postsocialist life. During the year I worked at Mari State University three students in the foreign-language department married men from the US or Mexico, with the expressed approval of older faculty members. The agencies also provided a welcome source of income to people with foreign-language skills. Several of my students and colleagues worked for them as translators. In fact, the few times that I heard people dream of opening their own business in Yoshkar-Ola, their idea was to open a matchmaking service.

The concerns I did hear people express over the exodus of brides from Russia were mainly of the sort alluded to in my epigraph: worries that the fact that Russian women were choosing Western men was a quality judgment on Russian men. . . . Whereas Gal and Kligman see debates over national reproduction as a context in which women become a focus of postsocialist politics, one of the arguments of this article will be that Russian debates over the demographic future of the nation, in which much attention is paid to the high mortality rates of men, are about masculinity at least as much as about femininity. Whereas the quantity and quality of Russia's male population figured prominently in women's discussions of why it was desirable to find a foreign husband, I did not hear residents of Marii El express worries over a possible lack of women caused by the out-migration of brides from the republic. Neither did they express the kind of condemnation of brides as traitors to the nation which has been a feature of the national press coverage of Internet matchmaking (Pilkington 1996: 208).

In this article I will consider the significance of Internet matchmaking for constructions of **gender** in post-Soviet Russia by looking at the largest matchmaking agency in Yoshkar-Ola, Virginia. I will place the services Virginia offers in the context of an international gendered and racialized division of labour, as well as in the local context, where the agency functions as a mediator of international connections. To understand why businesses like Virginia are able to flourish, we need to look at the changing expectations men and women in the former Soviet Union and in the West have of each other, and at changing imaginaries of the nation and the foreign in provincial Russia.

Virginia—The Agency

In an economically very depressed part of the Russian Federation—in 2001 the mean monthly per capita income in Marii El was the fifth lowest of the 89 subjects of the Russian Federation—Virginia has managed to expand from a family working from their home computer to a business employing about 70 people, offering a range of services in spacious offices on one of Yoshkar-Ola's central streets. Unlike [neighbouring republics], Marii El has no valuable mineral resources from which to generate income. The local economy under socialism relied heavily on arms production, and unemployment has been very high since the arms factories closed or sharply reduced production. . . .

The services offered by Virginia include matchmaking, local and international employment contracting, visa service and flight tickets for both foreign citizens visiting Russia and Russians travelling abroad, a digital photo studio, a real estate agency, and a language school. Each of the different branches has its own director, and the matchmaking agency even goes by a separate name, Maksim Introductions. But all are located in the same building, under the general directorship of the elder of two brothers who founded the company together with their mother in 1996, just months after the first Internet server became available in Marii El. At first, the family merely used email to send letters of introduction from local women to a small matchmaking agency in Wisconsin, but after one and a half years they created their own website, which allowed them to address Western men looking for a Russian wife directly. Since then Virginia has built up its own network of subcontractors at locations in Marii El, in the neighbouring republics[, and beyond]. Subcontractors place their customers' photos and biographical information on Virginia's website and use Virginia's bank connections to receive payments from abroad (in exchange for a commission which usually amounts to 50 per cent of the sum transferred).

Women who want to place an advertisement on the Web have to go to the office of Maksim Introductions in Yoshkar-Ola or to one of the subcontractors, where they pay for the digital photography and the webspace. When they start receiving letters from abroad, there are two possibilities for payment: if men who are not registered subscribers visit the site, view a "lady's" picture and short biography, and write to her, she has to pay for the letter when she picks it up, for the reply when she sends it, and additional fees for translations if she needs them. However, interested men are encouraged to register on the website and either pay a monthly or yearly subscription fee or [pay] a separate fee for each letter, in which case the "lady" incurs no charges. Subscribers receive extra benefits such as being able to request a report on a woman's English skills or to check whether other men have written to her or sent her an invitation.

The offer of special checkups on a woman's past indicates that many male customers worry about being cheated. The danger of being "scammed" by professional letter writers who place fake photographs on the Web in order to obtain money from a large number of men figures prominently on websites which offer advice to men interested in marrying Russian women. There is even a site which asks men to report agencies and individual women who deceived them. Virginia's director made a point of telling me that his agency accepted only profiles submitted in person by the woman, and only after

FIGURE 11.1　Sidewalk advertisement for Flash Plus photo studio in Yoshkar-Ola. The sign advertises photographs for "international acquaintances" as well as other products and services.

inspecting her passport, which gives information about her marital status.

Women in Yoshkar-Ola tended to suspect the agency, rather than their male correspondence partners, of fraud. There were many rumours about Virginia breaking up the correspondence of people who seemed to get along well, for the sake of keeping both partners as paying customers. It is also well known that Virginia makes a considerable profit on gifts purchased by male customers for their "ladies." Through the website, male customers can order gift baskets and flowers, pay for English classes at Virginia's own language school, or buy a monthly pass for Yoshkar-Ola's trolley busses. . . .

We are beginning to see how closely connected the different branches of Virginia are: the travel agency specializes in obtaining visas and passports necessary for romantic meetings arranged by the matchmakers or for people who have found work abroad through the job agency. For men who want to meet women in person rather than through email, the travel agency also offers a "Romantic Tour" package deal combining sightseeing in the Volga region with parties with single women. The real estate agency rents apartments to men who want to meet several women while they are in Yoshkar-Ola, or whose correspondence partner is unable to host them in her own home. The photo studio takes the digital pictures women need for their Web ads, and the language school offers English classes for women hoping to marry a foreigner. . . .

. . . Virginia's policy of allowing men to write to a "lady" free of charge, passing the financial burden on to her, may be an attempt to attract customers away from Western agencies, which typically require advance payment for each address or for access to a database. A comparison with a small sample of other Web-based matchmaking agencies in the former Soviet Union suggests that neither Virginia's price range nor its policy of allowing men to choose between paying for individual letters or purchasing a membership are unusual. However, not all agencies allow free initial contacts, and some offer the option of purchasing a woman's home address rather than conducting all correspondence through the agency. Agencies also differ in the range of services they offer. Some merely sell addresses, others equal Virginia by offering everything from digital photography and translations to visa and ticket services and English classes. Given the large number of agencies, the market must be quite competitive, and the strategy pursued by agencies like Virginia seems to be to become the one intermediary necessary for establishing relationships between Western men and Russian women. . . .

International Arranged Marriage and Female Migration

. . . In one chapter of her book on Russian–American marriages, Visson (2001: 213–25) describes the recent boom of couples meeting online. Visson . . .

heard about a case of abuse: a woman came to the US on a fiancée visa only to hear the man who invited her announce that he had no intention of marrying her. He forced her to live and sleep with him for the three months which her visa allowed her to stay, then bought her a plane ticket back to Russia. But far more of the problems which surfaced in her interviews with Russian–American couples living in the US sprang not from criminal intentions but from the expectations each spouse had of their life together: women from Russian cities languishing in the isolation of American suburbs, language problems, she turning out to be not as submissive and domestic as he had thought Russian women would be, his standard of living turning out to be not as high as she had hoped, or he discovering that she was more interested in making her own life in the US than in starting a family with him.

Beer (1996: 84) comes to similar conclusions in a study of German–Filipina couples, many of whom had also met through the services of marriage agencies, contact advertisements, or other conscious efforts to find a foreign partner. The problems couples talked about had to do with different notions about obligations to one's extended family, child rearing, or food preparation. While not denying that couples who do have abusive, exploitative relationships may simply be unwilling to be interviewed by an anthropologist, Beer argues that authors and activists who demonize mail-order marriages draw too easy a division between such arranged relationships and those which come about without professional intermediaries, as if the latter never involved unequal power relations or false preconceptions. . . .

It is . . . no accident that matchmaking services focus on bringing together *men* from the wealthy industrialized countries of Western Europe, North America, and Australia and *women* from the Third World and Eastern Europe. . . . Indeed, men whose letters I read and whom I met at the agency—US, German, and British citizens—said that the women of their countries were too emancipated, no longer believed in differences between men and women, and could not show or receive tenderness. In contrast, the photographs [through] which women are presented on Virginia's site—close-ups of the face and upper body shot slightly from above—create the impression of submissive, vulnerable creatures waiting to be rescued from their hard life.

The stereotype of "Russian" women ("Russian" serving as a label for women from the former Soviet Union—many of those advertising through Virginia are actually Tatar or Mari[1]) as being "feminine" and "submissive" is similar to the stereotype of Asian women, who were the major group promoted as "mail-order brides" before the collapse of socialism. The way Maksim Introductions advertises the "ladies" men can meet on their "Romantic Tours" would also fit the stereotypes of Asian women:

> You dream of meeting a real Russian family-oriented lady! You can find such ladies only in small towns in the centre of Russia! They are not spoiled by the life of big cities, they value family life and will make you happy for the rest of your life! . . . **WE GUARANTEE** that during our tour you will be exposed to HUNDREDS of beautiful ladies who are extremely interested in establishing relationships with Western men of all ages. This is not a "sex tour"! The women you will meet have high moral values. We do not concentrate on ladies of "elite class" (models, for example)—instead our goal is to introduce you to women of substance and values, with middle- and upper-class backgrounds who are as sincere about meeting you as you are them. . . . Typically there will be several ladies for every man in attendance. . . . Everything is centred around making you feel welcomed, comfortable, and relaxed, so that you can make the most of your time and reach your goal—meeting a woman of your dreams.[2]

Much of this could come from a website advertising Asian women—beautiful, caring, family-oriented ladies, unspoiled by luxury and typically appearing in large numbers, eager to please even the older Western visitor (cf. Wilson 1988). However, the emphasis on a middle-class background, suggesting similarity of status and outlook with the potential groom, already hints at a difference between Russian and Asian "ladies." . . . Women in Russia seem to offer all the traditional values men used to look to Asia for, but fit more neatly into the racial hierarchies of the US, and may be less readily recognized as "mail-order brides" when appearing with their husbands in public.

Although some women in Yoshkar-Ola laughed at letters in which men expressed the belief that Russian women were tender and submissive, most seemed to regard them as a reassuring answer to the question why there were so many seemingly healthy, seemingly well-off bachelors in the West. . . .

"All the Good Ones Are Taken"—On the Challenges of Putting One's Personal Life in Order

Contrary to the stereotype of the 20-year-old Russian beauty marrying an elderly American pervert, the ages of the women advertising through Virginia vary widely. In November 2002 the first 55 women on the site ranged in age from 20 to 53, with the largest group of women (21) between 31 and 40. All of them had post-secondary education. . . . Some 11 of the women had never been married, 24 were divorced, 1 was divorcing, 3 were widows, and 16 gave no information on their marital status. More than half the women (31) already had one or two children. According to Virginia's director, women between 25 and 35 with no more than one child and higher education have the greatest chances of finding a husband. The oldest woman who married through the agency was 57.

In describing their "ideal man" most women simply give an age span (typically starting at a few years older than they are and going to 10 to 15 years above that) and a minimum height (typically a little over their own height). Some add remarks such as "kind, caring, loving children," a desired country of residence, or a language that he should speak.

These standardized questionnaires are accompanied by one or two photographs and usually followed by a short letter of introduction in which the woman discusses her interests and aspirations. . . .

What motivates these women to look for a husband abroad? I have characterized international arranged marriage as a female migration strategy. That the desire to move to "the West" is a primary motivation for women who use the services of matchmaking agencies was assumed by many people I interviewed in Yoshkar-Ola. In a conversation with Rita and Lida,[3] two unmarried sisters, I was told with great glee the story of a failed migration. An American bridegroom arrived in Yoshkar-Ola to marry his chosen one, but liked the natural scenery of the republic so much that he stayed in her village, where the couple were still living more than a year after their marriage, much to the dismay of the bride. What made the story funny was the unspoken assumption that she had married him in order to move to the US, not to live in a Mari village with him.

On the other hand, women who were looking for a husband over the Internet, as well as some who were not, often explained the motivation for marrying a foreigner differently. Many women—whether young and unmarried or middle-aged and divorced—talked about being lonely, wanting to have a family. They would be happy to marry a Russian, many of them said, if they could find someone who was not a drunkard and would actually be a help and support rather than a big child who needed to be taken care of. Such men, they claimed, were almost impossible to find in Yoshkar-Ola, because they either got "taken" by other women . . . or moved away to find work in a bigger city.

Even if some women may simply have considered it more acceptable to describe their plans as emigrating in order to marry rather than marrying in order to emigrate, it may be worthwhile to take seriously what so many of them were saying and think of marriage as more than just a channel for migration. The very difficulty of starting and sustaining what these women considered a desirable family life may be one of the factors leading them to decide

to leave Russia. *"Obustroit' sebe lichnuyu zhizn'"*—to put one's personal life in order, to settle down with a stable family—was often mentioned as a woman's central concern in life, but just as frequent were complaints that post-Soviet life was *"takaya neustroennaya"*—so disorderly, uncivilized, and chaotic. Masha, a young woman who was very actively searching for a husband abroad, corresponding successively with several Americans and a German . . ., exemplifies the difficulties of creating the kind of orderly life she might have wanted in Yoshkar-Ola. At 21 years old, she had moved to Yoshkar-Ola from a smaller town, was working as a nurse, and [was] living in the apartment occupied by an uncle and his family. Since her monthly salary did not even cover the cost of groceries, she had no hope of ever being able to rent or buy her own apartment, so getting married to someone with access to his own housing was literally the only way for her to leave the obviously uncomfortable living situation with her relatives.

Another of the agency's customers, Olga, was a divorced librarian, living in a university dormitory with her 11-year-old daughter, since her former husband had kept their apartment. All her floor neighbours were male students, and she was concerned over her daughter sharing washroom facilities with them, but the only improvement of her living situation she could hope for in Yoshkar-Ola was persuading the administration to move her to a dormitory reserved for staff and faculty.

Whether these women might have been able to find husbands locally is another question. Male alcoholism has been discussed as a leading cause of illness and death throughout Russia for decades. . . . Another part of the problem is that even a reasonably sober young couple will have a hard time generating enough income to be able to establish their own household and live in some comfort. The options for finding any sort of employment which pays a living wage are very limited in Yoshkar-Ola. . . .

While there appears to be some truth to women's claims that eligible men are scarce in Yoshkar-Ola, part of the problem may be that men and women have adjusted their views of gender roles differently under the changing conditions of post-Soviet Russia. . . . [M]any men and women agree that it is desirable for the husband to be the main breadwinner, while women should work part-time or at least subordinate their careers to their family. However, . . . men and women differ in their interpretation of the breadwinner role. While women long for a man who will devote his energy and his income to taking care of his family, men see their earnings as a way to gain autonomy, and try to reserve part of them for sustaining social relationships outside the family—for instance, through social drinking with colleagues.

Such disagreements over gender roles between men and women in Russia lead some Russian women to look abroad in the hope of finding a man who is both able and willing to fulfill the breadwinner role she envisions. This does not mean that none of these women wants to work or study after marriage. During an English class which I attended at Virginia, the students—all women in their early or mid-twenties corresponding with Anglophone men through the agency—asked me whether American men minded if their wives worked, and the instructor, also a young woman, encouraged them to discuss this question with their correspondence partners. . . . [T]hese women combined dreams of a professional career with the expectation that the husband should be both the main source of material support and the person holding authority in a marriage.

In Yoshkar-Ola I rarely heard people condemn women for seeking to marry a foreigner, and I would like to suggest that this was due to a widespread recognition of the strain placed on male–female relationships by the conditions of post-Soviet life, as well as to a preoccupation with men as the weakest link in Russia's demographic future. While I heard only one instance of someone condemning women who search for a foreign husband as acting out of calculation . . ., I heard several young women complain that marriage between Russians had become more calculating. Young people used to get married when they felt like it, Rita explained, because they knew that their salaries were more or less assured,

[that] child care and education for their children would be provided, and that they would be assigned a state-owned apartment eventually, even if it would take a long time. Today, by contrast, people really needed to count whether they would be able to support themselves and children, how and where they would find housing, and how they would pay for their children's education. . . .

If financial insecurity is a relatively new concern for couples, the concern over a gender imbalance in Russian society predates the collapse of the Soviet Union, and was one of the reasons for the legalization of matchmaking services during the Brezhnev era [1964–1982]. The life expectancy of Russian men has been declining since the 1960s, a trend that increased in the 1990s. In 2001 life expectancy at birth was 58.6 years for men, compared with 72.1 for women. Since the mortality rate is especially high for men between 35 and 55, it is in this age bracket and above that women outnumber men. . . .

In the post-Soviet period this demographic imbalance has received increasing media and scholarly attention, along with the sinking birth rate and rising divorce rate. Matveeva and Shlyapentokh (2000: 145) speak of a post-Soviet "catastrophism" that focuses on fear of social, rather than natural, catastrophes, and Gal and Kligman (2000: 25) have identified the central role that public debates over reproduction—issues ranging from abortion legislation to stopping demographic decline—have played in the politics of most Eastern European states since 1990. They argue that taking up the issue of reproduction helps new governments gain legitimacy by constructing a link between the private concerns of citizens and the future of the state, and showing themselves as practising moral, responsible politics. For them, an important consequence of such debates is attempts at regulating women's sexual behaviour, and Russian feminist scholarship has also shown how the discourse on demographic decline blames women for not wanting to have children, and portrays reproduction as a female responsibility at the very time when the state is no longer offering much help to parents (Posadskaya, 1994; Issoupova, 2000). However, I found that much of the public anxiety in Yoshkar-Ola focused not on women but on the Russian man as an endangered species, weakened, just like Russian economic production, by the changing times and the demands of a Western lifestyle.

. . . I did not hear people in Yoshkar-Ola express worries that there would be a shortage of brides in the republic. The popularity of international marriages mainly raised anxieties over the quality of the nation's male members, who seemed to be rejected by consumers in much the same way as Russian products. This link is made in the parody of "buy Russian" slogans on the mug which I cite in my epigraph. It also came out during the International Women's Day celebration (8 March 2001) of our overwhelmingly female work collective at the foreign-language department of Mari State University. As the elderly colleagues were debating the question whether all the young, unmarried members of the faculty should better marry Russians or foreigners, Galina Aleksandrovna maintained that Russian men were best. She was silenced by Natal'ya Grigor'evna's question, "Yes, but where can they be found?," followed by a story about a drunken army officer on the bus. As the conversation turned to remembering how tasty the imported chocolates brought by recent guests had been, Galina Aleksandrovna interjected: "But sausages from Zvenigovo[4] are the best in the world!"

In this conversation between older women, Russian men and Russian products were the focus of attention, **symbols** of the nation's threatened economic and biological future. By implying that Russian women have to turn to foreign men because real Russian men have become a rarity, they relieved young women of the charge of betraying the nation but also made light of the problems these women faced. . . . Like the media discourse on Russia's gender imbalance and demographic decline, conversations such as these simultaneously reinforce the idea that it is a woman's foremost aim to find a husband and that it is very difficult to do so in Russia. Another subtext of this conversation is the opinion, expressed by scholars as well as by many of my female interlocutors, that men have been harder hit than women by the changes

of post-Soviet life, because male identities were tied more strongly to their status of worker in the Soviet economy. . . .

Commodifying Introductions: The Value of Foreign Connections

Lemon points to the ambiguous relationship of ex-Soviet citizens to Western commodities and money: while they have been seen as a threat to the integrity of Russian national substance, they have also formed the focus of fantasies about "possibilities of faraway exchange . . . of extensions of the self" (Lemon 1998: 29). In Marii El and other parts of provincial Russia the collapse of the Soviet Union has brought an explosion of (often contradictory) media images from and of "the West," while the difficult economic situation and visa restrictions still make travelling abroad impossible for most people, and foreign visitors remain rare. In this situation Internet matchmaking services offer a chance for some women to travel or move abroad, but they also create channels along which material and symbolic resources move into provincial Russia. For the mediators as well as their female customers, establishing such channels requires both new skills and the adaptation of modes of behaviour familiar from Soviet times. For instance, the matchmaking business is a way of enlarging social networks through introductions, reminiscent of the Soviet system of gaining access to goods and services through social relations (*blat*). But it differs from Soviet *blat* networks in several ways. The role of intermediary becomes commodified as a paid service, and the access provided is no longer to personal acquaintances but to technologies and skills which are needed to enter into contact with people who are unknown to the mediator as well as to the customer.

The number of Russian women who establish foreign connections through Virginia or similar agencies is greater than those who actually get married and emigrate. . . . Virginia's director would not give a success rate, since the process can take several years, and some women either give up along the way or marry locally. He claimed that any woman seriously pursuing the idea of finding a foreign husband could succeed eventually. This implies that female customers differ in their commitment to finding a husband through the agency, something I can confirm from the women I spoke to. Some were going to the agency once or twice a month to see whether they had received messages, while others were corresponding intensely with several men at a time, taking English classes to prepare for moving abroad, and even had telephone conversations with their correspondence partners. The first group of women seemed to treat the matchmaking service more like an insurance that might pay off in case of future need. For the agency itself, it is more profitable if a woman corresponds with men for a long time without getting married. . . .

Some women use the connections they gain through the matchmaking service without intending to emigrate permanently. Marina, a foreign-language instructor, presented the most striking example. When I met her in the autumn of 2000 she was recently divorced. . . . That autumn she spent a week in Italy at the invitation of one of her correspondence partners, whom she also asked to send her money for a new television set as a New Year gift. In the spring she married a local Russian. Placing an advertisement on the Internet opens up possibilities of travel and consumption for some women which would be closed to them without the material and legal support of a foreign contact. Even though for such women neither migration nor marriage is the immediate goal, they use the matchmaking agency to extend their network of connections abroad, helping make life in Yoshkar-Ola more pleasant. . . .

Other than the technology necessary for making international contacts, the Internet matchmaker also provides male and female customers with access to knowledge about each other's cultures, constructing a specific image of the gendered expectations of Western men and Russian women. On the English-language site of Maksim Introductions a monthly newsletter features articles on Russian

customs and holidays, with reminders of the possibility to purchase gifts and flowers for a "lady" through the agency. The agency's Russian-language pages also contain a calendar of holidays celebrated in selected Western countries, and the instructions for taking attractive pictures construct an image of the essentials of Western culture:

> No matter how sad you may feel, try to smile. The smile is an integral element . . . of Western culture, and without a smile you will receive far fewer letters. Do not transfer your problems onto your potential grooms.[5]

. . . This leads to a discussion of other pictures men may find attractive: although the agency discourages nude photographs on the publicly accessible web page, it suggests that women can place such pictures on protected pages accessible only to registered members. . . . Women are also urged to fulfill any requests "your friend" may make for pictures in specific attire or poses. . . . In letters I was asked to translate men frequently hinted that they would like to see what their correspondence partner looked like in a bikini. . . .

International matchmakers, even if they do not personally know their clients, provide each side with an introduction to the cultural environment of the other. Like all intermediaries, they depend on keeping two groups of people interested in each other as well as separated. In order to sustain this mutual interest, the agencies actively reinforce the idea that Russian women and Western men offer each other answers to crises in gender relations in their respective societies. By promising each side that they will find abroad what they have been looking for in vain at home, international matchmaking agencies both rely on and strengthen existing gender stereotypes in each society. . . .

In the perception of Virginia's female customers, the difficulty of "putting one's personal life in order" in Russia is due to the failure of many Russian men to act as responsible providers, and aggravated by Russia's depressed economy. If these women seek a solution through relationships with foreigners, they are embracing the idea of female dependence on a male breadwinner, fulfilling Western men's expectations of "traditional femininity." However, deciding to acquire the technical means and the cultural skills necessary for establishing Western contacts can also be a way to escape dependency and limited chances at home, as the examples of Masha and Olga and their housing situations show. . . .

Conclusion: Letters and Responses

I hope to have shown that Internet matchmaking in Russia is a socially and economically significant phenomenon that is part of more general changes in gender relations within Russian society and within the global division of reproductive labour. I have argued that the significance of this business to Russian women has not received the scholarly attention which it deserves, but is too often written off as just another part of an international network of trafficking in defenseless, victimized women. This does not mean that I deny the risks of abuse and dependency inherent in such marriage arrangements. But in Yoshkar-Ola I often felt unable to tell [women] that they had better alternatives than becoming a mail-order bride, because I could see for myself that local opportunities for supporting oneself or a family were very limited, and most channels for moving to a larger city or abroad seemed laden with similar risks of abuse.

. . . Whether they want to emigrate, find a way to have a family, or simply be invited to Italy for a vacation, these women are writing because they want a response, and they are writing to those people (Western men) who are both motivated to respond to them (because they dream of finding a beautiful, feminine Russian woman) and materially and legally able to respond (because they have the necessary funds to sponsor a bride and because their government's laws recognize a right of spouses to live together). For the sake of receiving a response, these women put on their most radiant smiles in the photo studio, no matter how sad it may make the social scientist to look at them.

References Cited

Beer, Bettina. 1996. *Deutsch–philippinische Ehen. Interethnische Heiraten und Migration von Frauen.* Berlin: Reimer.

Gal, Susan, and Gail Kligman. 2000. *The Politics of Gender after Socialism: A Comparative-Historical Essay.* Princeton, NJ: Princeton University Press.

Issoupova, Olga. 2000. "From Duty to Pleasure? Motherhood in Soviet and Post-Soviet Russia." In *Gender, State, and Society in Soviet and Post-Soviet Russia,* edited by Sarah Ashwin, 30–54. London: Routledge.

Lemon, Alaina. 1998. "'Your Eyes Are Green like Dollars': Counterfeit Cash, National Substance, and Currency Apartheid in 1990s Russia." *Cultural Anthropology* 13 (1): 22–55.

Matveeva, Susanna, and Vladimir Shlyapentokh. 2000. *Strakhi v Rossii v proshlom i nastoyashchem.* Novosibirsk: Sibirskii Khronograf.

Pilkington, Hilary. 1996. "'Youth Culture' in Contemporary Russia: Gender, Consumption, and Identity." In *Gender, Generation, and Identity in Contemporary Russia,* edited by Hilary Pilkington, 189–215. London: Routledge.

Posadskaya, Anastasia. 1994. "Self-Portrait of a Russian Feminist: An Interview with Anastasia Posadskaya." In *Women in Russia: A New Era in Russian Feminism,* edited by Anastasia Posadskaya, translated by Kate Clark, 183–201. London: Verso.

Visson, Lynn. 2001. *Wedded Strangers: The Challenges of Russian–American Marriages.* Expanded ed. New York: Hippocrene.

Wilson, Ara. 1988. "American Catalogues of Asian Brides." In *Anthropology for the Nineties: Introductory Readings,* edited by Johnnetta B. Cole, 114–25. New York: Free Press.

Notes

1. Tatar and Mari are Indigenous ethnic minorities in the Russian Federation. (Stern's note)
2. www.yoshkar-ola.com/e/services.shtml?romantic, read 4 September 2003. (Luehrmann's note)
3. All names in this article have been changed. (Luehrmann's note)
4. A small town in Marii El. (Luehrmann's note)
5. www.virginia.ru/marriage/private.shtml?photo, read 4 September 2003 (my translation). (Luehrmann's note)

Key Points to Consider

- Marriage is an important life-course event found in nearly all cultures. Marriage connects individuals as well as families, and it is a cultural institution widely regarded as important to the maintenance of social groups.
- Marriage migration tends to follow the same pathways as labour migration and occurs for many of the same reasons.
- The ubiquity of Internet access has encouraged the development of services that facilitate cross-border marriages. Operators of Internet-based matchmaking agencies tend to encourage gender stereotyping that matches the fantasies of their male and female clients.
- Cross-border marriages feed into moral panics in some, but not all, places.

Critical Thinking Questions

1. How do the residents of Yoshkar-Ola explain the growing incidence of cross-border marriages for local women? Did Luehrmann find evidence of a moral panic? Do you think that people in Yoshkar-Ola should be concerned that women are looking for foreign spouses?
2. In what way does the popularity of Internet matchmaking in Yoshkar-Ola reflect "changes in gender relations within Russian society and within the global division of reproductive labour"?
3. In your view, how do the customers of dating services like Match.com and eHarmony compare to those of Virginia? Does the fact that Virginia's clients are looking for international matches make their spouse-selection activities different from those of the clients of Internet-based domestic matchmaking services?
4. The phrase "mediated marriage" in the title of the article is a reference to the use of Internet-based services to negotiate (mediate) introductions of men and women interested in marriage. What other social institutions and practices facilitate matchmaking?

Suggestions for Further Reading

Abu Hashish, Shereen Ali, and Mark Allen Peterson. 1999. "Computer *Khatbas*: Databases and Marital Entrepreneurship in Modern Cairo." *Anthropology Today* 15 (6): 7–11.
Constable, Nicole. 2003. *Romance on a Global Stage: Pen Pals, Virtual Ethnography, and "Mail Order" Marriages*. Berkeley: University of California Press.

Luehrmann, Sonja. 2011. *Secularism Soviet Style: Teaching Atheism and Religion in a Volga Republic.* Bloomington: Indiana University Press.

Oxfeld, Ellen. 2004. "Cross-border Hypergamy? Marriage Exchanges in a Transnational Hakka Community." In *Cross-border Marriages: Gender and Mobility in Transitional Asia*, edited by Nicole Constable, 17–33. Philadelphia: University of Pennsylvania Press.

Stern, Pamela R., and Richard G. Condon. 1995. "A Good Spouse Is Hard to Find: Marriage, Spouse Exchange, and Infatuation among the Copper Inuit." In *Romantic Passion: A Universal Experience?*, edited by William Jankowiak, 196–218. New York: Columbia University Press.

Chapter 12

ARCTIC OCEAN

UNITED STATES

CANADA

PACIFIC OCEAN

UNITED STATES

ATLANTIC OCEAN

GULF OF MEXICO

MEXICO

0   300   600 km

United States of America

Introduction

Kinship is a matter of enormous importance to people. In small-scale societies, kinship may be the primary basis by which the society is organized and individual members' identities are formed. Large-scale, ethnically and socially diverse societies have many institutions through which people connect with one another, and in these societies, institutions other than kinship are often sources of identity, economic and emotional support, and **socialization**. However, despite the possibilities for religious, educational, class, ethnic, and social groups to provide many of the functions of family, kinship remains an institution that few people could imagine living without. Kinship remains privileged in culture and codified and validated in law.

American anthropologist David Schneider (1918–1995) asserted that the dominant ways that people in North America and Western Europe talk about kinship and assign kinship terms encourage people in Western cultures to think of kinship as a biological relationship. In other cultural groups, kinship is treated as a social rather than a biological relationship. Schneider argued that many anthropologists make an **ethnocentric** mistake of using Euro-American (and Euro-Canadian) models of kinship to interpret relationships in other cultures. For example, North Americans and Western Europeans often label kin relationships that are not created through marriage or descent as "**fictive kinship**." Adoption is sometimes also treated as fictive kinship. Schneider argued that anthropologists should look for the practices that symbolize kinship in different cultures rather than apply pre-existing Western categories to those cultures. He was correct: if we are true to our goal of understanding the world from the perspective of the people we study, we need to understand how and why *they* categorize some people as relatives and others as non-relatives. Along those lines, Arctic scholar Mark Nuttall observed that **Inuit** in North Greenland associate certain roles and obligations with particular kin relations—siblings treat each other one way, nephews and uncles another. North Greenlanders sometimes develop kinship relations with people who do not fit the category biologically, calling each other by the kin terms that reflect their shared affection and obligations as well as the activities they do together (Nuttall 2000). American anthropologist Mac Marshall (1977) noted something similar among the Trukese (Chuukese) people in the Marshall Islands.

Rather than treating kinship as biological relationships between people, it might be more appropriate to regard kinship as relationships among a group of people that, while often grounded in biology, most importantly entail enduring ties of affection as well as rights and obligations among group members and to the group as a whole. American anthropologist Kath Weston's research among lesbian and gay individuals living in San Francisco in the 1980s is illustrative. It is easy to forget that legal recognition of same-sex marriages is a recent development, and that it was (and in some cases still is) not uncommon for "out" gay and lesbian individuals to be estranged from their **natal** families. As well, when Weston was conducting her study, there was a widely held belief that the **affective** bonds of family were confined to heterosexual relationships. Weston, however, documented the symbolic and material ways that gay and lesbian individuals created "chosen families" out of friendships. At the same time, she showed that the lesbian and gay individuals she studied created familial relationships that drew on the building blocks of the American kinship system they had grown up with (Weston 1997).

New technologies that can map the human genome and do precise DNA matching may reinforce Westerners' pre-existing ideas about the importance of biological connections in kinship. At the same time, new assisted reproductive technologies (ARTs) mean that more and more infertile couples and individuals now have previously unimagined ways to have children. ARTs can involve the use of donated sperm or eggs, in vitro fertilization (IVF), a surrogate using her own or donor eggs, or some combination of these. These technologies make it increasing possible for parents and children to share no genetic material.

In vitro fertilization is an expensive and fairly invasive medical procedure involving a drug regime that causes a woman's body to produce mature eggs, physical extraction of up to forty eggs from the woman's ovaries, fertilization of the eggs with sperm in a petri dish, and finally implantation of two or more embryos (fertilized eggs) into the woman's uterus. Louise Brown, the first child conceived through IVF, was born in the United Kingdom in 1978. Since that time, IVF has become available to infertile couples in much of the world, including many developing countries. The widespread use of IVF has led to a spike in the birth of twins and triplets, but IVF also frequently fails to produce a pregnancy. According to anthropologist Elizabeth Roberts, who studied IVF in Latin America and the United States, "the take-home baby rate with IVF is a relatively low 30 per cent" (Roberts 2011: 235).

A single cycle of IVF often produces many more embryos than can be safely implanted in a woman and successfully carried to term. Initially, physicians destroyed the "extra" embryos. Since the 1980s, the development of cryopreservation techniques has permitted unimplanted embryos to be frozen for later attempts at pregnancy. There are many people, of course, who will never use all of their frozen embryos, raising the question of what should be done with the extra embryos. Elizabeth Roberts (2011) cites news sources that report the existence of 400,000 frozen embryos in the United States alone. Should these embryos remain frozen forever? Should they be destroyed? Should they be used for stem-cell or other medical research? Or should they be given to other infertile people who want to become parents?

The article by Chantal Collard and Shireen Kashmeri presented below concerns the last of these options. In particular, Collard and Kashmeri are interested in understanding how families who donate embryos and families who receive embryos think about and pursue kin relationships. What emphasis do they put on genetic connections among kin?

Under US and Canadian law, human embryos are considered property that may be transferred from one owner to another, but may not be sold. In fact, only a small percentage of unused frozen human embryos are transferred from the couples that produced them to other infertile people. The most common way this transfer happens is through embryo donations arranged by fertility clinics; the donors and recipients often have very little information about each other, and adoption agencies are generally not involved. Collard and Kashmeri studied people who donated and received embryos through an adoption program called Snowflakes established by a Christian adoption agency in California. From 1997, when the agency began arranging embryo adoptions, through early 2015, the program had resulted in the birth of nearly four hundred babies (Nightlight Christian Adoptions 2015). A similar embryo adoption program, called Beginnings, exists in Canada.

In the past, most adoption records in Canada and the United States were sealed—neither birth parents nor the child and her or his adoptive parents were able to know anything about the other. Adopted children were issued new birth certificates bearing the adoptive parents' names, officially erasing the fact that the child had been adopted. Most adoptions today are open adoptions in which all participants know one another's identity, the birth mother (or birth parents) can select who will adopt the baby, and the birth mother (or birth parents) may have ongoing contact with the child. Snowflake embryo adoptions are open adoptions that operate in the same way.

Collard and Kashmeri explore how the placing families and the adopting families involved in embryo adoption think about and value particular types of kin relations. In referring to the individuals who donated the embryos, the authors employ the term *placing families* rather than *genetic families* because some of these individuals used donated eggs and/or sperm to conceive and are not genetically related to the embryos. One consideration some families found to be significant is that through the processes of IVF and embryo adoption, genetic siblings may be born into and raised by different families. Another consideration is that IVF and cryopreservation make it possible for children to be conceived on the same date but born years apart, possibly confusing the sense of birth order.

The complicated biological facts of embryo adoption do not fit the **schema** or mental model that most North Americans have of how kinship is supposed to work. Building on the ideas of David Schneider, discussed above, Collard and Kashmeri try to understand how the families they studied reconciled the genetic facts with the need to establish their families as normal. In this regard, the authors make a distinction between "naturalizing kinship"—practices that emphasize the genetic ties between siblings—and "culturalizing kinship"—practices that emphasize the nurturing role of the family. As Collard and Kashmeri point out, some of the families draw on Christian religious models as they culturalize kinship.

Just as the gay and lesbian individuals studied by Kath Weston use American cultural models or schemas of kinship in creating families of choice, placing and adoptive parents also use existing schemas to imagine their families. Of course, due to death, divorce, and other circumstances, most North American families do not neatly match the model of the family that most people have in their minds. And so we often exercise **agency** to improvise within the range of what is culturally imaginable. The evidence Collard and Kashmeri present shows that placing and adopting Snowflake families also improvise and adjust as circumstances cause them to alter their expectations.

❖ About the Authors ❖

Chantal Collard recently retired from the Department of Sociology and Anthropology at Concordia University. Collard is from France and earned her degrees in anthropology from the University of Paris. She has lived in Canada since the 1970s. Collard has conducted fieldwork in Haiti, Cameroon, Quebec, and the United States on kinship and social organization, paying particular attention to practices of adoption.

Shireen Kashmeri is a PhD candidate at the University of Toronto. Her master's thesis at Concordia University examined surrogacy and assisted reproduction in an LGBTQ community of Toronto.

Embryo Adoption: Emergent Forms of Siblingship among Snowflakes Families

Chantal Collard and Shireen Kashmeri

In this article, we address new developments and issues in kinship and siblingship faced by genetic, or "placing," and adopting families who used the California-based embryo adoption program known as Snowflakes. We examine the choices these families made and their uncertainty and fears, too, especially as embryo adoption is still a relatively new procedure. For the families we studied, reproductive technologies have created the potential for two forms of siblingship that did not exist before: "batch siblings," that is, children conceived from the same gametes at the same time through in vitro fertilization (IVF) and born simultaneously as fraternal twins or triplets or in succession as a result of embryo cryopreservation, and "genetic siblings carried by different mothers," children created with the same genetic material, some of whom are born to their genetic mother and others to another woman as a result of embryo donation or adoption. . . .

We argue that the sibling relation is of the utmost importance both for those parents who relinquished embryos and those who adopted them. Although many placing families want to give their embryos a chance at life, they do not want to disperse them among several families. Instead, they strongly prefer to keep them together to increase the chances that at least two offspring will be born into the adoptive family. This desire correlates with adoptive parents' own partiality toward genetic siblingship in their family. In the case of adoptive families, siblingship becomes the core of the family, . . . reinforcing its genetic–biological basis and thus symbolizing its unity. Genetic siblingship also becomes the building block for the family's next generation, as the biological offspring of genetic siblings will also be genetically related, just as in most families. In this case, siblingship trumps descent, so to speak, at least for one generation. However, there are some exceptions to this model. For some adoptive parents, this genetic link does not matter so much, or, when it is not possible to have genetic siblings in the family, other strategies emerge to ensure that adopted children share a special relationship with at least one other child in the same situation. For instance, Snowflake siblings adopted from different placing families still share the same maternal womb and adoption history. Or, if the adoptive family has only one child, then the Snowflakes "family," composed of all the children born through the program, provides that child with the special bond of siblingship.

Placing parents think that embryos should not remain frozen forever and that the most moral course of action is to give them up to other parents, no matter how difficult this may be. In the process, the relations between these embryos and living brothers and sisters in placing–genetic families must

be [sorted out]. . . . But knowing of the existence of [genetic] siblings does not automatically imply contact between families. As far as relationships are concerned, two models emerged in our study. Some families keep in touch, redefining kinship relations and terminologies to create more distance between **consanguineously** related children and between [these children] and their "non-parents" in the other family. A second, more frequent model is that the genetic siblingship link is not activated during childhood, similar to the classic model of adoption. Instead, this contact is delayed until the children are old enough to make the decision and choose— or not—to include these "brothers and sisters out there" as more than virtual genetic siblings.

Our research findings are based on interviews with 44 participants. We conducted 14 interviews with genetic–placing parents and 17 with adoptive parents. Thirty-one participants were women; in 11 cases, husbands also participated. We interviewed 6 parents twice. We also met on two occasions with a coordinator at Snowflakes and had a lengthy interview with a religious leader—recommended by one of the adoptive mothers—who is also an academic and a public speaker. Interviews were done face to face in California, many of them in the participants' homes. . . .

The Snowflakes Embryo Adoption Program

Nightlight Christian Adoptions, a non-profit agency, provides domestic and international child adoptions as well as embryo adoption. The Snowflakes program distinguishes itself by providing open adoptions, unlike most fertility clinics, which provide very little identifying information to recipients of embryos. Nightlight considers an embryo similar to a live child. Embryos are thus "preborn children" or, rather, "potential preborn children," as not all of them survive the thawing, implantation, and pregnancy processes. . . .

Even though Nightlight is unabashedly Christian, and Christian values are featured prominently in its mission statement, its clients are not necessarily

Christian. The Snowflakes program's mandate is to save potential lives, which means it will accept couples from all religious backgrounds. Only married couples and single women are allowed to adopt embryos. Single men are ineligible to adopt, as it would require the use of a surrogate to carry the child. The logic of embryo adoption is predicated on the Christian notion that life begins at conception, and **supernumerary** embryos are, therefore, not just "extras" but, rather, unique and fragile, just like a snowflake (Nightlife Christian Adoptions Agency 2009). . . .

Kinship as Hybrid

. . . Anthropologists have long argued that only socially recognized family relations constitute kinship. However, following Strathern, we consider knowledge [of genetic ties to inform new understandings] of kinship because "once biological links are known, they cannot be laid aside" (1999: 79). True, biological links alone do not carry any weight as far as rights and duties are concerned (such as naming, citizenship, inheritance, and alimony). Yet,

once known, or even suspected, they definitely lurk in the background as far as incest prohibitions are concerned. Access to this form of knowledge was an important reason why Snowflakes parents chose embryo adoption over anonymous donation.

In terms of strategy, the primary goal of parents who use ARTs [assisted reproductive technologies] is to normalize their trajectories. "People start out on the fertility journey wanting to be a normal family and wanting others to see them that way. The question of how to proceed so that people see them as a normal family and the child as a normal child becomes the centerpiece of their efforts to become parents" (Becker 2000: 218). In building their families and writing their own kinship scripts, these parents do not innovate totally but, rather, use models of current practices around them, borrowing often from other ART and adoption practices, especially open adoption (Modell 2001), and from models of family recomposition after divorce (Simpson 1998).

Additionally, parents are concerned with acting morally (Collard and Kashmeri 2009; Konrad 2005; Roberts 2007). Several participants in the

FIGURE 12.1   Parents in Minnesota with the daughter they adopted through embryo adoption.

study spoke of consulting with religious leaders to "be honourable in front of God." Others talked of how they had thought long and hard about the best course of action for themselves and their future children in building their families. However, some placing parents admitted they had wanted a child so desperately that they did not think about the repercussions of IVF, such as creating supernumerary embryos, and reflected on them only afterward, once their families were completed.

Siblingship

Siblingship is one of the three basic kinship relations, together with descent and marriage. Yet, compared with descent and alliance in anthropology, it has been much less well studied, until recently. In classical anthropology, siblingship was frequently taken into account only as far as it affected the other two relations. . . .

Cultures differ in terms of how siblings are recognized and classified. Traditionally, in Euro-American kinship, "siblings are identified by genealogical or biological criteria, where full siblings have two biological parents in common and half-siblings share only one biological parent" (Cicirelli 1994: 8). Outside the case of identical multiples (such as identical twins), full biological siblings will, on average, share only 50 per cent of their DNA because each will receive half of each parent's set of chromosomes. . . . French sociologist Florence Weber (2005) refers to three coexisting criteria in Western kinship as "le nom, le sang, le quotidien" (name, blood, everyday living). . . .

Embryo adoption offers another basis for differentiating between genetic siblings: the gestational mother. If some cultures (especially **patrilineal** ones) downplay carrying and delivering a child, recognizing the maternal womb, for instance, only as a vessel or a container, others—quite to the contrary—recognize gestating a child as the most important criterion for filiation and siblingship. For example, in her study of the Kamea in Papua New Guinea, anthropologist Sandra Bamford notes, "Any children that a woman bears, regardless of who the father might be, are said by Kamea to be 'one-blood'

with one another. The same it should be pointed out does not hold true for a man. . . . Only persons born of the same womb are *jinya avaka*. To be 'one-blood,' then, is to have originated from the same maternal container" (2007: 61). Bamford acknowledges that she found this distinction unclear at first, as it seemed easily confused with the Western notion of genetic ties between parents and children.

> I initially confused the notion of "one-bloodedness" with Western ideas concerning the inheritance of biogenetic substance and assumed that the expression referred to the cultural fact that blood is the female contribution to conception. Kamea, as it turns out, did not share my fascination with the field of biology. Neither a woman nor a man is considered to be "one-blood" with their children; the term refers exclusively to having issued from the same woman's womb. (Bamford 2007: 61)

> . . .

In Euro-American kinship, however, we do not find such strong representations of the womb. Indeed, quite to the contrary, in the field of reproductive technologies, gestational surrogacy seems to have contributed to diminishing the importance of gestation as a marker of kinship (Delaisi de Parseval and Collard 2007; Kashmeri 2009; Ragoné 1994, 1996). . . .

Having the Pair: Siblings as the Core of the Family

One of the main observations from our study on embryo adoption is that siblingship connections are of the utmost importance to the participants and must be managed by both the placing and adopting parents. The adoption agency recommends adoptive parents not mix embryos in the implantation process, which hints at the importance of genetics. It also eases follow-up contact between the placing–genetic and adoptive parents and resulting child or children, both at the time of pregnancy and in the future. Placing parents try to ensure that embryos are kept in one adoptive family, that genetic siblings stay together and are not dispersed to many different families. To fulfill this goal, placing parents will actively look for adoptive parents who want to have multiple children and are willing to use all of their embryos. The importance of genetic siblingship in embryo adoption is illustrated by our conversation with Aubrey, a placing mother with two boys, who relinquished all 19 of her embryos to a single couple.

> We relinquished all of the embryos to [the adoptive parents] and in our terms, it was, we want somebody that will take all of the embryos and have more than one genetic sibling with those embryos. We wanted somebody that didn't have other kids, or they could have had other kids, but they want one or more children, because we had so many [embryos]. *I wanted them to stay in the same family. I didn't want them to go here and there and everywhere . . . because they're siblings* [laughs]. And I wanted somebody to have the siblings together because . . . Still I think [that] siblings should grow up together and I think you have a bond with your siblings that you don't have with other people.

This later caused much emotional difficulty because the adopted embryos resulted in only one boy, not a set of twins or sibling pair. This meant that Aubrey's sons were the adopted boy's only genetic brothers, but his adoptive parents were not open to the three boys meeting. Aubrey related that she had told the adoptive parents, "We would really like our sons to know him, because *our sons are the only genetic siblings that this child is going to have. Ever. And I would really like them to have a relationship*." However, the adoptive parents did not feel the same way and instead restricted contact to emails and pictures.

Adoptive mother Laurel, after thawing and transferring all the embryos from one family, decided to stop adding to her family through any type of adoption. This protected the integrity of the sibling relations between her two children based on their common genetic descent. She expresses her views on the importance of genetic ties clearly: "Oh, to me

it's very important because they are actually brother and sister. They are blood relatives . . . *they have a connection between them that we don't have with them.* So . . . it just means so much to us that they were genetically brother and sister."

Another adoptive mother, Sarah, also explains that it gives her much "peace" that her four daughters, all genetic siblings and Snowflakes, are related to each other:

> I feel a real peace because I know for me, I always try to put myself in their shoes, if I were adopted you know, what would I feel growing up and as an adult, and I think the biggest concern is "I'm not alone in the world." If they never get to have a relationship with the genetic parents, they at least have each other and they know that there is someone else like them so they are not alone.

However, Sarah remarks that the tight sibling bonds between the girls leave no room to add any fewer than two more adopted children.

> We've thought about adopting again and one of my biggest concerns is . . . Well, these four girls have such a connection, and if we adopted one, I'd kind of feel like we'd need to adopt two. They wouldn't be left out then. They wouldn't be like, "Oh, I'm the only one that doesn't have someone." *At least with these four I know that they all have that connection. They have the same story, the same family history, and it makes it easier for us not to have to trace too many outside families.*

Another adoptive mother, Ellen, contemplating having a second child from the same batch as her infant daughter, observed that the link between two genetic siblings would stand in [place] of genetic ties to the adoptive parents. The context of her embryo adoption is unique in our sample, because the embryos were created with both sperm and egg donation. This means that the placing parents are not genetically related to the embryos, and aside from the young boy in the placing family (and any potential half-siblings from each donor), there are no other genetic relatives.

I felt that they wouldn't, without having a biological tie to us as parents, they would have that tie to one another. Which would make the concept of embryo adoption a little bit easier for them. And that because they're, you know, with the embryo adoption, there are children that already are born that are biological siblings. I wanted them to have a biological sibling that they grow up with as opposed to some person that they've never met.

The sense that genetic siblings provide stable, enduring kinship relations was especially significant for older parents. For instance, Leslie, an older placing mother who used egg donation to conceive her fraternal twins, a girl and a boy, was very pleased the twins had each other.

And if we had had just the one child and embryos remaining we would have stopped with the one because of our age and finances. Since my husband is an only child and we're older it would have . . . *we're grateful that we have the two because they'll have each other.* And we're not young parents. I mean all parents probably won't outlive their children hopefully, but that was a blessing for us to have. . . . We were grateful that they had each other.

This does not mean that the genetic tie between siblings in a family remains important for all placing and adoptive parents. Some, instead, stress the value of socially constructed kinship and work to culturalize their children's ties to each other. In the following narrative, Lara observes the genetic tie between her two children is no longer significant to her idea of family.

When I had Simon, I desperately wanted him to have a genetic sibling, and I don't know why I wanted him to have that genetic sibling, but something inside me was just so desperate for him to have this genetic sibling. . . . Now that he has it, now that I know they're genetic, [if] these embryos don't come to be and we decide to either do a traditional adoption or maybe

adopt from China or go to foster care . . . it doesn't matter to me the same way as it did back when Simon was a baby.

She references her own family history to illustrate that genetic ties do not always result in "diffuse and enduring relations": "It totally has come to be in my head that I just don't believe that biology means that much any more. You know, I have family on both sides where the moms are not in the picture and want nothing to do with their children . . . and I just see that . . . blood relationship does not make you a mom . . . you know, it's a relationship, it's just so much more than blood."

In the case of adoptive parents Melissa and Ian, the same desire for genetic siblings was present but then changed when one of their twins died in utero. Initially, this twinship was highly gratifying and would have been their "first choice" because "these kids will always have each other and they're blood related and they're true sisters." Now that there are no embryos left from the same batch, and genetic siblings are no longer a possibility in their family, Melissa draws a parallel between affinity and social siblingship.

But I think at the same time, Ian and I aren't blood related and we're so close and family, you know? And then, I'm thinking, well, if we raise them to know that they're family, they might be better siblings to each other than some biological siblings. If we raise them to love each other and to care about each other . . . they're gonna be raised by the same parents. And I think that's what makes you siblings is being raised by the same parents and having to deal with the same family. It's all about what crazy things your parents made you do, like go camping.

In all the above narratives, the sibling pair, and not the married couple, is presented as the *core* (Schneider [1968] 1980) of the nuclear family. It is perceived as an enduring union, linking the family's present and future. Children of genetic siblings in an adoptive family will be genetically related cousins just as they would in a non-adoptive, genetically related family. In this sense, for the adoptive family, siblingship trumps common descent for one generation. For the placing family, minimizing the dispersal of embryos decreases the disruption of having siblings born into different families and ensures continuity of the sibling bond for the embryos adopted out.

As the above narratives illustrate, adoptive mothers in our sample do not emphasize womb siblingship between their adoptive children. However, elsewhere in their interviews, they do stress the joy of being pregnant and their feeling that their visible pregnancy displaces, for the rest of the world, the absence of genetic ties between them and the in utero adopted baby. Finally, these narratives of siblingship testify to the use of strategies that either emphasize the genetic tie between siblings (naturalizing kinship) or displace genetic and biological ties and highlight socially constructed kinship (culturalizing kinship). . . .

"Batch Siblings," Age, and Birth Order

Embryo adoption results in different kinds of emergent sibling relations, one of which is what we call "batch siblingship." Here, siblingship is the result of IVF and the simultaneous creation of embryos, but children are born at different times and, in this context, to different parents. This requires adoptive and placing parents to socially manage the perceived connection between embryos created the same day, in the same batch, with identical genetic material. In this section, we examine batch siblingship to show the elusiveness of siblingship and twinship and how it upsets a linear understanding of age and birth order.

Many of the adoptive parents we interviewed related their wonder at the time lag between the birth of their Snowflake and his or her siblings in the placing family. One such adoptive mother, Melissa, marvelled at this aspect of her daughter's conception: "In April of '94 is when her [adopted daughter's] biological mother got pregnant with her brother. She has a biological sibling. And he was born in January

of '95 and she was implanted into me on November tenth of 2005, so 10 and half years later!"

Brenda has a biological daughter and twin "Hispanic" boys produced from embryo adoption. At the time of her interview, she was considering implanting the remaining two embryos she had adopted, and she reflected on the birth order of her twins and their genetic siblings. Her narrative also illustrates the elusiveness of twinship when birth is delayed through embryo cryopreservation.[1]

> Technically they're [the two sets of twins in the adoptive and placing–genetic families] three years apart or however many years apart they are because of when they were born . . . and that's how we mark time from your birth day . . . not your conception day. . . . But I mean technically they are all twins, all four of them, they're quadruplets! Because they were all conceived at the same time, so yeah, that's really interesting. But who knows, these other two [frozen embryos] might be born in two more years or something, and you know they're six years apart from their own twins, it's crazy!

Adoptive mother Alyssa also remarked on the time lag between her two Snowflakes sons (she was pregnant with her second Snowflakes son at the time of the interview). "We joke that our two-year-old is actually seven! When he throws a two-year-old temper tantrum it's really easy to remember that he's only two! It's going to be interesting explaining to these boys that they were conceived the same day in the same petri dish, but they're 30 months apart." . . .

Anti-twinship and Culturalizing Siblingship Strategies

. . . A great concern for our participants . . . is managing the distinction between twinship and siblingship. We discussed the elusiveness of distinguishing between twins and siblings with the coordinator of the Snowflakes program.

COORDINATOR: Like they'll say, because they were conceived at the same time, even if they were born five years apart, or eight years apart, they say, "Oh, they're twins." But it's not the same sibling relationship, you know? I think the genetic parents, they see the children that are born through the Snowflakes adoption . . . as siblings to their children, because they often say, "My children's siblings will be raised in another family." But they don't necessarily see them as twins. The adoptive parents, I've heard them more often say, if they have two children, one born from the first frozen transfer, one born from a later frozen transfer, "Oh, they're kind of like twins!" Because they were conceived at the same time. But they don't say that this child that they have in their family is a twin to the sibling that was originally conceived at the same time that was born. They don't say that.

CHANTAL: So it's only twins in their family?

COORDINATOR: In their family . . .

In the interviews, we found that twinship was recognized within the family, and siblingship was acknowledged between families. The Snowflakes coordinator also noted that some adoptive parents work very hard to ignore the genetic link with the placing family to protect the siblingship links between the non-genetically related siblings in their own family. In this case, there is often an emphasis on legal kinship and everyday siblingship. . . .

This can be seen in the narrative offered by adoptive mother Brenda. She felt that her daughter would be "the" sister of her embryonic twin Hispanic brothers.

Yeah, I think who is your family, who is your mom, who is your dad, it's really the people who are with you day in and day out, that's your family. So, peo-ple from broken homes or step-parents or things like that you kind of define based on the relationship and on the commitment as family members. So for our boys, their sibling is going to be Cheryl. She's the one they're going to be with every day until they go off to college. So, as far as genetic siblings or even parents . . . they're not going to know them or have a relationship with them until they meet at some point, if that happens, and choose to have a relationship on their own later. But I think it's really just interesting as [in], *"Oh, that's interesting, they're my brother." I don't know if there's really any other kind of connection other than "We're genetically related, that's interesting." You know? But from a relationship standpoint there won't be, just because they're not around each other.*

Adoptive mother Delia, one of the first to complete an embryo adoption, took an even sharper position on the meaning of genetics in embryo adoption. In the following statement, she casts aside genetics and genetic siblings, drawing parallels to traditional adoption. Delia also demarcates a clear boundary between genetic or placing families (a language she too uses) and the adoptive family.

Because again [embryo adoption] is new and I've had a long time to think about this, and a lot of people would say that they are sisters and brothers, and, ok, let me tell you my take on that. When a placing family relinquishes, they are relinquishing parenthood and the child and parenthood is both the responsibilities and the blessings. . . . So what they have relinquished as well is sister, brother, aunt, uncle, mother, father. So, just because they share genes, you and I share genes.

Delia also introduces another dimension of culturalizing siblingship by emphasizing religious kinship through God. This works well with the ideological foundations of embryo adoption.

Really I feel like what I am saying is based in Scripture because, we tell Dominique this all the time, that she was adopted into our family, but that Mommy and Daddy are all adopted into God's family because [of] what Jesus did on the cross. . . .

The concept of "religious siblingship" was an important part of emergent siblingship for many of our participants, who often held strong Christian beliefs. If "we're all sons and daughters [of God]," then full genetic siblingship between placing and adopting families involves connections on a small or secular scale and is of little importance.

From the above testimonies, we see that three strategies are used to diffuse the importance of genetic siblings: excluding twinship between families, emphasizing the importance of everyday life in building siblingship, and stressing spiritual kinship. Again, an emphasis on biological exchanges during pregnancy was discernible in interviews but downplayed in comparison to siblingship within the same family.

Knowledge in Open Embryo Adoption and Incest Avoidance

Although Snowflakes distinguishes itself from embryo donation programs by providing open embryo "adoption," the degree of openness between adoptive and placing families varied along a continuum and was highly dependent on family dynamics. For some adoptive parents, the identity of the placing family, including the names of their children, was the only kind of "openness" that they wanted; this was welcome knowledge, whereas actually meeting or establishing close relations with the placing family was an unwelcome crossing of boundaries.

Delia, one of our key participants, asked us in a joint interview with another adoptive mother, "How do you define openness? Openness is just knowledge. It doesn't mean you have to spend Christmas together, you know?" Her friend, Vanessa, added, "Knowledge that when your Snowflake comes home from college and says 'I'm in love' that it's not a sibling. That's knowledge to me!" All participants in the study, both placing and adoptive parents, repeatedly made similar statements. . . .

Open Adoption: Contact

The degree of openness and contact we found between families is highly dependent on conceptions of siblingship. The idea that genetic siblings form a naturally stronger bond made it obvious to some adoptive parents that their son or daughter should have contact with the placing family. Adoptive mother Laurel shared with us that her family and the placing family have a fairly high level of openness and that the children have met each other.

I mean the way that they communicate with each other is just unbelievable—I mean even the way that the genetic family's children connect with our kids—it's like they don't really know and understand that they're genetically related . . . *but there's just something there that draws them to each other.* I mean, I don't know how to explain it, but there is something. *There's just a connection between all of them and you wouldn't know that they've never met and they don't know each other, it's like they've always been friends, you know?*

However, for some, the distance between the two families has to be managed. Lara, an adoptive mother whose family also has regular contact with the placing family and their children, employs a more culturalizing strategy by displacing kinship relations. Here, the genetic parents are called "uncle" and "aunt," and their children are viewed as cousins. This case is unique because the children in the placing family also call the adoptive parents "aunt" and "uncle." Lara did remark that the way the children are genetically related to each will be clarified for them when they are older. . . .

Open Adoption: Delayed Siblingship

Another strategy that adoptive and genetic placing parents employed to think about the relationships between genetic siblings living in different families is what we came to refer to as "delayed siblingship."[2] Parents gave several reasons why contact between genetic siblings raised in different families should be pushed to the future. One reason was that an adopted sibling shed light on batch siblingship, which suggests the randomness of embryo selection in transplantation and might destabilize the family (whether placing or adoptive). This point is expressed by placing mother Roxana.

> I would prefer my children not to know, because . . . I think it will just mess them up in the head a little bit. To know that their parents gave away their brother or sister. I mean, when they're older, I'm fine with them knowing, especially if the other children, the adopted embryo children want contact with us. That's fine when they're older, but not at this point. We just wanted our family unit to be normal and for them to feel loved and secure . . . and not like, oh, we could have been the embryo that was given away! They were the lucky one that got implanted!

Adoptive mother Ellen is also adamant that her adopted daughter Amy deserves to know about her conception, but not until she is older. "As she is able to understand . . . we will communicate . . . to her. Because it was expressed to me if you ever tell one person other than your spouse, be sure that you tell your child. . . . This is her history and she has a right to it . . . *I would certainly encourage her to explore it later in life. When she's able to understand the implications.*" . . .

Placing mother LeeAnn felt that it would be "natural" for her children to want to know their full genetic adopted siblings. This is partly why she chose an open adoption program versus a donor program. Moreover, she expects the contact between the siblings will continue after her death.

> Of course we would tell them that yes, they have a brother or sister or whatever somewhere, and explain the whole process . . . like I'm sure that child would want to know that they have full-blood siblings somewhere. So that's why it is important for me that they would have contact. Like when they're older . . . and my hus-

band and I are gone, I still would like them to write letters or even see each other.

Placing mother Louise indicates she also expects contact to occur in the future between the children and is willing to include the adopted boy in her family as a distant relative.

> So we figured well, we gave them [the embryos] a chance at life, and there you go, and I hope it worked out! *It wouldn't bother us to welcome someone when our kids were grown and they [the adopted son] were grown, to welcome them into the family, obviously they would have their family that they grew up with, but to welcome them as an extended family member.* So that's why we opted to sort of leave it like that, that if they wanted to we were certainly open about that. I wouldn't seek that out, I would let that be their option.

This emphasis on giving the child a significant role in deciding to initiate contact with his or her genetic siblings later in life is a repeated finding. Both genetic or placing and adoptive parents wait to see how their child's interest will play out. This can be seen in the following statement by adoptive mother Brenda.

> I guess we'll just have to play that by ear. They might be like, really interested in it and really like asking a lot of questions about it, wanting to know about them, or they might be like, whatever . . . those people are weird and I don't know them, you know? So I guess we'll just kind of play it by ear and take it based on what their interest level is in it. I'm not going to push it on them if they're uncomfortable with it.

She also makes an important point that was echoed by parents we interviewed who were either traditional adoptees themselves or who had completed domestic adoptions: Some adopted children have no interest in meeting their genetic families. . . .

Delayed siblingship in embryo adoption closely mirrors the model of deferred openness and contact in traditional adoption. However, in the case of embryo adoption, the place of future siblings is often seen as less threatening to the current family and less pressing because of the adoptive mother's pregnancy with the adopted child. Delayed siblingship, therefore, can involve both naturalizing and culturalizing strategies, as future siblingship is thought to naturally extend past the death of the genetic parents. . . . Frequently parents do not take kin knowledge to its conclusion and have genetic siblings meet, choosing instead to have the adoption agency act as a permanent gatekeeper of both parties' contact information.

Conclusion

In the context of ARTs, when bodily substances can circulate apart from direct contact between persons, the issue of siblingship has reemerged as vitally important in kinship and in need of urgent anthropological attention. Indeed, one of our main conclusions in this article is that the circulation of genetic material does not automatically make kinship relations non-existent, even if these relationships are not legally binding in terms of the kinds of parentage rights and duties that normally uphold siblingship in Western societies. . . .

In this case, for all Snowflakes participants, knowledge of full genetic siblingship acts as a rule as far as incest prohibitions are concerned. However, for many, relationships are optional, and we have to wait for the Snowflakes children to grow up to see if they will activate siblingship outside their parents' involvement in the future.

In this article, we have presented some of the main types of siblingship found in embryo adoption: genetic siblingship, batch siblingship, gestational siblingship, and delayed siblingship. We want to stress that the last two categories were not used by our participants directly, but helped us to make sense of the way siblingship emerges in relation to a diverse set of kinship issues. . . .

Another key conclusion is that, in embryo adoption, siblingship is of the utmost importance and becomes the core of adoptive families. However, different models of siblingship emerge in relation to a variety of kinship ideas. For some parents, having genetic siblings (minimally, a pair) is of the highest significance in the absence of common descent from a single ancestor. It ensures the cohesiveness of the adoptive family as well as the genetic relatedness of cousins in the next generation. Adoptive parents feel it contributes to the integrity of family relations and also helps make the "adoption story" more "understandable" for the children. . . .

In terms of the activation of siblings' relations, two models emerge. Not unlike family recomposition after divorce (Simpson 1998), in some cases, there is contact between both families early on and an extension of ties. This turns the child born from embryo adoption into, for example, a cousin or a special friend and non-parents into uncles and aunts. In other instances, there is a contraction of ties—a demarcation of siblings from each other on the basis of shared nurturing within the nuclear family, and it is left to the child to activate, or not, the sibling relationship later in life. We refer to this as "delayed siblingship," a model that also borrows from traditional adoption practices, in which finding one's origin later in life is common. In both cases, siblingship allows genetic–placing families and adoptive families to define their space and relations to each other.

References Cited

Bamford, Sandra C. 2007. *Biology Unmoored: Melanesian Reflections on Life and Biotechnology*. Berkeley: University of California Press.

Becker, Gay. 2000. *The Elusive Embryo: How Women and Men Approach New Reproductive Technologies*. Berkeley: University of California Press.

Cicirelli, Victor G. 1994. "Sibling Relationships in Cross-cultural Perspective." *Journal of Marriage and Family* 56 (1): 7–20.

Collard, Chantal, and Shireen Kashmeri. 2009. "'De embriones congelados a siempre familias': Ética del parentesco y ética de la vida en la circulación de embriones entre las parejas donantes y las adoptantes en el programa Snowflakes" ["'From Frozen Embryos to Forever Families': Kinship Ethics and Life Ethics in the Circulation of Embryos amongst Placing and Adopting Couples in the Snowflakes Program"]. *Revista de Antropología Social* 18: 43–66.

Delaisi de Parseval, Geneviève, and Chantal Collard. 2007. "La gestation pour autrui: Un bricolage des representations de la paternité et de lamaternité euro-américaines." *L'Homme: Revue Française d'Anthropologie* 183: 29–53.

Kashmeri, Shireen. 2009. *Unraveling Surrogacy in Ontario, Canada: An Ethnographic Inquiry of Surrogacy Contracts, Parentage Laws, and Gay Fatherhood.* Saarbrücken, Germany: VDM Verlag.

Konrad, Monica. 2005. *Narrating the New Predictive Genetics: Ethics, Ethnography. and Science.* Cambridge: Cambridge University Press.

Modell, Judith. 2001. "Open Adoption: Extending Families, Exchanging Facts." In *New Directions in Anthropological Kinship*, edited by Linda Stone, 246–63. Lanham, MD: Rowman and Littlefield.

Nightlight Christian Adoptions Agency. 2009. "Adoption Services since 1959." *Nightlight Christian Adoptions.* www.nightlight.org.

Ragoné, Helena. 1994. *Surrogate Motherhood: Conception in the Heart.* Boulder, CO: Westview.

———. 1996. "Chasing the Blood Tie: Surrogate Mothers, Adoptive Mothers and Fathers." *American Ethnologist* 23 (2): 352–65.

Roberts, Elizabeth F.S. 2007. "Extra Embryos: The Ethics of Cryopreservation in Ecuador and Elsewhere." *American Ethnologist* 34 (1): 181–99.

Schneider, David Murray. (1968) 1980. *American Kinship: A Cultural Account*, 2nd ed. Chicago: University of Chicago Press.

Simpson, Bob. 1998. *Changing Families: An Ethnographic Approach to Divorce and Separation.* Oxford: Berg.

Strathern, Marilyn. 1999. *Property, Substance, and Effect: Anthropological Essays on Persons and Things.* London: Athlone.

Weber, Florence. 2005. *Le nom, le sang, le quotidien: Une sociologie de la parenté pratique.* La Courneuve, France: Aux Lieux d'Être.

Notes

1. Brenda's case is interesting in that her twins through embryo adoption are "Hispanic" whereas she and her family are all Caucasian. She not only finds the time difference between twin births in placing and adoptive families "really interesting" but she also finds mixing embryos of different races and genetic parentage "the coolest thing." However, this mixing is not advised by the embryo adoption program. (Collard and Kashmeri's note)

2. Of course, delayed siblingship is evident in other ART contexts involving gamete donors, and DNA technologies are making known previously unacknowledged or unknown siblingship and half-siblingship. (Collard and Kashmeri's note)

Key Points to Consider

- North Americans tend to think of kinship as a biological or natural relationship. Other cultures emphasize non-biological factors such as nurturance, affection, cohabitation, and collaboration as important determinants of kinship.
- Religious beliefs can help establish the context of kinship practices. Many of the Snowflake families hold a religiously informed belief that embryos are potential, if not already living, persons. Some also employ religious language to extend kinship to non-genetically related individuals.

- New reproductive technologies that involve the use of donated eggs, sperm, or embryos have the potential to complicate kinship. Families who adopt embryos "culturalize" kinship in order to smooth out the complications.
- American families who have experience with embryo adoption tend to elevate relationships between siblings over relationships between parents and children.
- Embryos produced through IVF and frozen can produce a pregnancy many years after conception. Children conceived at the same time, regardless of when they are born, are "batch siblings." Snowflake families may talk about batch siblings as twins (or triplets, etc.) if they are born to the same family even if they are born years apart. They tend not to talk about batch siblings in different families as twins.

Critical Thinking Questions

1. Based on the information provided in the article, do adopting and placing families have different ideas about how kinship should be understood? What do the adopting families emphasize? What do the placing families emphasize? Drawing on the ethnography, what do you think accounts for the similarities and differences?
2. What do the authors mean when they write that some adoptive families "culturalize kinship"? How and why do these families do this? What is the alternative?
3. In your view, how important is it for children to be genetically related to their parents? Is it more important for children to share genetic material with their mothers or with their fathers? What leads you to think this way? Identify some of your cultural experiences that contribute to your thinking on this matter.
4. How do Snowflake families described in the article reconcile religious beliefs that embryos are living people with the reality that IVF creates many embryos that will never be born?

Suggestions for Further Reading

Collard, Chantal. 2009. "The Transnational Adoption of a Related Child in Québec, Canada." In *International Adoption: Global Inequalities and the Circulation of Children*, edited by Diana Marre and Laura Briggs, 119–34. New York: New York University Press.

Howell, Signe. 2009. "Adoption of the Unrelated Child: Some Challenges to the Anthropological Study of Kinship." *Annual Review of Anthropology* 38: 149–66.

Nuttall, Mark. 2000. "Choosing Kin: Sharing and Subsistence in a Greenlandic Hunting Community." In *Dividends of Kinship: Meanings and Uses of Social Relatedness*, edited by Peter P. Schweitzer, 33–60. London: Routledge.

Pashigian, Melissa J. 2009. "The Womb, Infertility, and Vicissitudes of Kin-Relatedness in Vietnam." *Journal of Vietnamese Studies* 4 (2): 34–68.

Roberts, Elizabeth F.S. 2011. "Abandonment and Accumulation: Embryonic Futures in the United States and Ecuador." *Medical Anthropology Quarterly*, 25 (2): 232–53.

Weston, Kath. 1997. *Families We Choose: Lesbians, Gays, Kinship*. New York: Columbia University Press.

Chapter 13

ARCTIC
OCEAN

Ulukhaktok

NUNAVUT

YUKON   NORTHWEST
TERRITORIES

★ Yellowknife

0   100 200 300
km

Northwest Territories

Introduction

If you attend a Canadian citizenship ceremony today, you will likely hear the judge refer to Canada as a "colourful tapestry." The metaphor of Canada as a tapestry that weaves together people of every **race**, every religion, and every national origin—their individual distinctiveness still visible, but combining to produce a beautiful, new fabric—is compelling. In 1971, Canada became the first country to officially recognize its **multiculturalism**, and in 1988 it enshrined multiculturalism in law with the passage of the Canadian Multiculturalism Act. Of course, all modern countries are multicultural, made up of peoples from diverse backgrounds who, while sharing a national identity and culture, maintain some distinctive cultural practices and norms that also contribute to a sense of self.

The 1988 Act asserted that "multiculturalism is a fundamental characteristic" of Canadian society and "an invaluable resource in the shaping of Canada's future" (Canadian Multiculturalism Act, SC 1988, c. 31). It directed government agencies to carry out their functions in ways that recognized and respected the racial and cultural diversity of Canadian society. It is no simple matter to govern in a way that gives weight to the distinct cultural heritages and identities of every group. Discussions about whether and how different cultural practices and values inform public policies are often emotional and highly politicized. Some critics of multiculturalism have complained that it goes too far in providing separate accommodations and amplifies the differences between Canadians. Others take the opposite position, arguing that Canadian multiculturalism is often limited to superficial matters such as supporting festivals that celebrate diversity, while government agencies continue to design most programs and policies in ways that conform to Euro-Canadian cultural sensibilities. Canadian sociologist Nandita Sharma (2011) goes further, suggesting that because official multiculturalism in Canada includes a **discourse** that "we are all immigrants," it excludes **Aboriginal** Canadians from making substantive contributions to public policies.

The article presented below concerns how taken-for-granted cultural values embedded in government programs and policies can have unintended consequences when the targets of the programs share cultural values that differ from those of the programs' designers. More specifically, I (Pamela Stern) suggest that a public-housing program meant to improve the economic security of Aboriginal communities in the Northwest Territories has, in recent years, contributed to increasing inequality and economic insecurity. This situation occurred, in part, because the program's design reflects Euro-Canadian ideals of the **family** rather than the cultural expectations of the **Inuit** and other Aboriginal Canadians who were meant to benefit from the program.

The particular example in the article concerns the Inuit in the town of Ulukhaktok in the western Canadian Arctic. The town, which was previously called Holman, is one of six Inuit communities in the Northwest Territories. (In 1999, the borders of the Northwest Territories were redrawn to create the territory of Nunavut. Approximately half of Canadian Inuit live in the 26 communities of Nunavut.) With a population of approximately 400, Ulukhaktok is smaller than most Canadian Inuit towns, but otherwise the residents, who call themselves Ulukhaktokmiut,[1] share a common history and culture with Inuit in other remote Arctic settlements.

Inuit are one of the three broad categories of Canadian Aboriginal peoples. (Other Aboriginal Canadians are known as **First Nations** and **Métis**.) Contemporary Inuit are descended from people who settled in Arctic regions of North America and Greenland around AD 1000. Historically, Inuit survived by hunting sea mammals, caribou, and other animals and by fishing. Today, all Canadian Inuit live in modern towns and participate in Canadian economic and social life. Yet **subsistence** hunting and fishing remain important parts of contemporary Inuit culture, valued as sources of high-quality food and for their connections to Inuit traditions.

My initial goal in writing the article was to change the way that anthropologists described contemporary Inuit subsistence work. I was bothered by what I regarded as **essentialist** discussions of Inuit subsistence work that were limited to hunting and fishing and the sharing of "land foods" (meat and fish). In addition, because most Inuit hunters were men, the discussions of subsistence and sharing almost always ignored the activities of Inuit women. There was also a tendency among anthropologists to write about sharing as voluntary. My **ethnographic** research suggested otherwise—first, I found that there was (and still is) a great deal of sharing that was difficult to observe and measure, and second, I found that Inuit felt moral obligations to share tied to their cultural identities as Inuit. As I dug into my field notes, I began to recognize connections among growing economic disparity, the loosening of sharing practices among some Ulukhaktok-miut, and the formulas used to determine how much a household paid for housing.

Permanent settlements in the Canadian Arctic are relatively new. Prior to the 1960s, most Canadian Inuit lived in a substantially traditional manner and had very limited access to the government services that most Canadians take for granted. It was only after World War II that the Canadian government began to take an interest in Inuit and their lands. It discovered Inuit living in fairly desperate conditions, suffering from very high rates of illness (especially tuberculosis) as well as some of the highest rates of infant mortality in the world. In response, the government determined to move Inuit into permanent towns and villages that it would administer. It used a variety of threats and enticements to encourage Inuit to move into the new towns. Public housing was one of the enticements.

Still today, there is very little private housing in the Canadian Arctic except in the very largest Inuit communities. As well, extremely limited employment opportunities combined with very high costs of food and other imports mean that public housing is very much a continued necessity. As I assert in the article below, the situation Inuit find themselves in today is undermining sharing practices that could even out economic disparity and contribute to community well-being.

There are no quick, easy, or cheap solutions. Few non-Aboriginal Canadians could or would want to live as their grandparents did; similarly, it is not realistic to think that Inuit or other Aboriginal peoples could take up the lifestyles of their ancestors as a way to improve their circumstances. In the final section of the article below, however, I propose that Inuit communities could use their authorities achieved through land-claims and self-government negotiations to develop programs and housing formulas that more closely match their cultural values.

❖ About the Author ❖

As a member of the Department of Sociology and Anthropology at Simon Fraser University, Pamela Stern studies the ways that individuals' work and sense of citizenship are tied together. She has done ethnographic fieldwork in Ulukhaktok as well as in non-Aboriginal towns in Ontario and British Columbia. Stern grew up in Florida and earned degrees in anthropology from the University of Florida, the University of Pittsburgh, and the University of California, Berkeley. She is the author of two books about Inuit history and culture and recently co-authored The Proposal Economy, *an ethnography about the ways that neoliberal governance has transformed how residents of a former silver mining town in Ontario enact their identities as citizens.*

The Nucleation of Inuit Households

Pamela Stern

Several years ago, anthropologists Jane Collier, Michelle Rosaldo, and Sylvia Yanagisako challenged a long-standing assumption that the family is a self-contained, socially, emotionally, and economically self-sufficient institution. Rather than accepting that the family is a universal institution that exists to meet universal human needs, Collier, Rosaldo, and Yanagisako argued that this image of the family arose relatively recently and serves as a "symbolic refuge from the intrusions [that threaten] our sense of privacy and self-determination" (Collier, Rosaldo, and Yanagisako 1982: 78). Canada, though officially multicultural, does not extend multiculturalism to all areas of public policy-making. For example, in family law, Canadian legal scholars have noted that law and public policy tend to assume that families are groups of "adults and children [whose relationship is] based upon a married heterosexual and procreative union" (Mykituiuk 2002: 776) rather than other arrangements that might be culturally valued among some segments of the population. Even where laws formally recognize other family forms, subtle policy practices reinforce the cultural ideal of a heterosexual **nuclear-family** household.

My interest in the family as a social and legal entity concerns the ways that Euro-Canadians' understandings of the nuclear-family household as self-contained and self-sufficient have been transferred to public policy in Canadian Inuit communities. The policies and practices of northern administration and governance in the latter half of the twentieth century ignored differences between Euro-Canadian and Inuit families or presumed the superiority of Euro-Canadian nuclear-family households. Inuit and Euro-Canadians both trace descent **bilaterally**, and both tend to reside in households based on the nuclear family. Where Euro-Canadians have tended to treat household and family as identical, however, Inuit have not. This aspect of traditional Inuit social relations has persisted despite involvement in the cash- and wage-based economy

and other institutions of the modern nation-state. Yet, a number of institutions of Western **modernity** work against the persistence of Inuit social relations.

This article, based on long-term ethnographic **fieldwork** in the community of Ulukhaktok (formerly Holman) in the Inuvialuit Settlement Region of the Northwest Territories (NWT), contrasts Inuit practices of sharing that reflect and reinforce Inuit models of the family with administrative practices associated with the allocation of housing that reflect and encourage a Euro-Canadian understanding of the family. Inuit models of **social organization** treat family as fluid and interdependent, and sharing is integral to this understanding. I focus on sharing because many Ulukhaktokmiut talk about it as socially and morally valuable, and many regard sharing as a traditional Inuit practice that distinguishes them, in a positive way, from the wider Canadian society. At the same time, many Ulukhaktokmiut encounter barriers to the kinds of regular sharing idealized through their discourse, and some have withdrawn from sharing networks.

Kinship, Sharing, and Social Relations

Historically for Inuit, production and consumption were organized through **kinship**, with activities often directed by a senior male or a senior couple. Kinship also provided the basis for political authority and, hence, for the maintenance of social order in the pre-settlement era. While not all relationships could be traced to actual ancestral or **affinal** ties, kinship terminology provided the metaphors through which social ties were established and maintained (Guemple 1972: 89–90; see also Nuttall 2000) through practices such as co-residence, co-operative work, and sharing.

In the past, Inuit had complex, formalized institutions for sharing game among kin and non-kin (Damas 1972; Remie 1984). In Ulukhaktok, as in many parts of the North, formal sharing partnerships or rules for dividing the catch no longer exist, although meat and fish continue to be shared. The sharing of game extends beyond kin networks, but it is within kin networks that most sharing occurs today (Collings, Wenzel, and Condon 1998). Sharing meat remains part of a set of morally valued behaviours, through which contemporary Ulukhaktokmiut and Inuit in other communities express their generosity, modesty, industry, and helpfulness, and through which they "create and maintain morally valued relationships" (Bodenhorn 2000: 28). Sharing is also reinforced by Inuit **cosmology**; animals were (and are still) thought to give themselves to hunters who share their catch (Bodenhorn 1990).

In contemporary Inuit communities, cash, tools, labour, and information, as well as meat and fish, are part of a moral economy of sharing. Historian E.P. Thompson (1963) used the phrase *moral economy* to describe the socially enforced obligations of landowners to landless labourers in pre-industrial England. The analogy is not perfect, but it approximates the Inuit expectations that individuals with a sufficiency of desirable goods make some of those goods available (through gifts, **generalized reciprocity**, and open pantries) to anyone, but especially kin, in need. Still, just as the Industrial Revolution transformed class relations in Europe, the economic transformations in the Canadian North affect Inuit social relations. In Ulukhaktok, sharing is a subject of local conversations that involve moral judgments about the generosity or stinginess of individuals. These conversations probably serve to encourage sharing, but they are also a way of envisioning and articulating what it means to be a good person.

Sharing is much more than economic (Mauss 1967), and it is not simply a pragmatic strategy for limiting risk in an uncertain environment. Women and men are enmeshed in sharing networks, made up primarily of extended kin, that regularly exchange money, clothing, household equipment, prepared foods, childcare, and other labour, along with meat and fish. Although sharing is affected by economic factors and has economic implications, sharing is not an economic practice in the narrow sense. Rather, *sharing is a form of Inuit social interaction that both binds people together and acts as a powerful **symbol** of those ties.*

I will illustrate this point with the example of the sharing network of one woman, Becky (a pseudonym), who was 34 years old in 2000. At the time, she lived alone in a two-bedroom public-housing unit and worked part-time as a cook at the Holman Eskimo Co-operative hotel, earning about $19,000 a year. Like many Inuit born in the 1960s, Becky attended school irregularly and eventually quit without graduating. Though she was intelligent, her low level of formal education limited the kinds of jobs for which she qualified. Other than babysitting and cleaning—both of which Becky had done—her only employment choices were clerking at one of the two local stores or her job in the hotel coffee shop.

Becky, like most in Ulukhaktok, lived in subsidized public housing. Her rent, computed on the basis of her income and her official household size of one, came to about 15 per cent of her take-home pay, a ratio that is considered comfortable by the dominant standards in North America.[2] Nonetheless, she found it a struggle to pay for rent and electricity, buy food, and keep up the payments on her cable television and telephone; and over the course of 2000, her phone and cable service were cut off.

Officially, Becky lived alone, but she had regular overnight visits from several of her nieces. In addition to feeding the children, she regularly washed their clothing and made sure that they got to school. Like several of her siblings, nieces, and nephews, Becky took her lunches at her parents' house. Usually the noon meal for adults consisted of game meat or fish served raw and frozen in the traditional Inuit style, but there was always store-bought food, consumed mostly by the children. On most days, 10 to 15 adults (including the author) and children arrived for lunch.

Once or twice a week, Becky helped herself to land foods (provided by a brother, brother-in-law, or nephews) from the chest freezer at her parents' house. More often she brought commercial food she had purchased and prepared to her parents' house where other kin consumed it. She loaned a portable telephone to an older brother when he told her he was planning to have his phone service reconnected, and she gave some of her furniture to a younger brother. Two of her siblings regularly asked permission to charge groceries to her co-op account. Becky also regularly purchased clothing for nieces and nephews.

Becky's parents' house was a regular gathering place for extended kin, and Becky was not the only family member who contributed cash and goods. Becky and several of her sisters pooled money to purchase a whole caribou[3] for her parents, which the extended kin group helped consume. One day she called my attention to the fact that one of her adult nephews (a regular at Friday evening drum dancing, but rarely present at lunchtime) was wearing a new pair of caribou-skin *kamiks* (boots). (The previous week Becky's mother had sold a similar pair to a tourist for a few hundred dollars.) The *kamiks* her nephew was wearing, she told me, had been made by her mother to sell, but her mother decided to give them to her grandson (Becky's nephew) "because he always helps them [her parents] out so much." This mundane, everyday sort of sharing involving cash, subsistence and commercial foods, and other goods occurs in other extended kin groups in Ulukhaktok, but it is not universal. In fact, some of Becky's siblings—the ones with the largest incomes—were not regular participants in this exchange. One reason Becky and some of her extended kin continued to participate was that her parents provided the centre and focal point in the moral economy of sharing. As will be discussed below, bureaucratic assumptions embodied in housing and other related policies made participation by individuals with large incomes difficult.

The culture of sharing is also reinforced in symbolic ways. I had the opportunity to observe a number of Inuit culture classes given by elders at the school. On one occasion, Mabel Nigiyok decided that she would teach a group of grade nine and ten students a game she called *Maq*.

The kids were asked to sit on the floor, close together in a semi-circle with their legs out straight—as if along the walls of a snowhouse. First, Mabel went along the line and lightly kicked each kid on the sole of the shoe. The kid was to respond, "maq." Then she asked each one a question about who made or where they got an item of clothing. Next Mabel asked the kids to hold out their hands and made silly comments

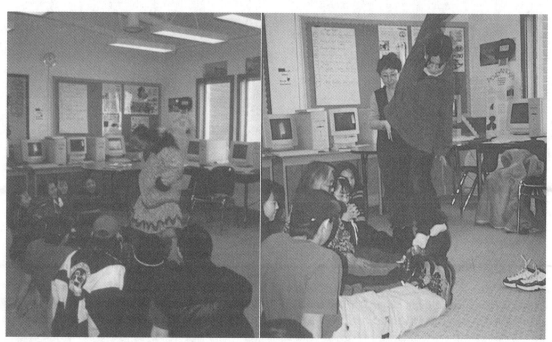

FIGURE 13.1   Grade nine and ten students in Ulukhaktok learn to play *Maq*.

about the color of their skin. The next step was to walk on the tops of their feet (as if on a balance beam!). This was followed by more questions such as, "Who made your hair?" or "Where did you get your nose?" The desired responses were clever silly ones. This round of questioning was to be followed by walking across the knees of the kids. (Stern field notes, March 2000)

I did not think to ask Mabel why she chose that particular game to share with the students, and she may not have had a particular purpose in mind. Nonetheless, teaching the game to the teens (as much as playing the game) offered symbolic reminders that sharing both clothing and genes is about social relationships, and that through sharing, people are entangled in webs of sociality.

As I will argue in the remainder of this paper, sharing and those webs of sociality are under pressure from growing economic disparity and from bureaucratic and administrative practices that regard individual households, and particularly nuclear-family households, as isolated social and economic units. The transition to a cash-based wage-labour and state-welfare economy has complicated sharing and placed the cultural values for sharing in tension with contemporary desires for individual accumulation. Money complicates sharing, but money is not the source of the tension. Rather, administrative practices, especially those surrounding housing, have favoured nuclear-family households. They have also made economic disparity between households appear to be the natural consequences of individual actions.

The Nuclear-Family Household in the Administration of the North

The community of Ulukhaktok was originally established as a mission and trading centre in 1939 and developed as a permanent settlement in the early 1960s. In the previous decades, Inuit in the region resided in seasonal hunting and trapping camps that included both related and unrelated individuals. Trapping white foxes for commercial trade, which was first practised in the 1920s, 1930s, and 1940s, was a more individualistic activity than subsistence hunting, and commercial trapping encouraged accumulation of private property. Even so, Inuit continued to share the products of subsistence hunting and fishing with both kin and non-kin through generalized reciprocity and formal exchange partnerships (Damas 1972).

With permanent settlement, the autonomy of nuclear families was taken for granted by government administrators. This assumption was likely encouraged by reports from anthropologists who used the terms *household* and *family* interchangeably. More than one ethnographer described sharing between households as sharing between separate families rather than as sharing by members of the same family residing in different households. For example, in 1923 Diamond Jenness wrote that "[c]hildren, as they grow up and marry, form new and distinct families of their own" (1923: 84). He continues with a detailed description of "distinct families" travelling and eating together, helping each other with childcare and chores, and sometimes sleeping in the same snowhouse or tent. In a more contemporary example, Richard G. Condon also described households as constituting distinct, if not quite independent, families:

> Most of these [older, actively hunting] households maintain a locker in the walk-in freezer where meat and fish is stored. The locker is sometimes shared with offspring living in other households. The general etiquette seems to be that these children may help themselves to meat or fish whenever they want. Not all the lockers are locked, but if they are, a son or daughter will simply go to the parent's house and take the key (with or without permission). For this reason, older active hunters generally have no idea how much meat and fish they share or how much land food they have remaining in their lockers. . . . Although some of these children can be a significant drain on the land food resources of their parent's house, they may also make deposits of meat and fish (Condon 1995a: 18).

Condon's interpretation that adult children "help themselves" to the food stores of parents contradicts the evidence of families such as Becky's in which resources are pooled across households without any strict accounting or assertions of ownership.

Multiple government policies and practices assumed that households were made up of families that were ideally independent, self-contained, and nuclear. Adult education materials prepared by the government for Inuit on everything from how to run a business to how to live in the new houses promoted a **hegemonic** view of the autonomous nuclear family. For example, a booklet entitled *Living in the New Houses* (Needham 1968) is illustrated with line drawings of a nuclear family eating meals together at the kitchen table and entertaining guests at the same table without food. The caption for the former reads, "Set a time for meals and let the family know you will be expecting them at that time" (Needham 1968: 20). In other drawings, the mother cleans the house, children do simple chores and sleep and study in their own spotless bedrooms, and the father hunts. Whatever the reality of Inuit household composition, the ideal family presented to and for Inuit readers of *Living in the New Houses* consisted of a breadwinner father, a homemaker mother, and three healthy, well-spaced children.

Wage Labour and Economic Disparity

The population of Ulukhaktok grew from 115 in 1963 (Usher 1965: 72) to approximately 400 in 2000 (author's census data). Over the same period, there was a reorientation of daily activity and focus from land-based subsistence hunting and trapping to town-based wage labour, recreation, and consumerism. In the early 1960s, according to Usher, no Ulukhaktokmiut relied upon permanent, full-time wage work; permanent wage-labour jobs simply did not exist for Inuit. Instead, people were engaged in subsistence hunting, fishing, trapping, and whatever short-term, casual wage work they could find. The adoption of snowmobiles and other expensive subsistence technologies as well as more and more consumer products depended upon a steady market for fox furs and sealskins as well as other cash income. This other income was usually women's earnings from handicraft production at the newly established Holman Eskimo Co-operative, but it also included men's earnings from casual labour or from the sale of carvings, as well as government aid. Subsistence hunting remained important, in part because it produced affordable, high-quality food that was not otherwise available.

Over time, permanent and additional casual work became available. Inuit also needed more and more cash to support themselves, but the time commitments of wage work were difficult to balance with those of subsistence hunting. As the population of Ulukhaktok grew, so did the number of wage-labour jobs, though job growth has not kept up with population growth. Consequently, just over half (55 per cent) of working-age adults had steady paid employment in 1979, but only 41 per cent were able to find permanent work 20 years later (author's census data).

Job growth during the 1980s was primarily the result of the 1984 incorporation of the town as a hamlet, a change that provided for local control of a larger municipal operating budget and new positions for municipal service workers. Minutes of Hamlet Council meetings from the late 1990s make frequent reference to the councillors' desires to create more jobs. Ulukhaktokmiut are also employed locally as teachers and health-care workers.

Wage work is now taken for granted as the route to a good and productive life. Subsistence hunting and fishing have continued, but at lower levels than were practised previously, and they are no longer universal activities. Ulukhaktokmiut, like other Canadians, now classify workers into career categories such as *office worker*, *teacher*, *artist*, and *truck driver*. Also included are the categories *casual worker* and *traditional*, as in "She's a traditional" or "I'm a casual worker." And for many people, casual work has become the only "real" work they can get. At the same time, *traditional* has taken on a new meaning as work done for money but requiring traditional Inuit skills. This work includes guiding sports hunters, sewing, carving, collecting samples for marine biologists, and running a two-week language camp for schoolchildren.

Wage labour has brought economic disparity. The disparity is largely the result of the severe shortage of regular paid employment opportunities. Less than half of the working-age population has any steady employment; the rest scrape by with irregular casual work and a variety of welfare programs. The job shortage is particularly disadvantageous to young adults and to women.

It is incorrect to regard subsistence hunting as Inuit and wage work as un-Inuit, but in its current short supply, wage employment presents challenges to the continuation of valued Inuit practices like sharing. Like other Canadians, Ulukhaktokmiut think wage work is simply the way people live and is necessary to maintain the community. In discussing the contributions of different kinds of workers, including seamstresses and hunters along with bylaw officers, teachers, and bookkeepers, a member of the Hamlet Council said, "Without all these people we would not have a community." In a similar vein, an elderly woman told me that there is no difference between people who work in town delivering water or running the town office and people who go hunting and bring back meat. She is thankful, she said, for everyone who works (Stern field notes, 1999).

The shift to wage labour has come with other modern changes including town-based temporal rhythms (Stern 2003), interest in other time-demanding activities including sports (Condon 1995b; Stern 2000), and cash-demanding consumption habits. At present, however, less than half of all working-age adults have a reasonable expectation of finding regular paid employment in the community. This critical shortage of employment opportunities is a source of personal and community distress and produces social cleavages, giving rise to a situation where many stop looking for paid employment. These discouraged workers and others come to see their poverty as a natural outcome of a failure to apply themselves, and thus deserved. Many Ulukhaktokmiut, like other Canadians, attribute regular employment and financial stability to individuals' motivations rather than to structural conditions. In the remainder of this paper, I turn to one of these structural factors—housing programs—and examine the policies and practices that promote social and economic isolation of individual households.

Housing Policy and the Social Isolation of Households

Since the 1960s, Canadian government officials have debated whether housing for Inuit should be provided as a social good regardless of residents' ability to pay, or whether housing is a market commodity that can be used to integrate Inuit into the social and economic fabric of Canada (Tester 2006). The question has never truly been resolved. In Ulukhaktok, the first public houses were welfare houses supplied without charge to domestic groups without a male hunter-trapper, which were thus presumed to be unable to provide for themselves. With the establishment of the Northern Rental Housing Program in 1966, and followed by the Northwest Territories Housing Corporation in 1973, the government undertook to provide houses for nearly all Inuit in the NWT. The result is that almost all housing in the smallest Inuit communities is provided through the public sphere.

Although policy-makers stated a desire to create housing that was socially appropriate for Inuit, it is not clear what they understood that to be. Inuit were not consulted with regard to design, size, or placement of the new houses. As time went on, houses grew larger and included an increased numbers of bedrooms and other spaces that emphasized privacy at the expense of either common areas or spaces "for cutting up meat, for food storage . . . and for the repair and storage of snow machines and other gear" (Department of Public Works n.d.: 16). According to Don Jossa, a design-development technical officer with the Northwest Territories Housing Corporation, doorways were purposely narrowed to prevent Inuit from engaging in activities such as snowmobile repair inside their houses (statement made during master's thesis examination at the University of Waterloo 16 December 2003). Housing needs were determined by bureaucratic formula.

In Ulukhaktok, all houses built before 1987, and most built since, have been detached "single family" structures. Since 1987, several two-bedroom duplexes and one-bedroom apartment units have been constructed, the latter specifically intended for the widowed elderly and for young singles. Ulukhaktokmiut referred to the complex for the elderly as "the old folks' home," and it was sited next to the Health Centre, presumably to facilitate house calls from the resident health workers. Up until the construction of "the old folks' home," the only elderly living by themselves were a few men who had never married or had no close kin in the community. To put this in context, a few years earlier several Ulukhaktokmiut and I watched a CBC news program describing the sad plight of some Canadian elderly living in nursing homes. After viewing the program, one woman, then in her mid-thirties, expressed her disbelief and disapproval that *qallunaat* (white people) would isolate the elderly in separate living facilities rather than care for them at home (Stern field notes, 1982).

The existence of apartment-style housing is one of several structural factors that have encouraged Ulukhaktokmiut to follow a Euro-Canadian model of family **life course** in which children grow up and establish their independence by moving out of the parental home, marrying, and forming new nuclear-family households. At the same time, the parents, supposedly seeking quiet leisure, grow old in houses without children.

While many Inuit communities have experienced severe housing shortages and overcrowding in recent periods, this has not been the case in Ulukhaktok. According to the Aboriginal Peoples Survey (APS), the mean household size in Ulukhaktok in 2001 was 3.1 persons, and there were no households that could be considered crowded (Statistics Canada 2001). The availability of houses in Ulukhaktok had important consequences for the way that public housing was allocated. In the late 1970s and early 1980s, with houses in relatively short supply, the allocation policy granted nuclear-family applicants preferential access to housing. Others, notably unmarried women with children, resided not in houses of their own, but with extended kin (Condon 1987: 155). Since the late 1980s, household composition has changed. Sibling groups, single parents, and young single adults all became eligible for houses, and once in their own houses, they also became eligible for other government benefits. At the same time, a new housing program provided private houses to wage-earning nuclear-family households.

Under the Northern Rental Housing Program and subsequent rental programs, the cost of housing was heavily subsidized. Rents, which included electricity, heating oil, water, and sewage and waste disposal,[4] were established on a sliding scale ranging from a very modest minimum to a maximum of 25 per cent of household income. At the upper end of the scale, rents were capped at between $500 for an older, smaller house and $800 for a new four-bedroom house. Housing was provided on the basis of need rather than on residents' ability to pay, but as noted, for a significant period of time, nuclear families were preferred in the housing-assignment practices.

In the mid-1980s, the Northwest Territories Housing Corporation introduced a home-ownership program for northern Aboriginal peoples. The program, dubbed HAP (for "Housing Assistance Program"), was a grant that included the materials and construction costs for a detached "single family" house. There were strict minimum and maximum income levels, so that only households with a full-time wage earner qualified, but those who qualified and applied received a house. Owners were required to live in the house for five years and to pay for their own utilities, heating oil, maintenance costs, and, more recently, an annual land-use fee. All of the successful applicants for HAP houses in Ulukhaktok were nuclear families. Seventeen nuclear families were able to take advantage of the program before it was replaced in 1993 with a far less generous home-ownership program called "Access."

In contrast to HAP, the Access program resembles a traditional home mortgage, but the required payments adjust to changes in household income. A different program (the EDAP, or "Expanded Down-payment Assistance Program") provides lump-sum down-payment grants and encourages prospective homeowners to seek traditional mortgages through banks. Sixteen Ulukhaktok families were purchasing Access or EDAP homes in 1999. All but two had applied as nuclear-family households. To be certain, there is symbolic value in home ownership. Although the houses must be chosen from a catalogue containing a very limited number of styles and sizes, there is some choice available. Furthermore, owners are able to customize and decorate them however they desire. Occupants of the 85 public-housing units do not have choices and can be (and occasionally are) asked to relinquish their house for other, more suitable tenants. As in southern Canada, home ownership signals social and economic success in Ulukhaktok.

The dual public–private housing system has contributed to an economic and social rift in the community, in which wage-earning nuclear-family households increasingly reside in private houses while public housing is occupied by the unemployed and the underemployed. More often than not, the public units are occupied by domestic groups other than nuclear families.

By the late 1990s, fairly significant disparities existed in housing costs as well as in incomes. Families living in public-housing units continued to pay a sliding-scale rent, but there were great inequities built into a system that was meant to prevent inequities. The formula used to calculate household income exempted old age pensions and most non-wage income. The latter worked to the advantage of households with income from unwaged, often unreported sources. The maximum monthly rent caps were also removed so that rents continued to rise as wage income rose. This led households with only moderate wage-based incomes to believe that they would be better off purchasing a house through Access or EDAP. *Significantly, the rent formula assumed that a household's economic obligation was to members of the household only*; it did not consider obligations to those outside the household. Yet, as the example of Becky shows, Ulukhaktokmiut participate in valued sharing networks that include individuals from many separate households. Individuals with steady employment income are often under tremendous social pressure to provide cash and other support for extended kin (see also Wenzel 2000), yet, because housing formulas do not consider these obligations, they find it difficult to participate.

Owners of Access and EDAP houses tend to pay the most for their residences. In 1999, it was typical for many of these homeowners to face housing costs that were well in excess of 30 per cent of their gross household income. Several Access and EDAP households

earned far less than they actually needed to cover their housing costs. To be certain, home purchasers in southern Canada also purchase homes beyond their means. A significant difference for homeowners in most Inuit communities is the absence of a functioning housing resale market. Any disruption in household income from the loss of a job or divorce leads almost inevitably to a mortgage default. The other difference—and my main point—is that Euro-Canadians do not feel cultural obligations to fund the needs of kin living in other households. In fact, there is a strong cultural preference against doing so. For many Inuit wage workers, housing has become so costly that it is extremely difficult to participate in culturally expected forms of sharing. Housing practices, thus, promote both a real and a symbolic insularity of nuclear-family households, and they encourage a "go it alone" mentality.

Inuit Public Policies to Promote Inuit Social Values

Ulukhaktokmiut have come to regard wage work as necessary and important to the achievement of personal goals and to the social stability of their communities. Nonetheless, wage labour has led to economic disparity between households that threatens the long-term persistence of kin-oriented sharing networks. Furthermore, long-standing social-housing policies and practices encouraged the establishment of nuclear-family households and at the same time declared those households to be socially and economically autonomous. There is no doubt that kinship continues to play a central role in the social life of Inuit communities, but in small places like Ulukhaktok where most people can trace some and often several kin ties to any other resident, people mobilize the relationships that have the most social and emotional salience for them. Sharing is one mechanism through which people create and maintain those ties.

There is also no doubt that Inuit social lives have been changed through their experiences with the Canadian government, but Inuit have not been passive recipients of Euro-Canadian governance practices. The elected Hamlet Council, which is the largest employer in the community, establishes the terms of employment and evaluates job performance for its employees. Similarly, public-housing assignments and rent adjustments are made by a Housing Committee composed of local residents. In both of these agencies of governance (and in many more), Ulukhaktokmiut could establish different policies that might be more supportive of their traditional values. But in Ulukhaktok, unlike in some other northern communities, these committees have tended to follow the bureaucratic principles inherited from the previous non-Aboriginal administration. Nonetheless, decisions about how many and what types of housing units to construct have been made by the Northwest Territories Housing Corporation rather than by the local Housing Committee. The same is true for the rent formula.

I began this essay with the claim that Canadian public policies privilege Euro-Canadian norms that treat nuclear-family households as independent and self-sufficient. The transition to wage labour was accompanied by policies and practices that encouraged Inuit households to think of themselves as socially and economically independent units. This is where I see the biggest threat to sharing and to the social stability of northern communities. Wage-earning, home-owning nuclear-family households may not have to cut themselves off from traditional sharing networks, but for some of them it becomes easier to do so than to accede to constant requests for assistance from needy kin. In the past, sharing was encouraged by living arrangements that enabled people to keep tabs on the fortunes and misfortunes of others. This is no longer the case, not only because modern houses afford more privacy to occupants, but also because information about earnings, expenses, and obligations is not public information. The

underemployed struggling to make ends meet may not understand or appreciate the financial struggles of others. Individuals with well-paid employment are imagined to be wealthy, in part because in comparison they are, but also their living expenses are not understood. Thus, I recorded multiple examples of gossip about the stinginess of individuals who were said to be living too well or to have access to special, unearned sources of income or other resources. Many of the targets of this gossip were people who did not regularly participate in sharing networks. Most of the gossip was simply that—gossip—but it reflects a tension between supposedly traditional values like sharing and supposedly modern forms of consumption and accumulation.

Because housing and employment practices are issues of policy, these are the places where Inuit, using the powers provided through self-government, can make changes that accommodate their values. The various land-claims agreements in Canada formally recognized Inuit cultures as distinct while simultaneously seeking to assimilate Inuit communities socially and politically into the Canadian nation-state. To date, education, housing, and other infrastructure, as well as labour practices and recreation, have been, for the most part, replicas of Euro-Canadian forms and practices. Significantly, these alien institutions involve new forms of consumption that require more and more cash and encourage households to see themselves and act as self-contained units. Inuit self-government might mean government as usual by Inuit, or it might mean government in accordance with Inuit values. As Inuit move forward with self-government, the opportunity arises to consider whether or not social policies such as those surrounding housing and employment truly conform to the cultural values they wish to promote.

References Cited

Bodenhorn, Barbara. 1990. "'I'm Not the Great Hunter, My Wife Is': Inupiat and Anthropological Models of Gender." *Études/Inuit/Studies* 14 (1–2): 55–74.

———. 2000. "It's Good to Know Who Your Relatives Are but We Were Taught to Share with Everybody: Shares and Sharing among Inupiaq Households." In *The Social Economy of

Sharing: Resource Allocation and Modern Hunter-Gatherers, edited by G.W. Wenzel, G. Hovelrud-Broda, and N. Kishigami. *Senri Ethnological Series* 53: 27–60.

Collier, Jane, Michelle Z. Rosaldo, and Sylvia Yanagisako. 1982. "Is There a Family? New Anthropological Views." In *Rethinking the Family: Some Feminist Questions*, edited by B. Thorne and M. Yalom, 25–39. New York: Longman.

Collings, Peter, George Wenzel, and Richard G. Condon. 1998. "Modern Food Sharing Networks and Community Integration in the Central Canadian Arctic." *Arctic* 51 (4): 301–14.

Condon, Richard G. 1987. *Inuit Youth: Growth and Change in the Canadian Arctic.* New Brunswick: Rutgers University Press.

———. 1995a. "I Always Let Him Have Danish: Modern Food Sharing Networks, Food Preference, and Community Integration in the Central Canadian Arctic." Paper presented at Second International Conference of Arctic Social Sciences, Rovaniemi, Finland, June.

———. 1995b. "The Rise of the Leisure Class: Adolescence and Recreational Acculturation in the Canadian Arctic." *Ethos* 23: 47–68.

———, Peter F. Collings, and George W. Wenzel. 1995. "The Best Part of Life: Subsistence Hunting, Ethnicity, and Economic Adaptation among Young Inuit Adult Males." *Arctic* 48 (1): 31–46.

Damas, David. 1972. "Central Eskimo Systems of Food Sharing." *Ethnology* 11 (3): 220–40.

Department of Public Works. N.d. *Housing in the Northwest Territories: Design/Construction Summary.* Yellowknife: Architectural Division, Project Management, GNWT.

Guemple, Lee D. 1972. "Eskimo Band Organization and the 'D.P. Camp' Hypothesis." *Arctic Anthropology* 9: 80–112.

Jenness, Diamond. 1923. *The Life of the Copper Eskimos.* Report of the Canadian Arctic Expedition. Vol. 12, part A. Ottawa: F.A. Acland.

Mauss, Marcel. 1967. *The Gift: Forms and Functions of Exchange in Archaic Societies.* Translated by I. Cunnison. New York: Norton.

Mykituiuk, Roxanne. 2002. "Beyond Conception: Legal Determinants of Filiation in the Context of Assisted Reproductive Technologies." *Osgoode Hall Law Journal* 39 (4): 771–815.

Needham, G.H. 1968. *Living in the New Houses.* Ottawa: Education Division, Northern Administration Branch, Department of Indian Affairs and Northern Development.

Nuttall, Mark. 2000. "Choosing Kin: Sharing and Subsistence in a Greenlandic Hunting Community." In *Dividends of Kinship: Meanings and Uses of Social Relatedness*, edited by P.P. Schweitzer, 33–60. London: Routledge.

Remie, Cornelius. 1984. "How Ukpaktoor Lost His Buttock and What He Got in Exchange for It: Cultural Changes amongst the Arviligdjuarmiut of Pelly Bay, Northwest Territories, Canada." In *Life and Survival in the Arctic: Cultural Changes in Polar Regions*, edited by G.W. Nooter, 97–120. Hague: Government Publishing Office.

Statistics Canada. 2001. "2001 Aboriginal Population Profile." http://www12.statcan.ca.

Stern, Pamela. 2000. "Subsistence: Work and Leisure." *Études/Inuit/Studies* 24 (1): 9–24.

———. 2003. "Upside-Down and Backwards: Time Discipline in a Canadian Inuit Town." *Anthropologica* 45 (1): 147–61.

Tester, Frank James. 2006. "Iglu to Igularjuagq." In *Critical Inuit Studies: An Anthology of Contemporary Arctic Ethnography*, edited by Pamela Stern and Lisa Stevenson, 230–52. Lincoln: University of Nebraska Press.

Thompson, E.P. 1963. *The Making of the English Working Class.* New York: Vintage Books.

Usher, Peter J. 1965. *Economic Basis and Resource Use of the Coppermine-Holman Region, N.W.T.* Ottawa: Northern Co-ordination and Research Centre, Department of Northern Affairs and National Resources.

Wenzel, George W. 2000. "Sharing, Money, and Modern Inuit Subsistence: Obligation and Reciprocity at Clyde River, Nunavut." In *The Social Economy of Sharing: Resource Allocation and Modern Hunter-Gatherers*, edited by G.W. Wenzel, G. Hovelrud-Broda, and N. Kishigami. *Senri Ethnological Series* 53: 61–85.

Notes

1. The suffix *-miut* means "people of" in the Inuit language. Therefore, *Ulukhaktokmiut* means "people of Ulukhaktok." (note added)
2. The Canada Mortgage and Housing Corporation regards housing costs equal to 30 per cent or less of gross household income as affordable. (note added)
3. At the time, there were few caribou in the area and local hunting was restricted. The local hunters and trappers association arranged to buy and resell caribou shot by hunters in Kugluktuk, a town to the south of Ulukhaktok on the mainland. (note added)
4. Electricity is no longer included in rent, but it is still subsidized for northern residents. (note in original)

Key Points to Consider

- Inuit today live in permanent communities and are integrated into Canadian economic and social life while continuing to practise many Inuit cultural activities and values.
- Generalized reciprocity, or "sharing," is highly valued in contemporary Inuit communities and is reinforced through practices that cause people to see sharing as a moral obligation.
- Inuit households are often made up of nuclear families, but familial obligations have traditionally extended beyond the household.
- In the ideal, multicultural societies enact policies and programs that take account of cultural difference. In practice, it is very difficult to accommodate distinct cultural values. Minority groups often find that they must accommodate to the norms and values of a dominant group.

Critical Thinking Questions

1. What kinds of sharing occur in contemporary Inuit communities? What is meant by the statement that "sharing is a form of Inuit social interaction that both binds people together and acts as a powerful symbol of those ties"?
2. Why would economic disparity make generalized reciprocity difficult? Explain your reasoning.
3. Make a list of the people you consider members of your family. (You could also draw your kinship chart.) What types of things are shared among this group? Do you share more with some people than with others? Could you consider your sharing to be generalized reciprocity? Why or why not? How does your sharing network reflect and/or reinforce your familial ties?
4. Think about what multiculturalism means to you. In what ways do you experience multiculturalism in your daily life? Are you aware of events or instances in which multiculturalism was encouraged? Discouraged? How was this accomplished? What were the effects?

Suggestions for Further Reading and Watching

Cousineau, Marie-Hélène, and Madeline Piujuq Ivalu. 2013. *Uvanga*. Montreal & Igloolik: Arnait Video Productions. Video recording, 86 min.

Searles, Edmund. 2002. "Food and the Making of Modern Inuit Identities." *Food & Foodways* 10: 55–78.

Stern, Pamela. 2010. *Daily Life of the Inuit*. Santa Barbara, CA: Greenwood Press.

——— and Peter V. Hall. 2015. *The Proposal Economy: Neoliberal Citizenship in "Ontario's Most Historic Town."* Vancouver: University of British Columbia Press.

PART IV

Rituals/Environment/
Economy

Chapter 14

Mexico

Introduction

If you have ever purchased Amway, Avon, or Herbalife products, you have participated in the form of direct selling known as multilevel marketing. The most successful multilevel marketers may not actually sell many cleaning products, cosmetics, or nutritional supplements. Instead, they earn the bulk of their sales income by recruiting others to become "independent distributors" (i.e., sellers) and supplying them with product to sell. These people, in turn, recruit additional distributors, with a portion of each sale filtering up the chain of distributors—hence, the phrase *multilevel marketing*. Globally, direct selling is big business; in 2013, it generated over US$178 billion in sales and involved more than 96 million sellers (World Federation of Direct Selling Associations 2014).

The article below concerns Omnilife, a Mexican multilevel marketer of nutritional supplements, and approximately fifty people who had signed on as distributors. Most were working-class and lower-middle-class urbanites. The original version of the article includes a long section detailing the history of multilevel marketing and earlier forms of direct selling (person-to-person sales outside a fixed store). Multilevel marketing has its roots in door-to-door peddling enterprises such as Fuller Brush and in companies like Tupperware and Mary Kay Cosmetics (also multilevel marketers), which sell products through home parties. Many of the best-known direct sales companies, including Fuller Brush, Amway, and Mary Kay Cosmetics, were founded by individuals who understood the companies to be extensions of their Protestant Christian beliefs. The managers of these companies often employ techniques to motivate sellers that are similar in form and content to Protestant evangelical messages about the constant need to strive for self-improvement.

Also omitted from the version included here is author Peter Cahn's description of his field site (Morelia) and research methods. Morelia, a UNESCO world heritage site, is a modern city of approximately 600,000 people. It is the capital of Michoacán State and is located immediately northwest of Mexico City, near the small city of Tzintzuntzan, where Cahn had previously done **fieldwork**. In fact, Cahn first learned about Omnilife while he was living in Tzintzuntzan, when he was invited to a sales party. Cahn's fieldwork in Morelia in 2003 and 2004 included **ethnographic** interviews with current and former Omnilife distributors (sellers). In addition, Cahn enrolled as an Omnilife distributor. Unlike many other distributors, he neither sold Omnilife products nor recruited others to sell them; nonetheless, his status as a distributor allowed him to attend the many sales and self-improvement workshops and rallies in Morelia and elsewhere. Like other distributors, he purchased and consumed Omnilife products.

Journalists and social scientists have noted that direct selling of Tupperware, Avon, and similar products expanded to formerly communist and developing countries with **globalization** and the spread of **neoliberal** forms of capitalism. Neoliberalism is an economic form that prioritizes competition and entrepreneurship among organizations and individuals. It became globally dominant in the 1980s and 1990s and is associated with globalization. Many assumed that people in developing economies were attracted to direct selling because it allowed them to learn new capitalist ideas; thus, direct selling seemed to be a "rational" response to the economic and social dislocations of globalization. According to Cahn, however, the appeal of direct selling is spiritual (almost religious) and emotional rather than rational.

Cahn's interpretation of direct selling as a kind of religious calling recalls Max Weber's (1864–1920) linkage of Protestant beliefs about spiritual salvation to the reorganization and intensification of economic activity that occurred with the development of modern capitalism. According to Weber, there is nothing natural or inherent in the desire for individual wealth. Rather, individuals' desires for more money, either for its own sake or for the opportunities it offers, are outcomes of cultural processes. Prior to the entrenchment of capitalism, businesses did not always seek to maximize their profits; nor did individuals always try to maximize their incomes. Weber argued that as capitalism developed, people had to learn to think about systematic work and the material benefits it brought as morally good. Weber saw this disposition as originating in the religious beliefs of European Protestants. Beginning in the sixteenth and seventeenth centuries, Protestants looking for evidence of their own salvation took economic success as a positive sign of God's favour. Belief in **predestination** had waned by the time Weber undertook his investigations in the first decades of the twentieth century, but individual labour, discipline, and the accumulation of wealth continued to be interpreted as evidence of moral virtue. These sorts of interpretations remain popular among many Protestants today.

Max Weber arrived at his understanding of the connection between Protestant salvation and modern capitalism long before advertisers and political leaders encouraged people to abandon frugality and modest lifestyles in favour of consumption as both a reward and an obligation of citizenship. With the development and spread of neoliberal economic practices since the 1980s, the association of industriousness, self-reliance, and wealth with moral correctness has intensified and spread further.

❧ About the Author ❧

Peter S. Cahn grew up near Sacramento, California, and studied at Harvard University, the University of Cambridge (UK), and the University of California, Berkeley. Through his ethnographic research, Cahn has examined religious and spiritual practices in contemporary Mexico. In addition, Cahn frequently contributes essays about academic life to The Chronicle of Higher Education. *He taught anthropology at the University of Oklahoma until 2010 and is now a senior administrator at Massachusetts General Hospital Institute of Health Professions.*

Building Down and Dreaming Up: Finding Faith in a Mexican Multilevel Marketer

Peter S. Cahn

Since the 1990s, mainstream media have reported on the legions of Avon ladies and Mary Kay beauty consultants fanning out across the developing world. They describe these bold door-to-door sellers with a wink to the [imagined] incongruity of selling lipstick in the Amazon, Brazilian slums, . . . [or] communist Vietnam. . . . Part of the curiosity is the unexpected presence of entrepreneurial activity in places often seen as hostile to capitalist ventures. . . .

According to an industry trade group, direct selling "is the sale of a consumer product or service, person-to-person, away from a fixed location" (Direct Selling Association 2002). Although it is a form of marketing most closely associated with a middle-class lifestyle that accompanied the expansion of North American suburbs after World War II, businesses that operate through direct selling have recruited millions of distributors from the developing world. Whereas Avon's sales flattened in the United States, for instance, sales in developing countries accounted for 38 per cent of the company's $4.5 billion in sales and 49 per cent of its pre-tax profit in 1995 ("Scents and Sensibility" 1996: 57). Similarly, Tupperware relies on its 100 foreign markets for four-fifths of its revenue and all of its growth (Hilsenrath 1996). Rather than seeing the brand and the home-party plan as old-fashioned, consumers in Asia, Eastern Europe, and Latin America embrace the opportunity to become distributors.

When academic writers have tackled the topic of the worldwide surge in direct selling, they have advanced the argument that direct selling prepares citizens of the developing world for full integration into global capitalist markets. They point to the resonance between direct selling's reliance on individual effort and the commodification of personal relationships with the tenets of neoliberal economics that have come to characterize modern capitalism. In this sense, participation in direct selling serves as an "instruction manual" for labourers making sense of a market-driven economy in which guarantees of **state** support no longer hold. These explanations, however, leave out the overt religiosity of direct selling that the participants describe so vividly.

Rather than understanding the explosive growth of direct selling around the world as a training ground for new economic subjects, I argue that it is through selling and consuming that distributors rebuild and fortify the foundations of their faith. All capitalist firms seek to exercise control over their employees, but direct-selling companies infuse [the] work . . . with spiritual significance. . . . For the company founders, direct selling may be a route to financial prosperity . . ., but for the millions of low-level distributors, the business represents an opportunity to replace systematized and anonymous labour with work that is transformative and fulfilling, characteristics that compensate for the uncertainty of material rewards. . . .

Converting to the Power of Positive Thinking

Cordless microphone in one hand and a yellow-tinged bottle of water in the other, Selene recounts to the 500-person audience her introduction to Omnilife. "Thanks to these blessed products, I've changed my life. I was fat. I was depressed. Since I was depressed, I ate more and got fatter. Who's been there?" I scan the packed hotel ballroom. As those in the predominantly female crowd listen to Selene's story, many take sips from Omnilife bottles in a range of shades from green to fluorescent orange. Unlike the imperturbable woman on stage in an elegantly tailored pantsuit, members of the audience shush squirming children and fumble for notebooks to copy down the diagrams shown in PowerPoint slides. But her testimony resonates with them. When she joined Omnilife, not only did Selene suffer from physical illness but she was also under financial stress: "I made gold jewellery. I had money and a house, but then there was an economic crisis in Mexico. I couldn't pay back my loans to the bank, so I went to private lenders, who charged 20 per cent interest. I couldn't pay them back, so the bank and the lenders fought over my house, and I was out on the street with two kids."

For five years, Selene lived with relatives while she searched for a way to support her children.

Her female cousins, who sold Avon cosmetics, Tupperware containers, and Stanhome household cleaners, invited her to join them. "I began leaving catalogues with clients," she continues, "and soon we won a prize from Tupperware. But I wasn't interested in plastic. I wanted money. I wanted what I used to have. I don't want to have to look at the price before I order from the menu." She appealed to God. "I said to God, 'Find me a job where I can support my children.' God listened to me. He put me in Omnilife. How great He is!" God's response came in the form of a newspaper ad promoting an Omnilife orientation session. When Selene learned about the products and began to consume them, she lost weight and gained the confidence to recommend them to others. "We have the security that this company will never fail, and, when I die, my children will keep receiving my paycheck." She pauses to acknowledge the applause from the audience.

Selene's appearance this Monday afternoon in Morelia, Mexico, targets both newcomers to Omnilife and veteran distributors. Before she segues into more technical advice on how to maximize earnings from the company's multilevel compensation plan, she slows her speech to make a final plea to the non-distributors:

God brought you here for a reason. Trust in God. I want you to close your eyes. Uncross your legs. Relax your arms. You enter a room and see people gathered around a coffin. As you get closer, you realize it's you they are mourning. You see your spouse crying, "Why did you leave us with so many debts?" Then you see your children. They are crying, "Why did you never give us the things you promised us?" Suddenly, you see the figure of a man. You can't see his face because the light is so bright. It's God. You turn to him and ask, "Please let me live again."

Selene puts down her microphone as the chords of a ballad called "Sueños" ("Dreams") fill the room. When the song fades, she instructs us, "Don't open your eyes until you know why you are living again, what motivates you. God gives us everything. We deserve abundance. I earn $40,000 a month." Two women and one man walk up onto the stage, declaring themselves ready to accept the opportunity to enroll in Omnilife as the audience welcomes them with sustained applause.

Although Selene's presentation borrows heavily from religious rhetoric of self-transformation and worship staples like call and response, her appeals to God lack any specific denominational reference. Only at the end of her four-hour talk do I perceive the overwhelming Roman Catholic affiliation of the audience. To illustrate her claim that success is "20 per cent work and 80 per cent attitude," she screens a short video clip profiling Tony Meléndez. A thalidomide baby born without

arms, Meléndez nonetheless learned to play the guitar with his feet. The climax of the biography shows Meléndez performing for Pope John Paul II. When the camera shows the pope's smiling reaction to the concert, the crowd in the hotel bursts into applause.

Learning the Lingo

[In order to begin fieldwork, and l]acking a personal connection to the company, I visit the Omnilife wholesale store in Morelia and ask for information. When the employee behind the counter cannot answer all of my questions, he refers me to a support centre located across the busy boulevard. A discreet Omnilife logo stenciled on the glass front identifies the office, which otherwise looks like a doctor's waiting room. . . .

Luisa, sitting behind the desk, greets me politely and gestures for me to sit. She is in her early thirties and is dressed in a summery pink-and-white outfit and white sandals accented with silver jewellery. She seems unfazed by my explanation that I am an anthropologist interested in learning more about Omnilife and invites me to try a cup of the company's Thermogen coffee. At first, she talks exclusively about the catalogue of nutritional products, which come in a bewildering range of flavours and have English names like "Fiber 'n Plus" and "Dual C Mix." The coffee I am drinking, she boasts, burns fat and helps prevent diabetes. "A man who suffered a heart attack drank the coffee and he felt better instantly. When you drink it, it's like you've been injected. It contains only vitamins, nutrients, and minerals—what your body needs daily. It goes directly to where your body needs it most and works in about ten minutes." She asks me searchingly how I feel after I finish drinking the coffee. The only difference I detect is a slight warmth, whether from the hot water, the burning of fat, or the sunny weather I cannot tell, but I answer her that I feel fine.

Over time, I learn more about Luisa's trajectory in Omnilife. Her parents, who ran their own business selling homemade facial creams, joined the company after participating in [a] marriage workshop [run by Omnilife founder] Jorge Vergara's cousin. Her mother suffered from osteoporosis so severe that she sometimes resorted to a wheelchair. The calcium-rich Omnilife products restored her to health, which persuaded Luisa to try them. Drinking a liquid called "OmniPlus" dissolved in water cured her of lifelong asthma that doctors could not treat and convinced her that the technology works. . . . Curious about these miraculous products' origin, I ask her who formulated them. She replies without elaboration that NASA scientists, the same researchers who patented the laser ray, designed them originally as food for astronauts.[1] Some people complain about their high cost, but Luisa reminds me that many patients willingly spend hundreds of dollars on medicines without any guarantee of recovery. "Your body was designed for nutrition, not medicine, am I right?" she asks me, leaving no room for disagreement. Since she joined Omnilife in 1991, she has not let a day pass without consuming the company's products in prodigious quantities.

The transformation she has experienced in Omnilife goes beyond the improvement in her physical health. She tells me that she studied to be a kindergarten teacher. If she had wanted relatively well-remunerated work in a government school, she would first have had to accept a year of service in a remote rural community. She opted to stay in Morelia and took a job in a private school that paid less than $200 a month. With that salary, she knew she would never realize her dream of buying a car. She supplemented her income by selling cosmetics via catalogue. When Amway came to Mexico, she signed up as a distributor, hoping to achieve the same affluence enjoyed by the leaders she saw at the presentations. Instead, she found that "it was all about appearances" and soon dropped out. The leaders had pressured her to buy an evening gown to appear prosperous, although she could not afford one. Omnilife, by contrast, "is about covering my needs" through regular profits from retail sales. It has the added benefit of promising health cures, something Amway's pricey soaps could not claim. In her first month and a half as an Omnilife distributor, Luisa's Omnilife

sales generated what it had taken her four months to earn as a teacher.

After she had devoted herself to Omnilife full-time for a few years, Luisa got married. In retrospect, she believes her desire to be a mother motivated her to wed and made her overlook the warning signs of a poor husband. The marriage produced a daughter, but by then Luisa had divorced her husband, who suffered from drug addiction and alcoholism. She moved in with her parents and her brother, all of whom worked full-time in Omnilife, and she enrolled in Omnilife's "basic school." In the name of "multidevelopment," Vergara had implemented a series of self-help workshops for distributors called "schools." Engaging in what one participant I spoke with called "interior work," trained counsellors lead groups segregated by sex through exercises designed to relieve grudges and to resolve family problems. Omnilife divides the schools into "basic" and "advanced" sequences, which take place over four weekends and can be repeated. Luisa attended the schools three times, hoping to deal with the failure of her marriage. By the third time, she knew when the session devoted to forgiveness was coming. She went outside the workshop meeting room and cried for a long time before she could rejoin the group and forgive her ex-husband.

The schools scarcely mention Omnilife products or the business plan, but Luisa considers them the key to her success. After graduating from the third school, she moved out of her parents' house and rented an apartment. "I live for my daughter. I want her to know that the two of us are a family." Following Selene's advice, she has a vision that moves her: a house. Sometimes she and her daughter imagine what their house will look like—two stories with a swimming pool and a garden. To save enough money for her house, Luisa keeps a harried pace. In the morning, after dropping her daughter off at school, she holds office hours at the support centre, makes phone calls, files paperwork, and answers questions from distributors who drop in. During the afternoon, she makes the rounds to visit her clients, checking on their health and replenishing their supply of vitamin powders. Even with several chugs from a bottle of Omnilife's energy drink, Luisa tires from the constant demands. Usually, she can spend no time with her daughter until the evening, but she knows she "must pay the price" to achieve her dream. Boosting her twice-monthly check is simply a matter of thinking positively and consuming the products consistently.

Vergara's "multidevelopment" plan, although not identified with any particular church, duplicates and enhances the spiritual message of rebirth through self-empowerment promoted by US–based multilevel marketers. In his public addresses, Vergara reduces the entire business plan to "using and chatting," claiming that the products practically sell themselves. Once a distributor consumes the products consistently, the effects are so salubrious that people notice the difference and ask for an explanation. In this way, selling Omnilife does not require either training in nutrition or knowledge of marketing. The sole requirement is a personal testimony of self-transformation that compels listeners to want to try the products themselves. In Luisa's well-rehearsed narrative, before Omnilife she was physically, financially, and emotionally ill. With the arrival of the products and company philosophy in her life, she recuperated her health and recalibrated her self-image into that of a successful, competent businesswoman who can surmount any obstacle. . . .

Training Capitalist Subjects?

Noticing the rapid growth of multilevel marketing in the developing world, [several] anthropologists have explained its success in terms of a different kind of transformation. They argue that participation in direct selling trains distributors in countries undergoing transitions to capitalism to accommodate new economic imperatives and connects them to transnational standards of self-presentation. Ara Wilson documents the popularity of Avon and Amway in Thailand during the Asian economic crisis of 1997. Selling there, she writes, "can provide a learnable system for working independently . . . and compelling templates with which to narrate one's possibilities in a shifting social order" (Wilson 2004: 174). . . . Other ethnographic accounts of direct selling in Asia have reached similar conclusions about its role in incorporating participants in a transnational capitalist network. Teenage girls in rural Thailand, Ida Fadzillah (2005) contends, use selling Amway and Avon cosmetics as a vehicle for their ambitions not to replicate the lives of their **peasant** mothers. Direct selling gives them geographic mobility, financial independence, and access to Western notions of cosmopolitan beauty. . . .

Chrissy Moutsatsos extends the argument about the role of direct selling in creating the conditions for new self-conceptions to Greek women who sell cosmetics for the Swedish company Oriflame. "Oriflame became a social space that enabled them to reframe their **subjectivity**. No longer 'merely' 'traditional,' they now became 'modern,' 'professional' women who stood closer to the ideals of the concept of modern Europeanness" (Moutsatsos 2001: 152). These accounts acknowledge only fleetingly the improbability of direct sellers considering a decades-old business model rooted in outdated notions of a gendered division of labour as an avatar of the modern. . . .

Focusing on the ways direct selling fashions rational economic actors in a modern marketplace obscures the explicit spiritual overtones that the participants themselves foreground. Anthropologists have demonstrated how traditional beliefs in the superhuman are central to the way people conceive of new economic arrangements (Comaroff 1985; Ong 1987; Taussig 1980). . . .

Instead of reading participation in direct selling as a rehearsal for more complete integration into a global, neoliberal economy, these studies reveal how it can be preparation for framing distributors' spirituality. Faith is an overriding concern in companies like Omnilife. So ingrained is faith in the efficacy of the products and in the generosity of the business plan that the lapsed distributors I met continued to consume the products and blamed themselves for failing to achieve success in the company. . . .

The proliferation of quasi-religious organizations like Omnilife exemplifies larger shifts in contemporary religious expression [throughout North America]. . . . In congregations from affluent suburbs to gritty inner cities, sermons resemble self-help tracts more concerned with individual therapeutic outcomes than with eternal salvation. In this environment of a personalized God, all religions come to resemble each other. A study conducted by researchers at Notre Dame University found that Roman Catholics were more than twice as likely to agree with statements of Protestant theologians than with pronouncements by Cardinal Ratzinger ([the future] Pope Benedict XVI; Wolfe 2003: 89). Other observers confirm that many people of faith in the United States consider themselves broadly spiritual rather than narrowly religious. . . .

The pursuit of foreign investment, free trade, and privatization of state industries in Latin America has forced an intensification in work patterns for [labourers and] white-collar employees. In each case, integration into a global economy has meant the erosion of state-supported services and an increasing [economic inequality]. Whereas some Mexicans have met these changes with violent confrontation, most have responded by adopting the logic of success through individual hard work. In this context of scarce resources, the motivational rhetoric of direct selling, although developed among evangelical Protestants in the United States, resonates strongly even with Roman Catholic Mexicans.

Luisa considers herself a practising Roman Catholic, attending Mass every Sunday, taking communion, and raising her daughter in the sacraments. Yet, in place of praying to saints and reciting the rosary in the morning, she repeats mantras to the "Infinite Intelligence" copied from a spiritual self-help book. To her, God is empathetic, not punishing. He gives his abundance to all humans equally. By addressing the Infinite Intelligence and instructing it to deliver the wealth

that is destined for her, she aims to maximize the riches that God provides.

This conception of a generous God to whom she can speak directly diverges sharply from the image inculcated by her religious education. Her life changed 13 years ago when she joined Omnilife, she declares. In attending Omnilife training sessions and reading the company literature, Luisa enrolled in an updated, more relevant "catechism" class. The new spiritual principles emphasize faith in the individual rather than institutions and strip away mediation between the divine and humans, allowing God's healing power to work directly on a person in crisis. That these tenets more closely resemble evangelical Protestantism than Roman Catholicism does not bother Luisa. . . . With her goal clearly envisioned, she feels confident she can reach it if she maintains her faith in herself.

Direct selling does not prepare her to be a more rational economic actor in a liberalized free market. Instead, Omnilife reorients and strengthens her spirituality so that emotional and material success depends on the manipulation of conditions under her individual control. . . .

Overcoming Internal Barriers

In the division of labour at Luisa's support centre, her father, Javier, conducts the business meeting on Thursdays for enrolled distributors. When I arrive at 5:00 p.m. one evening in June 2004, Javier is dressed casually in a white, short-sleeved polo shirt and navy slacks. He puts an Omnilife video in the VCR and sits in the audience to watch with his wife, Catalina. During the 20-minute presentation, distributors gradually fill up the rows of chairs. Many come straight to the meeting from the wholesale store across the street, toting plastic bags sagging with product.

The video, entitled *A Change for Your Entire Life*, features the story of Alejandro Pineda, a distributor in Mexico City. He recalls that he was a street cleaner and thought that he would be forever stuck in a demeaning job. The screen flashes to a desolate Mexico City street at night. Once he learned about Omnilife, he started taking the products. The video cuts to Pineda walking through the construction site for a spacious, two-story house. In the final scene, he tells the camera, "My family is more united now, and I recovered faith in myself." A graphic appears announcing the amount of his twice-monthly check from Omnilife: $13,000.

After he shuts off the television, Javier takes the microphone and perches on a stool in the front of the room while Catalina stays seated in the audience. He calls on several distributors to share what struck them most about the video. A few people demur, saying that they arrived late, but those who answer focus on the street cleaner's turnaround. A woman comments, "He conquered everything to get ahead." A man adds, "Sometimes I feel distressed that I'm falling behind, but I have faith that good things are coming to carry me to something larger." Suddenly, Catalina, on the verge of tears, volunteers her reaction: "What moved me was when he asked, 'Will my whole life be like this?' I felt the same. 'Don't I have the right to live better?' I asked myself many times. Like Pineda, we have this hunger to grow. I sometimes feel lost, but Omnilife is a light. This is what I wanted. We have to make a moral commitment." . . .

Javier continues, "When we forget to dream, we fall into the complex of 'I can't.' Dreaming is the most divine thing that can exist. When we stop dreaming, we lose that excitement. We all can, but we don't all want to." Turning to a middle-aged woman in the audience whose primary job is selling clothing at the municipal market, Javier asks, "What is your dream?"

"To work hard. I do it to help people. I feel good, so they also feel good."

Javier, unsatisfied, repeats, "What's your dream?"

She rephrases, "To get ahead, to earn a royalty check from Omnilife so I can leave the clothing stand."

Javier asks a man seated next to her, "Do you have a burning desire?" When the man is slow to respond, Javier counts aloud, "One second, two seconds. You, Silvia?"

Silvia, who enrolled only a month before, answers quickly, "To have enough product to nourish my children well."

Javier replies, "A burning desire is not about immediate needs." He points to a man in the audience, "You, sir, do you have a burning desire?"

"To have a lot of money."

"You need the exact quantity and the exact time by which you will earn it. Be very specific. It has to be something that doesn't allow us to sleep." He continues:

If I don't have a concrete idea of what I want in life, I won't go anywhere. In any business I need that motivation, that desire that moves me, that makes me agitated. It's like the light of a lens. It won't reach the paper if you hold the lens far away. But bring the lens closer, the light concentrates, and it burns the paper. This is the burning desire. We have to make it concrete.

We have to decide for ourselves to change our lives. Maybe you'll say I'm crazy. Each of us has to decide—it's a lot of work. It's not easy; it's not overnight. But it hurts more to be the person without the desire to change. What do I have to do? Look for my faults, identify what's held me back. What am I doing that doesn't allow me to advance? Then change my habits. We'll see results when we conquer our fears.

We all have fears. We see the butcher or the storekeeper and debate whether we should tell him about the [Omnilife] products, but fear paralyzes us and the moment passes. As the saying goes, "He who doesn't talk, God doesn't hear." What do we have to lose? Nothing. They'll either ask us to explain the products or say, "No, thanks." It's so simple; you don't need a professional degree. Just say, "I invite you to have a cup of coffee." Fear will make us conformist. We'll say, "Why risk it? I'm suffering, but I can manage." That's a sterile life. Who hasn't had problems? Do you know the only place there are no problems? The cemetery. To carry your problems around and not solve them is sad. We fall into a vicious circle, a carousel. We need to jump off. . . .

Javier controls the two-hour session deftly, never referring to notes or stifling audience participation. When it ends, he thanks us for our attention, and the 20 distributors socialize for a few minutes before dispersing to wait for their respective buses home.

This Thursday-evening meeting typifies the spiritual message of Omnilife and illustrates its appeal to working-class Mexicans confronting the challenges of neoliberal economic policies, which Mexico has pursued with vigour since the 1990s. Javier never studied beyond high school, and his wife dropped out of elementary school to help support her family. Although their two children pursued higher education, neither found professional employment that satisfied them emotionally or monetarily. Their experiences mirror the life histories of the men and women who frequent the support centre. . . . In Pineda's rise from street cleaner to homeowner and in Javier's late-model BMW parked conspicuously in front of the support centre, [these people] see examples of success attainable through "using and chatting."

. . . Javier emphasizes [that] fears, not structural impediments, prevent people from achieving their dreams. Distributors who have not duplicated the testimonials of changed lives featured in meetings, magazines, and videos should not fault the quality of the nutritional supplements or the soundness of the marketing plan. . . . [W]hen distributors find themselves stagnating, Javier advises them to identify their mental flaws and to modify their attitudes.

His recommendation forms part of a tightly organized campaign in the company to remake distributors' self-image and **world view**. The makeover starts with the nutritional supplements like the cup of coffee Luisa offered me. When she first

FIGURE 14.1   An Omnilife distributor attends a rally whose theme is "Cutting the Fear."

consumed the products, a chronic asthma that medicines had failed to treat disappeared. . . . What gives the powders their healing advantage over prescription drugs is that Omnilife interprets maladies as manifestations of mental disarray, not physical affliction. . . .

Once the company treats distributors' physical pain, it turns to correcting the attitudes that erode self-confidence and foster interpersonal conflict. . . . A man who left his job as a sales representative for a juice company to devote himself full-time to Omnilife recalls that he used to be a typical macho, quick-tempered and a steady drinker. He quarrelled with his wife and antagonized his clients. Worst of all, he could not fulfill his role as provider: "It hurts when my daughters ask for money, and I have nothing to give them." When his sister told him about Omnilife, he took it as an opportunity to transform his life, reading corporate publications and attending lectures in which company representatives portray machismo as cowardice, not manliness. To repair both his family relationships and his financial health, he must conquer the fears that limit his productive behaviour. At the 2003 rally, a mass ritual that draws some 20 thousand distributors to Guadalajara, he hears Vergara address the theme of how to eliminate fear. Although when we meet, his monetary troubles have not abated, he has assimilated Omnilife's message of personal transformation through internal reform. He states, "I don't want to ask for help. I had to suffer, but now I want to reap. I've changed so much, people wouldn't recognize me."

. . . Participation in the workshops, which cost a modest $11 for each session, is voluntary but is strongly encouraged in company literature and by meeting leaders. Taking a cue from quasi-religious 12-step programs, the first session begins with the axiom that "we don't know what we don't know," breaking down the egos of the participants so that they can be receptive to a new way of relating to the world. In successive sessions, the counsellors tell students not to assign blame to others for their problems and to "accept ourselves as we are," as one man told me. The final lessons aim to cultivate the habit of generosity, illustrating a karmic principle of reciprocity summed up by one alumnus as, "Those who give, receive." Graduation exercises take place at a beach resort in Mexico, uniting 1000 students from around the country. There, a motivational speaker dispenses fashion advice on the premise that external beauty reflects the newly ordered internal state. The weekend climaxes with the presentation of selected remade women and men, who appear on stage with their supportive families. . . .

Finally, Omnilife exhorts its adherents to affirm their new world view by teaching it to others. In business training sessions, leaders present overhead transparencies showing downlines of recruits as successive generations on a family tree. . . . Inviting others to join the company carries the responsibility of guiding recruits through the same shift in outlook and showing them how to impart the company's philosophy to their own invitees. This process strengthens the sponsor's commitment to the Omnilife world view while ensuring that recruits hear about the belief in a personal transformation from a familiar source.

Lest the spreading of the Omnilife message resemble Protestant proselytizing too closely, company leaders prefer the term *sharing*, defining the task as a charitable mission. In this way, the work of multilevel marketing delivers satisfaction and respect, benefits that traditional salaried employees lack. By privileging the non-material rewards that distributors accrue, Omnilife also blunts criticism that the pyramidal structure guarantees wealth only for those few at the apex of large organizations. Measuring success by the number of people distributors help, and not by the size of their paychecks, turns the insecurity of contemporary economic conditions into an asset. [While many employers in Mexico cannot] provide a substantial salary . . ., Omnilife at least offers a less concrete payoff that is available to all who want it: work that is spiritually significant and personally fulfilling.

Conclusion: Reintegrating Work and Spirituality

Throughout the developing world, workers thrust into a capitalist economy confront increasing competition and diminishing public support. Multilevel marketing **naturalizes** the magic of the free market, which turns money into more money for a fortunate few. . . . Yet to contend that a desire to function as more efficient moneymakers motivates participation in direct selling grants an instrumentality to these capitalist subjects that is not borne out by ethnographic data.

Little evidence supports the claim that earnings from direct selling surpass those from other forms of employment, especially because most distributors, unlike Luisa, devote only a few hours a week to the business. Despite testimonials of miraculous health cures, Omnilife's expensive nutritional powders prove a hard sell for many distributors. Earning high levels of income depends on building a network of thousands, a prospect at odds with the claim that no specialized training or social standing is necessary for success. Far more rewarding for direct sellers are the intangible, spiritual benefits. An Omnilife distributor who supplements the income from her work in a corner grocery store explains why she joined the company: "I was restless. I wanted more, and I wanted more." Omnilife's quasi-religious ethos supplies the "more," the connection between a source of income and a source for ordering the world.

Instead of aligning people's mental frameworks with the conditions of capitalist work, direct selling brings concordance between their work lives and their spiritual beliefs. Multilevel-marketing corporate philosophy masks the calculated pursuit of profit with a benevolent image of helping others. Rather than a rationalist guide to surviving in a neoliberal economy, direct selling suffuses its business practices with mystical qualities. . . .

To make the message believable, Omnilife borrows both rhetorical and ritual techniques from [religious] institutions. This emphasis on obedience to enlightened leaders and constant self-examination enhances corporate control over a two-million-member army of independent entrepreneurs. It does not represent sinister brainwashing; no matter how coordinated the spiritual campaign, distributors frequently defect from the organization without repercussions. Those who remain with Omnilife do so willingly because the quasi-religious work atmosphere resolves their inner struggles to extend goodwill to others while safeguarding their own self-interests. . . .

Seen as fostering continuity between professional activities and religious beliefs, direct selling in the developing world shares similarities with direct selling in the United States[, Canada,] and Europe. Although anachronistic in an age of Internet shopping and strip malls, home parties remain a vibrant sales strategy that allows distributors to perceive their work as a charitable mission. . . . Direct sellers' desire for self-improvement and spiritual significance through work felicitously matches the goals of corporate executives to cultivate loyalty and productivity among their distributors. This symbiosis ensures that quasi-religious organizations will continue as key players in contemporary capitalism.

References Cited

Comaroff, Jean. 1985. *Body of Power, Spirit of Resistance*. Chicago: University of Chicago Press.

Direct Selling Association. 2002. *What Is Direct Selling?* www.dsa.org.

"Scents and Sensibility." 1996. *Economist*, 13 July, 57–8.

Fadzillah, Ida. 2005. "The Amway Connection: How Transnational Ideas of Beauty and Money Affect Northern Thai Girls' Perceptions of Their Future Options." In *Youthscapes: The Popular, the National, the Global*, edited by Sunaina Maira and Elisabeth Soep, 85–102. Philadelphia: University of Pennsylvania Press.

Hilsenrath, Jon E. 1996. "Is Tupperware Dated? Not in the Global Market." *New York Times*, 26 May, C3.

Moutsatsos, Chrissy. 2001. *Transnational Beauty Culture and Local Bodies: An Ethnographic Account of Consumption and Identity in Urban Greece*. PhD diss., University of California, Irvine.

Ong, Aihwa. 1987. *Spirits of Resistance and Capitalist Discipline: Factory Women in Malaysia*. Albany: State University of New York Press.

Taussig, Michael. 1980. *The Devil and Commodity Fetishism in South America*. Chapel Hill: University of North Carolina Press.

Wilson, Ara. 2004. *The Intimate Economies of Bangkok: Tomboys, Tycoons, and Avon Ladies in the Global City*. Berkeley: University of California Press.

Wolfe, Alan. 2003. *The Transformation of American Religion: How We Actually Live Our Faith*. New York: Free Press.

Note

1. In reality, the original slate of products came from the line of "designer foods" promoted by Durk Pearson and Sandy Shaw, California-based longevity researchers. Early Omnilife publications make this explicit, but as the company introduced additional products, it obscured the provenance of the catalogue. Most commonly, distributors attribute the powders to "a team of international scientists." (Cahn's note)

Key Points to Consider

- Multilevel marketing remains a successful business model that has been expanding into global markets since the 1980s. The focus on individual entrepreneurial effort associated with direct selling is well suited to the neoliberal emphasis on competition.
- Individual distributors rarely make substantial sums of money, though they often become distributors believing that they will improve their economic circumstances.
- Multilevel marketing companies employ religious and spiritual messages and practices to sell their products and, more importantly, to motivate their sellers.

Critical Thinking Questions

1. What are the similarities between Omnilife's sales practices and Christian proselytizing? Are there differences that you can identify?
2. Cahn observes that most Omnilife distributors do not succeed in radically transforming their economic situations. Yet, he says that distributors are not being duped by the company. Why does Cahn believe that distributors stick with the company?
3. Neoliberalism emphasizes entrepreneurship and the desirability of individuals to be empowered to improve their lives while obscuring the obstacles to success that most individuals encounter. In what ways does the Omnilife message conform to this economic model?

Suggestions for Further Reading

Cahn, Peter S. 2003. *All Religions Are Good in Tzintzuntzan: Evangelicals in Catholic Mexico*. Austin: University of Texas Press.
———. 2008. "Consuming Class: Multilevel Marketers in Neoliberal Mexico." *Cultural Anthropology* 23 (3): 429–52.

————. 2011. *Direct Sales and Direct Faith in Latin America*. New York: Palgrave Macmillan.

Luhrmann, T.M. 2013. "Blinded by the Right? How Hippie Christians Begat Evangelical Conservatives." *Harper's Magazine*, April, 39–44.

Vincent, Susan. 2003. "Preserving Domesticity: Reading Tupperware in Women's Changing Domestic, Social, and Economic Roles." *Canadian Review of Sociology and Anthropology* 40 (2): 171–96.

Chapter 15

Ontario

Introduction

In 2008, a headline in *The Vancouver Sun* newspaper announced that because of student demands for sustainability, "university campuses all over the country are coming alive with green initiatives" (Scott and St Marseille 2008). In the years since, programs and projects identified as sustainability initiatives have become even more widespread, and you would probably be hard pressed to find a Canadian university that does not have one or more programs, degree certificates, or projects meant to promote sustainability. But what exactly do people mean when they talk about "sustainability" or "sustainable development"? Is *sustainability* a synonym for *environmentalism*, as the newspaper headline suggests?

The contemporary uses of the terms *sustainability* and *sustainable development* come from Chapter 2 of *Our Common Future*, a 1987 report by the United Nations' World Commission on Environment and Development (UNWCED 1987). The first sentence of the chapter defines *sustainable development* as "development that meets the needs of the present without compromising the ability of future generations to meet their own needs." The chapter continues with the assertion that in pursuing sustainability, "overriding priority" should be given to the needs of the world's poor. Thus, formal definitions of *sustainable development* generally note the need to balance economic growth, environmental protection, and social equity.

The article presented below makes a distinction between *environmental movements* and *environmental justice movements*. It is the former that have been dominant in Canada. The first environmental efforts in Canada were conservation-oriented. According to environmental historian Laurel Sefton MacDowell, Canadians have tended to regard the country's natural regions as an "abundant wilderness" (2012: 96) and to view natural resources—especially fish, forest products, and minerals—as the basis for the creation and maintenance of a strong industrial economy. From the late nineteenth century until the 1960s, conservation policies and practices in Canada were driven by industrialists' interests in managing resources in ways that would preserve them for industrial extraction.

The birth of the modern environmental movement is usually traced to the 1962 publication of Rachel Carson's book *Silent Spring*, which focused attention away from conservation of individual resources and toward the effects of pollution on entire ecosystems. The environmental movement that emerged took an ecosystem approach, but one that largely excluded humans from the natural environment. While Carson's work connected environmental pollutants to public health issues, the overall stress of the book was on the ways that human activities were degrading the natural environment. Similarly, some modern environmental organizations, including the Canadian-founded Greenpeace, have even protested more traditional activities such as **subsistence** hunting and fishing, which **Aboriginal peoples** across North America have practised since long before colonization. In recent decades, however, environmental organizations have been criticized as elitist for favouring urban dwellers' desires for "wilderness" protection over the needs of small-scale, generally poor, non-industrial users of natural resources.

The environmental justice movement, in contrast, links social concerns for equity to environmental activism. It grew out of the United States' civil rights movement through the recognition that communities of colour were (and still are) disproportionately burdened by land-use practices. These burdens include direct harms from proximity to toxic industries, highways, power plants, and waste dumps as well as lack of access to environmental improvements such as neighbourhood parks or other public amenities. Environmental justice movements have grown beyond the civil rights context of the United States to encompass the distinct contexts of inequality in other places as well as issues of global human rights such as the offshoring of toxic industries from wealthy countries to poor ones.

With the exception of **First Nations** reserves, Canada is not racially segregated to the same extent as the United States. It is, however, economically segregated in ways that enable disproportionately heavy environmental burdens on poor people. As well, the current political and economic system in Canada treats corporate profits as an unquestioned social good that benefits everyone. Yet recent events show that the pursuit of corporate profits can cause great public harm. In 2000, privatization of drinking water treatment in Walkerton, Ontario, resulted in thousands of illnesses and seven deaths from *E. coli* bacteria. In 2013, cost-cutting in the railroad industry led to a train derailment that killed 47 people and destroyed the central business district of Lac-Mégantic, Quebec. These are environmental justice issues because the decision to place corporate profits ahead of public health and safety benefitted a few corporate elites while raising the environmental risks for many. Although not only poor people are put at risk by such disasters, wealthier individuals are often better able to mitigate the harms they face.

The article below, by Anna Willow, concerns a successful environmental justice action undertaken collaboratively by a First Nations community (Grassy Narrows) and an environmental organization (Rainforest Action Network, or RAN). The people of Grassy Narrows First Nation are part of a larger Aboriginal group called Anishinaabe, whose members have traditionally made their homes in the north central woodlands of North America. Anishinaabe in Michigan, Wisconsin, and Minnesota are known as Chippewa or Ojibwa; the latter name, often spelled *Ojibway* or *Ojibwe*, was also applied to Canadian Anishinaabe in earlier eras. Approximately two-thirds of the 1500 registered members of the Grassy Narrows First Nation live on a small reserve in Northwestern Ontario near Lake of the Woods. Kenora, Ontario, 80 kilometres to the south, and Winnipeg, Manitoba, 275 kilometres to the southwest, are the closest cities.

Many troubling events characterize the history of Canadian colonial administration of First Nations. The Grassy Narrows First Nation has an especially sad history. Like the **Inuit** presented in Chapter 13, the people who formed Grassy Narrows First Nation maintained a relatively self-sufficient way of life involving subsistence hunting, fishing, and trapping; the gathering of wild plants; and occasional short-term wage work until the 1970s. Prior to that time, fishing for their own food and guiding non-Native sport fishermen had made up a substantial portion of their subsistence and cash economy. In 1970, however, the Grassy Narrows Anishinaabe learned that a serious health problem—a neuro-motor disorder called Minamata disease—was being caused by mercury contamination in the river and lake system that crossed the lands they hunted and fished on. For nearly a decade, a pulp and paper mill located hundreds of kilometres upstream in Dryden, Ontario, had been dumping mercury-laden effluent into the Wabigoon River, poisoning the fish that Grassy Narrows people depended on. Mercury is a heavy metal that **bioaccumulates** in an organism's body over time; humans and other top consumers are particularly susceptible to mercury poisoning because, through a process known as **biomagnification**, toxic substances tend to build up in higher and higher concentrations from the bottom to the top of a food chain. Because the local rivers and fish were contaminated with mercury, the Anishinaabe of Grassy Narrows lost a critical source of nutritious food as well as a source of cash, undermining other subsistence activities and the social relations that were built from them. Willow writes about the Anishinaabe connection to the boreal forest as "**emplacement**." She uses this term to describe the situation in which social relationships created through land-based activities like subsistence hunting and gathering build intense bonds between people and to the places where those activities occur.

Without doubt, the mercury contamination that the Grassy Narrows people suffered is an environmental justice issue. The article below, however, concerns a different issue—clearcutting of forests that, though not part of the Grassy Narrows reserve, are part of the Anishinaabe's traditional territories and are still used by Anishinaabe for hunting and trapping, for gathering wild rice and berries, and for collecting wood for baskets. According to the Anishinaabe, clearcutting puts these socially and culturally important activities at risk.

The article examines a collaboration between people from Grassy Narrows First Nation and non-Indigenous members of the Rainforest Action Network (RAN) to understand why this alliance was successful. In the full version of the article, Willow describes other successful alliances—in Brazil, Indonesia, and the United States—between non-Indigenous environmentalists and Indigenous communities, but she also notes that these sorts of collaborations often fail because the two groups have different concepts of the environment and different long-term goals. As well, many environmentalists have stereotyped ideas about Aboriginal people as "the original ecologists" and become disturbed by Aboriginal activities like hunting or by the realization that Aboriginal peoples do not live the ways their ancestors did. Collaborations that do succeed, Willow argues, do so because the parties recognize and accept the differences in their ultimate goals but have common interim goals. Willow suggests that in the Grassy Narrows–RAN collaboration, the environmentalists took the time to understand the Anishinaabe **world view** and, in doing so, also developed a sense of emplacement in the boreal forest.

⁂ *About the Author* ⁂

Anna J. Willow is from Wisconsin, where she worked with Anishinaabe communities to document culturally important natural resources. She holds degrees in anthropology and in environmental education from the University of Wisconsin and the University of Michigan. Willow teaches anthropology at The Ohio State University. Her current research program includes an ethnographic study of the social contexts and consequences of hydraulic fracturing ("fracking") for natural gas in rural Ohio.

Re(con)figuring Alliances: Place Membership, Environmental Justice, and the Remaking of Indigenous–Environmentalist Relationships in Canada's Boreal Forest

Anna J. Willow

The Trans-Canada Highway is the only major thoroughfare connecting dozens of Canadian cities and towns. Stopping its steady flow of travellers and truckers is a big deal. On 13 July 2006, Anishinaabe anti-clearcutting activists from Grassy Narrows First Nation joined forces with Rainforest Action Network's (RAN) direct-action environmentalists to block the highway just north of Kenora,

Ontario. For 43 months, Grassy Narrows residents had maintained a blockade on a logging road near their semi-remote reserve community—located 50 scenic miles [80 kilometres] to the north—that effectively prevented the passage of trucks and equipment, but industrial logging continued unabated in parts of the First Nation's traditional territory. The Trans-Canada event succeeded in returning public attention to Grassy Narrows' cause. Altogether, around one hundred protestors participated in the day-long blockade. A 30-foot [9-metre] tripod was erected in the highway at a strategically chosen site along the route taken by trucks carrying felled trees to one of Kenora's active mills. A RAN activist and a banner calling on spectators to "Save Grassy Narrows Boreal Forest" dangled from the formation.

Members of Grassy Narrows First Nation began publicly opposing industrial logging in the late 1990s. Residents responded to increases in logging operations' intensity and proximity to their 14-square-mile [36-square-kilometre] reserve with a growing sense of alarm. They were troubled by the threatened destruction of their land base and subsistence culture and argued that the ongoing clearcutting violated their treaty-guaranteed right to harvest resources throughout their 2500-square-mile [6475-square-kilometre] traditional territory.[1]

For several years, they expressed their concerns through conventional channels of letter writing and peaceful protest but felt they received no substantive response. By the end of 2002, a core group of dedicated activists had generated enough enthusiasm within their community to launch a blockade.

In May of 2003, I arrived in Northwestern Ontario with the goal of learning as much as I could about the blockade at Grassy Narrows and the cultural, political, and historical factors that inspired it. As my **ethnographic** project progressed, I got to know dozens of Anishinaabe activists. Less expectedly, I also became acquainted with a fluid assortment of non-Native supporters who spent time at the blockade site or attended blockade-related events in Kenora or Winnipeg, Manitoba.

In June of 2004, I met three . . . non-Native grassroots activists who attended an environmental gathering hosted by the First Nation and

FIGURE 15.1 A clearcut area near the Grassy Narrows reserve, Ontario, July 2003.

subsequently stayed on for much of the summer. These visitors talked, ate, and swam with Grassy Narrows residents and, more importantly, expressed a genuine commitment to understanding what mattered to them and why. In the months that followed, one of these individuals collaborated with RAN on an activist training course and was hired to work on the organization's Old Growth Campaign. Over time, the relationships established that summer nurtured an alliance considered successful by participants on both sides. Informed by my long-term study of the Grassy Narrows blockade and by more recent conversations with RAN campaigners, this article explores the motives and meanings of "environmental connections across difference" (Tsing 2005: x). . . .

Around the world, diverse human–environment relationship and divergent goals have [allowed] the formation of alliances that allow multiple parties to benefit in the immediate term. Yet critical observers of the international environmental movement have found that Indigenous–environmentalist partnerships have often been . . . asymmetrical[,] . . . perpetuating Indigenous peoples' systemic disadvantages and predestining promising partnerships for eventual disintegration. In the pages that follow, I describe how Indigenous–environmentalist alliances are being constructively re(con)figured in the context of recent anti-clearcutting activism in Northwestern Ontario. . . .

[Despite distinct perspectives], Indigenous activists and environmentalists have been able to develop respectful interpersonal relationships and imagine themselves as members of a diverse community united by [a shared] interest in boreal-forest protection. At the same time, an increasingly influential conceptual framework that fuses environmental and social concerns and redefines the environment to include humans and their activities has led to transformations in how the environmental movement formulates its . . . objectives. I argue that this . . . context not only facilitated the development of a strong alliance and an effective conservation campaign, but may also ultimately empower Indigenous communities to participate in environmental protection on terms that are closer to their own.

The Politics of Environmental Alliance

. . . [T]he ultimate goals of Indigenous activists— which tend to include political empowerment, self-determination, environmental health, and economic development in addition to environmental protection—often differ dramatically from the wildlands preservation orientation of most mainstream environmentalists. . . .

Diverse alliances sometimes collapse under the weight of competing interests alone, but the fact that environmentalists have often expected Indigenous peoples' goals to match their own has been even more damaging. As [Beth] Conklin and [Laura] Graham avow, "There is an inherent asymmetry at the core of the eco–Indian[2] alliance. Indians' eco-political value is bestowed from the outside— the product of a historical moment that has seized on Indians in general and certain Indians in particular, as natural symbols of ecologically harmonious lifeways" (Conklin and Graham 1995: 706). Instead of empowering Indigenous communities to present their own agendas, Indigenous–environmentalist partnerships have often been underlain by stereotypical images of contemporary Indigenous peoples as "Ecologically Noble Savages" . . . who feel an innate sense of spiritual connection to the environment and unfailingly act to conserve it.

As a result of these pervasive images [of Indigenous peoples as original ecologists], the short-term benefits of alliances are often outweighed by longer-term detrimental effects. When, for example, Penan people in the Malaysian state of Sarawak blocked roads to protest logging on their customary lands in 1987, they became the focus of an international environmental campaign. . . . In their quest to convey the situation to a sympathetic global public, environmentalists presented the Penan as they saw fit, converting the Penan into tools of persuasion capable of convincing supporters to send letters or money required, portraying them as endangered people intimately connected to an endangered forest (Brosius 1997). Instead of a dynamic and diverse group, the Penan were depicted as inherently ecological and, as a result, the political dimensions of their resistance were overshadowed by their alleged quest for natural harmony. Thus, although alliances with environmentalists bring advantageous attention to Indigenous causes, [the issues are] frequently formulated and communicated in terms dictated by non-Native members of Western industrial societies. . . .

. . . [A]lthough environmentalists' imaginings of Indigenous peoples as inherent ecologists have occasionally sown early seeds of productive working relationships, the same views have sparked heated clashes when living Natives inevitably fail to live up to unrealistic expectations, thus inciting charges of inauthenticity from those who think they know how "real" [Indigenous peoples] should act (see Muehlmann 2009). When, for example, members of the Makah tribe [who live in the Northwest Coast region of the United States] hunted a gray whale in 1999—a right specifically guaranteed by the 1855 Treaty of Neah Bay—some non-Native environmentalists reacted with astonished rage (Coté 2010). Hopi ceremonial harvest of golden eagles from Wupatki National Monument [in Arizona] has generated a similar outcry (Williams 2001).

Like Indigenous–environmentalist alliances in . . . Malaysia [and elsewhere], the partnership between Grassy Narrows and RAN united individuals with different ways of imagining the forest they sought to protect, different ultimate goals, and different strategic visions for accomplishing them. But whereas previous anthropological analyses have found that alliances often perpetuate the political asymmetries of north/south, colonizer/colonized, and centre/periphery (Doane 2007), activists in Northwestern Ontario appear to be moving closer to an equitable partnership. In the remainder of this article, I endeavour to explain how and why.

The Grassy Narrows/ Old Growth Campaign

. . . RAN is an established international environmental NGO, but it differs from traditional conservation organizations in several ways. While most North American environmental groups have historically excluded human activities and concerns from their agendas, RAN has incorporated Indigenous populations into its campaigns and articulated an organizational mission that includes supporting forest inhabitants and their rights since its early years in the mid-1980s. Correspondingly, RAN is also distinctive for its holistic focus on conserving entire ecosystems—which necessarily encompass human inhabitants and their activities—rather than just charismatic species or designated natural areas. Finally, RAN's direct-action marketplace and media-oriented tactics set the group apart from the legal and public policy emphases of most environmental NGOs (RAN 2010).

In early 2004, RAN was looking for its next corporate target. On the heels of an intense four-year campaign that convinced Boise Cascade to stop logging old-growth forests in the United States and adopt a global sustainability plan, the organization chose [to target] Weyerhaeuser, a Seattle-based logging giant that controlled vast tracts of North American old growth and had a reputation for environmentally destructive practices and conflict with communities in the regions it logged. RAN campaigners began by seeking specific sites where Weyerhaeuser was clashing with Indigenous boreal-forest communities. They found Grassy Narrows.

In the beginning, Grassy Narrows was one of many elements of a broad campaign that included events in Seattle and British Columbia and at the Toronto Stock Exchange. After months of informal collaboration, Grassy Narrows activists sat down with a RAN organizer to weigh the pros and cons of increasing RAN's level of support. The blockaders were enthusiastic about the public attention and new sources of support a stronger partnership could generate. From RAN's perspective, knowing the First Nation already had an anti-logging blockade in place, the strong relationships established in the summer of 2004, and the fact that Weyerhaeuser was purchasing softwood from the community's traditional territory combined to make Grassy Narrows a logical focal point. As [senior campaigner Annie] Sartor (interview, 13 April 2011) put it, "Everything kind of aligned and it made sense to throw a lot of support behind it."

Grassy Narrows and the surrounding boreal forest subsequently became the central focus of RAN's Old Growth Campaign. With support from RAN, Grassy Narrows activists released a letter on 28 February 2006 warning Weyerhaeuser and Canadian newsprint manufacturer Abitibi-Consolidated to stop logging the First Nation's traditional territory or "face a fierce campaign of resistance in the woods, in the streets, and in the marketplace" (RAN 2006a: 4). As anticipated, neither company halted its logging operations. In response, RAN put up outdoor advertisements and projections, launched a targeted website, organized an online petition, and released a report connecting "green" homes built by a Weyerhaeuser subsidiary to wood from clearcuts in Grassy's traditional territory (RAN 2006b). In April of 2006, Anishinaabe activists and RAN campaigners convened in Seattle for Weyerhaeuser's annual shareholders' meeting; they publicly challenged the corporation to "adopt independent Forest Stewardship Council certification, respect the rights of Indigenous communities, and adopt a comprehensive environmental policy to protect endangered forests" (RAN 2006c: 5).

That July, RAN helped finance and organize an environmental gathering that brought Grassy Narrows residents and supporters from across North America together at the blockade site. The gathering culminated in the Trans-Canada Highway blockade. Looking to prevent a racially charged local backlash in an area with a long history of tension between Anishinaabe and Euro-Canadian residents, RAN organizers filled most of the high-profile roles, but the guidelines and direction for the event came from Grassy Narrows.

With this prominent collaborative media action behind them, the alliance continued to gain strength. In January of 2007, Grassy Narrows declared a moratorium on clearcutting and other industrial activity within its traditional territory. Supported and publicized by RAN, Grassy's open letter was directed at government leaders and industry:

We now declare a moratorium on further industrial activity in our Traditional Territory until such a time as the Governments of Canada and Ontario restore their honour and obtain the consent of our community in these decisions that will forever alter the future of our people. . . . If you choose to ignore our rights, we will have no choice but to take more action with our supporters in the forest, in the markets, in the legislature, and in the courts to assert our rights as the Indigenous people of this land. We will determine the course of our own future, and we will care for our Traditional Territory.[3]

Meanwhile, RAN continued pressuring Weyerhaeuser to stop sourcing wood from the contested land by occupying the roof of a model home near Seattle and sending letters to investors disclosing the corporation's dismal environmental and human rights record.

The warm months of 2007 again saw a major outdoor demonstration, this time designed to influence the provincial government in Toronto. An event at the Ontario Legislature on 21 September brought RAN activists together with citizens from Grassy Narrows and dozens of other Ontario First Nations for a collaborative protest that would have been inconceivable in previous decades. RAN's explicit purpose was not, as most observers would expect, to call for stronger environmental regulations or the protection of ecologically sensitive areas, but to demand that the province recognize Indigenous rights. An enormous arrow-shaped banner reading "Native Land Rights Now" was unfurled and directed at the legislature building. Like the previous summer's Trans-Canada Highway blockade, the event attracted national media coverage in Canada (RAN 2008).

As the Old Growth Campaign progressed, RAN's strategy shifted to emphasize supply-chain logic: trees cut in Grassy's traditional territory travelled to Abitibi's mill in Fort Frances, Ontario, and later across the Rainy River to the Boise Cascade paper plant in International Falls, Minnesota, for processing. Because Boise owns two office-supply chains [OfficeMax and Grand & Toy] where paper products containing this wood were being sold, RAN organized an International Day of Action that drew protesters to [these] stores in 34 North American cities on 30 January 2008 (Tiner 2008). Less than a month later, Boise Cascade announced that it would no longer purchase wood from Grassy Narrows' traditional territory without the community's consent (RAN 2008).

Goals and Gains

On 11 May 2008, the Ontario Ministry of Natural Resources and Grassy Narrows First Nation entered into a memorandum of understanding to initiate formal negotiations—expected to take up to four years to complete—to resolve the ongoing blockade dispute.[4] Shortly thereafter, Abitibi announced plans to cease using wood from Grassy's traditional territory and relinquish its licence to log the area. Corporate representatives explained the decision in economic terms; with new sources of wood becoming available elsewhere due to a downturn in demand, waiting four years to determine the future tenability of logging in one location simply did not fit the company's business interests (Gorrie 2008). Because Abitibi was the official licence holder, the announcement also obliged Weyerhaeuser to stop using wood from the contested land (RAN 2008).

Activists at Grassy Narrows and RAN shared a sense of accomplishment and both [groups] acknowledged that they could not have succeeded alone. In the wake of the victory, J.B. Fobister—a respected Grassy Narrows subsistence harvester, business-owner, and anti-clearcutting spokesperson—commented publicly, "I'm really thankful for everybody that made this happen. We couldn't have done it without everybody's help over all these years." Similarly, RAN informed its donors that the organization was only partially responsible for the campaign's achievements by announcing, "This historic decision was the result of decades of lawsuits and peaceful protests by the people of Grassy Narrows, including the longest-standing Indigenous logging blockade in North America" (RAN 2008: 7).

Although both parties considered the withdrawal a positive outcome, their goals had never been identical. The strength of the Grassy–RAN alliance derived not from an obfuscation of diverse histories and interests but from a shared commitment to working within a circumscribed and co-created political space. Many of the RAN campaigners who worked closely with Grassy Narrows residents wholeheartedly supported the First Nation's right to self-determination, but RAN's organizational mandate ensured that logging—and especially ecologically valuable old-growth boreal forest—remained the group's primary concern. As Annie Sartor explained, RAN was inherently limited in the types of support it was able to offer, the particular issues it was able to back, and the duration of its involvement. She told me, "We were not a Grassy Narrows solidarity group. We were there to take on one particular logging issue" (interview, 13 April 2011). . . .

Clearcutting was the immediate consensus concern that united RAN and Grassy Narrows, but the people of Grassy Narrows face a much broader and longer-term array of challenges that go far beyond environmental issues to encompass environmental health, social justice, treaty rights, self-determination, and cultural revitalization (see Willow 2009, 2010, 2011, 2012). . . . Still, . . . the partnership between Grassy Narrows and RAN benefitted both parties. Collaborating with Grassy Narrows gave RAN an important political tool—Indigenous land rights—to complement its trademark corporate tactics. . . . Indigenous identity retains considerable representational and rhetorical power. Neither allies nor adversaries have challenged Grassy Narrows activists' status as Indigenous citizens. With increasing global public support for Indigenous rights and with many of Grassy's anti-clearcutting activists proudly reinforcing ties to traditional Anishinaabe cultural identity through linguistic and cultural revitalization projects (see Willow 2012), First Nation residents' uncontested Indigenous status enabled RAN to construct a compelling critique that extended beyond environmentalism and into the realm of human rights, a move that considerably enlarged the audience of prospective supporters.

Grassy Narrows, on the other hand, gained international media recognition and the tenacious backing of a multidimensional RAN campaign. The fact that RAN was aware of—and respectful of—the blockaders' complex set of goals influenced how the NGO conducted its campaign. Rather than forcibly integrating Anishinaabe activists' viewpoints into a predetermined agenda, Annie Sartor told me RAN campaigners "worked hard not to develop a campaign *alongside* them but to stand *behind* them. . . . We didn't reinvent anything RAN style, we just tried to pump up the volume" (interview, 13 April 2011). Activists at Grassy, for example, had considered utilizing boycott strategies since the blockade's early days. RAN was able to bring this idea to fruition. . . .

Imagining Place Membership

Relationships are processes, continuously negotiated and modified to meet complex . . . contexts and shifting . . . circumstances. . . . Some of the most constructive documented alliances between North Americans of Native and non-Native descent began as local responses to perceived outside threats that effectively redrew ethnic and cultural boundaries to encompass a shared sense of "**place** membership" (Grossman 2005: 25). . . .

Although the Grassy–RAN partnership bridged over 2000 miles [over 3200 kilometres] to unite an Indigenous boreal-forest community and a San Francisco–based NGO, the logic of place membership is valuable for illuminating the alliance's trajectory. Informed by their personal knowledge of the reserve and its residents, RAN staffers were aware from the beginning that Anishinaabe people . . . are members of a dynamic contemporary community who respond to complex challenges in diverse ways. As Brant Olson told me, RAN worked hard to ascertain a consensus position within the First Nation (interview, 28 April 2011). Although community members hold a variety of positions regarding logging—some are eager to see their people benefit from the associated economic development, while others oppose any type of industrial extraction—the consensus that emerged identified the ongoing clearcutting as a foremost concern. Right away, the logging companies harvesting wood from Grassy's traditional territory emerged as a mutual antagonist; even when longer-term goals diverged, removing Weyerhaeuser and Abitibi from the region provided an unambiguous and unanimous immediate objective.

Place membership grows from common commitment to a physical environment that is in some way shared, but it is as much about human relationships as about relationships between people and the places they care for. If place membership implies (as I propose it does) a willingness and ability to contribute to making a place what it is today and what it will become tomorrow, the most exemplary enactments of the place membership that grew from and guided the Grassy–RAN alliance—from time spent interacting in and around Grassy Narrows to collective participation in events that were simultaneously social and strategic—figure prominently in the story told here. Demonstrating a commitment to place that extended far beyond forest ecosystems and boreal biodiversity, RAN activists also contributed in ways that were less glamorous but just as significant by planting garden seeds, repairing structures, and entertaining children. Reciprocally, place membership additionally means allowing a place to influence one's attitudes and actions. As their sense of place and personal connection to Grassy Narrows and its people increased, some RAN campaigners became deeply committed to promoting the best possible future for the community and its citizens, sometimes over, above, and at odds with their organization's more abstract goal of forest protection.

. . . [T]he notion of place membership . . . extended in this instance to encompass an imagined community (Anderson 1983) composed of Indigenous activists and environmentalists who envisioned themselves as sharing a common interest in protecting Northwestern Ontario's boreal forest. Although RAN campaigners were well aware of their "outsider" status, their ability to speak to consumers of paper products and negotiate with logging companies informed this sensibility, as did their awareness that the physical systems that support human and non-human life—from the air we breathe to the water we drink—are interconnected and shared by all. Acknowledging that Grassy Narrows residents have more at stake than outside supporters ever could, one RAN forest campaigner put it this way: "Understanding that we are all dependent on the earth's ecological life-support systems and that we are all indirectly impacted by what happens in the forest allows us to understand that we all have a common interest in this work" (personal communication, 9 May 2011). Leaders of the Grassy Narrows blockade share a similar outlook; Judy DaSilva, a devoted anti-clearcutting activist and mother of five, once remarked that it's about "putting aside grudges and understanding that we're all in this together, whether we like it or not" (field notes, 10 November 2004).

A series of transformations in Grassy Narrows' relationship to mainstream North American society and recent technological developments made imagining [this type of] boreal-forest place membership possible. From the seventeenth century on, Anishinaabe people in Northwestern Ontario were active fur-trade participants. Consequently, the region's Indigenous subsistence base gradually shifted from hunting and gathering to a mixed economy. At Grassy Narrows, these changes accelerated in the 1960s and 1970s. In the early 1960s, the community was relocated and became accessible by road. When electricity reached Grassy Narrows in 1975, the arrival of television opened new channels for residents' exposure to mainstream ways of life, social attitudes, and pop cultural movements. By choice or by necessity, activists at Grassy Narrows are fluent not only in the English language but also in Euro–North American culture and the modes of interpersonal interaction that facilitate transactions with outsiders.

While the Grassy–RAN alliance would have been unfeasible in the absence of meaningful face-to-face interaction, the fact that both parties knew the other was only a phone call or email away was important to the imagined community's evolution. Although Grassy Narrows remains underdeveloped by Euro-Canadian measures, most households have telephone service and a handful of residents also have home Internet access. As a result, technologically facilitated communication that allows spoken or written words to flow across many miles has made sustained meaningful communication—and the genuine social relationships lauded as the key to the Grassy Narrows–RAN alliance's success—an achievable ambition. The creation of an electronic social network, webmastered by RAN but with regular contributions from Grassy Narrows residents, claimed collective territory for the alliance in the world of cyberspace in 2006 and is today the coalition's most active component. . . .

Redefining Environmentalism

Anishinaabe people, for the most part, do not think of themselves as environmentalists; even those who work tirelessly to defend their boreal forest homeland tend to see the environmental movement as an external phenomenon. . . . Over and above their concerns for ecosystemic integrity, they care about the viability of their land-based subsistence way of life and the distinctive sense of sovereign peoplehood it sustains. A complex system of reciprocal interactions between humans and more powerful "other-than-human-persons" has been documented as a central component of Anishinaabe human–environment relationships (Hallowell 1975). [Anishinaabe people live] as part of a natural world that is simultaneously social, spiritual, and economic, [and to them] Euro-American distinctions between environment, culture, and politics make little sense (see Willow 2009, 2012).

Non-Indigenous environmentalists are heirs to a very different set of historical and cultural baggage. The notion of wilderness, defined in the [United States'] 1964 Wilderness Act as "an area where the earth and its community of life are untrammeled by man, where man himself is a visitor who does not remain," has been central to the North American environmental movement (Wilderness Act 1964: Section 2c). Yet, as environmental historian William Cronon notes, only 250 years ago wilderness was seen as "the antithesis of all that was orderly and good" (1995: 71). . . .

In recent decades, a fundamental **paradigm shift**—essential to the development of the Grassy–RAN alliance—has transformed how environmentalists [regard] human communities and concerns in relation to the emplaced natural systems they seek to protect. Today, the formerly standard supposition that nature worth conserving exists only where humans and their activities do not is no longer defensible. . . . A fundamental acceptance of people as part of the world they work to protect now guides many environmental groups' organizational philosophies and operational strategies. In North America, this conceptual shift is most readily apparent in what has come to be called the environmental justice movement (EJM). . . .

EJM activists have long regarded the goals of the mainstream environmental movement—particularly the preservation of remote wild areas and endangered exotic species—as privileges available only to upper- and middle-class whites. Most decisively, they have charged the mainstream movement with defining the environment in a narrow way that precludes any consideration of issues that combine human and environmental concerns. Environmental justice offers a distinctive vision of what *environment* should mean and, consequently, of what environmentalism should strive to accomplish. In a speech at the First National People of Color Environmental Leadership Summit in 1991, movement leader Dana Alston articulated a coherent defining vision:

> The issues of the environment do not stand alone by themselves. They are not narrowly defined. Our vision of the environment is woven into an overall framework of social, racial, and economic justice. The environment, for us, is where we live, where we work, and where we play (Gottlieb 1993: 5).

Alston's statement remains the most common characterization of how movement participants view the environment and has influenced subsequent conversations that place social considerations like housing, education, safety, and employment alongside ecological issues (Checker 2005: 17).

EJM scholar Dorceta Taylor believes that in the short time since it emerged, this new paradigm has altered the nature of environmental discourse: "Because of environmental justice," she argues, "it is no longer considered appropriate for mainstream environmentalists to define and analyze environmental issues without considering the social justice implications of the problem" (2000: 523). The EJM's

challenge to the discursive power of mainstream environmentalism has succeeded in influencing how environmentalists define the places they seek to protect as well as what they are willing to accept as legitimate environmental issues. It has created a new cultural, social, and political space for the development of an agenda capable of encompassing and amalgamating formerly contrasting environmental perspectives, a middle ground with room for Indigenous activists and self-declared environmentalists to stand side by side. A relatively young organization with an energetic and engaged staff, RAN appears to have embraced this expanded, humanized environmental vision.

As Anna Tsing notes, far from implying homogeneity, collaborative movements can and do arise in the face of cultural and political difference, and "social mobilizations are facilitated by their appeal to diverse social groups, who find divergent means and meanings in the cause" (2005: 245–6). . . . Rather than attempting to discount the dissimilarities that divide non-Indigenous environmentalists and Indigenous world citizens, the Grassy–RAN alliance admitted and even encouraged difference as it constructed a shared political arena in which a common aim could be advanced. In the imagined cartography of this co-created world, Grassy Narrows was not peripheral but central.

Conclusion: Re(con)figuring Alliances

. . . In recent decades, cultural anthropology has directed [attention] to the venerable task of revealing the continuance and re-emergence of systemic inequities associated with global economic and cultural interchange. While this article is intended to inspire constructive **critical analyses**, I get the sense that many among us are also eager to find inspiration in stories of success. In this spirit, I have proposed that the achievements of the Grassy–RAN alliance can be attributed to a social context that made it possible for diverse participants to imagine place membership in a Northwestern Ontario boreal-forest community and a discursive context that reconceptualized the environment to include human activities and concerns. These are by no means the only factors that underlie this or other productive Indigenous–environmentalist partnerships, but they offer a starting point for those of us seeking to put academic knowledge to positive practical use. . . .

Ultimately, how members of Western industrial societies think about Indigenous peoples is bound to how they think about the environment. . . . Conklin and Graham (1995: 697) suggest that

support for Indigenous causes must "be founded on realistic understandings of Indians that will outlast the ebb and flow of popular enthusiasm and media fads." When conceptual gaps are narrowed, they can be bridged. Native activists can be approached not merely as . . . symbols, but as potential friends and collaborators in a common struggle. . . . When environmentalists refigure the categories that guide their relationships to the places they seek to protect, they also reconfigure the power structures underpinning their alliances with the Indigenous groups who call those places home.

References Cited

Anderson, Benedict. 1983. *Imagined Communities: Reflections on the Origin and Spread of Nationalism.* London: Verso.

Brosius, J. Peter. 1997. "Endangered Forest, Endangered People: Environmentalist Representations of Indigenous Knowledge." *Human Ecology* 27 (1): 47–69.

Checker, Melissa. 2005. *Polluted Promises: Environmental Racism and the Search for Justice in a Southern Town.* New York: New York University Press.

Conklin, Beth A., and Laura R. Graham. 1995. "The Shifting Middle Ground: Amazonian Indians and Eco-Politics." *American Anthropologist* 97 (4): 695–710.

Coté, Charlotte. 2010. *Spirits of Our Whaling Ancestors: Revitalizing Makah and Nuu-chah-nulth Traditions.* Seattle: University of Washington Press.

Cronon, William. 1995. "The Trouble with Wilderness; or, Getting Back to the Wrong Nature." In *Uncommon Ground: Toward Rethinking Nature*, edited by William Cronon, 69–90. New York: W.W. Norton.

Doane, Molly. 2007. "The Political Economy of the Ecological Native." *American Anthropologist* 109 (3): 452–62.

Gorrie, Peter. 2008. "Protest Prompts Abitibi Pullout." *Toronto Star*, 5 June. www.thestar.com/business/sciencetech/article/437156--protest-prompts-abitibi-pullout.

Gottlieb, Robert. 1993. *Forcing the Spring: The Transformation of the American Environmental Movement.* Washington, DC: Island Press.

Grossman, Zoltán. 2005. "Unlikely Alliances: Treaty Conflicts and Environmental Cooperation between Native American and Rural White Communities." *American Indian Culture and Research Journal* 29 (4): 21–43.

Hallowell, A. Irving. 1975. "Ojibwa Ontology, Behavior, and World View." In *Teachings from the American Earth: Indian Religion and Philosophy*, edited by Dennis Tedlock and Barbara Tedlock, 141–78. New York: Liveright.

Muehlmann, Shaylih. 2009. "How Do Real Indians Fish? Neoliberal Multiculturalism and Contested Indigeneities in the Colorado Delta." *American Anthropologist* 111 (4): 468–79.

Rainforest Action Network (RAN). 2006a. "Free-Grassy.net Launched in Support of Grassy Narrows." San Francisco: Rainforest Action Network.

———. 2006b. "American Dream, Native Nightmare: A Report on Weyerhaeuser." *Rainforest Action Network*. http://ran.org/content/american-dream-native-nightmare-report-Weyerhaeuser.

———. 2006c. *Old Growth Campaign. Putting the Rainforest into the Business Agenda: Rainforest Action Network 2006 Annual Report.* San Francisco: Rainforest Action Network.

———. 2008. *Old Growth Campaign. A Greenprint for Confronting Climate Change: Rainforest Action Network 2008 Annual Report.* San Francisco: Rainforest Action Network.

———. 2010. *Challenging Corporate Power: Corporate Campaigns and the Power of Grassroots Organizing. Greatest Hits, 1985-2010: Rainforest Action Network 2010 Annual Report.* San Francisco: Rainforest Action Network.

Taylor, Dorceta. 2000. "The Rise of the Environmental Justice Paradigm: Injustice Framing and the Social Construction of Environmental Discourses." *American Behavioral Scientist* 43 (4): 508–80.

Tiner, Tina. 2008. "Narrows Escape." *Now Magazine,* October. www.nowtoronto.com/news/story.cfm?content=163639.

Tsing, Anna. 2005. *Friction: An Ethnography of Global Connection.* Princeton, NJ: Princeton University Press.

Wilderness Act. 1964. Public Law 88-577 (16 US C. 1131-1136). 88th Congress, Second Session, 3 September.

Williams, Ted. 2001. "Golden Eagles for the Gods." *Audubon* 3 (2): 30–7.

Willow, Anna J. 2009. "Clearcutting and Colonialism: The Ethnopolitical Dynamics of Indigenous Environmental Activism in Northwestern Ontario." *Ethnohistory* 56 (1): 35–67.

———. 2010. "Cultivating Common Ground: Cultural Revitalization in Anishinaabe and Anthropological Discourse." *American Indian Quarterly* 34 (1): 33–60.

———. 2011. "Conceiving Kakipitatapitmok: The Political Landscape of Anishinaabe Anticlearcutting Activism." *American Anthropologist* 13 (2): 262–76.

———. 2012. *Strong Hearts, Native Lands: The Cultural and Political Landscape of Anishinaabe Anti-clearcutting Activism.* Albany: State University of New York Press.

Notes

1. The forefathers of Grassy Narrows First Nation signed Treaty Three [Treaty Three between Her Majesty the Queen and the Saulteaux Tribe of Ojibbeway Indians at the Northwest Angle on the Lake of the Woods with Adhesions] in 1873. Although the treaty stated that the signatory groups "shall have right to pursue their avocations of hunting and fishing throughout the tract surrendered," activists at Grassy Narrows argue that clearcutting impedes their ability to fully exercise these rights. (Willow's note.)

2. The term *Indian* as a name for Indigenous peoples is no longer used in Canada and is often considered pejorative here. Instead, most Indigenous Canadians are officially identified as *First Nations* in recognition that they, along with French and British settlers, contributed to the founding of Canada. The Conklin and Graham article, quoted by Willow, refers specifically to Indigenous peoples of Brazil, where *Indian* is still considered correct terminology. (Stern's note.)

3. This letter was signed by Grassy Narrows Chief Simon Fobister as well as blockaders, trappers, elders, and youth. It was posted online at www.amnesty.ca/grassy_narrows/voice_of_the_people.php (16 April 2010). (Willow's note.)

4. In December 2013, the Ontario Ministry of Natural Resources approved a new 10-year forest-management plan that could permit clearcutting to resume in the Grassy Narrows region. Earlier in the year, the Court of Appeal for Ontario overturned a Superior Court ruling in favour of the Grassy Narrows First Nation. In July 2014, the Supreme Court of Canada upheld the Court of Appeal's decision, ruling that as signatories to Treaty Three (1873), the Anishinaabe had agreed to cede land for mining, towns, forestry, and other provincially regulated activities. (Stern's note.)

Key Points to Consider

- Environmental justice movements differ from environmental movements in that the latter tend to see humans as separate from environments that need protection.
- Treaty Three (1873) between the Government of Canada and the First Nations bands of Northwestern Ontario granted the First Nations continued access to their traditional lands for subsistence purposes. However, forest clearcutting permitted by the Government of Ontario threatened this subsistence base. Various protests, including a 10-year blockade of a forest road, did not succeed in stopping the clearcutting.
- With support from a group of non-Native environmentalists, Grassy Narrows protestors were able to get attention for their case.
- The goal of the RAN environmentalists is to protect forests everywhere. The goal of the Grassy Narrows First Nation is to gain a measure of sovereignty over their local environment. The two groups were able to work together because they shared interim goals and because they learned to be respectful of their differences.

Critical Thinking Questions

1. Have you ever participated in a protest? What did your participation entail? What circumstances or kinds of injustice would move you to spend 10 years blockading a road?
2. Identify the protest tactics employed by the Grassy Narrows Anishinaabe and by the RAN activists. How do their tactics differ? Willow suggests that RAN activities were essential to getting attention to the Grassy Narrows people's cause. In what ways did Anishinaabe activities support the RAN cause?
3. What does Willow mean by "emplacement" or "place membership"? Do you agree with her that the RAN activists developed a sense of place membership in the boreal forest? Explain your reasoning.
4. What sustainability initiatives are being undertaken at your university or in your city? Would you characterize these as environmental or environmental-justice oriented? Explain your reasoning.

Suggestions for Further Reading

Checker, Melissa. 2011. "Wiped Out by the 'Greenwave': Environmental Gentrification and the Paradoxical Politics of Urban Sustainability." *City and Society* 23 (2): 210–29.

Crowe, Kelly. 2014. "Grassy Narrows: Why Is Japan Still Studying the Mercury Poisoning when Canada Isn't?" CBC *News*, 2 September. www.cbc.ca/news/health/grassy-narrows-why-is-japan-still-studying-the-mercury-poisoning-when-canada-isn-t-1.2752360. (This article contains links to a series of historical CBC reports on mercury poisoning on the Grassy Narrows reserve).

Ranco, Darren J. 2007. "The Ecological Indian and the Politics of Representation: Critiquing *The Ecological Indian* in the Age of Ecocide." In *Native Americans and the Environment: Perspectives on the Ecological Indian*, edited by Michael E. Harkin and David Rich Lewis, 32–51. Lincoln: University of Nebraska Press.

Turton, David. 2011. "Wilderness, Wasteland, or Home? Three Ways of Imaging the Lower Omo Valley." *Journal of Eastern African Studies* 5 (1): 158–76.

Willow, Anna J. 2012. *Strong Hearts, Native Lands: Anti-clearcutting Activism at Grassy Narrows First Nation.* Winnipeg: University of Manitoba Press.

———, Rebecca Zak, Danielle Vilaplana, and David Sheeley. 2014. "The Contested Landscape of Unconventional Energy Development: A Report from Ohio's Shale Gas Country." *Journal of Environmental Studies and Sciences* 4: 56–64.

Chapter 16

Peru

Introduction

Many people see mining as a destructive activity that radically reshapes the earth, levels mountains, poisons lakes and streams, sickens people and animals, and impoverishes traditional communities. At the same time, others see mining as a heroic activity that engages human ingenuity to extract the raw materials of the earth essential for **development**. In the latter interpretation, mining provides good jobs, inspires mass movements of people, builds communities, and creates enormous windfalls for individuals, corporations, and nations. While descriptions of mining are often filled with superlatives—the *biggest* operation, the *richest* deposit, the *largest* contributor to the regional economy, the *dirtiest* business, the *worst* violator of human rights—the actual experiences of people who live near mining sites are unlikely to be entirely good or entirely bad.

The article below, by Fabiana Li, concerns the ambivalence about mining expressed by women living near the Yanacocha gold mine high in the Peruvian Andes. Industrial mining today is very different from the famed gold rushes of history. The Yanacocha mine is one of the largest open-pit gold mines in the world. The gold found there is submicroscopic and could not have been recovered without recently developed chemical processes that employ cyanide to separate the tiny gold particles from the rock and other minerals. According to a PBS television documentary about Yanacocha, 30 tonnes of earth must be excavated for each ounce of gold recovered (*Frontline World* 2005). People living near the mine undoubtedly feel its impacts. Li's **ethnography** shows that community responses to development projects are complex and need to be examined in context. Her work also challenges some widely shared beliefs about **peasants** as conservative as well as beliefs that women feel a particular affinity to the natural environment.

Peasants live in many parts of the world and have long been the subject of anthropological investigation. They are small-scale agriculturalists who participate in market economies but use much of what they produce for household consumption. They are sometimes described as **subsistence** farmers, meaning that they often have little or nothing in the way of surplus produce. Many development projects, like the Yanacocha mine, are promoted by international organizations and national governments, in part to improve overall standards of living of a population. Development aims to increase agricultural yields, create new wage-employment opportunities, or extract natural resources for global markets. The promise of an improved standard of living may seem irresistible, but often individual households and communities find that despite greater opportunities for consumption, their lives are less secure. Globally, there have been many examples in which peasants have struggled against external development projects, contributing to a misperception of peasants as resistant to change.

Women and men often have different experiences with development that result from the practices of development agents as well from the distinct **gender roles** of each culture. The article below specifically addresses the experiences of rural Andean women (*campesinas* in Spanish) with extremely large-scale mining development. The women Li studied were very concerned about the environmental damage caused by mining, especially the damage to scarce water resources. Li, however, argues against those who suggest that women's roles as nurturers cause them to be more closely connected to and more defensive of the natural world than men are. Instead, she contends, people (men and women) develop their particular, often gendered, understandings of nature through the actual activities that they carry out in different environments. Li uses the phrase "socio-natural landscape" to recognize that these understandings are dynamic and grow out of tangible practices and social relationships.

※ *About the Author* ※

Fabiana Li was born in Peru and grew up in Canada. She studied at the University of Toronto, Simon Fraser University, and the University of California, Davis, where she earned her PhD in anthropology. Li's research examines how large-scale mining activities in Peru and Chile have contributed to conflicts between mining firms and local communities. One of the issues she studies is the way that mining firms employ environmental assessments to present themselves as responsible corporate citizens. She teaches anthropology at the University of Manitoba.

Negotiating Livelihoods: Women, Mining, and Water Resources in Peru

Fabiana Li

In Tual, a *comunidad campesina* (peasant community) neighbouring Peru's largest gold mine, Yanacocha, the women I spoke with told me that their irrigation canal did not carry as much water as it once did, and that the water had changed—they could no longer drink it, and they worried that it was harming their pastures and livestock. Dairy farming, sheep herding, and small-scale agriculture are the main economic activities for the majority of *campesino* families living in this area. All these activities depend on water, and many people blame the Yanacocha mining company for affecting the quantity and quality of water in a region where water scarcity has always posed a constant challenge.

The Yanacocha mining company is a joint venture between the Denver-based Newmont Corporation, the Peruvian company Buenaventura, and the World Bank's International Finance Corporation. Since the company's arrival in 1993, Yanacocha's open-pit mining operations have radically transformed the landscape and ways of life in nearby communities. More specifically, mining activity has had particular impacts on gender relations and women's lives, since *campesinas* (peasant women) play a key role in agricultural production, dairy farming, and the maintenance of the household. In representations of Andean **cosmology** as well as in contemporary discussions around women and the environment, water is sometimes associated with "feminine" principles. From this perspective, water is a source of life; it is linked to reproduction; and it is intimately related to domestic activities considered to be the domain of women. These symbolic and material connections could be used to argue (as Shiva and Mies 1993; Merchant 1990; Warren 2000; and others have done) that women's particular ways of relating to elements of Nature contribute to their marginalization and motivate them to act in its defence.

In this article, I want to critically examine the relationship between mining, water use, and women's roles. However, instead of starting from the assumption that women have a more direct affinity with Nature and a privileged role in the protection of water resources, I want to provide a nuanced account of women's experiences with mining and the ways in which they are affected by and respond to mining activity. While recognizing that women play an important role in defending their resources and ways of life, I want to show that their response to mining activity is sometimes marked by ambivalence and contradiction. As they struggle to negotiate their means of livelihood, people's relationships with the mining company oscillate between antagonism *and* co-operation.

Water, Irrigation Canals, and Mining Activity

Over the past two decades, a number of conflicts over mining activity have erupted throughout Peru. The proliferation of conflicts corresponds to a period of **neoliberal** economic restructuring in the 1990s aimed at attracting foreign investment and intensifying resource extraction. Alongside a favourable climate for investment that led to the privatization of state-owned enterprises and the development of large-scale mining projects, new technologies made it possible to mine deposits that had not previously been considered technically exploitable or commercially viable. In the gold industry, open-pit mining and cyanide leaching technologies made it profitable to extract low-grade ore containing microscopic traces of gold (sometimes called "invisible gold") in each ton of ore.

At the Yanacocha gold mine, located in the northern department of Cajamarca, 500,000 tons of ore are processed each day. The gold-containing ore is piled onto leach pads that measure 30 stories in height, which are watered with a cyanide solution that separates the gold. The Yanacocha mine is located at the headwaters of the watershed and is surrounded by communities that depend on natural water sources and irrigation canals for their livelihoods. Recent conflicts over mining activity have revolved around the mine's effects on the quality and quantity of water available for *campesino* communities and the nearby city of Cajamarca. Particularly troubling for Yanacocha's critics have been the mine's impacts on irrigation canals within Yanacocha's area of operations. I focus here on the case of the Tupac Amaru canal, one of six irrigation canals whose users have received compensation for damages caused by the mine's operations.

The Tupac Amaru canal runs almost 40 kilometres in length, and the water spring that is its source of origin is now located within the property of Yanacocha. In 2002, as the mine expanded its operations, run-off from the mine's waste-rock deposit contaminated one of the streams that feeds the canal, making it unsafe for human use. The company diverted the stream, reducing the amount of water available for irrigation. To make up for reduced flows, the company promised to pump chemically treated water from its water treatment plant into the canal. During my **fieldwork**, Tual residents informed me that the company awarded more than two hundred canal users US$4000 each and the equivalent of US$6000 per user in the form of community development projects. While company representatives thought that this agreement would settle the disputes with affected communities, a closer look at the canal and the complex relationships built around it might shed some light into why this has not been the case.

In Tual, one of four communities that use the water from the Tupac Amaru canal, most families rely on dairy farming—a task for which women are primarily responsible—as their main source of income. When the canal was constructed in the early 1980s by a group of *campesinos*, most people turned their agricultural fields into pasture for grazing dairy cows. For some families, the sale of milk to a transnational company that collects milk from local farmers became a more profitable activity than agriculture. The mine's construction of a highway connecting Tual to the city of Cajamarca made it possible for the dairy company's milk trucks to purchase small quantities of milk directly from individual farmers.

Today, the sale of milk provides families in Tual with a small but steady income. One woman I interviewed noted that while wage labour and mine-related employment are usually temporary and unstable, meaning that some men work only two or three months in the year, her paycheck from the sale of milk arrives punctually every two weeks. Families that no longer grow crops for their own consumption use the money earned from dairy farming to buy food in the city. Given that employment at the mine is limited and unreliable, women's contribution to the household economy through dairy farming is of vital importance, and their ability to provide for their families depends on the availability of clean water from the canals.

In areas surrounding the Yanacocha mine, a growing population, soil erosion, low crop yields, and small landholdings have made it increasingly difficult for people to make a living from agriculture and farming. The arrival of the mine created additional challenges and intensified the competition for resources. Producing enough pasture to feed the cows is a constant struggle, particularly during the dry season. In some cases, people's small plots of land do not provide enough pasture for their animals, particularly in communities that do not have access to irrigation water. The shortage of grass can be so severe that women must "rent out" pasturelands from other families. But for someone like Maria, an elderly woman whose sole cow provides a mere four liters of milk a day (after nursing its calf), paying to graze her animals means that the small amount of money that she makes selling milk is spent renting out pastureland. The availability of pasture limits the number of animals that a family can keep, since not having enough grass can mean having to sell an animal. Given people's dependence on dairy farming, it is not surprising that few topics are as recurrent in people's conversations as the availability of pasture, the coming of the rain, and the amount of water in the canals.

Milking the cows one morning, Bremilda, a woman in her late twenties, told me about the changes that led people in Tual to begin noticing the problems with the Tupac Amaru canal. She said people used to drink from the canal when they took the animals out to pasture and were far from other sources of water, but they had to stop doing so. The water didn't taste good any more, and when they irrigated the fields, the water left some yellowish specks on the grass. When people began to notice these changes in the quality and quantity of their irrigation water, canal users were quick to take action. At times, this meant soliciting the support of local **NGOs [non-governmental organizations]** to make their claims heard; at others, canal users resorted to more direct forms of protest to pressure the company to listen to their demands.

While women have had a visible presence in many of the protests organized against Yanacocha, they do not hold positions of authority in the community or in the administration of the canal. As in other Andean communities, women in Tual can be registered as canal users, but they do not usually hold positions of authority in community assemblies or in water users' associations. As a result, though women often feel the impacts on irrigation water most acutely, they do not fully participate in meetings and negotiation tables related to the mine's impacts on the canal. For example, in 2006, when fifty delegates were appointed by canal users to represent them in the latest round of negotiations with the company, only one of the delegates was a woman.

Between Conflict and Negotiation

Faced with the problem of contamination and reduced water flows in the canals, representatives of the Yanacocha mining company agreed to pump water from the mine's treatment plant into the canals. Following the 2004 agreement, however, canal users felt that the water being "returned" to them by the mining company did not adequately compensate for the water they had lost—neither in quality nor in quantity. The water they receive from the mine is treated to meet legal quality standards, but canal users complained that this water is different from the water they used to have—it had a different taste and coloration, and they could no longer drink it.

In response, Yanacocha's engineers argued that canal water is not *legally* required to be apt for drinking, since according to Peru's General Water Law, the water quality standards for irrigation water are different than those for [drinking] water. What this argument did not consider, however, was that before the mine's arrival, the canal [water] was used not only for irrigation, but also for cooking, washing clothes, and other household activities. In an area where water has always been scarce, it was common for people to drink from the canals when they were away from home or far from natural water springs. Regardless of its legal classification, *campesinos* had other uses for the canal and different criteria for determining if water was apt for human consumption: its taste, its source, and its effects on animals and pasture.

The case of the Tupac Amaru canal illustrates why water has become the centre of controversies over mining activity. While the Yanacocha mining company and government officials insist that mining can co-exist with agriculture and farming, and that the mine's environmental management plans guarantee water quality and quantity, the experiences of *campesinos* in Tual point to some of the reasons why the conflicts between communities and the mining company are so difficult to resolve. First, women's ability to contribute to the household economy through dairy farming depends on the availability of pastures, making irrigation water a necessary resource. Second, for *campesinos*, the chemically treated water being returned to the canals is not the same water that they once had, even if it meets the legal quality standards for irrigation water. Finally, water cannot be seen simply as a resource that can be replaced with compensation money and development projects. Water is part of a complex set of relationships between people and the landscape—relationships made through **affective** connections, people's investment in the construction and daily maintenance of the canal, and the social and political ties that the canal enables.

These complex ties contribute to an ongoing cycle of protest and co-operation, as people must denounce what they see as the mine's [harmful] effects on their irrigation water while knowing that their futures depend on their ability to pressure the company to provide them with other means of subsistence. Sometimes, this means collaborating with the company that has compromised their most important resource.

Since the mining company's arrival, the canal has become a means to negotiate new forms of livelihood: compensation packages, employment at the mine, charitable donations, and contracts for community-run businesses (*micro-empresas*) that provide services for the mine. For example, Bremilda's husband, Victor, purchased a van with two associates, and Yanacocha contracted them to transport workers from Cajamarca to the mine site. In addition, Bremilda was hired by her father's

FIGURE 16.1   The large-scale open-pit mining operations at the Yanacocha gold mine have radically transformed local landscapes and ways of life.

micro-empresa to provide packed lunches for a group of *campesinos* doing repair work on one of the canals in a nearby community (this, too, was a project paid for by the mining company). A sister-in-law, niece, and neighbour were recruited to help with the cooking. Though the job was short-lived, this opportunity was particularly welcome, since the mining company and service subcontractors mostly employ men for work that usually involves hard manual labour. Some women are hired as haul-truck drivers at the mine or for service-related positions, but the kind of short-term work in construction and canal maintenance that is mostly available to *campesinos* involves men almost exclusively.

In communities surrounding the mine, people's relationship with the mining company are not marked by firm opposition to mining activity, but by the constant and difficult negotiation of costs and benefits on which their livelihoods now depend. It is a relationship marked by contradictions, ambiguity, and ambivalence, as *campesinos* must resort to a variety of strategies to deal with the effects of mining activity, including negotiating for jobs, employment, and development projects. At the same time, as mining activity continues to expand, it irrevocably transforms the landscape and ways of life. The result is an ongoing cycle of protest actions and acquiescence that has come to characterize corporate–community relations in mining regions.

Conclusion

The case of the Tupac Amaru canal and the experiences of people living near the Yanacocha gold mine suggest that processes related to resource extraction have a significant effect on gender relations and women's lives. This is particularly evident given women's involvement in dairy farming and their dependence on water resources. In this article, I have focused on the particularities of women's experiences to show how the canal made the mine's impacts visible and motivated people to make claims against the mining company. At the same time, however, the canal enabled more ambiguous relationships with Yanacocha, providing a means to negotiate for employment, monetary compensation, and other benefits.

In protests against mining activity in Cajamarca, the recognition that "water is life" has helped mobilize people in unprecedented ways, for water helped bring together a wide range of actors with diverse (and sometimes contradictory) interests (on social movements in response to mining in Peru, see Bebbington and Bury 2013). Water has clearly been a powerful force for political activism; however, what drove people to defend their water resources was not necessarily an "environmentalist" ethic. When I spoke with canal users who had been part of the canal's construction and were now involved in its defence, what they emphasized was not a desire to recover a more "pristine" environment, but rather, their role in the making of this socio-natural landscape. *Campesinos* who participated in the construction of the canal felt a sense of pride and accomplishment for having used their own labour, knowledge of the landscape, and limited economic resources to channel water from a distant source. In *campesino* communities such as Tual, water is not simply an element of "Nature": it is embedded in a complex web of social, technological, political, and economic relationships that shape people's engagement with extractive industries.

References Cited

Bebbington, Anthony, and Jeffrey Bury, eds. 2013. *Subterranean Struggles: New Dynamics of Mining, Oil, and Gas in Latin America*. Austin: University of Texas Press.

Merchant, Carolyn. 1990. *The Death of Nature:*

Women, Ecology, and the Scientific Revolution. San Francisco: HarperOne.

Shiva, Vanadana, and Maria Mies. 1993. *Ecofeminism*. London: Zed Books.

Warren, Karen. 2000. *Ecofeminist Philosophy*. Lanham, MD: Rowman and Littlefield.

Key Points to Consider

- Resource-development projects often bring conflicts over land use. Mining is especially controversial because it radically reshapes the landscape.
- Men and women may have different perspectives about development activity that stem from their distinct gender roles and cultural practices.
- Improvements in standards of living from development are often unevenly distributed and can be highly disruptive of existing social relationships.

Critical Thinking Questions

1. Why does Fabiana Li use the phrase "Negotiating Livelihoods" in the title of the article? What are the different livelihoods being negotiated? Who are the negotiators?
2. Based on the information in the article, what were the benefits to Tual residents from the establishment and operation of the Yanacocha mine? What were the harms? How were women and men affected? In what ways did they respond to the opportunities and the harms?
3. How do newspapers in your region cover mining topics? Find some recent newspaper stories about mining and identify the issues discussed. What are the mined materials described? Is mining presented as a positive or a negative activity? Who or what is described as benefitting or being harmed? How?

Suggestions for Further Reading and Watching

Berreman, Gerald D. 1985. "*Chipko*: Nonviolent Direct Action to Save the Himalayas." *South Asia Bulletin* 5 (2): 8–13.

Frontline World. 2005. "Peru: The Curse of Inca Gold." Alexandria, VA: PBS. Online video, 31 min. www .pbs.org/frontlineworld/stories/peru404/.

Gill, Lesley. 2000. *Teetering on the Rim: Global Restructuring, Daily Life, and the Armed Retreat of the Bolivian State*. New York: Columbia University Press.

Kirsch, Stuart. 2007. "Indigenous Movements and the Risks of Counterglobalization: Tracking the Campaign against Papua New Guinea's Ok Tedi Mine." *American Ethnologist* 34 (2): 303–21.

Li, Fabiana. 2011. "Engineering Responsibility: Environmental Mitigation and the Limits of Commensuration in a Chilean Mining Project." *Focaal: Journal of Global and Historical Anthropology* 60: 61–73.

———. 2015. *Unearthing Conflict: Corporate Mining, Activism, and Expertise in Peru*. Chapel Hill, NC: Duke University Press.

Newmont Mining Corporation. 2014. "Operations and Projects: South America. *Newmont*. www.newmont .com/south-america.

Chapter 17

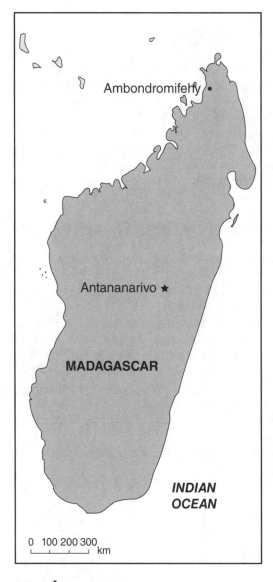

Madagascar

Introduction

In the 1930s, Canadian political scientist Harold Innis (1894–1952) showed that people who live in places where the economy is organized around **commodity** production (e.g., production of lumber, minerals, grains, furs, or fish) are vulnerable to booms and busts that have far-reaching effects on the organization of society. Innis developed this insight, known as "staples theory," through an analysis of how the fur trade shaped Canada's social, political, and economic development (Innis [1930] 1956). Though the fur trade that Innis investigated ended long ago, Canada remains a commodity-exporting country. According to analysis done by the Bank of Canada, commodities made up 63 per cent of Canadian exports in 2008–2010. In contrast, they made up an average of 44 per cent of exports from all countries in this same period (de Munnik, Jacob, and Sze 2012: 33). Canada's major export commodities now include wheat, unprocessed logs, minerals, and oil. Changes in global demand for these commodities have far-reaching effects on Canadians.

The article below, by Andrew Walsh, explores how people involved in commodity production in northern Madagascar experience life *after* a commodity boom. Madagascar, which was a French colony from the late nineteenth century until 1960, is an island nation off the southeast coast of Africa. Madagascar may be best known for its ecological diversity and as a destination for ecotourists, and as such the island is often imagined to be remote and isolated. But Madagascar is also a source of many global commodities. Over the last several centuries, Malagasy[1] people have supplied vanilla, tortoise shells, cotton, tropical woods, minerals, and other raw materials to international markets. Walsh's **ethnography** concerns residents of the town of Ambondromifehy, located near the northwestern coast of Madagascar, adjacent to Ankarana National Park.

In the late 1990s, newcomers anxious to share in the wealth generated by a local sapphire-mining rush flooded Ambondromifehy. By 2008, the rush was over; the frenzied economic boom that Walsh observed on his first visit to the town disappeared along with many of the people who had come during the boom. Curiously, the people who chose to stay did not see economic collapse. Instead, according to Walsh, they regarded the population decline and the economic downturn with ambivalence and, possibly, with a degree of optimism.

Small-scale, unregulated mining of the type done in Ambondromifehy is sometimes called *artisanal mining*, a phrase that depicts this activity as a highly skilled trade while downplaying its environmental and economic significance. An alternative term, *rat-hole mining*, in contrast, denotes its illegality and destructiveness. Independent, extralegal mining is not unique to Madagascar or even to poor countries, and it does not occur only in relation to the search for precious metals or high-value gemstones. The *New York Times*, for example, reported in 2014 that as many as three thousand independent miners in southwestern Poland were extracting coal one sack at a time from mines abandoned by corporate mining firms (Hakim 2014). Just as with the sapphire miners that Walsh describes, the independent Polish coal miners take on the health and legal risks of extraction while selling at low prices to middlemen who have better access to information about prices and markets.

Canada has a long-established legal framework for staking and registering mineral claims. Nonetheless, many of the famous Canadian gold and silver rushes of the last century were populated by individual fortune hunters using hand tools to dig on their own or with one or two partners in much the same way that Malagasy sapphire miners work. In some places, independent Canadian miners worked alongside well-capitalized corporations; and in a few cases, they succeeded to the point where they established mining corporations of their own. Large government-regulated corporations do the actual mining in Canada today, but there are still lone prospectors searching northern regions of the country for gold, silver, and especially diamonds.

There are other ways that Walsh's description of Ambondromifehy suggests similarities to resource towns in more prosperous places. The most obvious similarities are in the ways that both long-term residents and newcomers experience resource booms as simultaneously exciting and disrupting, chaotic and full of opportunity. In addition, the newspaper story that Walsh quotes at the beginning of the article, about the chaos of a mineral boom in another Malagasy town, could, with few changes, easily be about Fort McMurray, Alberta; Esterhazy, Saskatchewan; Minot, North Dakota; or any other North American town dependent on resource extraction. Further, resource-based economies everywhere are subject to booms and busts, both of which are disruptive to the communities where the extraction takes place, whether those communities are in wealthier or poorer areas.

Taking part in the sapphire trade is one way that people in Madagascar participate in global networks. But as Walsh's ethnography shows, globalization is an uneven process that differentiates people and places at the same time that it draws them into networks. Malagasy miners are incorporated into international trade networks through their relationships with foreign traders. The money they earn from sapphire mining also offers access to new opportunities for travel and consumption, new social relationships, and new aspirations. At the same time, these miners are disconnected from information about the economic and social value of the gems that might enable them to secure better prices for their labours. As Walsh observes, their lives are now characterized by uncertainty.

❧ About the Author ❧

Andrew Walsh studied anthropology at the University of Toronto and initiated his ethnographic fieldwork in Madagascar in 1992, while he was still a student. His current research contrasts how participation in ecotourism and sapphire mining shapes the lives of people in northern Madagascar. Walsh teaches anthropology at Western University in London, Ontario. His teaching includes a field course in environmental anthropology in Madagascar for university students from Canada and Madagascar.

After the Rush: Living with Uncertainty in a Malagasy Mining Town

Andrew Walsh

. . . "A Mad Gold Rush in Mangatany," reads the headline. Linking to the *Express de Madagascar* article [is] a striking photograph of thousands of Malagasy prospectors swarming over a desolate landscape of mud, pits, and tarpaulin shelters. "For several weeks," the article begins,

the village of Mangatany Fenoarivobe has been the site of a rush. A deposit of gold has been

drawing inhabitants from surrounding communities. Other [prospectors] are coming from still further away. In little time, the village has been transformed. The tents of fortune hunters have been popping up like mushrooms. The madness for gold is irresistible. (Solofonandrasana 2010)

The facts, figures, and people quoted tell of a chaotic place, each sentence of the article distancing this "community" (quotation marks used in the original source) further from normalcy. Tens of thousands of people have arrived in a matter of weeks. . . . The suffering is great. There is no drinking water and no "respect for hygiene and order." And yet people continue to flood the place. "I heard about it through the mass media," one fortune-hunting prospector is quoted as saying. He has "migrated here in hope of a better life."

However shocking it is made out to be, the story of this place is as common in Madagascar as it is elsewhere in Africa. . . . And everywhere [mining rushes] are found, [they] attract attention; fortune-hunting prospectors, it seems, aren't the only ones to find such places "irresistible." Governments see in mining rushes the potential to lure foreign investment; international investors see in them new, untapped "mining destinations"; and journalists see in them some of the most disturbing aspects of Africa's increasing reliance on the output of its resource frontiers. . . .

My own first encounter with a mining rush came one day in 1997 when the bush taxi in which I was travelling through northern Madagascar slowed to a crawl on a stretch of highway that it once would have sped along. This was Ambondromifehy, a roadside boomtown that had emerged following the discovery of sapphires in its vicinity a year earlier. It took us almost half an hour to drive the single kilometre of highway from one end of town to the other. The pavement ahead of us was crammed with trading stalls, food stands, vehicles taking on and dropping off passengers and freight, and hundreds of people (young men, mostly) wandering back and forth from stall to stall with little bluish-green stones to sell. Having previously worked mostly in small, quiet villages in the region, where people make their living from growing rice and raising cattle, I had never seen anything like this, and, like many of the miners and traders I would end up interviewing over the following years, I was drawn in by the vitality and possibilities of the place. I wound up conducting four months of ethnographic research in Ambondromifehy in 1999, and [I] followed up with regular visits over the next 11 years. . . .

. . . [M]ining rushes exhibit qualities that tend to make for good front-page news—they happen quickly, tweak readers' imaginations, and pose urgent problems. Stories of what happens after a rush, on the other hand, are rarely told. . . . Comparing notes from one of my most recent visits (in 2008) to Ambondromifehy to those gathered in 1999, quantitative indicators of decline are easy to come by. At the height of the boom, my favourite lunch spot, the Hotel Relax, served at least two hundred meals of rice and stew a day. In 2008, they served only twenty-five. Snack sellers who once sold up to fifty *kapohaka* (the measure of a condensed milk can) of peanuts a day were selling only ten a day by 2008. A bush taxi that had regularly travelled between Ambondromifehy and the nearby regional centre of Ambilobe eleven times a day now made only three trips. . . . [K]ey figures, like population estimates . . . [or] the number of abandoned houses, . . . [seem] to point down the same precipitous slope: Ambondromifehy is in decline. Numbers tell only part of the story, however. Qualitative data pulled from conversations with restaurateurs, peanut sellers, and bush taxi drivers, among others, suggest a more complicated reality; there is more than just decline going on. . . . Take, for example, the fact that Ambondromifehy's population is now less than a third of what it was in 1999, surely as unambiguous a sign of the town's decline as any. To those who have stayed behind, however, this drop in population is just as likely to be discussed in positive as in negative terms. . . . Many of those who have stayed have . . . spread out into the abandoned lots of former neighbours, either expanding their own homes or courtyards, or planting fenced gardens of fruit trees, manioc, and greens. This population drop has also, by all reports, made Ambondromifehy a much safer place to be. Indeed, many of the miners and traders I spoke with on my most recent trip, in 2010, indicated that they much preferred living here than in other, newly emerging, mining boomtowns for this reason alone.

That many of those who have stayed behind in Ambondromifehy . . . seem to be finding an upside to the town's apparent decline is enough to make me question whether *decline* is, in fact, the right word

FIGURE 17.1   Residents outside houses in Ambondromifehy, Madagascar.

for what it is that people are experiencing socially in this place. There is no doubt that the local sapphire trade is less vigorous than it once was, and that, as a result, there is less money being made here now (in 2010) than before, but the people with whom I have been speaking in Ambondromifehy have not been communicating [a] profound sense of abjection [despair]. . . . Many who have stayed on have resigned themselves to the unlikelihood of ever making a life-changing fortune in this place. "Here you can find enough to eat," said one miner in 2006, echoing the views of others who had decided to stay after the rush had passed. "If you're okay with making money enough to eat, then you'll be okay here." This is by no means wild optimism, but it is not quite abjection either. So what is it?

. . . I propose that it is most obviously *uncertainty* that the people of Ambondromifehy have had to contend with in the aftermath of the rush that brought them to this place. I do not mean by this that such people are not sure as to whether or not the local sapphire trade has declined over the past decade; it certainly has, and they know it. Nor am I implying that there is any doubt as to the significant changes in population, snack sales, and bush-taxi service, among other indicators, noted above. In highlighting the significance of uncertainty in people's lives I mean only to suggest that living in a place marked by years of decline does not necessarily mean living only in the shadow of better times. Those who have stayed behind in Ambondromifehy after the end of the rush continue to look ahead as they make meaningful lives for themselves. And in doing so, they are inevitably faced with a range of uncertainties that are easily overlooked from a distant or retrospective vantage point that emphasizes general trends at the expense of lived realities. . . . [I]t is a mistake to assume too much of purported, and implicitly **teleological**, trends like industrialization, urbanization, and modernization [Ferguson 1999]. . . .

Northern Madagascar's Sapphire Rush and Slowdown

The village of Ambondromifehy was originally founded in the early twentieth century by young men who had come to the far north of Madagascar from the island's east coast to watch over herds of cattle grazing in the region. As the place's few long-time resident elders—*tompontanana* or people "responsible for the community"—described it in 1999, these young men saw opportunities here and settled, began growing rice, married and had children, and eventually died and were entombed here. . . . Everything changed, however, when sapphires were discovered nearby in 1996. First came attempts at large-scale mining about 10 kilometres east of the village. Soon after came the first foreign and Malagasy sapphire buyers, and then, as word spread, the first independent Malagasy miners and traders. . . . Dozens of new arrivals quickly turned to hundreds, and then hundreds turned to thousands. The rush was on.

Like most small-scale mining towns, Ambondromifehy was a magnet not just for the mobile risk-taking men who appeared to dominate the place, but also for school teachers, shopkeepers, petty traders, farmers, and a wide range of others from throughout Madagascar, all of them intent on earning the fortunes rumoured to be accessible in this place. Ambondromifehy, in other words, became a place in which many different kinds of people wound up "meeting when grown," an expression commonly used in the region to describe the

circumstances of internal migrants who find themselves pursuing livelihoods alongside others with whom they share no roots or family connections. Meeting when grown is a good thing, one recent arrival told me in 2006, in that it enables people to learn things that they never would have learned in the places they hail from. . . . Meeting when grown also has its downside, though. One older long-time resident of Ambondromifehy complained that a place in which people meet when grown is better described as a place "without parents," meaning, as he saw it, a place in which juniors greatly outnumber seniors, and the authority of elders (for whom he spoke) doesn't count for much. . . . While the very first arrivals had reportedly done the appropriate thing by asking permission to settle and seek livelihoods from local land, those who followed soon became so numerous that control was out of the question. . . .

For those who did meet when grown in Ambondromifehy, the relationships necessary to carry out the work that had brought them there developed quickly. Mining was commonly carried out in teams, usually consisting of young men working co-operatively and sharing what they could find in pits they had dug themselves. In other cases, miners found safety and support in numbers as they searched for sapphires in the depths of the region's many caves. Buying and selling sapphires in the local market . . . also [required] that newcomers establish reasonably trustworthy ties with miners and fellow traders. . . . In some cases, traders took on the role of patrons, supplying food and other supplies to teams of miners with the expectation of being able to buy whatever sapphires they came up with. . . . By 2006, however, things had changed considerably. Like others I spoke with that year, one miner I interviewed recalled the early years of the rush with nostalgia, pining for the days when one could find sapphires "on the grass" and then blow the great amounts of money earned from their sale "dreaming" over rounds of beer at a town bar or on visits to the discos of cities near and far.

. . . I should stress that what many remember as the mining town's best years were anything but good for all. Long-time resident elders of the place were not the only ones concerned over the effects that the sapphire trade was having in the region. International and Malagasy conservation organizations charged with managing local protected areas were also concerned, and with good reason. In the early months of the boom, the Ankarana Special Reserve—a protected area located only a few kilometres from Ambondromifehy—became well known as one of the best locations in which independent miners might work. . . . [A]lthough protected on paper, the reserve was, in fact, largely unprotected on the ground, meaning that prospectors could come and go from what conservationists had termed the "taboo forest" with little concern over being caught. This easy access was short-lived, however. In the face of the unprecedented destruction caused by so much human activity inside the reserve, the local office of the National Association for the Management of Protected Areas requested government support to keep miners out. Support came, but even local outposts of police and military in Ambondromifehy could not keep these trespassers out of the reserve. . . . Outside of town, meanwhile, the dominant image of Ambondromifehy was anything but flattering. Press and popular reports of the place during the rush years employed many of the same images as the newspaper article cited earlier, portraying it as an anarchic, polluted nightmare. More significantly, perhaps, Ambondromifehy was deemed unworthy of the sorts of public service projects (digging wells or building schools and clinics, for example) that the **state** and **NGOs [nongovernmental organizations]** were undertaking in other, far less populous, communities in the region.

. . . By 2006, local officials estimated that the population of the town had fallen by at least two thirds since the height of the boom, to around 5000 inhabitants. In 2010, a local government office had collected the names of 1347 residents, though this number came with the assurance that many more had not been counted. . . .

While there is no doubt that the supply of locally mined sapphires has declined in Ambondromifehy's slowdown years, . . . the most attentive

observers of recent developments in the local sapphire trade . . . tend to stress that it is the drop in the number of foreign buyers coming to the region that has had the greatest effect on the local economy. Here it should be noted that almost all of the sapphires mined locally are destined, ultimately, for foreign markets (Walsh 2010). . . . Given how susceptible the trade in Ambondromifehy is to fluctuations in the trade in Thailand—where the bulk of Madagascar's sapphires are processed and transformed into jewellery—as well as to market shifts in consuming countries like the US, China, Japan, and Great Britain, it isn't surprising that Ambondromifehy was hit particularly hard by the global financial crisis of 2008, during and after which foreign buyers adapted to the uncertainties of the time by buying fewer sapphires and paying less for them. . . .

On my most recent visit to Ambondromifehy in 2010, I asked people their thoughts on what will become of this place over the next decade. The overwhelming response was that the town is not, as many outsiders have been predicting for years now, on the verge of complete collapse. This modest optimism surprised me. Only a year earlier, the town had been largely abandoned when a new find of demantoid—a rare sort of green garnet—only 150 kilometres down the highway drew thousands of its remaining residents away. The place was empty, I heard from one older man who had stayed behind during this new rush; you could bathe out in the open by the side of the road, he reported, and didn't have to worry about anyone seeing you. Once again, though, people came back; mining and trading demantoid during a rush, it seems, did not offer the same opportunities as mining and trading sapphires in the midst of a slowdown. While no one I spoke with in 2010 imagined that Ambondromifehy would ever be the place it had been during the rush of the late 1990s, no one imagined that it would ever be anything but a place dependent on the mining and trade of sapphires, either. The sapphires are still there, I was assured again and again, and there is still a market for them. Indeed, shortly before I arrived on this most recent visit, a group of four miners had sold several days' worth of stones (3 kilograms in total) for 120 million Malagasy Francs (around $12,000) to a group of Malagasy traders. Commenting on this and other indications that the local trade might, in fact, be reviving, a trader put the conditions necessary for Ambondromifehy's survival simply. So long as there are still people overseas interested in buying sapphires, he said, there will be people here willing to dig them up. And so long as there are success stories to be told, sapphire work will remain attractive among a limited set of options, and Ambondromifehy will remain a draw. Indeed, what surprised me most during my 2010 visit was meeting several people who had arrived in town *for the first time* in the previous few months. . . .

Living with Uncertainty

All people, no matter what their circumstances, live with uncertainty. In Malagasy communities in which I have worked in the past, for example, people concern themselves with everything from the vagaries of weather and its effects on crop yields, or the unpredictable outcomes of national political developments, to the deeper-lying uncertainties inherent in social relationships. . . . In suggesting that people living in Ambondromifehy have been "living with uncertainty," then, I am not suggesting that they are altogether exceptional. That noted, a careful consideration of the particular set of uncertainties that people face in this town reveals a good deal about what makes a place like this distinct. In this section I focus especially on how the uncertainties of the town's slowdown years are connected to, and in some cases extensions of, those that prevailed during its boom times. The intended point is simply that whatever else has changed in this place through years of decline, certain difficulties inherent in navigating life in and around the local sapphire trade remain. Let me begin with the uncertainties associated with "meeting when grown."

Based on the limited description offered in the previous section, some might infer that boom-time residents of Ambondromifehy managed to create reasonably functional and productive social and work networks despite having met only when grown. They did, but always in the face of the uncertainties that come with such arrangements. People who meet when grown in communities like this don't generally know their neighbours very well, let alone whether they can trust these people as workmates or trading partners. As I have described elsewhere (2009), this means that the decisions of boom-time residents of Ambondromifehy to engage in **reciprocity** with one another—to give with the expectation of a return—were always questionable. . . . During the early years of the rush, the dangers that can come with putting too much trust in people one doesn't know and cannot track were especially apparent in widely circulating stories of "red suitcase" women who, legend has it, would enter working, trusting, spousal relationships with men under false pretences, only to skip out on them with all of their shared earnings in hand. Ten years later, stories collected from women in town suggested that it was, in fact, men who were more likely to abandon relationships and obligations in Ambondromifehy. In either case, the fact that such relationships involved people whose connections with one another tended to be both relatively recent and shallow was especially problematic. Indeed, in a place of people who have met when grown, the story of the red suitcase woman warns, one can't even be sure that one's spouse is the person that she or he claims to be.

The uncertainties inherent in relationships among Malagasy people in Ambondromifehy were even more pronounced in connections between Malagasy traders and foreign buyers. At the beginning of the rush, foreigners (Thais and West Africans in particular) were the only ones taking sapphires out of the country, and they were thus in a powerful bargaining position vis-à-vis the Malagasy traders from whom they bought. Foreign traders were able, for example, to take stones out of the country on credit, offering nothing more than promises of return payments to the Malagasy traders with whom they dealt. So long as the trade was working and demand was high, this system worked reasonably well. . . . As the tide of the local trade shifted, however, foreign traders began leaving with valuable stocks of stones and then not coming back at all, leaving local exchange partners high and dry.

Early on in the rush, Ambondromifehy's inhabitants attempted to mitigate the uncertainties inherent in their relationships with others in town and in the trade by establishing associations that draw people with common interests together. The most successful of these have been mutual-aid associations made up of people who come from the same region of origin. . . . [T]hese associations function mostly as a means for raising money necessary to provide members with support in times of illness or death. In Ambondromifehy, as in other migrant communities in the region, such associations are especially attractive to people concerned with the possibility that they might die far from home and without the means to have their bodies repatriated. Less successful have been associations that aim to encourage members to invest more in the community of Ambondromifehy itself. The parents' association connected with the local public elementary school, for example, has never managed to garner much local support for building much-needed facilities, despite repeated requests by teachers and association representatives. Since 1999, I have also observed three separate efforts at organizing miners and traders into co-operatives begin with high hopes and end in disappointment. . . . Particularly problematic have been efforts at establishing a single marketplace in which affiliated miners and traders would be expected to carry on their dealings with one another and foreign traders in a public and transparent way. . . .

Making money from mining and trading sapphires in Ambondromifehy has never been easy. . . . [M]iners I met in 2008 were struggling just as much as they had in previous years with a question that faces small-scale gemstone miners everywhere: when to abandon mining sites in which they have already invested their labour. As the hand-dug pits and tunnels in which miners around Ambondromifehy work get deeper and longer, they not only become more difficult and dangerous to navigate, but

also harder to leave. There is always the chance that today's efforts in a particular pit will be more profitable than yesterday's return.

Trying to make a living from buying and selling sapphires is no less complicated than trying to make a living from mining. First, traders must know about the distinctive qualities of the sapphires they have or should be looking to buy for resale. Unlike gold and other mined commodities that can be sold by weight for a single standard price, every sapphire is unique and must be evaluated and priced as such. The problem is that knowledge about the more and less valuable qualities of sapphires being mined around Ambondromifehy comes ultimately from buyers further along the exchange chain in whose interest it is never to reveal too much of what they know. In the early years of the boom, this fact of the trade made it easy for knowledgeable foreign and Malagasy buyers to amass fortunes by paying ridiculously little for stones that sellers had no way of knowing were worth much more than the buyer's price. Over the years, the advantage enjoyed by the most knowledgeable few has lessened as more Malagasy traders have obtained the technology (special flashlights and magnifying devices, for example) and the expertise necessary for discerning the internal qualities of sapphires, but this increase in knowledge has not always translated into an increase in profits across the board. After all, it is not only the qualities of stones that determine what will be paid for them. Also important are a number of other factors over which people in Ambondromifehy have no control and about which they have little access to certain knowledge: the state of distant markets for the stones mined locally, currency exchange rates, international fashion trends, or the output of other sources of sapphires elsewhere in Madagascar and in other supplier countries. Since global demand for what is coming out of the ground around Ambondromifehy appears to shift frequently, and today's unwanted or low-cost stones could well be worth considerably more in the future, Malagasy traders have tended to speculate in the local marketplace by stockpiling what they think might be undervalued stones. As time goes by, however, and fewer foreign buyers come to town every week, such investments appear increasingly foolhardy. As with miners, though, traders have a hard time knowing when to give up on something in which they have already invested so much.

In the face of the many uncertainties inherent in the local sapphire trade, miners and traders are frequently on the lookout for signs of what their futures might hold in the town. Unfortunately, their readings of the signs they encounter are not always accurate. Take, for example, the fact that Thai traders had built solid, cement-walled houses in Ambondromifehy in the midst of the town's apparent decline—as sure a sign as any to many I have spoken with since 2006 that the local trade is destined to continue well into the future. Why would these foreigners build such houses if they weren't intending to stay here, and keep buying, over the long term? In fact, these houses were built more for the sake of short-term convenience than with long-term intentions. As the boom passed and profit margins fell, it became both safer and more economical for Thai buyers to live permanently in town than it had been in the past, when they were forced to commute regularly from the far more expensive provincial capital of Antsiranana, a hundred kilometres away. In other words, what has been taken by some as a sign that Ambondromifehy is "developing" (a term several **informants** invoked when speaking of these durable structures) was, in fact, more the product of the local trade's decline.

Thai buyers were not the only ones to appear to be investing in this town despite the decline of the local sapphire trade. Malagasy miners and traders have done the same over the years, whether by building solid houses of their own, contributing to the digging of wells, or taking over the building plots of neighbours to plant gardens. As of 2006, a number had even begun growing rice in the region, either sharecropping with long-time residents or renting land on which to grow. Although it is tempting to read these investments as signs of people's long-term intentions in this place, we must be careful not to overstate the case. People may, for example, have been building more solid and comfortable houses over the years, but they have also

continued to invest even more in portable forms of wealth (cars, generators, mining equipment, and, of course, gold jewellery and gemstones) that they can take with them should they up and leave someday. Similarly, these settlers' gardens tend to be planted with quick-growing trees that will give fruit in short order, they do not keep rice seed from year to year, and none of them appear to have any interest in amassing cattle locally—all indications that they are thinking ahead, certainly, but always with the possibility of a future move in mind.

Luc's Story

As should be evident from the preceding section, living with uncertainty in Ambondromifehy is not a matter of living in a constant state of denial or abjection. It is, rather, living on the edge of whatever is next. To illustrate this simple point further, I conclude by discussing one miner/trader's decade-long stay in this town. I first met Luc in 2004, several years after the end of the boom. In the years since, I have visited, phoned, and interviewed him frequently, surprised at each encounter to find that, despite all I had been hearing of the town's impending collapse, he was not only surviving but making a decent living in Ambondromifehy. While Luc is by no means representative of all who have stayed on long after the end of the rush, I hope that in presenting some of his story I may provide readers with a better sense of what living with the uncertainties described above can be like.

Luc first arrived in Ambondromifehy at the age of 23 in 1998. He had come from a village on Madagascar's northeast coast knowing nothing about sapphires but intent nonetheless on making enough money from these little stones to set himself up for life. Like so many others, he began by mining illegally within the "taboo forest"—the conservation area west of Ambondromifehy in which, at the height of the rush, young men risked being shaken down by local gangs or arrested and imprisoned by national police. . . .

Within a couple of years of arriving, Luc successfully transitioned from mining to trading, acting first as a *demarcheur*—a mobile trader who mediates exchanges between sellers and buyers—and then, as he learned more and made more connections, buying and selling for himself. In the early 2000s, he also developed a close relationship with a Thai trader, named Deng, for whom he began collecting particular kinds of stones from among the miners and fellow traders with whom he had existing relationships. . . . Over the years, and despite a language barrier that prevented them from discussing much but trade, Luc and Deng became quite close. . . . And yet Luc also complained of having been "burned" by this friend—more than once, Deng didn't pay what he said he would for stones for which Luc could never have found another buyer. By 2010, Luc's dealings with Deng had fallen off significantly. . . .

Luc met and married a woman in Ambondromifehy in 2000, and he had two children with her in 2001 and 2003. Joining his new wife's church, he converted to Seventh Day Adventism. . . . [He adopted a] common trader strategy of supplying teams of miners with provisions of food, gifts of cigarettes, and occasional loans of money, with the expectation that they would bring him whatever they had to sell before showing it to anyone else. As problematic as certain aspects of the trade are to him—as an Adventist he is especially conscious of the fact that making a living from trading sapphires requires him to lie to others—he claims that there is no better way for someone like him to make the money he needs to support his children. By 2010, his wife had taken up with another trader and moved to another boomtown.

In 2005, Luc built a solid, cement-floored house on the side of the highway that runs through town. He spent about seven million Malagasy Francs (about $700) on the structure, expensive by some standards, but nowhere near the cost of the cement-walled structures that Thais were building up the road at around the same time. Other Malagasy traders in town, he told me, were sending all their money away to build houses in the regions from which they had come. His thinking was different.

What are you going to do? Build a nice house far away and then live in a small, poorly built house here? . . . Even the foreigners, the Thais, have built cement houses here even though they are people from overseas. Why are we Malagasy people here in our own land not doing this . . . building strong houses?

This was typical of his decisions around investment and consumption in that it came out of the realization that, despite his initial plan to get in and get out quickly, he had *already* settled in Ambondromifehy and might as well start living like it. Beginning in 2008, he even started growing rice locally on land rented from one of the town's original inhabitants. "I've been here ten years now," he told me in 2008. "I'm not a visitor but a *tompontanana* [a person responsible for the community]." Claiming this status, however, did not mean that he always agreed with others in town . . . who were interested in seeing the community "develop." . . . Bringing electricity, running water, and more public services to this place, he worried, would raise the cost of living in the town. As it stood in 2010, Ambondromifehy had, in his view, many of the attractive qualities of bigger towns or cities (ease of access, plentiful consumer goods and food markets, distractions, possibilities for generating income, and so on) without any of the associated costs or bureaucratic hassles. . . . [T]his was his . . . home. "When I return from a visit to the place of my parents," he noted in 2008, "I tell people I am returning home—to Ambondromifehy."

Like so many others in town, Luc's most recent brush with abandoning Ambondromifehy came in May 2009 when he was drawn by the promise of new fortunes to be made from a new strike of demantoid (green garnet), 150 kilometres away. As he had done a decade earlier, he entered this new rush as a miner and then, quickly, moved into trading, putting some of the money he had earned from sapphires to work. . . . Ultimately, though, this new rush was just not conducive to the sort of life he had come to appreciate in Ambondromifehy. "It isn't orderly there," he told me a year after his return.

"People from here weren't happy there." Ambondromifehy, by contrast, can "make one happy. It isn't hard to make enough money to get by."

Luc's return to Ambondromifehy should not be taken as a sign that he had given up his goal of making a life-changing fortune. He was just as ambitious in 2010 as he had been when I first met him [six] years earlier. In our last conversation, he told me that he had his sights set on taking advantage of "people who don't know anything yet about [the] stones [they are mining or trading]." . . .

To make his fortune in this way . . . will require that he leave town. When might this [time] come? Luc didn't know more than that it might take a while. "None of us [who came during the rush and are still living here now] expected to be here so long," he reminded me. . . . All he was certain of in 2010 was that despite his recent investment in a house in town, and regardless of his attempts at growing rice on local land, he has no intention of living here for the rest of his life. "Ambondromifehy," he once told me, "is an easy place to live in, but it is an easy place to leave."

Luc is certainly not alone in making a home for himself and his children in a place that he only provisionally calls home, a place that is "easy to leave." In fact, Simone's recent work (2003; 2004; 2006) on the interconnected realities of migration and urban life elsewhere in Africa suggests that Luc and others in Ambondromifehy are less "mad" or unusual than news reports might lead us to imagine. Many of the uncertainties precipitated by the mining and trade of sapphires destined for foreign markets are those long faced by Africans living an urban life that, Simone reminds us, "was primarily generated out of the imposition of an external world upon local economies" (2004: 29). And for Luc, as for other urban Africans, such uncertainties may not be as repellent as many assume. While there is no doubt that the "mobility and flexibility" that characterize places like these can have "disintegrating effects" on "customary modes of affiliation" (Gotz and Simone 2003: 126), these same features also precipitate new opportunities for people like Luc to improvise. . . . Fundamentally, though, contexts like the one I have described here are . . . not simply places of decline or stagnation, but places in which people abide and aspire in the face of uncertainty. And waiting in contexts like this is not necessarily any less active than moving. . . . [S]taying put after a rush [is] not . . . a matter of being left behind. In Ambondromifehy certainly, and perhaps elsewhere, abiding the familiar uncertainties of a place that may appear to be in decline can make more sense than exploring the possibilities, and unfamiliar uncertainties, of a next new thing.

References Cited

Ferguson, James. 1999. *Expectations of Modernity: Myths and Meanings of Urban Life on the Zambian Copperbelt.* Berkeley: University of California Press.

Gotz, Graeme, and AbdouMaliq Simone. 2003. "On Belonging and Becoming in African Cities." In *Emerging Johannesburg: Perspectives on the Postapartheid City,* edited by Richard Tomlinson, Robert A. Beauregard, Lindsay Bremner, and Xolela Mangcu, 123–47. London: Routledge.

Simone, AbdouMaliq. 2003. "Moving Towards Uncertainty: Migration and the Turbulence of African Urban Life." Paper presented at the Conference on African Migration in Comparative Perspective. http://pum.princeton.edu.

———. 2004. "Critical Dimensions of Urban Life in Africa." In *Globalization and Urbanization in Africa,* edited by Toyin Falola and Steven J. Salm, 11–50. Trenton, NJ: Africa World Press.

———. 2006. "Pirate Towns: Reworking Social and Symbolic Infrastructures in Johannesburg and Douala." *Urban Studies* 43 (2): 357–70.

Solofonandrasana, Stephane. 2010. "La folle ruée vers l'or à Mangatany." *AllAfrica,* 5 July. http://fr.allafrica.com/stories/201007051220.html.

Walsh, Andrew. 2009. "The Grift: Getting Burned in the Northern Malagasy Sapphire Trade." In *Economics and Morality: Anthropological Approaches*, edited by Katherine E. Browne and B. Lynne Milgram, 59–76. Lanham, MD: Altamira Press.

———. 2010. "The Commoditization of Fetishes: Telling the Difference between Natural and Synthetic Sapphires." *American Ethnologist* 37 (1): 97–113.

Note

1. Malagasy is the name of the people and of the language of Madagascar.

Key Points to Consider

- Local economic adaptations that involve resource extraction are subject to booms and busts tied to economic activities in distant places.
- Taking part in the sapphire trade is one way that Malagasy people participate in globalization. Miners are disadvantaged by their limited access to information about the value of the stones, and they are often cheated by traders, yet they continue to see sapphire mining as a chance to become wealthy.
- Globalization is a process that links dispersed people and places together in ways that allow them to exchange ideas, finance, media, technologies, and consumer goods. Globalization also involves differentiation through uneven access to information, technologies, and financial resources.

Critical Thinking Questions

1. What evidence do residents of post-boom Ambondromifehy point to when they describe the future of the town as hopeful? Does Walsh think that they are mistaken? Does he think that their lives would be better if they abandoned the town? Why or why not?
2. According to Walsh's informants, what are the benefits of living among people who met "when grown"? What are the problems?
3. What does Luc mean when he asserts that he is "a *tompontanana*" ("a person responsible for the community")? How is that status related to the decisions he makes about where and how to live?
4. Walsh asserts that residents of post-boom Ambondromifehy "live with uncertainty." Do you agree that *uncertainty* is an appropriate term for the situation he describes? What would it be like to live with certainty?

Suggestions for Further Reading

Hakim, Danny. 2014. "The Mines Have Shut Down. The Miners Haven't." *New York Times*, 29 March. www.nytimes.com/2014/03/30/business/energy-environment/the-mines-have-shut-down-the-miners-havent.html?_r=0.

Walsh, Andrew. 2005. "The Obvious Aspects of Ecological Underprivilege in Ankarana, Northern Madagascar." *American Anthropologist*, 107 (4): 654–65.

———. 2006. "'Nobody Has a Money Taboo': Situating Ethics in a Northern Malagasy Sapphire Mining Town." *Anthropology Today* 22 (4): 4–8.

———. 2012. *Made in Madagascar: Sapphires, Ecotourism, and the Global Bazaar*. Toronto: University of Toronto Press.

PART V

Global Lives/Local Identities

Chapter 18

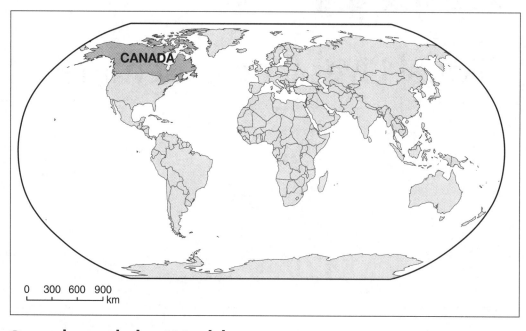

0 300 600 900
km

Canada and the World

Introduction

How do you know when you are an adult? Is adulthood conferred at a certain age, say 18 or 25? Do you consider yourself an adult now?

Some societies create elaborate rituals to mark an individual's transition from youth to adulthood, but in Canada and many other places there are no specific **rites of passage** to adulthood. Instead, we generally associate being an adult with a series of **life-course** changes. The term *life course* refers to the somewhat messy process of how lives actually unfold at different places and different times rather than to a fixed set of life stages. The activities we usually associate with becoming an adult in North America include completing school, starting a career, moving out of our parents' home, marriage, and becoming a parent ourselves. The timing of these events and the order in which we do them (and even whether we do them at all) depend upon both individual and external factors. The expectations we have about how our own lives will (or should) proceed guide the individual decisions we make about school and work and family.

A person's family history is influential in determining his or her life course, but the experiences and attitudes of peers may matter even more. Indeed, the "typical" life course of one generation differs from that of previous generations. For example, when I (Pamela Stern) was a child, I was often told a story about my maternal great-great grandmother. She was married at the age of nine and was told that as a "married woman" she could no longer play with her dolls. The story of my great-great grandmother served to help me understand that my opportunities, expectations, and choices would be different from hers. **Agency** or individual choice matters for our life-course decisions, but **structural factors** (social class, economic conditions, demographics, etc.) help establish the parameters of the choices available to each of us. Culture, too, helps to create the models or **paradigms** that shape our understandings of how our lives will unfold and guide the actions we take.

In the article below, Vered Amit examines some of the life-course paradigms of contemporary Canadian youth. Demographers and other social scientists have reported that over the last few decades, there has been a significant upward shift in the ages at which young people in Canada and other wealthy countries take up adult roles and identities. The average ages at which young Canadians are recognized as adults is about the same today as it was 100 years ago, higher than in the 1950s, 1960s, and 1970s. Scholars have offered many different explanations for the current shift. In the full version of her article, Amit observes that despite a vast literature describing the extension of the period between childhood and adulthood, our general understanding of what it means to be an adult has not changed. For example, social psychologist Jeffrey Arnett advocates for recognizing a new life stage that he calls "emerging adulthood," which is characterized by exploration and instability. But as Amit points out, Arnett and other scholars (and many of the youth Amit studied) continue to treat adulthood as an inflexible endpoint on the life course.

The Canadian youth discussed in the article below are, in many respects, quite privileged. They are university educated, and they have the economic means and the **social capital** to travel abroad. In addition, the young Canadians Amit and her colleagues spoke with expressed a sense of security that they would be able to seamlessly take up adult roles and responsibilities whenever they chose to do so. This is not the case for all young Canadians. To begin with, not all are able to attend university; in fact, only about 30 per cent of contemporary Canadian youth earn university degrees by the time they reach their late twenties (Shaienks and Gluszunski 2009). Further, relatively few young Canadians have the resources to travel to foreign countries, and many do not feel secure about their future prospects. In less affluent countries, young people are even less likely to have the opportunities afforded to the youth Amit discusses. In many places, youth do not so much choose to delay "settling down" into adulthood as they find that economic or social conditions block their abilities to move through the life course as they had anticipated. Some scholars have suggested that the protests that marked the Arab Spring of 2011 were, in large part, a result of the unfulfilled desires of large numbers of youth to "settle down" and begin adult lives. British anthropologist Paul Richards (2001) has suggested that the protracted civil wars in Sierra Leone and Liberia during the 1990s were, in part, caused by an absence of employment for large numbers of educated rural youth.

One of the questions that Amit considers is how much actual choice the privileged young Canadians she encountered are exercising. For example, when they quit seemingly "good jobs" in order to travel, are they exercising agency, responding to structural factors, or following a cultural model? Amit did not do **participant observation** to pursue the answers to these questions—that would likely not have been possible. Her method is, nonetheless, **ethnographic** because she has sought to understand the actions of travelling youth from their own perspectives, taking their social and cultural contexts into account.

✦ About the Author ✦

Vered Amit grew up in Montreal and Israel. She studied at McGill University and the University of Toronto and earned a PhD at the University of Manchester in England. Amit's research concerns the personal implications of transnational mobility (the movement of people across borders) and transnational identity (affiliation with two or more countries). In addition to the research described in the article below, Amit has studied Armenian migrants in London, England; high-school students in Quebec; and Canadians who purposefully choose employment that involves long sojourns abroad. She is currently conducting research on the ways that young Canadians who inherit dual citizenship make decisions about where in the world they will live and work. Amit teaches anthropology at Concordia University.

"Before I Settle Down": Youth Travel and Enduring Life-Course Paradigms

Vered Amit

Um, I've always wanted to travel, and that's kinda, I just decided to do it now, 'cause I wasn't attached to a job or anything. And at the time that I made the decision to travel, I wasn't attached to um, any guy either, but that changed before I came. So I just thought, I'm young, I can do it, and before I settle down and get, you know, started in life, I'll come over and travel.

Maureen's explanation of why she embarked on a working holiday in Edinburgh at the age of 24 invokes a theme that recurs in the literature on youth travel. . . .

But what does such an expectation of "settling down" imply for broader perceptions of life-course phases?

The designations of certain forms of travel as configured around youth, that is as "youth travel," implicitly entail particular conceptions of the life course. Thus, emergent forms of contemporary youth mobility have often been identified with more general developments involving a supposed extension of youth and delayed transitions into adulthood in affluent Western countries. In many respects, therefore, the ways in which these young travellers experience and account for their voyages could serve as a textbook illustration for some of the key shifts in the roles associated with, and the duration of, youth noted by many social scientists over the last three decades. And yet, running through these young travellers' renderings of "settling down" is an implicitly conservative set of expectations about the nature of adulthood that seems fairly impervious to the possible implications of their own experiences of travel, work, and study abroad.

The insistence by many of these youthful travellers that an extended sojourn abroad is possible only when one is young and unfettered can be juxtaposed against a range of studies in which people actively seek out opportunities for travel and extended stays abroad at many ages and points of their life course. The young travellers' expectations that in due course they will return home and take up stable long-term work and family commitments can also be set against scholarly and institutional renderings of uncertainty and mobility as an inescapable entailment of the entire life course in a "post-traditional cosmopolitan world" (Beck 2000: 211). But at the same time, Maureen's expectation that sooner or later she will settle down and "start life" by establishing a home, [a] family, and a stable career can also be viewed as converging with another kind of scholarly and institutional **discourse** that emphasizes the extended duration of youth in affluent Western contexts, without redefining the goal posts of adulthood. . . .

Changing Life Course or Changing Youth?

In their review of sociological and anthropological perspectives on the life course, Hockey and James contrast "classical" social science notions of the life cycle as a "series of fixed stages and roles through which every individual moved as they aged" with the perspective of . . . contemporary theorists . . . "who are more likely to highlight a diversity and fragmentation of paths, rather than a commonality and continuity of experience, as the outcome of life's turning points" (2003: 11). . . . [T]he emphasis [in the latter view] is on the increasing importance of individual

agency and self-reflexivity in the construction of the self. Nothing can be taken for granted, it is a state of being that encompasses an augmentation of both individual freedom and risk. Thus Beck argues that in the shift from the understanding of **modernity** rooted in the European Enlightenment to the "cognitive insecurity" and the "risk regimes" of what he calls the "second modernity," "people are expected to make their own life-plans, to be mobile and to provide for themselves in various ways. The new centre is becoming the precarious centre" (Beck 2000: 70).

For Beck, an integral feature of this paradigmatic shift has been a move away from the standardization of **Fordism** toward notions of flexible work. . . . [T]he archetype of the flexible worker presumes a mobile person who changes employment frequently and, if necessary, residence as well, going "where the jobs are" (Beck 2000: 30). This version of contemporary modernity, hence, intrinsically links the individualization of the life course with the ongoing normalization of uncertainty and associated pressures for mobility.

However, as Hockey and James note, in spite of more fluid contemporary processes of age classification and life-course transitions, there are many ways in which "the more rigid pattern of the modern Western life course which emerged in the mid-nineteenth century" continues to claim a powerful hold on Western imaginations (2003: 57). . . . [At the same time,] across a number of scholarly disciplines, there appears to be a wide consensus that in affluent, post-industrial societies there has been a general shift in the ages at which key transitions to adulthood are being enacted. According to a *Canadian Social Trends* report produced by Statistics Canada:

> In recent years, social scientists have found that the transition to adulthood is taking longer to complete. Young people are living with their parents longer, are more highly educated, and attend school for more years than their parents did. The age at marriage has been rising, fertility rates have been falling, and the age at which women have their first child has been increasing. (Clark 2007: 13)

At first glance, Jeffrey Arnett's [2000] conception of "emerging adulthood" seems to draw away from the kind of social science consensus on an extended youth that Clark cites above in favour of an emphasis on exploration and uncertainty. . . . But a second glance quickly makes clear that far from [simplifying] the life course, Arnett is simply adding another phase to it. Thus, Arnett has argued that in Western industrialized countries, demographic changes have made the years between 18 and 25 a distinct period of the life course, and he proposed the term "emerging adulthood" for this phase, which he characterizes as a period of both greater instability and possibility. . . . In this period it is not demographic transitions such as establishing stable residences, finishing school, settling into a career, or marrying that matter to one's subjective sense of adulthood but "individualistic *qualities* of character" (Arnett 2000: 472–3). Nonetheless, it is to these kinds of demographic transitions that Arnett turns in explaining why his conception of "emerging adulthood" cannot simply be folded into a general phase of "young adulthood":

> The period from ages 18 to 25 could hardly be more distinct from the thirties. The majority of young people ages 18–25 do not believe that they have reached full adulthood, whereas the majority of people in their thirties believe that they have (Arnett, in press). The majority of people ages 18–25 are still in the process of obtaining education and training for a long-term adult occupation, whereas the majority of people in their thirties have settled into a more stable occupational path. The majority of people ages 18–25 are unmarried, whereas the majority of people in their thirties are married. The majority of people ages 18–25 are childless, whereas the majority of people in their thirties have had at least one child. The list could go on. The point should be clear. Emerging adulthood and young adulthood should be distinguished as separate developmental periods. (Arnett 2000: 477)

In other words, what most distinguishes "emerging adulthood" is that it is *not* adulthood and adulthood is defined in terms of the same goal posts identified by Clark as marking out the extension of youth. Where people between the ages of 25 and 29 fit into this paradigm is unclear, but what Arnett's distinction between "emerging" and "young" accomplishes is that it leaves the criteria of adulthood unchanged even while a larger number of people are defined as outside of it.

While Arnett's theory of "emerging adulthood" has attracted a good deal of interest, . . . [it has] also elicited criticism. . . . Bynner (2005) has argued that the psychological orientation of "emerging adulthood" . . . tends to downplay the importance of structural factors in shaping and stratifying roles and identities. Drawing on British surveys, Bynner (2005) contended that more privileged youths are responding to the increasing emphasis on formal qualifications through extended participation in postsecondary education and the postponement of family commitments, while their less advantaged counterparts are pursuing a more "traditional" route to adulthood with rapid and early transitions from secondary school to work. In a later comparison between Canadian and British survey material, Côté and Bynner (2008) contended that while Arnett had correctly identified young people's tendencies toward individualization and destandardization, his emphasis on *choice* and the emergence of a new development stage to frame these trends was misplaced. Instead, Côté and Bynner viewed these orientations as *reactions* to structural processes of **globalization** and technological transformation that have undermined the social supports available to young people as well as increas[ed] the uncertainties and ambiguities of trajectories toward adulthood. Rather than viewing young people as freely choosing to prolong their transitions toward adulthood while experimenting with identities, Côté and Bynner argued that young people have been forced to respond to a set of historical processes of economic exclusion and marginalization, which have made financial independence harder to achieve. Rather than entering a new stage of development, young people are, in this perspective, simply trying to cope with a particular set of institutional changes. . . .

Student-Youth Travel

In this paper, I draw on material collected as part of a larger project, which involved collaboration with Noel Dyck and the assistance of several graduate students, particularly Heather Barnick, Kathleen Rice, and Meghan Gilgunn. The project was a multi-locale study (Canada, Australia, the US, and the UK), which focused on three forms of Canadian student and youth travel and sojourns abroad including university exchanges, working holidays, and athletic scholarships. Some students and youths were interviewed in Canada as they prepared to embark on, or more commonly after they had returned from, one or more of these kinds of opportunities for travel abroad. Others were interviewed while they temporarily spent time abroad respectively on a "working holiday" in Britain, on a university exchange or on a more extended period of study in Australia, or completing a program of study in an American university supported by an athletic scholarship. Altogether we interviewed 99 Canadian students and youth travellers. Each of our graduate research assistants also completed an ethnographic study of 4 to 6 months duration with Canadian working holidaymakers in Edinburgh (Kathleen Rice), exchange and international students in Melbourne (Heather Barnick), and university athletes in Boston (Meghan Gilgunn). In addition to our encounters and exchanges with student and youth travellers, we also interviewed 43 government, university, and **NGO [non-governmental organization]** officials who were involved in developing, administering, or promoting programs for student and youth mobility in Canada, Australia, the UK, and the US. In this paper, however, I will be concentrating primarily on the young people in our study that participated in working holidays and university exchanges.

University student exchanges, which have been a feature of the postsecondary educational landscape since the Second World War, have more recently received . . . new [attention] as part of general calls for "internationalization." But the ubiquitous mention of internationalization in the mission statements of universities in many countries does not necessarily connote either agreement about its definition or indicate what kind of priority it is actually accorded in practice (Welch and Denman 1997). Nevertheless, if there is not much clarity about "internationalization," it is still reasonably clear that its most substantial aspect involves the mobility of students. While much of the institutional (i.e., universities, government, academic advocacy groups, etc.) interest in student mobility has usually concerned international students seeking to complete a full degree in their host university, there has also been talk of, and in some cases more or less concerted effort expended at, increasing the numbers of students who participate in short-term international exchanges of a semester or two. The students participating in such exchanges are still, however, very much in the minority; in Canada, probably around 2 per cent of postsecondary students participate in these forms of extended stays abroad.

One of the most common rationales in the field of "international education" for encouraging students to participate in these kinds of exchanges is offered by Daly and Barber:

> It is widely acknowledged that in the globalizing marketplace, organizations are seeking employees with skills and characteristics that enable them to be more competitive in the international arena. . . . One of the most effective means for graduates to develop "international skills" and communication competencies is through international academic programs such as study abroad and student exchange. (2005: 26–7)

Echoes of such arguments can also be heard with respect to work-abroad opportunities. Thus, according to a Canadian official with whom I spoke whose work involves the development of bilateral exchanges enabling students and youths to temporarily work abroad, young people taking up these possibilities:

> gain experience in the workforce and once you return to Canada you become more attractive to Canadian employers as part of a knowledge-based economy because the employer looks at

the participant and sees an individual who is open-minded, who has seen other things, who is actually also open to new ways of doing things and is willing to accept changes, which is very important for an employer these days.

Another Canadian official administering a work-abroad program argued that it is important to convince young participants:

> that nowadays fields of study tend to vary over one's career, right? A lot of people are in two, three careers even in this day and age and it's probably going to stay that way for some time. But more importantly, we try to get across to them that, look, it doesn't matter what the overseas work experience is, it's the fact that you've done it.

In short, official discourses tend to emphasize that one of the benefits of extended stays abroad for young Canadians is the training it can provide for future work in a globalized marketplace that often demands versatility in work practices, roles, and occupational choices.

. . . [T]his kind of official rationale for extended stays abroad does not necessarily conform to the motivations enunciated by young people for such mobility. I and others have reported that more than training for future professional or occupational roles, young travellers are likely to represent their journeys as [a time out] before they move to take on—or in some cases resume—the commitments they associate with adulthood or, in Maureen's words, "get my life started." While this "time out" may have resonances with the period of **liminality** . . . associated with rites of passage, it does not necessarily effect either the socially recognized shift in status van Gennep ([1908] 1960) associated with this period or the more radical personal and social transformations that Turner (1969) thought could be generated by this experience of between-ness. Instead, for many of the young Canadians we spoke with, who had taken up opportunities for work or study abroad, their journey was noteworthy for the "temporary reprieve it seemed to offer from social

expectations of a predictable progression through educational and career commitments" (Amit 2010: 64). A stay abroad did not so much facilitate a passage to other statuses and phases as stave them off a little longer.

In sharp distinction to Côté and Bynner's construction of extended youth as an effort to cope with processes of economic marginalization and exclusion, our study included examples of young people who had left what they considered to be "good" jobs in order to take up opportunities for an extended stay abroad. Rhonda was 24 years old, had already completed an undergraduate degree in journalism, and had worked in her chosen field of media relations and event coordination when, after visiting some friends in Europe, she decided to spend a period of time abroad on a working holiday in Edinburgh.

> I just absolutely fell in love with the city, and the travelling, so, um, I had a really good job back home, and I just decided last year that it wasn't the time for me to have that nine-to-five job and sign the government contract, you know, so I just decided to take up the working holiday visa, and come to Europe and work.

She had, she explained, just put her career "on hold." Rosanne was 28 years old and had left a job she had occupied for three and a half years as an assistant bank manager of a large branch in order to take up, like Rhonda, a working holiday in Edinburgh. After being repeatedly promoted in her job at the bank, she had arrived at a point

> where it was time to take the management courses and move up again. And [I] was definitely feeling the pressure from my big bosses. I don't really feel that's where I want to go with my career, so I was thinking of a career change anyway when I came here.

Rosanne's primary aspiration for her stay in the UK was to "have a good time and relax," but she also felt that "professionally, it's obviously not that great of a career move. It's not really fabulous on your resumé to sort of work your way up, and then leave and come back and so, it's not a career move, it's just to get experience. Life experience, I guess." So rather than the "resumé enhancer" that a student travel official used to characterize working holidays, for Rosanne at least, this journey was a resumé interruption that in due course she felt she would probably need to justify to future employers.

Similarly in his study of backpackers, Sørensen noted that while many of these young people were embarking on these travels at a crossroad in their lives, in most cases, this transitional period was "self-inflicted, brought about by a desire to travel" (2003: 853). They had quit a job, broken up with a partner, or effected some other break to facilitate the backpacking journey they were planning.

. . . [I]n this paper I want to focus more particularly on the constructions of adulthood implicated in the rationales often crafted for youth travel. In other words, what light do the constructions of particular forms of youth travel shed on the ways in which young travellers comprehend the life course and articulate their expectations of adulthood? One might be forgiven for assuming that . . . the willingness of young people to interrupt "good" jobs or careers for an extended period abroad indicates a shift toward non-linear and individualized representations of the life course. But in fact one of the most consistent subtexts of youth travel representations reasserts a very conventional and conservative notion of the life course.

Like Maureen, whose comments opened this paper, in one form or another many of the young travellers we interviewed or encountered represented their stay abroad as something they could do only before they "settled down." Rosanne, who had interrupted a job as a bank manager to work temporarily in an Edinburgh youth hostel, did not think it was likely that she would go on this kind of extended travel again because

> you eventually at some point have to get into your job, and get married, and have kids, and do all of that. And once you have kids to do extended travel would be difficult. So it may be

in retirement, it's a possibility, but not in the next twenty years.

Rhonda, who had put her career on hold to travel to Europe, similarly felt that

> I know I have to settle down for a bit and do my Master's. But I tell myself, I give myself until at least the age of 28 or 29, 30 and then really like, settle down and really like, you know, maybe think about buying a house and the job and everything. But until then I don't think I'm ready.

John had embarked on a university exchange at an Australian university in spite of the likelihood that it would extend the duration of his undergraduate studies. But in his view, a certain kind of travelling definitely had a "best before" date:

> Yeah, basically what I'm trying to do right now is stay single and travel while I can. You know what I mean—cause like when you're 35, you can't really go around and travel in hostels and stuff like that so . . . I kinda want everything out of life. So I want to be young and have fun now, travel, you know go do the hostelling thing, do all that, and then still have the education and what not to get back to Vancouver and, you know, work an office job and earn however much money and settle down with a family and kids and stuff like that.

At 24, Melissa was working in Montreal after several longer journeys abroad, first on a backpacking trip through Europe, then on a university exchange in Paris, and finally, when she had completed her BA, to teach English as a second language in Japan. She was enjoying her job in Montreal but had applied to go back to university for a second qualification and was also thinking of eventually spending a further year on a working holiday before she reached the age of 30. She did not feel ready to settle down yet, but "if I fall in love with someone . . .". Meanwhile, her parents, who had encouraged her travels, also reminded her that "yes, I want you to go and explore and you're young and go, but at the same time, remember at some point, you will have to make a decision to be able to solidify a good salary and secure yourself some equity or something."

The notion that an extended sojourn abroad is something that you do when you are young, before you settle down, is a theme that also resonates in other studies of youth travel. Sørensen quotes Mark from Britain, who explained the urgency to travel "before it is too late":

> It's a question of now or never. Since graduating from University a couple of years ago, I've made good money, so I can afford to travel. I thought that if ever then now, because 10 years from now I may be tied up with wife, kids, mortgage, and all the rest of it. (2003: 853)

Similarly, Desforges quotes Jenny, one of the young travellers in his own study of "long-haul" travellers:

> [p]eople want more from their lives and something for themselves first, to go and see the world while they're young and stuff, I guess. I know I do. There's a lot to see and a lot to do. . . . I think everyone I've spoken to has wanted to go away again and is not ready to settle down into a life, because they want to see the world, and there's more important things in life than commuting up to London every day. (1998: 190)

Fixing Adulthood

The flip side of the insistence on travelling when you are young is the presumption that it will not be possible to do so when you are older and have "settled down." This determined construction of adulthood as immobile and fixed is all the more striking when it is set against contemporary adulthoods that are integrally organized around ongoing movement. Harrison's (2003) study of 33 Canadian travel enthusiasts included individuals ranging in age from 30 to over 75 years old. One third were retired and about half were married, some divorced. Their incomes ranged from about $20,000 to well

over $180,000 per year and almost all were working or had worked at a professional or managerial job in occupations ranging from business to engineering. The forms of their travel varied considerably from package tours to independent travel, with different ranges of frequency and duration of trips. But their travels were central to their identity while not excluding a commitment to other important pursuits and connections.

My own study (Amit 2006, 2007) of transnational consultants included people whose work involved repeated travel to a variety of destinations. They too ranged in age from people in their thirties to those in their sixties. While for the most part they maintained a principal residence in Canada, their work might keep them abroad for months in any given year. Most had deliberately sought out this kind of [travel-dependent] career, working hard to establish their profile and competence in this kind of transnational workscape.

Notwithstanding these kinds of mobile leisure and occupational practices, while a few of the younger travellers we encountered in our study expressed an interest in developing a career that allowed for travel, most viewed their journeys as a function of youth. In effect, they were defining a transition to adulthood, at least in part, in terms of bringing their participation in extended travel to a close. But as we can see from the comments by the youthful travellers I cited earlier, this insistence on what Hockey and James have called a "chronologised, **modernist** life-course project" is not restricted to travel (2003: 115–16) but also takes shape around presumptions regarding certain key elements of home, family, and work. . . .

But this version of the life course revolves around a particular [view] of adulthood, which appears to be shared by many people including youths, their parents (see Melissa's earlier comment), educational authorities, scholars, and so on. What these perspectives share is a fairly pervasive notion of "settling down" as entailing certain key transitions around work, marriage, setting up an independent household, curtailing travel, and so on. When these kinds of transitions do not happen at all or else happen at a different age, then the goal posts of adulthood are pushed back through the extension of youth. What this means is that while the definition of youth is being repeatedly revised in terms of age range, duration, appropriate activities, and so on, adulthood remains socially and conceptually fixed as the attainment of certain key roles and statuses. Thus the extension of youth allows a concomitant arresting of adulthood as particular versions of "settling down." The more you change the definition of youth to reflect changing patterns of work, residence, education, or travel, the less you have to change the definition of adulthood.

Accordingly, as I noted earlier in this paper, Arnett justified the distinction he is positing between "emerging adulthood" and "young adulthood" as revolving around the relative proportions of people between 18 and 25 who are still obtaining education and training, have not yet married, and are childless, as opposed to the ratios of people in their thirties who have settled into a more stable occupational path, married, had at least one child, and so on (2000: 477). This rendering of adulthood stands in marked contrast to the late capitalist rhetoric of flexibility . . . in which mobility, insecurity, reinvention, and re-education are treated as lifelong necessities. Yet, as I also noted earlier, scholars such as Côté and Bynner (2008) who are trying to explain the extension of youth often account for this [delayed entry into adulthood] in terms of the same factors of economic restructuring and globalization that are used to buttress the rhetoric of economic flexibility. And likewise, as I noted earlier in this paper, the emphasis on versatility often cited by officials promoting or administering programs for youth travel would appear to be oriented toward a similar notion of the impact of globalization and economic restructuring. That is to say, this kind of "international experience" is seen as instilling a capacity for flexibility necessary in globalized economies.

There is thus a fundamental contradiction vested in certain scholarly and official notions of an extended youth. They at once stress the impact of post-industrial economic restructuring in reshaping the nature of youth even as they reaffirm a long-standing modernist chronology of the life course. It is, however, a contradiction that seems to be accepted, even asserted, by many of the young travellers that participated in our research project. Why? I suspect that this is a version of youth and of the life course that offers a more reassuring notion of what is at stake in being young and mobile.

Elsewhere I have suggested that what is most attractive about international university exchanges and working holidays is that, however exploratory, they put very little at risk (Amit 2010). If you do not like your job on a working holiday, you can just go home. Many of the university exchanges in which Canadian students participate stipulate minimal pass/fail requirements and in any case usually last for little more than a semester. Youths embarking on these kinds of extended stays abroad are overwhelmingly from middle-class-family backgrounds, in fact, providing evidence of a certain level of parental or personal financial resources is usually a visa requirement. Parents often, in one way or another, provide financial backing for these journeys, either directly funding them as is usually the case for academic exchanges or providing a measure of backup support. Thus most of the young people participating in working holidays do not expect to return to their countries of origin with much, if anything, in the way of accumulated savings. But they know that in most cases, their parents will likely provide them with temporary accommodation or support while they work out their subsequent plans for work, education, or residence. If it is an adventure, it is a fairly safe one.

However, if this travel was to be viewed as not just an interlude but also the shape of things to come, it might well take on very different connotations. Quitting a "good" job to embark on a temporary sojourn abroad or extending the duration of one's studies to enjoy a semester or two abroad is not a risky proposition if you believe that when you return to Canada, you will easily be able to find another job or finish your degree and then begin an attractive career or, in short, "settle down." Some scholars appear to assume that an extension of youth reflects perceived difficulties in attaining particular signposts of adulthood. But is it possible that one of the factors encouraging these kinds of interludes is precisely a continued faith in a "chronologised, modernist" life course? Very few of the young travellers we talked to expressed any doubt or uncertainty that when they were ready, they would be able to settle down. It is this confidence in the eventual prospect of a certain kind of adulthood that imparts to their travels the . . . aspect [of individual choice] noted by Arnett. An extended but still contained youthhood can present a much more reassuring prospect than an adulthood in which jobs, residence, family, and marriage continue to be constituted as uncertain, insecure, and fluctuating processes over the course of your whole life. [These young people] can be youths for a while longer because they are still confident that in due course they will be able to become a certain kind of adult. And this confidence is bolstered by a range of official discourses, scholarly constructions, media images, and parental reminders. What will they think or do if it turns out not to be altogether true?

References Cited

Amit, Vered. 2006. "Claiming Individuality through 'Flexibility': Career Choices and Constraints among Traveling Consultants." In *Claiming Individuality: The Cultural Politics of Distinction*, edited by Vered Amit and Noel Dyck, 90–109. London: Pluto.

———. 2007. "Globalization through 'Weak Ties': A Study of Transnational Networks among Mobile Professionals." In *Going First Class? New Approaches to Privileged Travel and Movement*, edited by Vered Amit, 53–71. Oxford: Berghahn.

———. 2010. "The Limits of Liminality: Capacities for Change and Transition among Student Travellers." In *Human Nature as Capacity: An Ethnographic Approach*, edited by Nigel Rapport, 54–71. Oxford: Berghahn.

Arnett, Jeffrey Jensen. 2000. "Emerging Adulthood: A Theory of Development from the Late Teens through the Twenties." *American Psychologist* 55 (5): 469–80.

Beck, Ulrich. 2000. *The Brave New World of Work*. Translated by Patrick Camiller. Cambridge: Polity.

Bynner, John. 2005. "Rethinking the Youth Phase of the Life-Course: The Case for Emerging Adulthood?" *Journal of Youth Studies* 8 (4): 367–84.

Clark, Warren. 2007. "Delayed Transitions of Young Adults." *Canadian Social Trends 84* (Winter). Statistics Canada Catalogue No. 11-008.

Côté, James, and John M. Bynner. 2008. "Changes in the Transition to Adulthood in the UK and Canada: The Role of Structure and Agency in Emerging Adulthood." *Journal of Youth Studies* 11 (3): 251–68.

Daly, Amanda J., and Michelle C. Barber. 2005. "Australian and New Zealand University Students' Participation in International Exchange Programs." *Journal of Studies in International Education* 9 (1): 26–41.

Desforges, Luke. 1998. "'Checking Out the Planet': Global Representations/Local Identities and Youth Travel." In *Cool Places: Geographies of Youth Cultures* edited by Tracey Skelton and Gil Valentine, 175–92. London: Routledge.

Harrison, Julia. 2003. *Being a Tourist: Finding Meaning in Pleasure Travel*. Vancouver: University of British Columbia Press.

Hockey, Jenny, and Allison James. 2003. *Social Identities across the Life Course*. Basingstoke, UK: Palgrave Macmillan.

Sørensen, Anders. 2003. "Backpacker Ethnography." *Annals of Tourism Research* 30 (4): 847–67.

Turner, Victor. 1969. *The Ritual Process: Structure and Anti-Structure*. Ithaca, NY: Cornell University Press.

van Gennep, Arnold. (1908) 1960. *The Rites of Passage*. Translated by Monika B. Vizedom and Gabrielle L. Caffee. Chicago: University of Chicago Press.

Welch, Anthony, and Brian Denman. 1997. "Internationalisation of Higher Education: Retrospect and Prospect." *Forum of Education* 52 (l): 14–27.

Key Points to Consider

- In North America, the definition of youth has changed with respect to age range, duration, appropriate activities, and so on, but the definition of adulthood has remained socially and conceptually fixed as the attainment of particular roles and statuses.
- Global economic and social trends to regard flexibility as a desirable personal attribute may encourage youth to strive for greater mobility.
- University and government officials encourage youth to travel as a way for them to build skills and social connections; young travellers, however, tend to regard their sojourns as a "time out" from real life.

Critical Thinking Questions

1. What institutional rationale(s) do government and university officials give for encouraging youth travel? What motivations for travel did the youth Amit spoke with offer? Do you regard these as compatible or incompatible? Explain your reasoning.
2. Amit observes that the life-course patterns that arose in the late nineteenth century in the West continue to have a "powerful hold on Western imaginations." In other words, these old patterns still structure the ways that most people in the West think about the normal life course. What do you think about this observation? How do you expect your life to change in the next decade or so? What does Amit mean when she says that many young Canadians have conservative expectations about the nature of adulthood?
3. Are you an adult now? If not, how do you define your place in the life course? How did you reach this assessment? What part does your gender or ethnicity play in the path(s) you expect your life to follow?
4. What does the phrase "settling down" mean to you? Think of some specific "official discourses, scholarly constructions, media images, and parental reminders" that give the phrase meaning for you.

Suggestions for Further Reading

Amit, Vered. 2006. "Claiming Individuality through 'Flexibility': Career Choices and Constraints among Travelling Consultants." In *Claiming Individuality: The Cultural Politics of Distinction*, edited by Vered Amit and Noel Dyck, 90–109. London: Pluto Press.

Amit-Talai, Vered. 2002. "The Waltz of Sociability: Intimacy, Dislocation, and Friendship in a Quebec High School." In *Academic Reading: Reading and Writing across the Disciplines*, 2nd ed., edited by Janet Giltrow, 233–51. Peterborough, ON: Broadview Press.

Brown, Ryan A., Daniel J. Hruschka, and Carol M. Worthman. 2009. "Cultural Models and Fertility Timing among Cherokee and White Youth in Appalachia: Beyond the Mode." *American Anthropologist* 111 (4): 420–31.

Richards, Paul. 2001. "War and Peace in Sierra Leone." *Fletcher Forum of World Affairs* 25 (2): 41–50.

Chapter 19

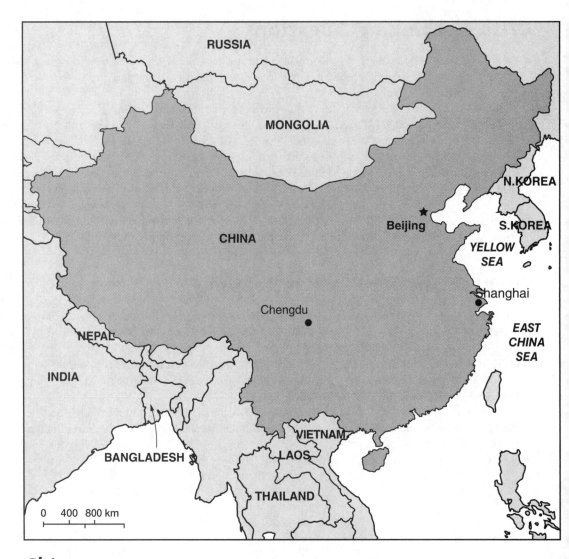

China

Introduction

Some of the most common questions that anthropologists are asked have to do with the logistics of ethnographic **fieldwork**: "How did you explain your research to the people you studied?", "What did they think about you?", "How do you cope with people who do not want to participate in your research?" Indeed, sometimes individuals or entire communities do not want to co-operate with an anthropologist's intrusive or annoying questions. Or they find that having a nosy, culturally incompetent outsider around is a burden. Some years ago, Canadian anthropologist Jean Briggs described being ostracized and ignored for several months when the **Inuit** family she was living with, which had "adopted" her as a daughter, became tired of her and upset about her inadvertent violations of their norms of polite behaviour (Briggs 1970). Though at the time Briggs found banishment from social interactions to be extremely distressing, she was never in any danger, and the experience actually helped her understand Inuit cultural preferences for emotional restraint more fully than otherwise might have been possible.

Briggs's situation was an extreme case, and most of the time people willingly co-operate with anthropological investigations. In fact, the codes of ethics that professional anthropologists have developed over the last several decades require us to ensure that **informants** understand the goals of the research and are willing participants. In other words, these codes require us to make sure that the people with whom we are working have given their "informed consent" to participate in the study. Individuals or groups of people we would like to include sometimes rebuff us, but this is not a serious or widespread problem. A research question that depends on the co-operation of any specific individual or group is probably too narrow to be of much intellectual or practical interest. As well, it is increasingly common for anthropologists and community organizations to collaborate to propose, design, conduct, and analyze **ethnographic** research. **Participatory research**, as this type of research is known, is not exclusive to anthropology.

Aside from taking part in participatory research, which often aims to benefit participants and their communities in some way, why do informants co-operate with anthropologists? One of the effects of **globalization** is that many of the people that contemporary anthropologists study know something about anthropology and often read and critique the things we write about them (Brettell 1993). Still, people often come up with their own theories to explain why the anthropologist is there and what she or he is doing. Individual informants may have personal reasons for engaging with an ethnographer. Sometimes they find the anthropologist interesting. Alternatively, they may relish the opportunity to tell their story, or they may believe that there are advantages to building a relationship with an outsider. While research participants are sometimes paid for their time, current ethical protocols require that this payment be minimal, so that people participate because they want to rather than for monetary or other compensation.

The article below considers some of the dilemmas an ethnographer might encounter when it appears that informants anticipate some special benefit from assisting her or him with the research. Anthropologist John Osburg was in Chengdu, China, from 2002 to 2006 to study ways that economic reforms and globalization were redefining the routes to status and success in that area. Chengdu is the capital of Sichuan province in southwestern China. It is a rapidly growing commercial and financial centre with more than 14 million people in its metropolitan area. Osburg was especially interested in Chengdu's new entrepreneurs, many of whom had become quite wealthy. In part, Osburg was responding to calls from within the discipline of anthropology to study the powerful as well as the poor.

Anthropologists have long acted as advocates for disadvantaged people, and many think that this advocation is an important function of anthropology. Osburg refers to this inclination as "our anthropological instincts to side with the disenfranchised." He also refers to a famous article by Laura Nader entitled "Up the Anthropologist." Nader called on her colleagues to "**study up**"—that is, to use anthropological tools to study powerful individuals and institutions—in order to uncover the ways that power and wealth are institutionalized and treated as ordinary and natural. Nader observed that it is much harder to study elites than it is to study poor people, but that studying only the poor leaves important topics that affect various people—including the poor—unexamined.

Osburg wanted to "study up." As he describes in the article, he conducted some of his fieldwork in bars frequented by management professionals and other white-collar workers. In the course of doing ethnography, he was taken in by some businessmen who made no secret of the fact that many of their business activities were criminal in nature. It turned out that understanding the workings of criminal gangs helped Osburg learn how wealthy Chengdu entrepreneurs build and maintain the social networks that are part of succeeding in business.

But spending time with members of criminal gangs presented Osburg with ethical problems. First, he worried that his informants would pressure him to assist them with money laundering, smuggling, or getting visas to visit the United States. Fortunately, Osburg seems to have been able to successfully avoid these forms of direct **reciprocity**. He is less clear about how he resolved a second problem: that he might lose his "critical perspective," his ability to recognize, from a researcher's perspective, the relations of power that his informants enacted. Doing good ethnography demands that we try to understand the world from the perspective of the people we are studying. This aim frequently leads us to identify with the people we study; we want others to like them or at least understand them the way that we do and see their seemingly strange practices as sensible. Osburg calls this sort of identification, which can distort our perspectives, "ethnographic seduction," and he worried about succumbing to it. Of course, not every informant is likeable, but ethics demands that we treat each humanely.

In his discussion of research ethics, Osburg mentions an institution he labels an "IRB." *IRB*, which stands for "institutional review board," is the contemporary American term for what used to be called the "human subjects committee." In Canada, these same bodies are usually called "offices of research ethics," and they are found at all universities and many hospitals and research centres. Their task is to help researchers design and conduct studies in which both the participants and the researchers are protected from physical, psychological, legal, or social harm. As Renée Sylvain (Chapter 1) and others have observed, the ethical protocols developed by research ethics boards do not always offer clear guidance for every situation that an ethnographer may confront during fieldwork.

Osburg is not the only anthropologist to have studied criminals and criminal activities, and the corruption Osburg describes is not unique to Chengdu or even to China. Ethnographies of individuals who commit crimes are important. Most people, including the people who make and enforce laws, make assumptions about the motivations and practices of criminals; ethnographies can provide these people with deeper, close-to-the-ground information and **critical analysis** on which they can build more informed opinions and approaches. Like "studying up," however, studying criminals presents ethical challenges. The anthropologist has to figure out how to act humanely toward individuals who engage in activities that are widely regarded as despicable. At the same time, the anthropologist does not want to endorse violent or criminal practices. For example, in his study of crack dealers in New York City, Philippe Bourgois (2003) struggled with how to present fairly violent men in a way that showed their vulnerabilities. Other ethnographies of crime have revealed the intimate connections between activities understood as legal and good and those treated as illegal and bad. Carolyn Nordstrom's ethnography of global trade, for example, showed that smuggling is ubiquitous and occurs alongside and as part of legal trade (Nordstrom 2008). Like Nordstrom, Osburg notes here that it is very difficult to sort out the "relationships between [the] 'legal' and [the] 'criminal,'" and indeed they may be two sides of the same coin.

❖ About the Author ❖

John Osburg teaches anthropology at the University of Rochester in New York. After finishing his BA at Columbia University, he went to China to teach English. Osburg conducted the research presented here for his PhD studies at the University of Chicago. Part of that field research involved co-hosting a variety show for a television station in Chengdu. The full ethnography, Anxious Wealth: Money and Morality among China's New Rich*, includes an analysis of changing gender relationships among the new elite in China.*

Meeting the "Godfather": Fieldwork and Ethnographic Seduction in a Chinese Nightclub

John Osburg

Introduction

Early on during my fieldwork in Chengdu, China, I met two wealthy businessmen in a bar that was popular with white-collar workers. Their shaved heads and leather jackets made them stand out among the polo shirts and jeans, and one explained that his girlfriend, an entrepreneur who exported rare mushrooms from the highlands of Sichuan to Japan, had brought them there. After treating them to drinks, I explained why I was in Chengdu and described my research, hoping they might be of assistance. One of them, who I later came to know as *Chen Ge* (Big Brother Chen), kept offering to introduce me to a side of society that, in his words, I wouldn't be able to access on my own. Not understanding his implied meaning and rendered immodest by our drinking, I explained that I had been in Chengdu for a while and claimed that I knew people from all levels of Chengdu society. He continued to hint at the nature

of this group: secret, not open to all. Slowly I realized he was talking about what ordinary Chinese people referred to as the *heishehui* ("black society"), and understood by outsiders as the underworld of organized crime.

The next day, Mr Chen called to invite me to see his furniture company's showroom, which was one of his many businesses in addition to nightclubs, smuggling, antiques, and protection rackets. Mr Chen showed me some of his furniture and asked if their products suited American consumers' tastes. After we had sat around watching his *xiong-di* ("brothers," junior members of his organization) play cards, Mr Chen invited me to dinner, but I had already made plans for that evening. As he escorted me to a place where I could get a taxi, he mentioned that he would like to introduce me to his group's *jiaofu*, using the Chinese translation of the English term *godfather*. He explained, "Meeting the godfather is more valuable than meeting the mayor. You know, in China there is no law. Relationships are the law." He told me that winning the favour of the "godfather" would boost my career and would guarantee me prosperity. Big Brother Chen explained that he liked me and would do whatever he could to help me. Yet his sudden expression of affection and interest in my well-being was unsettling. Thinking back to my anthropological education on reciprocity, I interpreted his gesture as a deliberate strategy to put me into a relationship of indebtedness to him, and I became anxious about potentially being approached for favours by a powerful criminal boss. When I meekly replied that I wished I could do something for him in return, but I'm just a poor graduate student, he laughed and told me, "Don't worry, we're [i.e., his organization] not that opportunistic" (field notes, 7 February 2004).

Conventional anthropological fieldwork methods and ethics are ill-suited to navigating a relationship with someone like Big Brother Chen and his associates. Building rapport is usually portrayed as the anthropologist winning the trust of the reluctant locals and as something the anthropologist does, rather than something that is done to him or her. While most anthropological ethics and guides to methods (see, for example, Bernard 1994) assume a power asymmetry between anthropologist and informant, in which the anthropologist has the upper hand, during my time with Chen (and later his boss, "the godfather"), I was never entirely sure if I was studying "up" (Gusterson 1997; Marcus 1983; Nader 1972) or "down." My relationship with Chen and his associates generated a particular set of ethical, emotional, and **epistemological** issues that ready-made professional ethics or IRB guidelines were little help in navigating. I argue that studying "illegal" actors presents a peculiar power dynamic and renders anthropologists particularly vulnerable to what Antonius Robben terms "ethnographic seduction" (1996). Finally, I suggest that studying illegal practices requires that we be wary of taking terms such as *illicit, illegal, marginal,* and *criminal* at face value because these terms often obscure the complex interconnections and mutually constitutive relationships between "legal" and "criminal" domains.

The "Godfather"

A few weeks after Big Brother Chen's offer to introduce me to the godfather, he gave me the mobile phone number of an individual who I later came to know as *Pang Ge* (Brother Fatty). When I met him, Brother Fatty was a permanent resident of the United States and spent six months each year in New York to maintain his residency status. After my first few weeks of meeting with this group, people began to hint that my role would be to help Brother Fatty in America, and that this was one of their reasons for "courting" me. When introducing me, Brother Fatty would explain, "He's going to help me in America," or "He's going to teach me English."

My anxieties about reciprocity and indebtedness diminished somewhat, however, as it became clear that Fatty and Chen felt like they gained *mianzi* ("face") simply by having an American in their entourage, especially one who spoke Chinese and performed deference to their organizational hierarchy.[1] Their associates were often surprised and impressed when I appeared with Fatty's group, and both Fatty and Chen hoped that my presence would indicate to outsiders that their group possessed "international" connections and a "global" reputation. After a few months, however, Fatty started talking about setting me up in a business in Chengdu, explaining that he would provide the necessary start-up capital. He and Chen suggested that I open a Western restaurant, which, I inferred, would likely function to help them launder money.

Fatty presented himself as a generous and selfless man, whose sole purpose was to help those around him. He referred to himself as a "man who could get things done" and who could summon powerful individuals from all domains of society with his mobile phone. Fatty frequently alluded to, or boasted about, his connections with various **state** agencies. He talked about having dinner with *Gong An Ju* (Public Security Bureau)[2] representatives and negotiating his organization's permissible activities with them. Police were present many of the evenings when Fatty and his group entertained business associates in their nightclub, and some introduced themselves as members of the police, making no attempt to hide their status. Like most underworld organizations in China, Fatty had many official patrons who tipped him off about any anti-crime campaigns and helped him avoid prosecution.[3]

I often asked Fatty's *xiongdi*, as well as interviewees outside of the underworld, why the police or the military do not crack down on criminal organizations in China. Most emphasized that shutting them down was costly due to the considerable resources required for launching an investigation and amassing evidence. There were also the social costs of disrupting a large sector of the **informal economy** and the risk of causing thousands of undereducated young men with a propensity for violence to lose their livelihoods. The *heishehui* (Chinese criminal underworld) therefore provide effective forms of governance beyond the state's formal reach. Not only do they regulate vice—drugs, prostitution, gambling, etc.—and generate considerable unofficial revenue for the police in the form of bribes, they also govern one of urban China's most dangerous and difficult-to-control **demographic** groups: young, undereducated bachelors who have left their rural hometowns for the cities. Since Fatty's group was organized by **ideologies** of loyalty, brotherhood, and subservience to hierarchy, Fatty's *xiongdi* were largely subject to his command. Furthermore, state agencies and real-estate developers frequently employ junior members of the *heishehui* to force reluctant residents from land marked for new developments. In addition, local state agencies use them to quash public protests and to intimidate their organizers.[4] Thus, while underworld leaders cultivate relationships with members of the state for protection, insider access, and government privileges, state officials rely on underground forms of force to achieve the aims of development, govern the underground economy and its unruly actors, and generate unofficial incomes to support the extra-bureaucratic "face" appropriate for a powerful official in the reform period.

Legitimization and Ethnographic Seduction

When colleagues or students learn that I conducted research with underground criminal bosses, they are often impressed that I was able to "access" such a presumably secretive group. My chance meeting with Big Brother Chen no doubt gave me a point of entry that I would not have had otherwise. However, once I was introduced to Fatty, my problem quickly became not how to deepen my relationship with his group, but precisely the opposite—how to maintain distance. Fatty, Chen, and their *xiongdi* subordinates were masters of a type of relationship-building referred to in the Sichuan dialect as *goudui*, which can be understood as a form of courtship for some instrumental purpose. They frequently invited me to dinner and drinks at their nightclubs, offered me gifts and introductions to women, and presented me with business opportunities. When I returned to the United States for the holidays, Fatty called me minutes after my plane landed to ask if I had a safe trip, and on Christmas morning he called to wish my family and me a "Merry Christmas." Given their seductive onslaught of gestures of care and generosity toward me, maintaining distance in a way that did not threaten to undermine our relationship became a serious challenge.[5] In the end, United States permanent-residency regulations unexpectedly resolved my growing anxiety—Fatty left to spend six months in the United States, and I stayed in China to finish my research. And by the time he returned to China, I was preparing to leave.

Fatty had much more money than I will likely ever have, and he certainly wielded considerable informal power in Sichuan. By most definitions he was a local, if not regional, elite. Yet he eagerly sought the forms of **social**, **symbolic**, and **cultural capital** that I embodied because of his perceived marginalization by global racial, linguistic, and educational hierarchies. Even within Chinese society, Fatty was simultaneously marginal (as a criminal with a **peasant** background who spoke with a thick rural accent) and powerful (through his wealth and access to the police and government officials). It was thus difficult for me to find the correct ethical and epistemological stance to take toward his accounts of himself and his group's activities. I vacillated between a mode of empathy, in which I felt the need to give voice to Fatty and his group, and a more critical mode of unmasking, in which I felt the need to pierce through their self-proclaimed *yiqi* (righteousness) and their ethics of *renqing* (relationships) to document how Fatty's organization perpetuated forms of domination and oppression in contemporary China. Was he a marginalized ex-peasant struggling against an oppressive, unjust system and thus vaguely situated in the righteous bandit tradition in China (see Ownby 1996)? Or was he an integral part of the violent side of state domination and accumulation in China? If the latter, does approaching Fatty from a [position] of "empathetic understanding" run the risk of "humanizing" state terror (Sluka 2000: 27)? Was he worthy of a relativistic sympathy, or was I a victim of (partially deliberate) "ethnographic seduction" (Robben 1996)?

By being "won over" or "seduced" by our informants, we may risk legitimizing their claims to morality, virtue, or honour at the expense of more critical perspectives.[6] According to Robben (1996), "Seduction prevents interviewers from probing the discourse of the interviewee and, instead, makes them lose their critical stance toward the manifest discourse" (72). Robben points out, however, that a desire for seduction is inherent in anthropological research. He states, "[A]nthropologists want to be seduced because it gives them the desired feeling of gaining access to a hidden world" (97). I confess to the giddy feeling of finally "gaining access" sitting next to Fatty at his nightclub as he bragged about his sometimes-violent exploits. Studying the "hidden worlds" of illegal activity might make seduction more likely since illicit actors may hope to actively recruit the anthropologist in order to legitimize their activities or **world views**. Informants deemed outlaws by the state might be eager to "tell their side of the story" to the outside world or to use the anthropologist to "lend a halo of objectivity" to their accounts (Robben 1996: 84). While Fatty was not particularly concerned with using me to set the historical record straight, my status as a well-educated American made me attractive for legitimizing his businesses and burnishing his reputation.

My experience with Fatty highlights two issues that emerge when studying actors at the margins of respectability and legality. First, our professional ethics (which presume a less powerful, vulnerable subject) and the lessons of studying "up" (which presume a powerful, reluctant, and secretive subject) both leave us ill-equipped to handle members of the underworld who might be marginal in certain domains but quite powerful in others. Furthermore, while IRBs require that we determine in advance who is vulnerable, illegal actors might be both victims and perpetrators of violence, and therefore both "vulnerable" (by IRB definitions) and complicit (see Clarke 2010). Second, illicit actors might not only have a special interest in building their own forms of rapport with an anthropologist to further their own agendas, but may, as in the case of Fatty, be especially adept at doing so. These conditions might render an anthropologist who spent many of his free moments during graduate school watching episodes of *The Sopranos* and *The Wire* particularly vulnerable to ethnographic seduction.

In addition to the dangers of ethnographic seduction, my experience with Fatty revealed that we also run the risk of missing ethnographic opportunities if we uncritically accept dominant, state-generated constructions of the "illicit." Rather than being seduced by a hidden, "difficult to access" world and by our anthropological instincts to side with the disenfranchised or being misled by "state thought" (Bourdieu 1994) that insists on the marginality of these worlds to the everyday workings of the nation-state, the economy, and the wider society, we need to investigate the ways in which such worlds might be intertwined (Heyman and Smart 1999). Instead of structuring our analyses around the binaries of legal–illegal and licit–illicit, we need to be attentive to how these binaries are produced through processes of illegalization and the ways in which they obscure a messier, interconnected field of power. Furthermore, studying seemingly illicit actors requires that we suspend, at least initially, our modalities of studying "up" or "down" and that we operate with a more flexible framing of our subjects. While I was initially seduced by Fatty's self-presentation as a righteous bandit, my growing awareness of his organization's decidedly unrighteous activities ultimately put a damper on his attempted courtship of me. Instead of formulating ethical axioms for studying illegal practices, our studies should foreground the fraught process of conducting research on illegality and the various ethical and epistemological shifts such research both requires and enables.

References Cited

Bernard, H. Russell. 1994. *Research Methods in Anthropology: Qualitative and Quantitative Approaches.* 2nd ed. New York: Altamira Press.

Bourdieu, Pierre. 1994. "Rethinking the State: Genesis and Structure of the Bureaucratic Field." *Sociological Theory* 12 (1): 1–18.

Clarke, Kamari. 2010. "Toward a Critically Engaged Ethnographic Practice." *Current Anthropology* 51 (S2): S301–12.

Gusterson, Hugh. 1997. "Studying up Revisited." *PoLAR: Political and Legal Anthropology Review* 20 (1): 114–19.

Heyman, Josiah, and Alan Smart. 1999. "States and Illegal Practices: An Overview." In *States and Illegal Practices*, edited by Josiah Heyman, 1–24. New York: Berg.

Hu, Hsien Chin. 1944. "The Chinese Concepts of 'Face.'" *American Anthropologist* 46 (1): 45–64.

Kipnis, Andrew. 1995. "Face: An Adaptable Discourse of Social Surfaces." *Positions* 3 (1): 119–48.

Marcus, George. 1983. *Elites: Ethnographic Issues.* Albuquerque: University of New Mexico Press.

Nader, Laura. 1972. "Up the Anthropologist—Perspectives Gained from Studying Up." In *Reinventing Anthropology*, edited by Dell Hymes, 284–311. New York: Vintage.

Ownby, David. 1996. *Brotherhoods and Secret Societies in Early and Mid-Qing China: The Formation of a Tradition.* Stanford, CA: Stanford University Press.

Robben, Antonius. 1996. "Ethnographic Seduction, Transference, and Resistance Dialogues about Terror and Violence in Argentina." *Ethos* 24 (1): 71–106.

Sluka, Jeffrey A. 2000. "Introduction: State Terror and Anthropology." In *Death Squad: The Anthropology of State Terror*, edited by Jeffrey A. Sluka, 1–45. Philadelphia: University of Pennsylvania Press.

Notes

1. *Mianzi*, in its broadest sense, can be understood as social prestige or reputation. For key anthropological analyses of the concept of face, see Hu (1944) and Kipnis (1995). (Osburg's note.)
2. Gong An Ju is the Chinese state agency responsible for policing and public safety. (Osburg's note.)
3. These patrons were referred to as his *baohusan* (protection umbrellas). (Osburg's note.)
4. Referred to as "mass incidents" in the state-run media, these protests are most often sparked by inadequate compensation for land and housing reappropriated by the state, wage disputes, and concerns about polluting factories. Many [Communist] party officials fear that these incidents might metastasize into larger political movements. (Osburg's note.)

5. Deepening my rapport with Fatty would likely have generated even thornier ethical dilemmas. In particular, if I agreed to open the restaurant, Fatty would have likely initiated me into his organization, forcing me to swear an oath to a set of relationships, ethics, and practices that would be in direct conflict with the code of ethics of a professional anthropologist. (Osburg's note.)

6. For Robben (1996: 73) the term *seduction* has multiple connotations. In the context of his fieldwork in Argentina, he uses it to refer to the ability of some of his more powerful informants to charm, captivate, or persuade him. By using *seduction*, he is also invoking its literal meaning, which is "to be led astray from an intended course" (73). (Osburg's note.)

Key Points to Consider

- Anthropologists are concerned with conducting ethical research. It is difficult to maintain the objective distance from informants that allows for "critical perspective" while also getting close enough to do good ethnography.
- Informants and other research participants have their own reasons for co-operating with an ethnographer. Understanding what those reasons are may help the ethnographer avoid ethical problems.
- The efforts by Osburg's informants to incorporate him into their social and economic networks presented ethical challenges, but these efforts also provided him with insights into how those networks functioned.

Critical Thinking Questions

1. Why did Osburg find Big Brother Chen's interest in him to be "unsettling"? Do you think he was correct to be concerned? Why or why not?
2. Osburg writes about the danger that anthropologists might be "'won over' or 'seduced' by our informants" so that we uncritically accept "their claims to morality, virtue, or honour." Is this concern particular to the study of elites, or is it a potential problem in any ethnographic situation? Explain your reasoning.
3. In what ways does Osburg regard criminal gangs as serving an important regulatory function in Chengdu? Does he excuse their criminal activities? Did Osburg successfully avoid "seduction," or does he seem to glamourize the criminal gangs? Explain your reasoning.
4. Do you think that a policy of minimal or no compensation to people who participate in ethnographic studies is ethical? Why or why not?

Suggestions for Further Reading

Bourgois, Philippe. 2003. *In Search of Respect: Selling Crack in El Barrio*. 2nd ed. Cambridge: Cambridge University Press.

Briggs, Jean L. 1970. "Kapluna Daughter." In *Never in Anger: Portrait of an Eskimo Family*, 225–307. Cambridge: Harvard University Press.

Nordstrom, Carolyn. 2008. *Global Outlaws: Crime, Money, and Power in the Contemporary World*. Berkeley: University of California Press.

Osburg, John. 2013. *Anxious Wealth: Money and Morality among China's New Rich*. Stanford: Stanford University Press.

Chapter 20

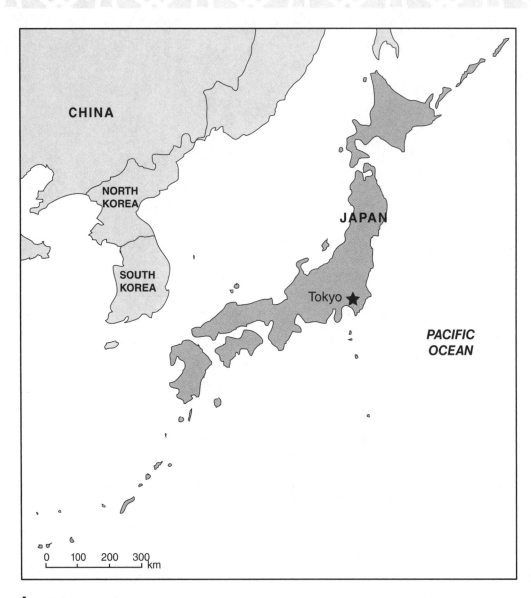

Japan

Introduction

More than half of the world's population today live in cities, and in some countries, including Japan and Canada, urban dwellers make up far more than 50 per cent of the populace. Thus, it might be somewhat surprising to realize that in both Japan and Canada many of the national **symbols** and iconic sites are in rural places. The creation and promotion of national symbols is something that is actively cultivated by governments to encourage shared sentiments of **nationalism**, nostalgia, and identity.

Corporations also draw on and cultivate national symbols to sell their products. Some of the best examples of Canadian national (and nationalist) symbols in advertising are associated with the Olympic Games, an event that is itself an opportunity for nationalist fervour. A television commercial for the hardware and building-supplies chain RONA, for example, presented during the 2012 London Olympics consisted of a cross-country relay with a screwdriver in place of the baton. The relay began in Vancouver and ended on a fishing dock in Newfoundland. Along the way, the relay participants encountered, and mirrored in sport, iconic Canadian images: a bear, a prairie field, a train, whitewater rapids, a herd of buffalo, the CN Tower. In another example, a commercial for Molson Canadian beer begins: "When you think about Canadians, you might ask yourself, 'Why are we the way we are?' Well, the answer is laying [sic] right under our feet, literally. The fact is, it's this land that shapes us." The accompanying visuals include Canadians engaged in active, even extreme, recreational activities at sites meant to be representative of the Canadian landscape—jumping off a cliff into a lake, whitewater rafting down a turbulent river, hiking in rugged wilderness, playing hockey on a frozen lake. Toward the end of the commercial, a shot of an unpeopled field of golden grain appears, representing the beer. As these images flood by, the voiceover states that Canada has "more square feet of awesomeness per person than any other nation on Earth" and that both Canadians and their beer—Molson Canadian, of course—are "made from Canada." Similarly, a Hudson's Bay Company ad intersperses images of voyageurs and Olympic athletes, past and present adventurers traversing a difficult, snow-covered landscape. The voiceover reminds viewers that "We didn't just survive the elements; together, we thrived in them."

These advertisements, and many other forms of popular media, draw on and reinforce connections that Canadians have learned to make between the Canadian landscape and the Canadian people. There is a tendency for Canadians to imagine themselves as settlers in a masculine wilderness, struggling against rugged nature and, in the process, absorbing a bit of the strength, power, and wildness of the land. Tellingly, in the RONA relay, two of the three urban shots—one of Toronto and one of Montreal—feature what are arguably feminized sports, synchronized swimming and race walking. The **trope** that unites the Canadian landscape with the Canadian people is what anthropologist Sherry Ortner (1973) labelled an "elaborating symbol." According to Ortner, elaborating symbols bring together a number of ideas important to a group of people in a way that tells a story about those people or is otherwise significant to them.

The article below, by Nelson Graburn, considers symbols that Japanese citizens recognize in the landscape of Japan, and it examines how these individuals identify those symbols as representative of an authentic Japan. Just as Canadians see themselves in the Canadian landscape, Japanese conceive of their identities in relation to the Japanese countryside. Leisure, recreation, and tourism in rural Japan are the focus of Graburn's analysis; he shows how leisure activities are essential to the ways that Japanese have come to see the land as a representation of "Japanese-ness." Japanese people are often stereotyped as consumed with work, and as Graburn points out, as a group Japanese do work long hours and take few vacations. Nonetheless, it is through leisure rather than work that Japanese express what they believe to be their true selves.

In the full version of this article, Graburn includes a description of recent rural-to-urban migration in Japan. This sort of migration is a global phenomenon, but it is especially prevalent in Japan, where 92 per cent of the population live in cities (by comparison, 82 per cent of Canadians live in urban areas). All over the world during the past half century, urban migration that began with the Industrial Revolution has proceeded at an accelerated pace. This **demographic** transformation reflects changes in culture as well as in economic and social organization. Changes in the technologies used in primary industries such as farming, forestry, mining, and fishing have greatly increased productivity while employing far fewer people. One, perhaps ironic, effect of what economists would regard as increased economic efficiency is the decline of many previously vibrant rural places. In Japan, Graburn reports, only 10 per cent of farmers are able to make a living primarily from agriculture. The remainder "are 'weekend farmers' who have full-time jobs, usually in nearby towns and cities" (Graburn 1988: 197). Rural women, even more than men, have fled the countryside rather than find themselves managing a farm alone while their husbands commute to jobs in urban centres. Rural-to-urban migration is a complex phenomenon involving alterations in family size and household configuration, **gender roles**, education, consumption patterns, work, and, as shown in this article, alterations in the practices and meanings of leisure activities.

The government of Japan responded to the declining fortunes of rural villages first with grants for "village revitalization" and later by encouraging (with rhetoric and with financing) projects designed to develop rural areas as sites for domestic recreation and tourism. To the extent that a rural tourist industry has developed in Japan, it is due, in large part, to government campaigns to encourage urban Japanese to reaffirm their connections both to "wild" nature and to places designated *furusato* or "old home places." Over time, Graburn shows, Japanese urbanites' attachments to their specific rural places of origin have been replaced with more general attachments to rural places that "look and feel 'homey' to the urban middle classes." Thus, contemporary Japanese tourists—particularly those who hail from large cities—are attracted to places that for them symbolize an idealized, "authentic" Japan, seemingly untainted by the **globalization**, the stressful hustle and bustle, or the foreign influences found in Japanese cities.

❖ About the Author ❖

Nelson Graburn grew up in rural England. After studying natural sciences and anthropology at Cambridge University, he continued his studies in anthropology at McGill University and then at the University of Chicago. He has worked at the University of California, Berkeley since 1964 as a member of the Department of Anthropology, a curator of the Phoebe A. Hearst Museum of Anthropology, and a founder and director of the university's Canadian Studies program. He has been a major scholar in Inuit studies, especially of Inuit art, and is a founder of the anthropological study of tourism. The article presented below concerns his special interests in the cultural practices and symbolic importance of domestic tourism in wealthy countries, especially Japan.

Work and Play in the Japanese Countryside

Nelson Graburn

This [article] is concerned with the development of the Japanese countryside into a site for recreation. I have entitled it "Work and Play" because the countryside was, until a few decades ago, the site of work for the majority of the population and because, [since the 1970s], the growth of tourism and recreation in the countryside has in part been planned specifically to provide work opportunities for the population whose previous occupations—farming, forestry, and fishing—have encountered serious declines.

The [article] consists of three parts: first, a consideration of what the countryside is and the ways in which it may be conceived; second, an account of the planning of non-agricultural developments and of which recreational and tourist activities take place there; and third, a consideration of the discourse of new meanings of the countryside in contemporary Japanese culture.

The Japanese Countryside

The landscape of Japan, though penetrable (by tunnels or winding roads), consists of steep and often volcanic mountains covering nearly three-quarters its area. There are many narrow valleys, but the few densely populated fertile plains contain most of both the agricultural and the urban areas. In Japan, land usage follows topography: according to the *Japan Statistical Yearbook* (Statistics Bureau 1993: 505, 526) 77 per cent of the surface of Japan is forested (over 10 per cent of the mainly forested areas are now incorporated into national, quasi-national, and prefectural parks), only 14 per cent is farmed and cultivated, while 2.6 per cent is given over to residential areas and less than 1 per cent to industry.[1]

As the focus of this [article] is play or recreation (*rejâ*) in the countryside, we are given pause when we think of the Japanese term for it—*inaka*, as expressed by the two kanji [written characters] that might

otherwise be pronounced *ta* (rice field) and *sha* (household or house), that is, "fields and houses" for short. In her . . . *Rice as Self*, Ohnuki-Tierney (1993: 92–3) . . . states that *inaka* was and still is an urban construction, encompassing those parts of Japan likely to be visited by urban people when they leave their towns and cities. What about the other 77 per cent, the relatively uninhabited landscape? This might be thought of as *hikyô*, the hidden or unexplored (i.e., uninhabited regions), or *henkyô*, the frontier, in the historical sense of not yet settled regions, or even *arechi*, waste or good-for-nothing land where humans could never settle.

The conception of *inaka* may have undergone change as less and less of Japan's land is cultivated, and the former dominant occupation in the largest area, forestry, has become a moribund industry. On the other hand, new uses for the land, such as skiing, trekking, and golf, may have revived, or brought into habitation, or at least into familiarity, areas that were otherwise "empty" or unknown. Thus it is likely that the countryside where the recreation now takes place is not exactly the same *inaka* where farmers live and where so many urbanites once had their *furusatos*, their home communities.

Japan has long been a relatively urban, densely populated nation, with the metropolis of Edo (Tokyo) reaching more than 1,000,000 people even before the end of the Tokugawa era [1603–1867]. The power to define categories of life and land, and hierarchies of moral value, lay with the powerful . . . and showed remarkable continuity until the last few decades. Though *inaka no hito*, the people of the countryside, might have been looked down upon, ambivalence was expressed because in the official moral hierarchy it was the farmers who were placed after the *samurai* and noble elite, above the craftsmen and business people of the towns and cities.

The relation of the countryside to the cities began to change in the Meiji era of Western-inspired industrialization (1868–1912). Then, and again particularly since World War II, the inhabitants of the rural areas have flocked to the bright lights and the many jobs proffered by the cities. By 1930 the rural population, *inaka no hito* (engaged in agriculture, forestry, and fisheries) dropped below the 50 per cent mark, and in the 1950s rural unemployment was higher than 10 per cent in many areas. By 1970 only 25 per cent of Japan's population lived in the rural areas. . . .

Many kinds of rural occupations have diminished or disappeared. There is little need for anyone to keep farm animals such as bullocks and horses, as these have been replaced by motorized vehicles. Charcoal makers were important in forestry before the arrival on the scene of kerosene and electricity. Even though Japan has done a wonderful job in restoring its forest areas since their devastation in World War II, lumberjacks are a dying breed because they are hardly needed now that Japan relies on the much cheaper wood from much larger trees that it harvests or buys in foreign [places] such as Burma [Myanmar], Borneo, and the New Hebrides.

The national spotlight, however, is on rice farmers and the disappearance of rice-growing acreage. The Occupation-ordered land reform of the late 1940s[2] put farmers in charge of their own land, motivating them to switch to other crops for greater profit. . . . By the 1960s, Japan was not only able to feed herself with rice but also to produce large surpluses that forced the central government to find storage and begin price supports. The government then started a financial incentive scheme to rotate the rice paddies, always leaving some fallow.

. . . With fewer fields in use, with industrial and housing developments encroaching upon rural areas, coupled with increasing numbers of farmers farming only part-time or weekends, rice production has actually fallen in recent years. In 1965 farmers planted over 3 million hectares of paddy to produce 12.4 million tons of rice, but by 1991 these figures had dropped to 2 million hectares and 9.6 million tons, representing an increase in productivity but an overall decline in production.

However, rice consumption has also dropped. Japanese want more variety in their diet and increasingly look toward bread, pasta, and such substitutes. Government-distributed rice is, even with a subsidy, at least five times more expensive in Japan than on the world market. Even government school lunches include rice only two or three times a week. Certain segments of the populace and the government have always claimed that they want Japan to be self-sufficient in rice even if only at uneconomical prices—following the experience of starvation after World War II—and their fears were borne out in the summer of 1994 when the rice crops failed massively and Japan was forced to buy foreign rice from Southeast Asia, the United States, and other countries.

I was in Japan during that time, and I was amazed at how many people—family and friends—told me (coming from California) with great glee that they each had a sure supply and didn't have to eat that *gaimai*, that foreign rice! As Ohnuki-Tierney's *Rice as Self* (1993) stresses, it is not the monetary cost (which is not expensive to the affluent Japanese) nor the nutritional value of rice (which is on a par with other available foods) that concerns Japanese; it is the key symbolic value of rice: rice as bright green in watery terraces; rice loaded with golden grains; rice as *sake*, the drink of the gods; rice as the earth; rice as the water; rice as the labour of the hardworking Japanese countryman. As . . . Michael Foster (1994) suggested, we should perceive . . . rice and rice farming [in Japan] as an art form central to [Japanese] heritage, not as an industry.

Planning Recreation in the Countryside: Making Work

At the national level there have been two kinds of plans to boost the economy of the lagging Japanese countryside: First are Tokyo-generated plans for the decentralization of industry by attracting [factories] to the countryside, . . . plans for new recreational areas [and] resort areas, and even [considerations of] moving the capital from Tokyo to the hinterlands (Tabb 1995: 169–97). The [first of these approaches], the dispersal of Japanese industry, has not been as successful as hoped; major industry and . . . highly trained workers are still attracted primarily to the metropolitan zones (Keener 1992; Tabb 1995). However, to examine this process would be marginal to the present project because it turns countryside into urban areas. This process often leads to widespread loss of "rural character" and a proliferation of ugly sights. Due in part to historical patterns and in part to the American influences of the [post–World War II] Occupation period, Japan has very weak zoning laws. For instance, farmers generally hang on to their land as long as possible, both for sentimental reasons and because it is subsidized, but when they do sell their land—and many have become very rich doing so—they can sell it to a factory, to a *pachinko* [gaming] parlour, to a supermarket, to practically any enterprise. Thus lovely rural valleys often sprout haphazard development in all directions (the converse also occurs, tiny enclaves of farming may remain in the midst of a huge city).

Second, there has been a redistribution of national (and later prefectural) tax moneys specifically to village . . . governments along with a growing nostalgia for *furusato* "old/home village" culture, with the assumption that somehow the core of the "real Japan" lies in peripheral, rural communities. This is expressed in a national and regional—economic and ideological—*mura okoshi*, "village revitalization," movement: this "pro-countryside" movement has real adherents, with strongly moral and ecological principles—there are meetings, national organizations, and somewhat anti-establishment schemes—as well as governmental status. Prime Minister Takeshita created a "Furusato Foundation" to give 100,000,000 yen (approximately $700,000 at that time) to each village as *mura okoshi* development grants. The villages were, however, free to choose in what way they would spend this money.

Villages all over Japan chose to spend their money differently: improvement of roads and road signs, improvement of schools and health clinics, building of facilities for the recreation and care of the growing population of old persons, advertising of resort attractions, loans or grants to improve inns, campgrounds, hot spring resorts, and so on. But the most famous and financially rewarding was a village in Hyogo-ken (near Kobe) that turned its cash into a solid gold ingot that was put on display in the community hall. Locals and visitors were challenged to pick it up (under the eye of guards)—a clever idea that brought in reporters, TV crews, and tourists in large numbers.

The central government passed the "Law of Development of Comprehensive Resort Areas," which came into effect in June 1987. In turn regional governments began applying for this funding, and by 1991 over 18 schemes had been approved. The purpose of this law is, like the title of this [article], two-fold: to foster the construction of resorts and leisure facilities in order to revitalize regional economies *and* to provide more leisure opportunities for the workaholic Japanese. . . .

For instance, one scheme was the Nagano Prefectural Government's proposal, called the Fresh Air Shinshû Chi-Kumagawa plan. It called for the construction of seven golf courses on 180,000 hectares of mountainous land. This provoked a reaction from the locals who feared that these recreational facilities would lead to the pollution of sources of drinking water (more on this later).

Another scheme, in co-operation with the Forestry Agency, is called the "Human Green Plan," which proposes more flexible use of the national forest to include resort areas and sports facilities such as ski runs, golf courses, tennis courts, botanical gardens, and bird sanctuaries, as well as tourist accommodations. It encourages private investment in these public lands.

[Since 1970], Japan has developed superb albeit expensive urban and interurban public transportation systems. However, outside of the urban areas the infrastructure is relatively inadequate. Great effort and expense has been forthcoming in an attempt to supply this missing infrastructure so that the urban population will venture into the local countryside for recreational purposes. Unfortunately sometimes the building of roads cannot keep up with the growing number of cars. In 1978, Ronald Dore, in describing the rural valley that led to the village of Shinohata, wrote, "Ten years ago, when the trunk road was first completely metalled all the way to the next prefecture, there were express buses, but no longer. Now the roads are so crowded that express would be a mockery. . . ." (Dore 1978: 17). By 1992, 78 per cent of Japanese families owned a personal car, and that number rose to over 87 per cent in rural areas (Statistics Bureau 1993: 50, 305).

Domestic mass tourism [in Japan] has a long history. . . . The task of the government has been to open up means of communication from the dense metropolitan areas and to encourage the provision and publicity of rural tourism and recreational facilities which, in turn, should employ local people. [Since 1980], the government has instigated an extensive national road-building effort, both for expensive intercity toll roads (and bridges) and [for roads] into previously isolated hinterland areas. The recent abundance of cars and the national highway and bridge construction program have made more accessible some of the more remote country areas, and consequently visitor numbers have risen dramatically. . . .

Attractions of the Hinterlands

There is a vast range of attractions for visitors to the Japanese hinterlands. Some are historically traditional like pilgrimages to famous temples and shrines; most of them are newly installed and thoroughly secular. It is convenient to divide these recreations into two kinds: *rejà* and *kenbutsu*—that is, active and passive forms of tourism. The former appeals to younger people and the latter to older people, each having different conceptions of the countryside. **Class** and **gender** are also significant factors.

For instance, the mildly active sport of golf is one of the more popular rural recreations, but nearly all players are upper-middle-class professionals, and only 15 per cent are women. Golf, which has an annual turnover of over 2 trillion yen and has over twelve million players in 2000 clubs (1990 figures), was also one of the first issues resisted by locals because of the metropolitan planning for outlying recreation and resorts (Yamada 1990). The spate of building golf courses, even by levelling mountain tops, for the sake of relatively rich, middle-aged men, has threatened the landscape with pollution and change. Golf courses now occupy more than 1.25 per cent of Japan's *total* landscape, an area larger than Greater Tokyo, which is home to thirty million people! Due to lavish use of pesticides and herbicides, run-off pollution [from golf courses] often threatens nearby fishing areas and water supplies.

Hot spring (*onsen*) bathing is popular with all ages but does not quite fit the "do" versus "see" classification; it is passive rather than active, but the senses involved are feeling and smell as much as sight. [Since the 1970s there has been] an *onsen bûmu* (hot spring boom) in resorts, most of which were formerly used by local rural people or a few upper-class visitors. Though the natural waters were often said to have curative, or at least recuperative, powers, most of the eighty million Japanese who annually partake of *onsen* do so purely for relaxation. . . .

Domestic tourism, with over sixty million participants and three hundred million trips a year, supplies the countryside with some of its active and most of its passive visitors. Many of the attractions, in contrast to the ones mentioned above, are site specific—that is, people go to particular, well-known, often historical places. Famous natural scenery, equal in popularity to *onsen* bathing, is even more popular than visiting famous man-made attractions. But we must not forget that all attractions are man-made in the sense that they have been socially constructed and validated as attractions (MacCannell 1976; Berque 1986). These culturally certified natural features most prominently include mountains, volcanoes, waterfalls, cliffs, caves, and shores, most of which are the habitations of powerful *kami* (gods), with shrines for praying to the *kami* usually to be found nearby. Other natural attractions are less site specific, such as river boating, whale watching, and, of course, the seasonally appropriate viewing of nature—cherry blossoms, wild azalea, autumn maples.

Historical sites of many kinds have long formed the backbone of Japanese domestic tourism (Graburn 1983a; Ishimori 1989; Vaporis 1995). In addition to the famous shrines, temples, and castles, which are often found in urban or urbanized rural areas, specifically rural attractions are becoming very popular: most of these are obsolescent or obsolete structures, including archaeological sites [and] old farm houses . . ., either in *situ in* villages or, more often, brought together in "old house parks" somewhat similar to European eco-museums. Some are made more appealing for a wider range of people by including restaurants or traditional crafts activities and sales of souvenir *omiyage*. One of the most spectacular is the fairly new *Yu-no-kuni-no-mori* in Kanazawaken, a group of restored thatched [farm houses] brought together in a landscaped park, each hosting a traditional crafts activity such as lacquer ware, pottery, paper making, country cooking, and so on. This was erected at great cost a few kilometers from a popular *onsen* resort by the wealthy owner of the local taxi companies.

Some whole villages, lucky enough not to have been "modernized," remodel themselves on traditional styles but not as museums. Chiran, the lovely tea-growing village south of Ibusuki, combines the nostalgic attractions of thatched houses, manicured gardens, and neat rows of tea bushes, with the, for some, equally nostalgic national memorial to heroic Kamikaze pilots and their selfless widows. This makes the very important point that any particular tourist trip may well not be limited to one type of attraction: one often finds the old with the new, the familiar with the strange, or "nature" and culture in interesting combinations.

Rural Recreation and Japanese Culture: Making Hay (Play)

In this final section, I shall consider the factors in contemporary Japanese society that have impelled the population into rural recreation and tourism, and how it has been done. Using the model of recreation and tourism as a **ritual of reversal**, we infer that the attractions are pull factors that appear to provide relief or **liminal** compensation (Graburn 1977; 1983b) for some push factors in contemporary urban living, and that the advertising and publicity systems make the actors aware of either the potential relief and pleasure to be enjoyed or of some kind of pain (or guilt) engendered by city life—for example, not tending to family graves back in the *furusato* village. . . .

Lebra (1993: 13) has . . . noted that internationalization, *kokusaika*, is a phenomenon that many Japanese feel has been thrust upon them, causing distaste, if not anxiety. . . . Internationalization is more apparent in the modern city, increasingly in the form of . . . guest workers and other foreigners. After World War II and the end of the Occupation, the overwhelming

presence of foreigners subsided, but the urban way of life became increasingly "foreign," that is, at least superficially more Western. The Tokyo Olympics in 1964 brought in many foreigners and coincided with the relaxation on buying foreign money. This, in turn, allowed Japanese tourists to go abroad in increasing numbers, itself a self-imposed *kokusaika*, but the vast majority did not go abroad. *Kokusaika* had become a more insistent policy by the 1970s. Lebra (1993: 13) claims that this spurred attempts at retrenchment by self-discovery: This threat to national identity was soon countered by domestic tourism. As Ivy (1995: 40–8) shows, the JNR [the Japanese National Railways, which was run by the government], tied up with Dentsu, the world's largest advertising agency, began the "Discover Japan" campaign in 1970. Actually this followed the decade-older but smaller commercial campaign by JTB [Japan Travel Bureau] (Nihon kôtsû kôsha [Japan Travel Bureau] 1960).

Part of the effort to get citizens to travel out from the [cities] was the *furusato* campaign of the 1970s, which urged urbanites to travel *back* to the villages and small towns from which they or their families had migrated. *Furusato* is an inherently nostalgic concept implying alienation, which I have translated as "old/home village." As Ivy points out, the idea of *furusato-mairi*, going back to the old/home village, parallels the common appellation of the "Discover Japan" campaign—*Nihon no saihakken*—which literally means "*Re*discover Japan."

This campaign depended on the idealized construction that all Japanese families had or ought to have had a cozy rural or small-town community of origin. The campaign was probably not aimed at youths, nor was it particularly effective for them. However, for those who do maintain contact with relatives back home, there are at least two annual occasions when they should return home for family/ritual purposes. These are *oshôgatsu*, the week starting with the New Year's Eve visit to the local Shinto Shrine, and *obon*, the Buddhist mid-summer "All Souls Day." Family members are supposed to worship and to care for the graves on these occasions and at the time of the spring and autumn equinoxes.

As the reality of *furusato-mairi*, the annual pilgrimage home has become less compelling for families who have lived in cities for generations—or has been replaced by the desire to go elsewhere, even abroad—the metaphor of *furusato* itself has broadened and the travel to them has become less personal. *Furusato* has been promoted as a cultural conception that might be devoid of "real" historical or genealogical links. Trips out of the city may be aimed at "*furusato*-like" places, places that look and feel "homey" to the urban middle classes. The resulting cultural construction of *furusato* has resulted in a major rural industry. There is even a *Furusato Fair* now in Tokyo.

One might suggest that the end of the "Discover Japan" campaign, which was replaced by "Exotic Japan" according to Ivy (1995: 48), perhaps coincided with the point when the possibility of having a "real" *furusato* faded and gave way to the rise of a multiplicity of possible socially constructed *furusatos*. Although Ivy focuses on the new campaign's attempt to find and promote the exotic or foreign in Japan . . . (Ivy 1995: 50), we could also say that the countryside was foreign and exotic rather than "home" for a majority of Japanese. Thus, the countryside has become an exciting place to explore, just like a foreign country, in multitudes of promotional television programs.

This idea that rural/*furusato* is in some ways "foreign" to younger, urban Japanese is strengthened by Rea's (1996) insightful discussion of the significance that at least two foreign rural places have been labelled *furusato*—Anne of Green Gables's (*Akage no Ann*) "home" country and that of her author, Lucy [Maud] Montgomery, in Prince Edward Island, Canada, and Hill Top Farm in the Lake District [of England], the former abode of Beatrix Potter, the writer of "rural" children's books. . . . According to Rea, the words and actions of the thousands of Japanese tourists who go [to these foreign locations]—crying, meditating, feeling the soil—lead one to believe that for many the "real" nostalgic moral centre may no longer lie in the Japanese countryside but in someone else's.

John Knight's . . . "Rural *Kokusaika*" paper (1993) shows how one rural area in Oku Kumano has invented new traditions (cf. Hobsbawm and Ranger 1983) in its relation to the city. Among other things, it has a campaign to get footloose urban folks to "adopt" the village as their *furusato*. Urbanites regularly receive packages of country produce

and a newsletter. The illusion is further instilled by visiting and, possibly, even planning to retire there.

But the **ideology** of *furusato*, originally a national advertising campaign, reached its peak when Prime Minister Takeshita [disconnected] the idea of *furusato* from its country and small-town moorings and declared that every place in Japan—city districts, suburbs, small towns, or villages—should become *furusato*—that is, communities with sentimental relationships of long-term loyalty based on face-to-face interaction. This has achieved a partial success, for instance among groups of mothers who "naturally" gather to send their children to school together, as well as in community recreation and health centres, playgrounds, [and] sports and hobby groups. . . .

Dozens of surveys in the past decade found that tourist travel within Japan (summer, winter, hot springs, etc.) was the second-highest-ranked leisure activity of the Japanese (Yano 1994: 302), second only to eating out. Though I agree with Kanzaki (1992) that the Japanese have always liked to travel within their country, my point is that increasingly, recreational travel is to places that were previously too bucolic, too remote, or previously unmarked on road maps. We have to ask the question: If these displacements result from urban alienation, what do the attractions of the countryside mean? Most of the above-quoted writers suggested that if the city is modernity, then the countryside must denote the traditional past.

Ohnuki-Tierney (1993: 120) gives us a clue. "A crucial dimension of rice symbolism in Japanese culture is the rice paddies that stand for agriculture, the countryside, and the past—all symbolizing nature with its soil and water and, ultimately, the Japanese nature and its people." I contend that it cannot be just the rice paddies but the whole way of life that can provide the "antidote to urban civilization."

There has been a further tipping of the moral hierarchy, ironically instigated by the Western-influenced romantics like Yanagita, Yanagi, and Hamada (Foster 1994; Moeran 1984). One might summarize this as an ideological shift from the idea "rich city/poor village," to "poor city/rich village" (Knight 1993: 211). This ascendency in things rural representing tradition has coincided with a parallel trend toward the "natural" in food and drink, in "greenery," and in the countryside—for example, the emphasis on fresh, locally available foods such as *sansai* (mountain vegetables).

Not surprisingly, an analysis of representations in the advertising for these domestic tourism institutions does suggest the elimination of "modern/Western" phenomena—a kind of ideological ethnic cleansing and, conversely, the nostalgic highlighting of the condensed symbols of Japanese-ness (Moeran 1983).

Conclusions

To fill these recreational amenities and to provide the income and employment for the people of the rural areas, the "supply side" must be considered, the opportunities for urban people to use them. Even today, most Japanese have very short vacation periods, scattered fairly evenly throughout the year, many of which workers do not take. Adult's and children's vacations often do not coincide. There has been a rapid increase in the affluence and an ageing of the population. There has also been some increase in leisure time available to residents in urban and suburban areas—spurred by the government's effort to reduce the work week (to five and a half days) and to increase the length of vacation time *actually taken*.

But young unmarried adults are one group that has increasing free time and spending money. They often travel to the countryside in peer groups—OLs (office ladies [i.e., women who work in offices]) living [with their parents], particularly, have money to spare.

Older people, especially older women, are a growing segment. They have the money and the freedom. I would suggest that older people have a modern conception of the countryside *inaka* and its *furusato*, and that the urban youth might have the more recently "culturally constructed" set of conceptions discussed in this [article].

What can we learn, then, about Japanese culture through an examination of leisure activities in the countryside?

First, at the economic/demographic level, we have seen an exchange in which traditional rural activities are increasingly replaced by new service industries serving tourism and recreation. The rural population crash accelerated the depopulation of many rural communities and the growth of urban and suburban areas. Moon's (1989) account of a Tôhoku ski resort illustrates a successful example of tourism development countering population loss.

Second, at the cognitive level, for the urban population the country life of their ancestors has become increasingly remote. Actual attachments to particular places, *furusato*, and to their rural populations have increasingly been replaced by simulations that have been manipulated by the national and local authorities in pursuit of the policies outlined above. At the same time, the mental conception of the countryside itself, *inaka*, has expanded, especially for younger, urban people whose parents were no longer able to talk about their upbringing and life in the countryside. *Inaka* has expanded to include many formerly uninhabited areas, where recreational activities such as skiing, river boating, surfing, and trekking now take place.

Third, at the moral level, there has been an increasing, sometimes nostalgic, appreciation of the value of country life, of the countryside, and of "nature" (*shizen*) itself. . . . [M]anaged nature has come to represent tradition in a very positive sense. Not only are (both traditional and novel) "natural foods" increasingly popular, but there is a new appreciation of natural phenomena for their own sake. . . . Modern urban "separation from nature" is now deemed to be like a disease, to be countered at the private level by increasing tourism and recreation in the countryside, and at the governmental level by the creation of camps and schools in the countryside where cycles of urban children attend a few days at a time to learn at first hand "what nature is like."

References Cited

Berque, Augustin. 1986. *Le sauvage et l'artifice: Les Japonais devant la nature*. Paris: Gallimard.

Dore, Ronald. 1978. *Shinohata: A Portrait of a Japanese Village*. New York: Pantheon.

Foster, Michael. 1994. "Yanagita and Yanagi: An Exploration into Some of the Ideas of Two of Japan's Folklorists." Berkeley, Manuscript.

Graburn, Nelson H.H. 1977. "Tourism: The Sacred Journey." In *Hosts and Guests: The Anthropology of Tourism*, edited by Valene Smith, 17–32. Pittsburgh: University of Pennsylvania Press.

———. 1983a. *To Pray, Pay and Play: The Cultural Structure of Japanese Domestic Tourism*. Aix-en-Provence, FR: Centre des Hautes Études Touristiques.

———. 1983b. "The Anthropology of Tourism." Special Issue of *Annals of Tourism Research* 10 (1).

Hobsbawm, Eric, and Terence Ranger, eds. 1983. *The Invention of Tradition*. Cambridge: Cambridge University Press.

Ishimori, Shuzo. 1995. "Tourism and Religion: From the Perspective of Comparative Civilization." In *Japanese Civilization in the Modern World IX: Tourism* (Senri Ethnological Studies 38), edited by Tadao Umesao, Harumi Befu, and Shuzo Ishimori, 11–24. Suita: National Museum of Ethnology.

Ivy, Marilyn J. 1995. *Discourses of the Vanishing: Modernity, Phantasm, Japan*. Chicago: University of Chicago Press.

Kanzaki, Noritake. 1992. "The Travel-Loving Tradition of the Japanese." *Japan Echo* 19 (4): 66–9.

Keener, Christopher R. 1992. *Grass Roots Industry in the Town of Sakaki: An Alternative Perspective of the Japanese Post-war Miracle*. PhD diss., University of California, Berkeley.

Knight, John. 1993. "Rural *Kokusaika*: Foreign Motifs and Village Revival in Japan." *Japan Forum* 512: 203–16.

Lebra, Takie S. 1993. *Above the Clouds: Status Culture of the Modern Japanese Nobility*. Berkeley: University of California Press.

MacCannell, Dean. 1976. *The Tourist: A New Theory of the Leisure Class*. New York: Schocken.

Moeran, Brian. 1983. "The Language of Japanese Tourism." *Annals of Tourism Research* 10: 93–108.

———. 1984. *Lost Innocence: Folk Craft Potters of Onta, Japan*. Berkeley: University of California Press.

Moon, Okpyo. 1989. *From Paddy Field to Ski Slope: The Revitalization of Tradition in Japanese Village Life*. Manchester: Manchester University Press.

Nihon Kôtsû Kôsha (JTB). 1960. *Rural Life in Japan*. Tokyo: JTB.

Ohnuki-Tierney, Emiko. 1993. *Rice as Self: Japanese Identities through Time*. Princeton, NJ: Princeton University Press.

Rea, Michael. 1996. *A Furusato Away from Home*. Berkeley: Manuscript.

Statistics Bureau (Japan). 1993. *Japan Statistical Yearbook*. Tokyo: Statistics Bureau, Management and Coordination Agency.

Tabb, William K. 1995. *The Postwar Japanese System: Cultural Economy and Economic Transformation*. Oxford: Oxford University Press.

Vaporis, Constantine. 1995. "The Early Modern Origins of Japanese Tourism." In *Japanese Civilization in the Modern World IX: Tourism* (Senri Ethnological Studies 38), edited by Tadao Umesao, Harumi Befu, and Shuzo Ishimori, 25–38. Suita: National Museum of Ethnology.

Yamada, Kunihiro. 1990. "The Triple Evils of Golf Courses." *Japan Quarterly* 37 (3): 291–7.

Yano Tsuneta Kinenkai, ed. 1994. *Nihon kokuseizue '94/'95*. Tokyo: Kokusei-sha (no. 52).

Notes

1. In the period between 2005 and 2012, forests occupied 66.3 per cent of Japan's land surface, 12.2 per cent was cultivated farmland, 3.1 per cent was residential, and 0.4 per cent was industrial (*Japan Statistical Yearbook 2015*, www.stat.go.jp). (Stern's note)

2. Following Japan's surrender at the end of World War II, the Allied forces took control of the country until 1952. (Stern's note)

Key Points to Consider

- The form and style of domestic tourism varies from country to country as well as by tourists' age, gender, and social class.
- The ways that people participate in tourism are culturally and socially informed. Tourism activities are not merely matters of individual choice.
- In Japan, urbanization has led to rural depopulation and rural economic decline. Nonetheless, many Japanese feel an emotional connection to rural places, which are perceive as representing true "Japanese-ness."
- The meaning of the term *furusato*, which Graburn translates as "old/home village" has changed from being a specific rural place where an individual came from to being a more generalized site of nostalgia for an idealized, romantic rural past. Tourism provides individuals with a way to express that nostalgia.

Critical Thinking Questions

1. Think about a vacation trip you took recently. Where did you go? What activities did you engage in? How did you select this particular destination? Had you been there before? Was it recommended by friends? What did you know about the culture in your destination before you went? How well did what you found match your expectations? Do your friends and family share your ideas about what makes a good vacation?
2. What are the key symbols of Canadianness or of another country where you have lived? Where and when do you encounter these symbols? Are they connected to particular places, activities, foods, or relationships? What kinds of emotions do they evoke?
3. In this article, Nelson Graburn observes that Japanese conceive of the Anne of Green Gables tourist site in Prince Edward Island as one of two authentic *furusato* places located outside of Japan. What do the Japanese mean when they describe a place as *furusato*?
4. Many Canadians think of Vimy Ridge (in France) as special, even sacred. Do you feel this way? Why or why not? What institutions and practices are involved in shaping your ideas on this subject?

Suggestions for Further Reading

Graburn, Nelson H.H. 1977. "Tourism: The Sacred Journey." In *Hosts and Guests: The Anthropology of Tourism*, edited by Valene L. Smith, 17–32. Philadelphia: University of Pennsylvania Press.

———. 1995. "The Past in the Present in Japan." In *Change in Tourism: People, Places, Processes*, edited by Richard Butler and Douglas Pearce, 47–50. London: Routledge.

———. 1998. "Weirs in the River of Time: The Development of Historical Consciousness among Canadian Inuit." *Museum Anthropology* 22 (1): 18–32.

Ortner, Sherry B. 1973. "On Key Symbols." *American Anthropologist* 75 (5): 1338–46.

Television Commercials Discussed in the Introduction

Hudson's Bay Company. 2010. "We Were Made for This." HBC. Online video, 1 min. www.youtube.com/watch?v=dLsFkZKj63U.

Molson Canadian. 2010. "Made from Canada." Molson. Online video, 1 min. www.youtube.com/watch?v=X_yW4-cgG4g.

RONA. 2012. "Olympic Relay TV Commercial." RONA. Online video, 1:35 min. www.metatube.com/en/videos/148348/RONA-2012-Olympic-Relay-TV-Commercial.

Chapter 21

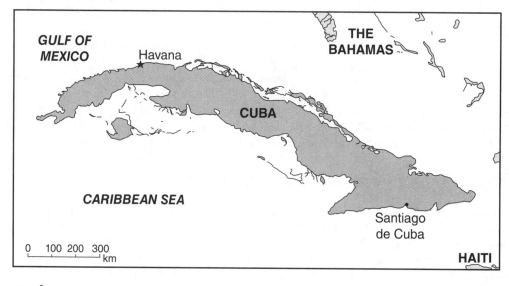

Cuba

Introduction

The dissolution of the Soviet Union in 1991 brought an end to the **Cold War**, ushering in the current era of **globalization** that has drastically transformed economic activities, patterns of interaction, and flows of people, goods, money, and ideas throughout the world. In addition to setting off changes at the global scale, the collapse of the Soviet Union had specific effects on individual countries that had depended on the Soviet Union for economic and political support. One of these countries was Cuba.

The Cuban Revolution in 1959 established a centralized socialist economy that allowed Cuba to become one of the most **egalitarian** countries in the world. Cubans enjoyed nearly full employment as well as high standards for health care, education, and other social services (Mesa-Lago 1998: 869). This remarkable achievement was supported by trade and economic subsidies from the Soviet Union. Significantly, this support enabled the revolutionary government of Cuba to survive a very strict economic boycott imposed by the United States beginning in 1960.

Yet Cubans' economic equality came at the social cost of an authoritarian government that criminalized both political dissent and individual economic activity. The political leadership maintained its authority through severe censorship and a **discourse** of continuous revolution that penetrated every institution and aspect of social life on the island. Music, dance, theatre, and other forms of **expressive culture** were all organized by the **state** and harnessed in support of the ongoing revolution.

The collapse of the Soviet Union and the subsequent loss of trade and subsidies created a severe economic crisis in Cuba. Cubans refer to this crisis, which lasted throughout the 1990s and early 2000s, as the "Special Period." During this time, the Cuban government sought to replace the lost trade with the Soviet Union by encouraging foreign investment, especially in tourism. It also, for the first time, permitted Cubans to receive **remittances** from family members living abroad and to engage in private entrepreneurial activities. These actions eased the economic crisis, but they also caused economic inequality to return.

The article abridged below describes a genre of Latin American dance music—reggaetón—that has become wildly popular in Cuba since the beginning of this century. The author, Alexandrine Boudreault-Fournier, argues that the loosening of state economic controls along with the economic inequality that followed created the conditions for reggaetón to flourish in Cuba. Boudreault-Fournier studied the activities of reggaetón musicians and producers. These reggaetoneros, as they are known, are mostly dark-skinned young men, often from the eastern provinces of Cuba, who are widely disparaged for their youth, their **race**, and their poor musicianship. They and their music are mostly excluded from state-supported performance venues and recording studios. Boudreault-Fournier makes the interesting observation that rap music, which is supported by the state, has been losing out to reggaetón, which is not. In this article, Boudreault-Fournier concentrates on a group she refers to as "mature reggaetoneros"—musicians who had previous success as rap artists but have abandoned rap for reggaetón.

One of the central questions addressed in the article concerns whether reggaetoneros feel socially marginalized and are experiencing a "crisis of faith" in the state, as some Cuban intellectuals have claimed. Boudreault-Fournier considers what she learned in her conversations with reggaetoneros as well as her analysis of reggaetón performances to suggest that these young Cubans are not in a state of despair. She observes that many reggaetoneros, through their dress and their actions, embody an individualism and a consumerism antithetical to Cuban revolutionary socialist principles, which

Boudreault-Fournier refers to as "the dominant social formation." At the same time, she notes that although they are not filled with revolutionary zeal, they have absorbed the nationalist sentiments and **symbols** promoted by the revolutionary leadership. Rather than despair, Boudreault-Fournier suggests that reggaetoneros are engaged in "a marginal **nationalist rhetoric**" that is neither supportive of nor directly opposed to dominant official discourses. This position she calls an "**ideology** of escape" that allows reggaetoneros to reinterpret national symbols in ways that diverge from the official ideologies without posing a real challenge to the existing social order.

❧ About the Author ❦

Alexandrine Boudreault-Fournier teaches anthropology at the University of Victoria. Cuba has been her primary fieldwork site since 2000; there, she has explored the political and economic aspects of music production and consumption. Boudreault-Fournier's MA project at Concordia University included an ethnographic film called State the Rhythm, *which looks at Haitian dance groups in Guantánamo and Santiago de Cuba. She completed a PhD in social anthropology and visual media at the University of Manchester and has continued to include filmmaking as part of her ethnographic research. Recently, she has applied her media and ethnographic skills as part of a team of researchers investigating health-care delivery in impoverished sectors of Quebec.*

Positioning the New Reggaetón Stars in Cuba

Alexandrine Boudreault-Fournier

At the beginning of the 2000s, reggaetón, a Caribbean musical phenomenon influenced by Panamanian ragamuffin, Jamaican dancehall, and Spanish speaking hip hop, arrived on Cuban shores. Reggaetón rapidly became the favourite [music] . . . for a majority of young Cubans, overtaking timba[1] in popularity in regions such as Santiago de Cuba. Yet this phenomenon, associated with individualist and market-oriented values, has been regularly denigrated by prominent Cuban intellectuals and professional musicians. Reggaetón was also criticized by the press . . . as being anti-cultural, banal, vulgar, and trashy (see for instance Medel 2005). . . . [R]eggaetón lyrics are about love, sex, and consumerism, rather than issues of social concern. But despite such criticisms in a context in which censorship is often exercised, little was done to limit the diffusion of the music.

The recent reggaetón invasion generated deep clashes within Cuban hip-hop circles as many rappers who previously adhered to a more politicized philosophy joined the reggaetón craze; they were subsequently accused of embracing a superficial form of expression. This article focuses on . . . former rappers who began to produce reggaetón in the city of Santiago de Cuba; they are referred to in this article as "mature reggaetoneros." Most of them are men in their early twenties who started as rappers in the 1990s, and who decided to adopt reggaetón aesthetics in the 2000s to increase the commercial viability of their music production. They tend to be more serious about making a living from the music and acquiring professional status than younger reggaetoneros [are]. Most reggaetoneros active in the Santiago reggaetón scene are not recognized as professionals, which means they cannot legally sign contracts and receive payments for their performances. Significantly, only one active reggaetón group in Santiago, Candyman, is officially recognized as professional by state music institutions.

In contemporary socialist Cuba, the commercialization of a music genre that is not officially supported by the revolutionary leadership, such as reggaetón, implies that producers must rely heavily on their involvement in informal networks and illicit activities, such as recording music in unauthorized homemade studios, copying and distributing CDs in the street without copyright considerations, and performing illegally at local dance halls in exchange for undeclared payments.

While reggaetón music has obtained unprecedented dissemination through underground channels, reggaetoneros are almost exclusively active in parallel networks, which allow them to commercialize, promote, and distribute their music outside of state regulations. The participation of reggaetoneros in such alternative networks of production and distribution, in addition to their general antipathy toward state institutions, . . . has contributed to the general conception that reggaetoneros represent only the most marginal of all youths. However, even though reggaetoneros participate in alternative networks that are on the margins of legality, they still coexist and even collaborate with state infrastructures when it is convenient to do so. The first section of this article focuses on how reggaetón music is produced and distributed in homemade recording studios. The exploration of reggaetoneros' parallel networks illustrates how these actors have constructed a niche that is neither within nor against the dominant [system].

. . . Similar to their participation in alternative networks of music production and distribution, reggaetoneros [express] a marginal nationalist rhetoric that is not directed against dominant official discourses. Reggaetoneros express nationalist sentiments through subjects that appear "non-political." . . . Two such subjects . . . [are] sport and sexuality[, the former of which is] briefly discussed [below].

Finally, reggaetoneros' position toward the [ongoing Cuban] revolutionary project is addressed. Reggaetoneros transform, adapt, reject, and combine dominant and alternative ideological principles, which at times may bring them closer to the revolutionary project . . ., but *most of the time* seem to distance them from [official political rhetoric]. . . .

Santiago: The Cradle of Cuban Reggaetón

Santiago is located [on] the east[ern part] of the island and is the second most populated city after the Cuban capital, Havana. The eastern part of the island, what is often referred to as the Oriente, includes the provinces of Las Tunas, Granma, Santiago, Holguín, and Guantánamo. The provinces of Santiago and Guantánamo—located on the south coast and facing the Caribbean—are known to be racially "blacker." Waves of migrations from Haiti and Jamaica to the eastern part of the island in the nineteenth and twentieth centuries explain the significant presence of people of African origin in the region. Cultural and artistic currents . . . from these neighbouring islands . . . have historically influenced the city's cultural landscape. Radio waves from Jamaica are easily caught on the outskirts of Santiago, and it is reported that at the end of the 1990s many rappers from the region used to listen to Jamaican radio programs with the help of homemade antennas. . . .

The majority of the first reggaetoneros to acquire [national] popularity . . . are from Santiago. . . . What is produced in the Oriente, however, receives little coverage in the Cuban state media, reflecting the institutional bias of the Cuban system toward the capital. By and large, reggaetón in the Oriente remains a local phenomenon, partly because of a lack of promotion in the national media and a lack of interest in the genre on the part of state institutions.

In Santiago—as opposed to Havana—reggaetón is often considered a part of hip-hop culture, in spite of the fact that . . . relation[s] between rappers and reggaetoneros [have] not always been [easy]. But while rappers officially received institutional and ideological support from the [state] (see Fernandes 2003, 2004, 2006; Baker 2005), reggaetoneros do not. Thus reggaetoneros are forced to find alternative venues and networks for performing and producing their music. At the same time, rappers seem to be losing ground. Many in Santiago argue that rap is on the verge of disappearing; in Havana, only a few groups are still active. . . . In Santiago, rappers who were active at the end of the 1990s have not necessarily stopped performing, but many have transformed their musical production toward a more danceable *mezcla* (mix), a fusion of various Caribbean styles, including reggaetón. . . .

Home-Based Studios and Transnational Networks

This section provides a broad portrait of how reggaetoneros and reggaetón producers have been able to construct alternative networks that allow them to produce and distribute their music without depending on state institutions, but without rejecting collaboration with the cultural infrastructure with which they might in fact maintain relations.

The sole recording studio in Santiago, managed by the state EGREM (Empresa de Grabaciones y Ediciones Musicales [Recordings and Musical Editions Enterprise]) and called Siboney, has recorded very few underground rappers and reggaetoneros. . . . This has in turn motivated many producers to record underground rappers and reggaetoneros in unofficial studios. While reggaetoneros tend to be computer illiterate, a clan of producers has emerged who are both technologically and musically savvy. Producers take a central role in the creation of the song and the sound. The acquisition of the technology to produce and record music electronically has been achieved incrementally since the end of the 1990s with the help of foreign[ers]. . . . Homemade studios equipped with basic computer equipment, speakers, and microphones have become the primary spaces in which rappers and reggaetoneros produce and record music. . . . One of the most basic elements of reggaetón music is the rhythm section, commonly referred to as the background track: a percussive mix, usually produced electronically, on top of which the voice is superimposed. These homemade studios are spaces where producers create the background tracks and then record reggaetoneros' voices.

In addition to being spaces of creation and production, home studios are also central spaces of **socialization**—places where reggaetoneros meet, discuss, sing, debate, and collaborate with each other and with producers. . . . Conversations among reggaetoneros may be related to Santiago's latest venue, rumours about performance opportunities, the arrival of a foreign impresario [event organizer] in town, and the like. The casual atmosphere of the home studio allows for spontaneous and informal meetings to take place. . . .

Many reggaetoneros work in close collaboration with professional musicians who may have privileged contacts with foreigners and access to recording equipment. One example is given by Alejandro, a professional musician who played with the famous son[2] band Son 14. A few years ago, Alejandro decided to leave the band to become a full-time music producer because it was more economically advantageous. His allegiance, however, did not lie necessarily with reggaetón. He began his recording career producing salsa music, before switching to the more lucrative production of reggaetón. . . . [B]ecause most reggaetoneros are not professional by state standards, they don't have access to state studios, increasing their reliance on such unofficial recording spaces. Because of his music training, Alejandro can produce complex melodic arrangements, incorporating brass instruments and rhythmic variations. . . . Yet Alejandro does not particularly like reggaetón, and he considers the genre as evidence of a social decadence provoked by the hardships of the Special Period.

Alejandro owns a well-equipped studio located in his family house, which he acquired bit by bit thanks to friends and family living abroad. To access the studio, one has to climb a small, hidden staircase located at the back of the kitchen. The studio is awkwardly located; one gets the impression of being in an in-between floor because of the room's low ceiling. Nonetheless, the small studio is well equipped by Cuban standards. The space is spotless, isolated from outside light and sound, and the entire room is covered with carpet (to improve sound insulation). There is no decoration and few personal effects. The only articles on the table, apart from his computer, are used for music production and recording (such as CDs, keyboard, speakers, etc.). Among reggaetoneros, Alejandro's illicit business is considered one of the best equipped in the city. His studio contrasts with the basic bedroom studios encountered throughout Santiago.

Homemade-studio businesses are considered illicit in Cuba, although no concrete attempts to dismantle them have been put forward. . . . It is not legal for professional musicians to record music that is not their own for commercial purposes. Musicians who [operate] such illicit businesses legitimize them by arguing that they are for personal use and artistic experimentation. But Alejandro is conscious of his precarious status before the law, and he applies severe self-censorship to what he produces. He told me during an interview, for instance, that he would never record a group that promoted anti-revolutionary messages for fear of shutdown. This fear leads him and other home producers to police reggaetoneros' lyrics, a process that offers no more expressive freedom than the state itself. . . .

Another category of producers is made up of reggaetoneros who have been able to acquire the technology to produce and record reggaetón. One of the best known in Santiago is Kiki. . . . Kiki has siblings in Florida and he received his first computer from them a few years ago. Apart from his basic third-generation computer, Kiki's bedroom studio is equipped with just two speakers and a

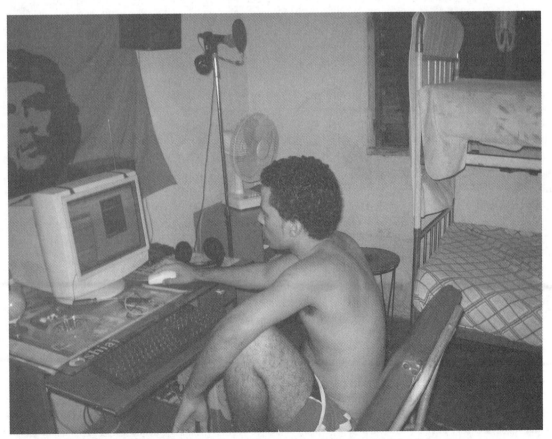

FIGURE 21.1   Background-track producer Kiki's bedroom studio in Santiago de Cuba, Cuba.

shaky microphone. His bedroom is small and often crowded with reggaetoneros and friends. A bunk bed is located to the side of his working table and, unlike Alejandro's tidy studio, the whole space is filled with personal effects, clothes, and CDs.

In 2006, Kiki was part of an underground rap and reggaetón group called Magia Negra, but he dedicated most of his time to creating background tracks and recording bands from Santiago. He claims to have produced more than two thousand background tracks, usually producing one background track per day, with the actual recording taking one additional day. Kiki taught himself how to use the technology and never received formal musical training. The background-track-creation process takes place in Kiki's bedroom, in collaboration with reggaetoneros who first perform the song for Kiki without a background track. While hearing the melodic patterns, Kiki plays with scales, rhythms, and sound effects on his computer. Most of the time, a background track is produced only after Kiki hears a specific song, but at other times a band may buy a background track from him and subsequently get inspiration from its rhythmic patterns to create vocal arrangements. All admit that one of the advantages of producing reggaetón is that it is fairly simple. The background track is entirely electronic, and it follows a repetitive rhythmic pattern; there is no need to record live instruments. Voice arrangements are usually simple, involving one to three reggaetoneros and occasionally female backup vocals. In less than two days, one can create a background track, record, and mix a song. The idea is to keep it simple—and make it danceable.

A few years ago, a foreign impresario approached Kiki to create a company that would promote groups from the Santiago region abroad. This company, called Trespeso and headquartered in New Zealand, commercializes the final reggaetón recordings and takes . . . half of each song's royalties. All of the groups approached by the impresario were keen to sign contracts. The negotiations took place outside of the Cuban [legal] framework. In other words, the company's business—and the whole process of signing contracts, buying music

and background tracks, and copyrighting—took place without the involvement of Cuban authorities. In the case of Trespeso, the contracted groups have not received any royalties yet, but the foreign impresario has sporadically provided them with MP3s, turntables, computers, and other electronic devices.

Since the emergence of reggaetón, five foreign companies are known to have recorded reggaetón in Santiago. Some have acquired a better reputation than others, but a bitter feeling remains among reggaetoneros who believe that many of the contractual obligations were not respected and among those who were not entirely aware of the consequences of signing such contracts (often written exclusively in English). But as a consequence of working outside official regulations, reggaetoneros do not have the legal protection to launch an appeal. Although reggaetoneros are aware of issues related to copyright, they rarely register their songs with the local ACDAM (La Agencia Cubana de Derecho de Autor Musical [The Cuban Agency for Musical Author Copyright]). Kiki, who claimed to have produced more than two thousand reggaetón background tracks, has never registered any of them. Instead, he sold them to local reggaetoneros, who most likely didn't register them either, for 200 Cuban pesos (approximately $8) each. Kiki controls the price of his production and negotiates with reggaetoneros directly, without intermediaries or agencies. The freedom of being able to commercialize and manage their own production is valued highly by reggaetoneros who believe foreign impresarios make money with their products.

In Santiago, reggaetoneros have put in place a network of . . . Cubans and foreigners to build up their credentials and increase the potential for commercializing their music. Even though reggaetoneros have been able to articulate their own interests within a quasi-independent system, many do not reject involvement with the official [state] system. For instance, reggaetoneros might perform at concerts organized by the AHS (Asociación Hermanos Saíz [the Association of Young Vanguard Artists]) and actively seek official recognition so that they can more easily sign contracts, receive remuneration for their performances, and travel abroad. Hence many stubbornly apply for membership to the state music agency in Santiago . . . that represents professional musicians. Others also seek recognition through the amateur system, increasing their opportunities to perform (for free). . . .

Reinforcing the marginality of reggaetoneros is the fact that reggaetón is not perceived as quintessentially Cuban by most state functionaries concerned with culture. The reggaetón promoted in the Cuban media (mostly broadcast out of Havana) remains a copycat of Puerto Rican aesthetics. Even radio stations broadcasting from Santiago tend to prioritize reggaetón made in the capital. . . . Its "foreigner" status prevents reggaetón from being accepted and supported by the revolutionary institutions. To make matters worse, most reggaetoneros . . . lack formal music training and are not recognized as professional musicians, an official endorsement that would allow them to earn money legally for their performances.

. . . [R]eggaetoneros are often perceived as opportunists who are involved in illegal and unconventional networks for the sole aim of cashing in on this lowly genre's popularity abroad. For instance, Alpidio Alonso (2004: 7), the national president of the Asociación Hermanos Saíz, publicly denounced the "lamentable" nature of reggaetón during the eighth congress of the Young Communist Union in December 2004. From a state-institutional perspective, reggaetón's artistic dimension is simply not acknowledged. It remains a "foreign pseudo-culture" oriented exclusively toward consumption and commercialization, relying almost exclusively on parallel (illegal) networks of production and distribution led by opportunists and marginal youth groups. . . .

Social and racial prejudices further prevent the inclusion of reggaetoneros in institutional programming. Many [officials] working in local cultural institutions describe reggaetoneros as "young, black, male delinquents," and most dislike reggaetón music. Thus there is a strong aversion on the part of most local state institutions . . . to deal with this

young clientele. Indeed, the collaboration of reggaetoneros with local institutions is an accommodation of convenience rather than an ideological allegiance; they rely on cultural institutions only when it is convenient to do so. . . .

Sport: An Alternative Articulation of Nationalism

It is in seemingly non-political realms that reggaetoneros articulate strong nationalist rhetoric, which overlaps with dominant ideologies in an unpredictable and disjointed fashion. In order to illustrate these alternative articulations, I examine . . . reggaetoneros' identification with the national Cuban baseball team. . . .

Reggaetoneros often express a need for their music to be recognized as an authentic form of Cuban cultural expression. MC [Master of Ceremonies] Camerun clearly states that: "we have to assign reggaetón its national brand, assume reggaetón as part of the national culture." In the Cuban context, this implies, among other things, that reggaetón incorporates typical Cuban musical traditions. Nationalism is also expressed by reggaetoneros during their performances. The Cuban flag is often exhibited on stage, and reggaetoneros commonly shout, "*¡Esto es reggaetón a lo cubano!*" (This is Cuban reggaetón!). Reggaetoneros are proudly identifying their form of expression as the most popular dance music in Cuba, and they emphasize the importance of recognizing their importance to the genre's evolution in the island. Considering the lack of official recognition for reggaetón, the attempt to nationalize reggaetón [has] political implications.

Reggaetoneros, and Cuban youth in general, express an alternative nationalist rhetoric through baseball fanaticism. Baseball entered Cuba in the second half of the nineteenth century (González Echevarría 1999), and it remains a central [symbol] of Cuban nationalism. . . . The significance of baseball as an emblem of Cuban nationality reached its [peak] in March 2006, when Cuba played against Japan in the finals of the first World Baseball Classic in San Diego, California. In Santiago, rumours about the Cuban team's participation in the Baseball World Classic permeated social life in the lead-up to the championships. The Cuban team was allowed to take part in the World Classic . . . after the United States unsuccessfully attempted to block Cuba's participation. . . . There were reports that in response to this attack, Castro had defiantly announced that if Cuba won, the money awarded (believed to be millions of dollars) would have been donated to Hurricane Katrina victims in New Orleans. This rumour coincided with a general feeling of disgust among Cubans at the Bush administration's handling of the disaster. These events, which took on a humorous note, bolstered Castro's image among youths as a bold political leader who challenged imperialist insolence.

Around the same time as the Baseball World Classic was taking place, the reggaetón song "Pitchea" (to pitch), by the group Eminencia Clásica from the province of Cienfuegos, became the biggest musical hit in Santiago. The song—associated with a simple choreography (promoted by the video clip) in which dancers imitate swinging a baseball bat to hit a ball that finally ends up breaking a window (heard in the soundtrack)—highlights the popularity of baseball among young Cubans. In Santiago de Cuba, most young people knew the dance moves, which were constantly re-enacted every time "Pitchea" was played. . . .

Reggaetoneros' support for their national team is further expressed through their attire. Many reggaetoneros wear baseball jerseys . . . emblazoned with "Cuba" on the front. Baseball jerseys are extremely expensive in Cuba and can be purchased only in dollars and at tourist stores, although they can also be found in illegal clothing networks. Few Cubans have the financial means to acquire such a strong symbol of Cuban nationalism. Among reggaetoneros, however, the jersey is commonplace. These are usually acquired through revenues generated by foreign contracts,

or they are given to reggaetoneros by foreigners. By wearing Cuban baseball jerseys, reggaetoneros project an image charged with contradiction: on one hand, the jersey is an outward gesture of pride and support for the national team; on the other, it is a status symbol, signifying reggaetoneros' socioeconomic position as hard-currency holders. By wearing an expensive commodity that most Cubans cannot even dream of owning, reggaetoneros identify themselves with a national sport and team, while at the same time distancing themselves from the rest of the population. The jersey, when worn by a young Cuban, is thus a paradoxical [symbol], expressing nationalist sentiments that run counter to the official revolutionary principles of social and economic equality for all. . . .

Crisis of Faith or "Ideology of Escape"?

In his analysis on reggaetón in Havana, Baker maintains that "reggaetón artists tend to stand outside socialist principles altogether, *refusing to engage with ideology on any level*" (forthcoming; my emphasis). In referring to timba, Moore (2006: 133) in turn maintains that youths "reject" socialist rhetoric because it runs counter to the values of hedonism, sensuality, and materialism, which permeate the genre. Moreno Fraginals (1997) pessimistically claims that contemporary Cuba is confronted by a dark period of "disintegration" rather than "transition." He refers to young *balseros*[3] in Guantánamo and the increase of suicide among youths as examples of accumulated despair and resentment of the Revolution. Is Cuba therefore facing a post-ideological moment represented by its lost youth? Is Cuban youth in a "crisis of faith," as one representative of the Asociación Hermanos Saíz in Santiago [claimed] to me?

These are fair questions. The conscious conversion of underground rappers, whose lyrics were deeply engaged in politics, to a more commercial type of music might suggest a decline in political engagement. Reggaetoneros are, in many ways, the embodiment of market-oriented and individualistic values—interests that diverge from the official socialist teachings of the Revolution. But reggaetoneros are not, however, in a state of despair. By establishing sophisticated alternative networks, they have organized a system that meets their needs. Such networks involve an array of actors and relationships, which allow reggaetoneros to produce and distribute their music in accordance with norms and conventions that differ from those of the dominant social formation. Furthermore, instead of arguing that reggaetoneros are driven by a crisis of faith and that they are not involved in the articulation of ideology, I maintain that reggaetoneros interact with the dominant revolutionary system by [expressing] what Carolyn Cooper (1993) called an "ideology of escape." In other words, reggaetoneros tend to express interests that position them on the margins of—but not necessarily against—the dominant formation. Articulating an "ideology of escape" implies that reggaetoneros oscillate between being close to the revolutionary project and distant from it.

Making and having money, and the aspiration to become rich, provide reggaetoneros with a form of escape from the political, a kind of detour that allows them to bypass the many regulations that characterize Cuba's revolutionary system of consumption. It has been argued . . . that there is an "urgency" among Cuban youths to acquire material goods and become rich (Clarke, Micken, and Hart 2002: 29). This tendency is markedly pronounced in the reggaetón scene. It is generally believed among Cubans that—unlike [with] rap—"easy" money can be made with reggaetón. Such a belief, reinforced by mythical success stories, is also shared by most reggaetoneros.

[Reggaetonero] Mikael's rhetoric provides a good example of such a desire to escape from the political. Mikael's entire family lives in the United States; he is "the only one left here," as he once said. Mikael does not have a job inside the state system and he is not a member of his local Comité de la Defensa de la Revolución (Committee for the Defence of the Revolution). When asked if he would like to move to the United States in order to join his family, he answered: "Why would I leave Cuba? Here the weather is wonderful, there is no violence. . . . This country is a paradise when you have the money to get what you want!" Mikael is one of the few reggaetoneros in Santiago who manages to make a living with his music. He also receives financial help from his family abroad. This does not imply that Mikael would not like to travel abroad. On the contrary, most mature reggaetoneros—and most Cubans in general—dream of travelling abroad. . . .

While reggaetoneros [express] interests that are often contradictory, these must be considered in the context of the post-Special Period, which is [also] characterized by . . . antithetical ideological principles. Indeed, reggaetoneros' desire to acquire money is not exceptional if one considers that the revolutionary government during and after the Special Period also adopted capitalist-oriented policies, which were justified by the argument that they would help maintain the socialist system. Abel Prieto, the . . . minister of culture, explained that the "new [state] approach to the arts constitutes commercialism, not capitalism. Cuba's dollar economy is merely a sign of 'complicated' times, not political upheaval" (reported by Cantor 1999). . . . Indeed, a distinction has to be made between the guarded and pragmatic commercialism of the state and the materialist desires of reggaetoneros. Yet this illustrates that the contemporary Cuban [situation] is characterized by . . . contrasting values.

Reggaetoneros' desire to make money is further combined with a fascination for the outside world, which is another form of escape. In addition to [being attracted] to Caribbean and North American popular cultures, many reggaetoneros maintain relations with foreigners who visit the island. These exchanges give reggaetoneros a glimpse of other trends in fashion and musical style, and visitors often bring with them the electronic equipment necessary for the production of reggaetón music (ranging from MP3 recorders to computers). Such expensive products are in high demand among reggaetoneros because they were not available on the official market until recently. But contact with young foreigners has also significantly altered reggaetoneros' identification with revolutionary figures.

Despite their conversion to a market-oriented form of music production, many "mature reggaetoneros" . . . remain faithful to the figure of Ernesto Che Guevara, exhibiting his icon on stage, on T-shirts, and on other products. . . . However, the meaning behind the adoption of such a symbol contrasts with how it is promoted by the revolutionary government. . . .

In Cuba, Ernesto Che Guevara is a pillar of the Revolution. At the end of the 1950s, Che fought side by side with Fidel Castro and other young revolutionaries . . . [to] overthrow the dictatorial regime of Fulgencio Batista. Che was part of the vanguard, the embodiment of revolutionary commitment. From the beginning of the Revolution, he was associated with the ideal of a New Man born of a socialist system. . . .

Today, Che is ubiquitous: his image constantly appears on television; the days of his birth and death are officially recognized every year; "*seremos como el Che*" (We will be like Che) is recited by young pupils at school on a daily basis; and the song "Hasta Siempre Comandante," written by Carlos Puebla and dedicated to Guevara, is taught to children as young as five years old attending [day]care. One may question how meaningful such a motto or song is to Cuban children (Blum 2005), but the revolutionary figure of Che is nonetheless endorsed strongly by the state.

The famous Che icon, taken from Alberto Korda's 1960 photograph, has acquired a different symbolic connotation outside of Cuba. Although it remains an emblem of resistance and anti-capitalist struggle, it has largely been divorced from its political [meanings], likely because of its overuse in commercial contexts. A revamped image of Che, promoting a range of products from wine to snowboards, has therefore acquired a commercial rather than a political significance for most international youths. The use of Che's image by rappers in the United States and its exhibition by young . . . tourists in Cuba have had a direct impact on Cuban rappers who found in Che a symbol of rebelliousness at a global scale.

What are we witnessing at this point in time? Many converted reggaetoneros seem to maintain their identification with Che, even though their practices and associated discourses have changed drastically. Isnay, a rap and reggaetón producer from Santiago, maintained that rappers' and "many reggaetoneros" identification with Che has nothing to do with the Cuban Revolution per se. Rather, it signals a deeper identification with the symbols and values inherent to the process of social revolution in general. . . . Kiki similarly explained to me that the reason he identifies with Che is because "Che was real, he was a man of principles, and also he was an internationalist." Kiki added, "Che was not Cuban, he came here to fight for his principles, and then went away to pursue them." Therefore, many rappers and mature reggaetoneros admire Che for sticking to his principles and values, and for pursuing the struggle around the world in order to spread his ideals.

It is the global scale of Che's actions that impresses rappers and many mature reggaetoneros. And it is the prevalence of his image among young tourists and North American rappers that has encouraged Cuban rappers and mature reggaetoneros to regard him as such. The meanings attached to this symbol diverge from the official narrative. . . . [O]n one hand, the image of Che is not conceived of as strictly commercial or drained of political [value]; mature reggaetoneros regard it as an emblem of principled rebelliousness. On the other, this image has been adopted as it is perceived and exhibited by young tourists who visit the island. The latter emerges as a mix of commercialism, revolutionary romanticism, and anti-capitalist sentiment. Each facet is expressed at different intensities and in different contexts, highlighting the complexity of such a symbolic attachment.

Conclusion

There is no evidence to suggest mature reggaetoneros from Santiago de Cuba collectively position their practices and discourses against the dominant system. As I have maintained throughout this article, reggaetoneros tend to articulate alternative nationalist discourses that position them on the margins. In addition, their involvement in parallel networks of production allows them to capitalize on the advantages of both systems and negotiate each system's respective norms and conventions. Furthermore, reggaetoneros are not confronting a "crisis of faith" per se, because they articulate sound ideological principles that are appropriate to the post-Special Period. Their adoption of market-oriented and individualist values may yet challenge the tenets of socialism; but official policies adopted since the Special Period, in many respects, reflect similar values, highlighting the paradoxical context in which mature reggaetoneros produce and distribute their music. . . . But despite the various and often-contradictory ideological components of reggaetoneros' discourses, it is clear that alternatives to the values promoted by the orthodox revolutionary project are emerging, adding colour to the palette reggaetoneros use to give shape to their reality.

References Cited

Alonso, Alpidio. 2004. "El objetivo último de todo este esfuerzo es transformar, mejorar al hombre." *Juventud Rebelde*, 5 December, 6–7.

Baker, Geoffrey. 2005. "Hip Hop, Revolutión! Nationalizing Rap in Cuba." *Ethnomusicology* 49 (3): 308–402.

———. Forthcoming. "The Politics of Dancing: Reggaeton and Rap in Havana, Cuba." In *Reggaeton*, edited by Raquel Z. Rivera, Deborah Pacini Hernandez, and Wayne Marshall. Durham, NC: Duke University Press.

Blum, Denise. 2005. "¿Venceremos o Venderemos? The Transnationalization and Neiman Marxistization of the Icon of Che Guevara." In *Cuba Transnational*, edited by Damian J. Fernández, 165–178. Gainesville: University Press of Florida.

Cantor, Judy. 1999. "Welcome to the Bureaucracy: Why Cubans Call the Ministry of Culture the 'Mystery of Culture.'" *Miami New Times*, 24 June. www.miaminewlimes.com/Issues/1999-06-24/news/feature2_full.html.

Clarke III, Irvine, Kathleen S. Micken and H. Stanley Hart. 2002. "Symbols for Sale . . . at Least for Now: Symbolic Consumption in Transition Economies." *Advances in Consumer Research* 29 (1): 25–30.

Cooper, Carolyn. 1993. *Noises in the Blood: Orality, Gender and the "Vulgar" Body of Jamaican Popular Culture*. London: Macmillan Caribbean.

Fernandes, Sujatha. 2003. "Island Paradise, Revolutionary Utopia or Hustler's Haven? Consumerism and Socialism in Contemporary Cuban Rap." *Journal of Latin American Cultural Studies* 12 (3): 359–75.

———. 2004. "Fear of a Black Nation: Local Rappers, Transnational Crossings, and State Power in Contemporary Cuba." *Anthropological Quarterly* 76 (4): 575–608.

———. 2006. *Cuba Represent! Cuban Arts, State Power, and the Making of New Revolutionary Cultures*. Durham, NC: Duke University Press.

González Echevarría, Roberto. 1999. *The Pride of Havana: A History of Cuban Baseball*. New York: Oxford University Press.

Medel, Osviel Catro. 2005. "¿Prohibido el reguetón?" *Juventud Rebelde*, 13 February. www.bdi.cu/internet/jrebelde/2005/enero-marzo/feb-13/prohibido.html.

Moore, Robin. 2006. *Music & Revolution: Cultural Change in Socialist Cuba*. Berkeley: University of California Press.

Moreno Fraginals, Manuel. 1997. "Transition to What?" In *Toward a New Cuba? Legacies of a Revolution*, edited by Miguel Angel Centeno and Mauricio Font, 211–16. London: Lynne Rienner Publishers.

Notes

1. Timba is a form of Cuban dance music that is similar to salsa, but with more complex rhythms. Timba was popular in Cuba in the 1980s and 1990s but, unlike some other Cuban musical styles, did not penetrate the global music scene. (Stern's note)

2. Son is an Afro-Cuban musical style that was one of the precursors to salsa. (Stern's note)

3. *Balseros* are people who flee Cuba on makeshift rafts. (Stern's note)

Key Points to Consider

- Reggaetón is a Latin American musical genre that has become extremely popular among Cuban youth, particularly those who are socially and economically marginal.
- Unlike other Cuban musical genres, reggaetón is generally not supported by state cultural institutions. Reggaetoneros have limited access to state performance venues and recording studios.
- Even though they are marginalized, reggaetoneros participate in discourses of Cuban nationalism through their music and through their actions.
- The collapse of the Soviet Union in 1991 had wide-ranging consequences around the world. Unlike in Eastern Europe, communism did not end in Cuba, but Cuba did make economic changes that brought about economic inequality within its own borders.
- International tourism to Cuba is one avenue through which Cubans participate in globalization, particularly through access to foreign ideas, consumer products, and foreign currencies.

Critical Thinking Questions

1. What does Boudreault-Fournier mean by the statement that the "collaboration of reggaetoneros with local institutions is an accommodation of convenience rather than an ideological allegiance"? What are some examples that illustrate reggaetoneros' accommodations to official institutions?
2. What examples does Boudreault-Fournier provide to argue that reggaetoneros identify with the Cuban nation without identifying with the ongoing Cuban revolution?
3. Boudreault-Fournier asserts that reggaetoneros express an "ideology of escape." What are they escaping? How successful are they?
4. Boudreault-Fournier mentions that reggaetoneros share "mythical success stories" that fuel their dreams of becoming rich and famous. Do similar stories of "easy money" exist in Canada? In what contexts? Do you think that myths are empowering or disabling in these contexts? What evidence supports your reasoning?
5. Based on Boudreault-Fournier's descriptions, does reggaetoneros' attachment to baseball seem similar to Canadians' attachment to hockey? Why or why not? Provide specific examples to explain you assessment.

Suggestions for Further Reading and Watching

Boudreault-Fournier, Alexandrine. 2003. *State the Rhythm*. Online video, 48 min. http://vimeo
.com/69070249.

———. 2010. *Golden Scars*. Cimarron Productions. Online video, 61 min. http://vimeo.com/69532639.

Fairley, Jan, and Alexandrine Boudreault-Fournier. 2012. "Recording the Revolution: Fifty Years of Music
Studios in Revolutionary Cuba." In *The Art of Record Production*, edited by Simon Frith and Simon
Zagorski-Thomas, 247–67. London: Ashgate.

Glossary

Aboriginal people People descended from any of the cultural groups that inhabited a land prior to its colonization. In Canada, there are three main categories of Aboriginal people: **Inuit**, **Métis**, and **First Nations**; these groups have somewhat different histories as well as distinct relationships to the Crown.

affective Relating to the expression or experience of emotion.

affinal kinship Relationships created through marriage.

agency Human beings' ability to exercise choice within the constraints of their culture.

apartheid Literally "apartness" in Afrikaans. A system of laws and social practices in South Africa and Namibia that enforced **racial** distinctions and physical and social separation of people classified as belonging to different racial groups. In South Africa, apartheid ended in 1994.

applied or practising anthropology The use of anthropological research methods and insights to solve practical problems between and within cultures.

asceticism A lifestyle characterized by avoidance of physical pleasures in order to achieve spiritual or moral uplift.

autoethnography The application of anthropological methods and forms of analysis to interpret aspects of one's own life.

bilateral descent The practice of tracing one's heritage equally from both mother's and father's kin.

bioaccumulation The gradual buildup of toxic substances within a biological organism.

biomagnification The buildup of toxic substances in higher and higher concentrations from the bottom to the top of a food chain.

Cartesian dualism Representing the world as divided between two fundamentally different and separate components such as *mind* and *body*. The notion derives from the ideas of French philosopher René Descartes (1596–1650).

class A ranked group within a hierarchically stratified society whose membership is defined primarily in terms of wealth, occupation, and/or access to power.

Cold War, the The period between 1945 and 1991 of militaristic competition between the United States and the Union of Soviet Socialist Republics (Soviet Union) and their allies for global economic and political domination. Although the term *Cold War* implies an absence of military engagement, the two sides engaged in multiple proxy wars during this period.

commensality The practice of eating together, thought to contribute to a sense of connection among participants.

commodity A raw material or agricultural product that is traded in the market.

communitas Shared, temporary feelings of intense emotion and togetherness, often accompanied by the suppression of status differences.

conjugal bond An assumed emotional attachment between spouses, based on romantic love.

consanguineous Literally, "of the same blood"; genetically related.

cosmology A theory of the universe as an ordered whole and the laws that govern it.

critical analysis In anthropology, research that takes account of power relations and the ways that these are reflected in social life. Critical analysis should not be regarded as a form of critique.

cultural assimilation Absorption of one cultural group into another so that the distinct cultural traits of the absorbed group disappear.

cultural capital Context-appropriate knowledge that helps a person improve his or her economic or social status.

culture shock The feeling of physical and mental dislocation/discomfort a person experiences when in a new or strange cultural setting.

culture-specific syndrome An illness or a set of symptoms restricted to a specific group of people; also referred to as *culture-bound syndrome*.

demographer A social scientist who studies the measurement of populations and various aspects of population change.

demographic Pertaining to the structure and/or measurement of populations.

development Directed change intended to improve peoples' standards of living.

diaspora Migrant populations with a shared national origin living in a variety of different locales around the world.

discourse Collective understandings of meaning represented in language. More generally, the manner in which ideas are discussed.

egalitarian The absence of formalized differences in power, wealth, and influence.

embodied knowledge Cultural knowledge that is preserved and transmitted through lived experiences (rather than through written texts or audio or video recordings).

embodiment The manner in which an individual's culture and sense of self are presented in and through her or his physical body.

emic Concerning an insider's interpretation of meaning.

emplacement A culturally produced sense of belonging in a place.

enculturation The process by which individuals learn to think and act in ways that are considered appropriate in their particular cultures.

epistemology The study of knowledge and how people acquire knowledge.

essentialism The belief that a person or a thing has certain "essential" characteristics or qualities because that person or thing is understood to fit into a certain category. When applied to human beings, essentialism often results in overly simplistic and stereotyped assumptions about people.

ethnicity An individual's or a group's sense of identity connected to ancestry, geographic origin, religion, cultural heritage, and/or language.

ethnocentrism The universal tendency to assess the beliefs and behaviours of other peoples from the perspective of one's own culture.

ethnography In-depth study of the ordinary, everyday behaviours and beliefs of a group of people in an effort to understand the world from their perspective.

expressive culture Music, art, dance, sport, and other creative practices through which people express their beliefs and identities.

family Two or more people who consider themselves to be related through descent, marriage, adoption, common experience, or sharing.

fieldwork An extended period of close involvement with people in whose way of life anthropologists are interested.

fictive kinship The relationship between people who identify as kin even though they are not connected by biology, adoption, or marriage.

First Nations One of the three main divisions of **Aboriginal peoples** in Canada. First Nations peoples' relationships to Canada are governed by the Indian Act as well as through the Canadian Constitution and various treaties.

foodways Culturally and socially produced practices related to the production, preparation, and consumption of food.

foragers People who live by gathering wild plants, fishing, and hunting; sometimes called hunter-gatherers.

Fordism Assembly-line mass-production in which the employer carefully managed every aspect of the work process. Over time, Fordism has become associated with labour unions, good wages, and job security to balance the risks from dull or dangerous industrial manufacturing.

formal economy Economic activities that are recorded in a country's official statistics.

Foucauldian Relating to the ideas of French social theorist Michel Foucault (1926–1984). Foucault used historical methods to show how individuals in modern societies act in ways that benefit the powerful.

gender The social and culture qualities associated with each sex. These associations vary cross-culturally.

gender roles Behaviours and practices associated with being male or female or a "third" gender. Gender roles vary cross-culturally.

generalized reciprocity A mode of exchange in which individuals exchange goods and/or services without strict accounting under the assumption that the exchanges will eventually balance out.

globalization   The reshaping of local conditions through global exchanges and connections on what seems to be an ever-intensifying scale.

governmentality   The idea, developed by French social theorist Michel Foucault, that modern people willingly govern themselves in ways that maintain the existing social order.

hegemony   A system of leadership in which rulers persuade subordinates to accept the **ideology** of the dominant group by offering accommodations that nevertheless preserve the rulers' privileged position.

holism   The perspective that all aspects of culture are integrated into a complex system that can be fully understood only in context.

hunting and gathering   An economic adaptation based on collecting plants, fishing, and hunting to meet material needs for food, clothing, tools, and shelter; also known as **foraging**. Until approximately 12,000 years ago, all peoples in the world were foragers.

ideology   A set of beliefs that allows a person to navigate and/or justify the kind of life he or she leads.

informal economy   Economic activities that are not included in a country's official statistics. Informal earnings can include unreported, un-taxed income from barter exchanges and working "under-the-table" as well as the proceeds of crime.

informants   People in a particular culture who work with an anthropologist in ways that provide the anthropologist with insights about their way of life; also called *respondents*, *interlocutors*, or *collab-orators*.

interpellate   To come to recognize oneself as a member of a certain group or as the target of a particular program. (Note: This term should not be confused with the term *interpolate*, which is used in mathematics.)

intifada   Arabic word meaning "uprising." While the term can be applied to any kind of rebellion or protest, it is most commonly used by non-Arabic speakers to refer to two recent periods of Palestinian resistance to Israeli occupation.

Inuit   One of the three main divisions of **Aborig-inal peoples** in Canada. Inuit peoples' relationship to Canada is governed by the Canadian Constitu-tion and various treaties, but not by the Indian Act. The Inuit traditional home is the treeless regions of northern Canada and Alaska as well as Greenland and the Russian Far East.

Keynesianism   An economic and governance sys-tem based on the ideas of British economist John Maynard Keynes (1883–1946). Keynesianism, which fell out of favour in the 1980s, involved pro-gressive taxation in order to provide publicly funded social services as a right of citizenship.

kinship   Socially recognized ties among people, most commonly derived from mating, birth, and nurturance.

language   A form of communication that is a systematic set of arbitrary **symbols** shared among a group and passed on from generation to generation. It may be spoken, signed, or written.

language ideology   Shared ideas about what constitutes "good" language and evaluations of the prestige attached to a language (and its speakers).

legal citizenship   The rights and obligations of individuals accorded by the laws of a state.

lifeways   Culturally and socially produced ways of living.

life course   A culturally shared understanding of the passage of human lives as linked to those of other individuals and cultural practices as well as through individual accomplishments and **rites of passage**.

liminality   An ambiguous transitional state in a **rite of passage** in which the person or persons un-dergoing the ritual are outside their ordinary social positions.

marriage   A culturally sanctioned relationship be-tween two people (usually adults) that transforms the status of the participants, carries implications about sexual access and/or rights to any offspring, and establishes connections between the kin groups of the participants.

material culture   The physical things that people produce and use.

matrilineal   Tracing descent through female an-cestors.

medicalization   Labelling a problem or disorder that may have social or economic causes as a medi-cal disorder.

Métis One of the three main divisions of **Aboriginal peoples** in Canada. The category includes people who have a mixed **First Nations** and European cultural heritage as well as the descendants of some First Nations women who lost their "Indian status" through marriage to non-Aboriginal men.

modernist A supporter of modernism (i.e., modern ideas, expressions, and practices); or, characteristic of modernism.

modernity The quality of being modern. In the West, modernity is often considered to be a state of social organization characterized by complex economic and political institutions, a market economy assumed to adhere to recognized standards, and a division of labour in which roles and statuses are depersonalized.

modernization A social transformation marked by the acceptance of standardization, depersonalization, mass production, and the centralization of authority.

moral panic Shared fears that social order is under threat from the failure of some group of people to adhere to the norms of correct behaviour.

multiculturalism Cultural diversity; the extension of citizenship rights to include cultural difference.

natal kinship Relationships inherited at birth.

nation A group of people who conceive of themselves as sharing the same history, culture, and **language**, and even the same physical/biological substance. Political scientist Benedict Anderson describes nations as "imagined communities."

nationalism Strong feelings of attachment to one's **nation** or country.

nationalist Of or relating to **nationalism**. Also, one who supports political independence for the nation to which she or he feels strongly attached.

nationalist rhetoric Language that is meant to produce feelings of **nationalism**.

naturalization The process by which social differences or certain practices created by human beings come to be thought of as ordinary, unremarkable, and possibly arising from nature.

neoliberalism A form of governance that prioritizes capitalist forms of competition among organizations and individuals rather than collective action. Neoliberalism, which is associated with the political programs of Margaret Thatcher (1925–2013; prime minister of the United Kingdom from 1979 to 1990) and Ronald Reagan (1911–2004; president of the United States from 1981 to 1989), is currently the dominant form of governance in the world.

NGO See **non-governmental organization**.

non-governmental organization (NGO) A private agency that engages in service delivery or development work. NGOs sometimes act in place of the state to provide social services, education, or health care.

nuclear family A kin group made up of parents and their minor children.

paradigm A shared set of assumptions or way of thinking about reality.

paradigm shift A dramatic change in the underlying assumptions or way of thinking about phenomena.

participant observation A data-collection method, common in anthropological studies, involving living and working with the people being studied and participating in their culture in order to learn about the world from their perspective.

participatory research A category of research in which the subjects of the study participate in designing and conducting the research. A subcategory of participatory research known as "participatory action research" or PAR is usually organized around testing interventions for ameliorating social problems.

patrilineal Tracing descent through male ancestors.

peasant A subsistence farmer, fisher, or artisan who may also produce for the market.

pedagogy The method and practice of teaching.

phenomenological Concerning human consciousness and direct experience from the point of view of the individual.

pidgin language A special-purpose **language** created through the ongoing interactions of people who speak different languages.

place In certain contexts, a location and all of its human and physical attributes. (This definition is borrowed from the discipline of geography.)

political ecology The study of human environmental interactions that prioritize the role of political, economic, and social forces.

potlatch   A complex of social and religious activities performed by **First Nations** peoples along the Northwest Coast region of North America. At potlatches, which often mark important transitions, hosts feed, entertain, and give gifts to the guests.

pragmatism   A philosophy based on the ideas of American educator John Dewey (1859–1952) and others that holds that thought derives from the pursuit of practical goals rather than from passive observation.

praxis   The integration of theory and action.

predestination   A theological tenet of some Protestant sects that holds that an individual's spiritual salvation is predetermined by God.

race   Social groupings of humans, usually based on overt physical characteristics, culture, and/or geographic origins, that are treated as originating in biology.

racial   Of or relating to **race**.

racism   The systematic oppression of members of one or more socially defined "races" by another socially defined "race."

reciprocity   A mode of exchange in which individuals exchange goods and/or services in a way that builds social bonds and obligations. See also **generalized reciprocity**.

remittances   Money sent as a payment or a gift. In globalization discourse, the term often refers to money sent by global workers and immigrants to family and friends in their countries of origin.

rite of passage   A ritual that serves to mark the movement and transformation of an individual from one social position to another.

ritual of reversal   A ritual in which ordinary social order and roles are temporarily reversed.

salvage anthropology   A type of ethnographic data collection, common in North America in the early twentieth century, that was concerned with documenting the cultures that were thought to be disappearing.

schema   A culturally produced mental model that represents or conveys ideas about social phenomena.

sex   A biological state of being male or female.

sexual identity   An individual's erotic aims and desires as integrated into her or his personality.

sexuality   Culturally informed feelings and practices involving sensual aims and gratifications associated with the sex organs.

social capital   The personal networks and accumulated favours owed to a person that may contribute to his or her economic well-being.

socialization   The process of learning how to think and act as (and be) a member of a particular group.

social organization   Systems and institutions that make up the various ways that people in a society relate to each other and recognize status differences.

state   A stratified society that possesses a defined territory within which it establishes institutions of government to enforce laws, collect taxes, and administer the population and the territory.

structural factors   Enduring economic and social institutions that contribute to differentiation in the life chances and experiences of members of a population.

study up   Make a conscious effort to study powerful people and institutions in order to understand the sources of their power and its effects.

subjectivity   An individual's awareness of his or her own agency and position as a subject.

subsistence   Production and consumption outside of capitalist modes of exchange. In the field of Inuit studies, the term is generally used to describe traditional economic activities associated with hunting and fishing. In other contexts, the term is used to describe small-scale farming and/or fishing.

substantive citizenship   The actions people take, regardless of their legal citizenship status, to assert their membership in a state and to bring about political changes that will improve their lives.

supernumerary   More than the expected, usual, or required number.

symbol   A thing that stands for something else.

symbolic capital   Prestige or honour that can become a resource to enhance one's material well-being.

teleological   Treating the outcome of an event as natural and inevitable.

temporal regime   A system of time regulated by institutions and/or through repetitive actions.

time discipline   Culturally distinct ways of organizing time so that it is regarded as correct, even moral.

transgender   A gender identity that does not match one's biological sex.

transnational migrant   A person who physically moves from one nation-state to another while maintaining social connections to both places.

trope   A figurative representation or recurring theme; often, an oversimplified and stereotyped representation of a phenomenon.

value-added economic activities/opportunities   In the context of trade, manufacturing or other processing of raw materials prior to export.

world view   An encompassing picture of reality created by members of a society.

References

APA (American Psychiatric Association). 2013. *Diagnostic and Statistical Manual of Mental Disorders.* 5th ed. Arlington, VA: American Psychiatric Publishing.

Black, M. 1970. "The Round Lake Ojibwas: 1968–1970." In *The Round Lake Ojibwa: The People, the Land, the Resources, 1968–1970,* edited by J. Watts, 154–378. Toronto: Ontario Department of Lands and Forests.

Bordo, Susan. 2013. "Not Just 'a White Girl's Thing': The Changing Face of Food and Body Image Problems." In *Food and Culture: A Reader,* 3rd ed., edited by Carole Counihan and Penny Van Esterik, 265–75. New York: Routledge.

Bourgois, Philippe. 2003. *In Search of Respect: Selling Crack in El Barrio.* 2nd ed. Cambridge: Cambridge University Press.

Brettell, Caroline, ed. 1993. *When They Read What We Write: The Politics of Ethnography.* Westport, CT: Bergin & Garvey.

Briggs, Jean L. 1970. "Kapluna Daughter." In *Never in Anger: Portrait of an Eskimo Family.* Cambridge, MA: Harvard University Press.

B'Tselem. 2012. "The Separation Barrier—Statistics." *B'Tselem—The Israeli Information Center for Human Rights in the Occupied Territories.* www.btselem.org/separation_barrier/statistics.

Hugh-Jones, Stephen. 2005. *Lectures on Religion and Ritual ("Symbolic and Real"),* Lecture 3, "Time." Cambridge: Cambridge University. www.dspace.cam.ac.uk/handle/1810/114588.

CIA (Central Intelligence Agency). 2013. "West Bank." *The World Factbook.* www.cia.gov/library/publications/the-world-factbook/geos/we.html.

Citizenship and Immigration Canada. 2013. *Facts and Figures 2012—Immigration Overview.* www.cic.gc.ca.

Constable, Nicole. 2004. "A Tale of Two Marriages: International Matchmaking and Gendered Mobility." In *Cross-border Marriages: Gender and Mobility in Transitional Asia,* edited by Nicole Constable, 166–86. Philadelphia: University of Pennsylvania Press.

———. 2007. *Maid to Order in Hong Kong: Stories of Migrant Workers.* Ithaca, NY: Cornell University Press.

Creese, Gillian, and Brandy Wiebe. 2009. "'Survival Employment': Gender and Deskilling among African Immigrants in Canada." *International Migration* 50 (5): 56–76.

de Munnik, Daniel, Jocelyn Jacob, and Wesley Sze. 2012. *The Evolution of Canada's Global Export Market Share.* Working Paper 2012-31. Ottawa: Bank of Canada.

Department of Manpower and Immigration. 1966. *1966 Immigration Statistics.* Ottawa: Department of Manpower and Immigration, Canada Immigration Division.

Dods, Roberta Robin. 1998. *Prehistoric Exploitation of Wetland Habitats in North American Boreal Forests.* University of London. http://discovery.ucl.ac.uk/1317920.

———. 2000. "Boundary Markers, Cultural Divisions, and Economic Landscapes." In *Selected Papers of Rupert's Land Colloquium 2000,* compiled by David G. Malaher, 69–83. Winnipeg: The Centre for Rupert's Land Studies at the University of Winnipeg.

———. 2002. "The Death of Smokey Bear: The Ecodisaster Myth and Forest Management Practices in Prehistoric North America." *World Archaeology* 33 (3): 475–87.

———. 2003. "Wondering the Wetland: Archaeology through the Lens of Myth and Metaphor in Northern Boreal Canada." *Journal of Wetland Archaeology* 3: 17–36.

———. 2004. "Knowing Ways/Ways of Knowing: Reconciling Science and Tradition." *World Archaeology* 36 (4): 547–57.

———. 2007. "Pyrotechnology and Landscapes of Plenty in the Northern Boreal." In *The Archaeology of Fire: Understanding Fire as Material Culture,* edited by Dragos Gheorghiu and George Nash. Budapest, HU: Archaeolingua.

Douglas, Mary. 1966. *Purity and Danger: An Analysis of Concepts of Pollution and Taboo.* New York: Routledge.

Frontline World. 2005. "Peru: The Curse of Inca Gold." Alexandria, VA: PBS. Online video, 31 min. www.pbs.org/frontlineworld/stories/peru404/.

Gessen, Masha. 2014. *Words Will Break Cement: The Passion of Pussy Riot.* New York: Riverhead Books.

Giddens, Anthony. 1990. *The Consequences of Modernity.* Stanford: Stanford University Press.

Graburn, Nelson H.H. 1998. "Work and Play in the Japanese Countryside." In *The Culture of Japan as Seen through Its Leisure,* edited by Sepp Linhart and Sabine Fruhstuck, 195–212. Albany: SUNY Press.

Gusterson, Hugh. 1996. *Nuclear Rites: A Weapons Laboratory at the End of the Cold War.* Berkeley: University of California Press.

Hakim, Danny. 2014. "The Mines Have Shut Down. The Miners Haven't." *New York Times,* 29 March. www.nytimes.com/2014/03/30/business/energy-environment/the-mines-have-shut-down-the-miners-havent.html?_r=0.

Harvey, David. 2005. *A Brief History of Neoliberalism.* Oxford: Oxford University Press.

Ho, Karen Z. 2009. *Liquidated: An Ethnography of Wall Street.* Durham, NC: Duke University Press.

Innis, Harold A. [1930] 1956. *The Fur Trade in Canada: An Introduction to Canadian Economic History.* Toronto: University of Toronto Press.

Jankowiak, William, ed. 1995. *Romantic Passion: A Human Universal?* New York: Columbia University Press.

Langlois, Kellie A., Andriy V. Samokhvalov, Jürgen Rehm, Selene T. Spence, and Sarah C. Gorber. 2011. *Health State Descriptions for Canadians: Mental Illnesses.* Ottawa:

Statistics Canada. www.statcan.gc.ca/pub/82-619-m/82-619-m 2012004-eng.pdf.

Leach, Edmund. 2000. "Time and False Noses." In *The Essential Edmund Leach*, Vol. 1, edited by Stephen Hugh-Jones and James Laidlaw, 182–6. New Haven, CT: Yale University Press.

Lee, Richard B. 1968. "What Hunters Do for a Living, or, How to Make Out on Scarce Resources." In *Man the Hunter*, edited by Richard B. Lee and Irven DeVore, 30–48. Chicago: Aldine.

Linton, Ralph. 1936. "One Hundred Percent American." In *The Study of Man*, 326–7. New York: D. Appleton-Century.

Luhrmann, T.M. 2012. *When God Talks Back: Understanding the American Evangelical Relationship with God*. New York: Alfred A. Knopf.

MacDowell, Laurel Sefton. 2012. *An Environmental History of Canada*. Vancouver: UBC Press.

Mackey, Eva. 2002. *The House of Difference: Cultural Politics and National Identity in Canada*. Toronto: University of Toronto Press.

Marshall, Mac. 1977. "The Nature of Nurture." *American Ethnologist* 4 (4): 643–62.

Mayo Clinic. 2015. "Anorexia Nervosa: Causes." *Diseases and Conditions*. www.mayoclinic.org/diseases-conditions/anorexia/basics/causes/con-20033002.

Mesa-Lago, Carmelo. 1998. "Assessing Economic and Social Performance in the Cuban Transition of the 1990s." *World Development* 26 (5): 857–76.

Millar, Kathleen. 2012. "Trash Ties: Urban Politics, Economic Crisis and Rio de Janeiro's Garbage Dump." In *Economies of Recycling: The Global Transformation of Materials, Values and Social Relations*, edited by Catherine Alexander and Joshua Reno, 164–84. London: Zed Books.

Nagle, Robin. 2013. *Picking Up: On the Streets and behind the Trucks with the Sanitation Workers of New York City*. New York: Farrar, Straus, and Giroux.

Nightlight Christian Adoptions. 2015. "Snowflakes Embryo Adoption and Donation." *Nightlight Christian Adoptions*. www.nightlight.org/snowflakes-embryo-donation-adoption.

Nordstrom, Carolyn. 2008. *Global Outlaws: Crime, Money, and Power in the Contemporary World*. Berkeley: University of California Press.

Nuttall, Mark. 2000. "Choosing Kin: Sharing and Subsistence in a Greenlandic Hunting Community." In *Dividends of Kinship: Meanings and Uses of Social Relatedness*, edited by Peter P. Schweitzer, 33–60. London: Routledge.

Ong, Aihwa. 1987. *Spirits of Resistance and Capitalist Discipline: Factory Women in Malaysia*. Albany: SUNY Press.

Ortner, Sherry B. 1973. "On Key Symbols." *American Anthropologist* 75 (5): 1338–46.

Poerksen, Uwe. 1995. *Plastic Words: The Tyranny of a Modular Language*. University Park: Pennsylvania State University Press.

Richards, Paul. 2001. "War and Peace in Sierra Leone." *Fletcher Forum of World Affairs* 25 (2): 41–50.

Roberts, Elizabeth F.S. 2011. "Abandonment and Accumulation: Embryonic Futures in the United States and Ecuador." *Medical Anthropology Quarterly* 25 (2): 232–53.

Rogers, Edward S. 1962. *The Round Lake Ojibwa*. Royal Ontario Museum Occasional Papers, no. 5. Toronto: Royal Ontario Museum, Art and Archaeology Division.

——. 1972. *Ojibwa Fisheries in Northwestern Ontario*. Toronto: Ontario Ministry of Natural Resources.

Ryan, Andrew. 2013. "Most British Children Will Be Born out of Wedlock in 2016." *Globe and Mail*, 11 July. www.theglobeandmail.com/life/the-hot-button/most-uk-children-will-be-born-out-of-wedlock-by-2016/article13136180/.

Schinkel, Willem. 2011. "The Nationalization of Desire: Transnational Marriage in Dutch Culturist Integration Discourse." *Focaal—Journal of Global and Historical Anthropology* 59: 99–106.

Scott, Marian, and Jill St Marseille. 2008. "Student Movement a Sustainable Success: University Campuses All Over the Country Are Coming Alive with Green Initiatives." *Vancouver Sun*, 28 June, N14.

Shaienks, Danielle, and Tomasz Gluszynski. 2009. *Education and Labour Market Transitions in Young Adulthood*. Ottawa: Statistics Canada. www.statcan.gc.ca.

Sharma, Nandita. 2011. "Canadian Multiculturalism and Its Nationalisms." In *Home and Native Land: Unsettling Multiculturalism in Canada*, edited by May Chazan, Lisa Helps, Anna Stanley, and Sonali Thakkar, 85–101. Toronto: Between the Lines.

Shulman, David. 2007. *Dark Hope: Working for Peace in Israel and Palestine*. Chicago: University of Chicago Press.

Speck, F.G. 1915. *Family Hunting Territories and Social Life of Various Algonkian Bands of the Ottawa Valley*. Canada Department of Mines, Geological Survey, memoir no. 70: 1-10. Ottawa: Government Printing Bureau.

Turner, Terence S. 2012. "The Social Skin." *HAU: Journal of Ethnographic Theory* 2 (2): 486–504.

UN (United Nations). 2014. "Troop and Police Contributors." *United Nations Peacekeeping*. www.un.org/en/peacekeeping/resources/statistics/contributors.shtml.

UNWCED (United Nations' World Commission on Environment and Development). 1987. *Our Common Future (Brundtland Report)*. Oxford: Oxford University Press.

Verdery, Katherine. 1996. "The 'Etatization' of Time in Ceaușescu's Romania." In *What Was Socialism, and What Comes Next?*, 39–58. Princeton, NJ: Princeton University Press.

Weston, Kath. 1997. *Families We Choose: Lesbians, Gays, Kinship*. New York: Columbia University Press.

WHO (World Health Organization). 2015. *International Classification of Disease* (ICD-10). www.who.int/classifications/icd/en.

World Federation of Direct Selling Associations. 2014. *Global Direct Selling—2013 Retail Sales*. www.wfdsa.org/files/pdf/global-stats/Sales_Report_2013.pdf.

Zaloom, Caitlin. 2006. *Out of the Pits: Traders and Technology from Chicago to London*. Chicago: University of Chicago Press.

Credits

Readings

Chapter 1: Sylvain, Renée. 2005. "Loyalty and Treachery in the Kalahari." In *Auto-Ethnographies: The Anthropology of Academic Practice*, edited by Anne Meneley and Donna J. Young, 25–38. © University of Toronto Press Higher Education Division 2005. Reprinted with permission of the publisher.

Chapter 2: Glass, Aaron. 2004. "The Thin Edge of the Wedge: Dancing around the Potlatch Ban, 1921–1951." This abridged version of the essay was first published in its entirety in *Right to Dance/Dancing for Rights*, Naomi M. Jackson, ed. Published in 2004 by Banff Centre Press.

Chapter 3: Heller, Monica. 2011. "Brewing Trouble: Language, the State, and Modernity in Industrial Beer Production (Montreal, 1978–1980)." In *Paths to Post-nationalism: A Critical Ethnography of Language and Identity*, 74–93. Oxford: Oxford University Press.

Chapter 4: Meneley, Anne. 2008. "Time in a Bottle: The Uneasy Circulation of Palestinian Olive Oil." *Middle East Report* 248 (Fall 2008): 18–23. Reprinted with permission.

Chapter 5: Ervin, Alexander M. 2012. "A Green Coalition versus Big Uranium: Rhizomal Networks of Advocacy and Environmental Action." *Capitalism Nature Socialism* 23 (3): 52–69. Reprinted by permission of the publisher (Taylor & Francis Ltd, www.tandfonline.com).

Chapter 6: Blackwood, Evelyn. 1998. "*Tombois* in West Sumatra: Constructing Masculinity and Erotic Desire." Reproduced by permission of the American Anthropological Association from *Cultural Anthropology*, Volume 13, Issue 4, pages 491–521, November 1998. Not for sale or further reproduction.

Chapter 7: Irwin, Anne. 2012. "'There Will Be a Lot of Old Young Men Going Home': Combat and Becoming a Man in Afghanistan." In *Young Men in Uncertain Times*, edited by Vered Amit and Noel Dyck, 59–78. 2012 Berghahn Books Inc. Reproduced by permission of Berghahn Books Inc.

Chapter 8: O'Connor, Richard A., and Penny Van Esterik. 2008. "De-medicalizing Anorexia: A New Cultural Brokering." *Anthropology Today* 24 (5): 6–9. John Wiley and Sons.

Chapter 9: Ameeriar, Lalaie. 2012. "The Sanitized Sensorium." Reproduced by permission of the American Anthropoligical Association from *American Anthropologist*, Volume 114, Issue 3, pages 509–20, September 2012. Not for sale or further reproduction.

Chapter 10: Phinney, Harriet (2006) "Asking for a Child: Refashioning Reproductive Space in Post-war Northern Vietnam," *Asia-Pacific Journal of Anthropology* 6 (3): 215–30. Reprinted by permission of the publisher (Taylor & Francis Ltd, www.tandfonline.com).

Chapter 11: Luehrmann, Sonja. 2004. "Mediated Marriage: Internet Matchmaking in Provincial Russia." *Europe-Asia Studies* 56 (6): 857–75. Taylor & Francis. Reprinted by permission of the publisher (Taylor & Francis Ltd, www.tandfonline.com).

Chapter 12: Collard, Chantal, and Shireen Kashmeri. 2011. "Embryo Adoption: Emergent Forms of Siblingship among Snowflakes Families." Reproduced by permission of the American Anthropological Association from *American Ethnologist*, Volume 38, Issue 2, pages 307–22, May 2011. Not for sale or further reproduction.

Chapter 13: Stern, Pamela. 2005. "Wage Labor, Housing Policy, and the Nucleation of Inuit Households." *Arctic Anthropology*, 42 (2): 66–81. © 2005 by the Board of Regents of the University of Wisconsin System. Reproduced courtesy of the University of Wisconsin Press.

Chapter 14: Cahn, Peter S. 2006. "Building Down and Dreaming Up: Finding Faith in a Mexican Multilevel Marketer." Reproduced by permission of the American Anthropological Association from *American Ethnologist*, Volume 33, Issue 1, pages 126–42, February 2006. Not for sale or further reproduction.

Chapter 15: Willow, Anna J. 2012. Reproduced by permission of the Society for Applied Anthropology from Willow, Anna J., "Re(con)figuring Alliances: Place Membership, Environmental Justice, and the Remaking of Indigenous-Environmental Relationships in Canada's Boreal Forest", *Human Organization* (2012), 71(4), pp. 371–82.

Chapter 16: Li, Fabiana. 2008. "Negotiating Livelihood: Women, Mining and Water Resources in Peru," Reprinted by permission of the author. This abridged version of the article was first published in its entirety in 2008 in *Canadian Woman Studies* 27(1): 97–102.

Chapter 17: Walsh, Andrew. 2012. "After the Rush: Living with Uncertainty in a Malagasy Mining Town." *Journal of the International African Institute* 82 (2): 235–51. Reproduced with permission.

Chapter 18: Amit, Vered. 2011. "'Before I Settle Down': Youth Travel and Enduring Life Course Paradigms." *Anthropologica* 53 (1): 79–88. Reprinted by permission of the author.

Chapter 19: Osburg, John. 2013. "Meeting the 'Godfather': Fieldwork and Ethnographic Seduction in a Chinese Nightclub." *PoLAR: Political and Legal Anthropology Review* 36 (2): 298–303, John Wiley and Sons.

Chapter 20: Graburn, Nelson H.H. 1998. "Work and Play in the Japanese Countryside." Reprinted with edits by permission from *The Culture of Japan as Seen through its Leisure* edited by Sepp Linhart and Sabine Fruhstuck, the State University of New York Press © 1998, State University of New York. All rights reserved.

Chapter 21: Boudreault-Fournier, Alexandrine. 2008. "Positioning the New Reggaetón Stars in Cuba: From Home-Based Recording Studios to Alternative Narratives." Reproduced by permission of the American Anthropological Association from *The Journal of American and Caribbean Anthropology*, Volume 13, Issue 2, pages 336–60, November 2008. Not for sale or further reproduction.

Maps

Chapter 1: Namibia, adapted from "Namibia," *The World Factbook*, CIA, https://www.cia.gov/library/publications/the-world-factbook/geos/wa.html.

Chapter 2: British Columbia, adapted from "Canada," *The Atlas of Canada*, Natural Resources Canada, http://ftp2.ctis.nrcan.gc.ca/pub/geott/atlas_tif/atlas6/Reference/Bilingual/canada02.pdf.

Chapter 3: Quebec, adapted from "Canada," *The Atlas of Canada*, Natural Resources Canada, http://ftp2.ctis.nrcan.gc.ca/pub/geott/atlas_tif/atlas6/Reference/Bilingual/canada02.pdf.

Chapter 4: Palestine, adapted from "Map of the West Bank, Settlements and the Separation Barrier, June 2012," B'Tselem, www.btselem.org/maps.

Chapter 5: Prairie Provinces, adapted from "Canada," *The Atlas of Canada*, Natural Resources Canada, http://ftp2.ctis.nrcan.gc.ca/pub/geott/atlas_tif/atlas6/Reference/Bilingual/canada02.pdf.

Chapter 6: Indonesia, adapted from "Indonesia," *The World Factbook*, CIA, https://www.cia.gov/library/publications/the-world-factbook/geos/id.html.

Chapter 7: Canada and Afghanistan, adapted from "The World," *The Atlas of Canada*, Natural Resources Canada, http://ftp2.cits.rncan.gc.ca/pub/geott/atlas_tif/atlas6/Reference/Bilingual/world01.jpg.

Chapter 8: North America, adapted from "North America," *The World Factbook*, CIA, https://www.cia.gov/library/publications/the-world-factbook//graphics/ref_maps/political/jpg/north_america.jpg.

Chapter 9: Ontario, adapted from "Canada," *The Atlas of Canada*, Natural Resources Canada, http://ftp2.ctis.nrcan.gc.ca/pub/geott/atlas_tif/atlas6/Reference/Bilingual/canada02.pdf.

Chapter 10: Vietnam, adapted from "Vietnam," *The World Factbook*, CIA, https://www.cia.gov/library/publications/the-world-factbook/geos/vm.html.

Chapter 11: Russia, adapted from "Russia," *The World Factbook*, CIA, https://www.cia.gov/library/publications/the-world-factbook/geos/rs.html.

Chapter 12: North America, adapted from "North America," *The World Factbook*, CIA, https://www.cia.gov/library/publications/the-world-factbook//graphics/ref_maps/political/jpg/north_america.jpg.

Chapter 13: The Territories, adapted from "Canada," *The Atlas of Canada*, Natural Resources Canada, http://ftp2.ctis.nrcan.gc.ca/pub/geott/atlas_tif/atlas6/Reference/Bilingual/canada02.pdf.

Chapter 14: Mexico, adapted from "Mexico," *The World Factbook*, CIA, https://www.cia.gov/library/publications/the-world-factbook/geos/mx.html.

Chapter 15: Ontario, adapted from "Canada," *The Atlas of Canada*, Natural Resources Canada, http://ftp2.ctis.nrcan.gc.ca/pub/geott/atlas_tif/atlas6/Reference/Bilingual/canada02.pdf.

Chapter 16: Peru, adapted from "Yanacocha," BBC News, http://newsimg.bbc.co.uk/media/images/41207000/gif/_41207399_peru_yanacocha_map203.gif.

Chapter 17: Madagascar, adapted from "Madagascar," *The World Factbook*, CIA, https://www.cia.gov/library/publications/the-world-factbook/geos/ma.html.

Chapter 18: Canada and the World, adapted from "The World," *The Atlas of Canada*, Natural Resources Canada, http://ftp2.cits.rncan.gc.ca/pub/geott/atlas_tif/atlas6/Reference/Bilingual/world01.jpg.

Chapter 19: China, adapted from "China," *The World Factbook*, CIA, https://www.cia.gov/library/publications/the-world-factbook/geos/ch.html.

Chapter 20: Japan, adapted from "Japan," *The World Factbook*, CIA, https://www.cia.gov/library/publications/the-world-factbook/geos/ja.html.

Chapter 21: Cuba, adapted from "Cuba," *The World Factbook*, CIA, https://www.cia.gov/library/publications/the-world-factbook/geos/cu.html.

Photos

Chapter 1: San girls in Namibia, Wikipedia Creative Commons, http://commons.wikimedia.org/wiki/File:Namibian_Bushmen_Girls.JPG. Public Domain Dedication CC0 1.0 http://creativecommons.org/publicdomain/zero/1.0/deed.en.

Chapter 2: A Hamat'sa dancer performs in a Kwakwaka'wakw big house, © Rolf Hicker Photography.

Chapter 4: Palestinian women harvest olives in October 2004 after being granted permission from the Israeli Defense Forces to cross the separation barrier to reach the olive orchard, © David Silverman/Staff/Getty Images

Chapter 5: Members of Clean Green Saskatchewan sweep mock spent fuel-rods under the carpet to protest a proposal to locate a nuclear-waste-storage facility in the province. Photo: Robbie Davis, The Sheaf

Chapter 7: Canadian soldiers from Princess Patricia's Canadian Light Infantry outside "the wire" in Afghanistan in July 2002, US Military Photo, retrieved from http://commons.wikimedia.org/wiki/File:Canadian_soldiers_afghanistan.jpg.

Chapter 10: Mothers and babies in the northern province of Bac Ninh, Vietnam, © HOANG DINH NAM / Staff / Getty Images

Chapter 11: Sidewalk advertisement for Flash Plus photo studio in Yoshar-Ola. The sign advertises photographs for "international acquaintances" as well as other services. Courtesy Sonja Luehrmann.

Chapter 12: Minnesotan family created by embryo adoption, photo courtesy of the Woodbury Bulletin.

Chapter 14: An Omnilife distributor attends a rally whose theme is "Cutting the Fear." Photo by Peter S. Cahn.

Chapter 15: A clearcut near Grassy Narrows, July 2003. Photo by Jon Schledewitz.

Chapter 16: Large-scale open-pit mining operations at the Yanacocha gold mine. © imageBROKER / Alamy.

Chapter 17: Residents outside houses in Ambrondromifehy. © Laura Tilghman / Gems and Environment project, University of Vermont, 2005.

Chapter 21: Background-track producer Kiki's bedroom studio in Santiago. Courtesy Alexandrine Boudreault-Fournier.

Index